King Lear

and the Naked Truth

King Lear

and the Naked Truth

Rethinking the Language of

Religion and Resistance

Judy Kronenfeld

Duke University Press Durham and London

1998

© 1998 Duke University Press

All rights reserved

Printed in the United States of America

on acid-free paper ∞

Typeset in Monotype Dante with Frutiger Black display

by Tseng Information Systems, Inc.

Library of Congress Cataloging-in-Publication

Data and permissions appear on the last

printed page of this book.

For David

Contents

Preface

In the sixties, as a scholarship student from a working-class background at Smith College, attending my first literature seminar, I suggested there must be *some* connection between eighteenth-century material and economic conditions and the world of *Moll Flanders;* I vividly recall the shunning silence. Some years later, as a teacher, I offered to give a course in Anglophone West African literature under the auspices of an English department and was dismayed to be told it was not a viable subject, "simply not done." Yet, now, when the political and social meanings and values of literature are the dominant interest of the discipline, and the canon has been thankfully broadened or transcended, I sometimes find we've created new excesses in our attempts to correct old ones, and I am dismayed at the small place given to questions of textual evidence and reasoned argument—and at the assumption that those matters are always and inevitably merely subjective. Hence this book. It has been written on the boundaries of— or outside of—disciplines or academic institutions over a long period of time. The advantages of such liminality perhaps include a disinclination to work within institutionalized frameworks of thought, which, in turn, can lead to a close re-examination of the taken-for-granted texts on which that thinking may be based.

This book does critically examine many of the assumptions about language and history that shape poststructuralist historicist criticism, as well as the research methods particular critics use in following up on those assumptions. Yet I must also say that I share with the critics I challenge their profound sense of the embedment of literature in the thought, beliefs, practices, and habits of perception of its historical and cultural moment, and have been enormously stimulated by their models for, insights into, and questions about these interconnections.

My thanks go to Edgar Schell for his extremely useful response to my first bibliographical queries—many years back; to Stanley Stewart, for reading and insightfully commenting on some of my essays from which this book grew; to Joan S. Bennett for her unfailingly sound pragmatic advice, support, and enthusiasm; to Herbert S. Lindenberger for his interest in my projects from early on; and to Robert S. Montgomery for his helpful concern. Most of all, my gratitude and appreciation go to Debora Shuger for her detailed and extraordinarily helpful response to the manuscript on two separate occasions—not to mention her pointing the way to more useful references than it is possible to acknowledge.

The staff of the Huntington Library, San Marino, where most of the research for this book was done, were, as always, unfailingly helpful. John Bloomberg-Rissman, in the Center for Bibliographical Studies at the University of California, Riverside, kindly stopped his work more than once to help me track down obscure and needed information, as did Robert P. Lang.

Parts of this book incorporate expanded and revised earlier work. Chapters 1, 3, and 4 make use of my essay "Post-Saussurean Semantics, Reformation Religious Controversy, and Contemporary Critical Disagreement," as well as some smaller use of my earlier essay, "Probing the Relation between Poetry and Ideology: Herbert's 'The Windows'"; chapter 3 also incorporates parts of my article "Enlightening Linguistics, Actual Reference, and the Social Nature of Language, or Yes, Virginia, There IS a World." Chapter 7 is based on another essay of mine (also briefly echoed in the introduction), "'So Distribution Should Undo Excess, and Each Man Have Enough': Shakespeare's *King Lear*—Anabaptist Egalitarianism, Anglican Charity, Both, Neither?" I would like to thank the editors of *Assays: Critical Approaches to Medieval and Renaissance Literature*, the editors of the *John Donne Journal*, the editors of the *Associated Writing Programs Chronicle*, and the editors of *ELH*, respectively, for permission to reprint material from these published works.

I come, then, to family—the community of most support. My parents, liminal too, whom the facts of twentieth-century history sent across borders, within and from Europe—my father from Nazi Germany in 1934—did not have the opportunity to receive the education they valued, but blessed me with their values, their perspectives, and their respect for the scholarship I love. I am saddened that my mother did not live to see in print the book she advertised to everyone, in and out of hospitals, during her last difficult year. I also have my children to thank for their confidence and love, and for taking time out from their own busy schedules. My son, Daniel, kindly read several chapters from an early manuscript version and provided precise editorial suggestions and queries (as well as delightfully outrageous remarks and drawings).

My daughter, Mara, prodded me for explanations, and offered, in her conversation, a continuing education in the concerns and values of the present moment. My greatest debt is to my husband, David, for his endless listening, his endless encouragement, his almost endless faith, and the occasional sharp prod ("Do it!"). This book is for him.

Note on Modification of Sources

References to act, scene, and line of *King Lear* and other plays of Shakespeare appear parenthetically in the text; all such citations are from *The Riverside Shakespeare*, edited by G. Blakemore Evans (Boston: Houghton Mifflin, 1974). However, where the *Riverside* text of *Lear* differs in any conceivably substantive way (thus, not normally, for example, where the difference is only in spelling) from either the 1608 Quarto or the 1623 Folio (as given in *The Parallel King Lear, 1608–1623*, prepared by Michael Warren [Berkeley: Univ. of California Press, 1989]), I give the Q or F reading in a note. Biblical quotations are from *The Geneva Bible: A Facsimile of the 1560 Edition* (Madison: Univ. of Wisconsin Press, 1969), unless otherwise indicated.

For the sake of readability I have modernized the spelling in quotations from Renaissance sources, including the Geneva Bible, even when these sources are quoted by modern critics. In certain cases, however, I retain the original spelling, although I do normalize *u/v, i/j, vv* for *w*, long *s*, contracted forms such as the ampersand, and (in Renaissance sources) the thorn, þ. In particular, for the reader's convenience in locating older works, I retain original spelling in titles—whether of parts of works (individual poems, speeches, etc.) or of whole works. And I do not modernize spelling in quotations from the Quarto or Folio *Lear*, or in quotations in Middle English (and in the latter, I keep the thorn). I have silently corrected obvious misprints in modern texts.

I keep the original punctuation in all quotations from Renaissance sources (except that I do introduce apostrophes for possessives), but regularize punctuation in titles for the sake of consistency. I eliminate the random use of italics and follow modern conventions of capitalization throughout. The only exceptions to these rules appear in quotations from the Quarto or Folio *Lear* and from Middle English; in these I neither use modern capitalization nor introduce apostrophes for possessives.

Introduction

History, Language, and Postmodern Criticism

of the Renaissance

For well over a decade, many literary critics have either looked for alternatives to what they see as false claims of objectivity or universality in meaning—alternatives that they have sometimes located in the slippery slide of meaning itself—or traced how meanings are determined by (purportedly) hegemonic cultural systems. Both kinds of projects in historicist and politicizing criticism—and indeed the conception of their very opposition—rest on particular assumptions about language and history. It is these assumptions that this book questions. Most importantly, it also offers a reasoned theoretical and practical alternative to both radical relativism and simplistic objectivism.

On the particular and practical level, this book investigates the images and metaphors of nakedness and clothing (and the material realities to which they relate) in Renaissance religious, political, and literary culture, and applies the resulting understanding of that metaphor field to *King Lear*. Both Reformation religious discourse and scholarly discussion of the play and its period suggest the semantic field of nakedness and clothing implicates religiopolitical positions or "sides" in Tudor and Stuart England (e.g., ceremony-rejecting Puritans or radicals who prefer "the naked truth" versus ceremony-loving Anglicans or conservatives who prefer outward splendor).[1] Thus to investigate this semantic field is also to investigate—and to reevaluate the nature of—the relationship of Shakespeare's play to the religiopolitical controversy of his time, the subject of so much contemporary political criticism.

As a study in historical semiotics, this book also offers two theoretical contributions that shaped, and were shaped by, the investigation of that semantic field. First, it sets forth a theory of meaning grounded in a way of thinking about language that is post-Saussurean, but not deconstructionist. Among other things, that theory addresses the task of interpreting our own interpretations, that is, of understanding how and why we continue to find these metaphoric images of nakedness and clothing—or other metaphoric images—tempting and meaningful. Second, this book explores a case for distinguishing "our meanings" from "their" meanings, that is, the case for a language-based historicism built on the proffered theory. This historicism would plausibly oppose both the infinite regress of deconstruction and the theoretical plethora of contingent or "local" readings based on differing political positions in several new historicisms; it also would plausibly oppose the alternative, in other new historicisms, of monolithically closed and inevitably imprisoning cultural codes.[2] It seeks to distinguish the particular multiplicities of meaning that are historically likely from those that are not.

Indeed, this historicism attempts to mediate the very opposition between subject and system, "slippery signifier" and "implacable code," in a new and specific way by reassessing the linguistic model on which — according to the poststructuralist view — that opposition is built. The opposition between culture or language as either a repressive totalizing system, an inescapable set of prescriptions and codifications, or an unbounded realm of polyvalency and free play has certainly provoked an unease — at least on the theoretical level — in some discussions of poststructuralism.[3] My approach addresses that unease; it seeks to preserve the meaning of the concept of culture — as collective, shared — and yet also specifically to explain how creativity may occur, and how a range of new opinions may be voiced and understood within cultural parameters. It shows how the same language may be used by opposed sides with different referents and, hence, meanings in mind, and yet how that language is shaped by shared cultural values and constraints.

Finally, unlike some new historicism — as well as some old historicism, albeit in a different way — my approach does not encourage reading "culture as a text" with "tropological relations" among the "objects of study" (Montrose, "New Historicisms," 401); it seeks comprehensive evidence before connecting cultural forms of expression such as politics, religion, and art on the assumption that they have been shaped analogously by underlying cultural codes. Thus the discussion in this book of the cultural thematics of "nakedness and clothing" in *King Lear* derives from an approach that tries to be at once painstakingly semiotic and painstakingly historical.

My focus is on nakedness and clothing as signs within Renaissance written discourse and within other cultural practices, and my questions are about the meanings of these signs, as well as about the general nature of the systems or semantic fields in which they commonly occur. With what other signs is each of these (syntagmatically) linked? With what other signs does each of these (paradigmatically) contrast?[4] And how do these other semantic relations connect to the basic polarity of "naked versus clothed"? What are the focal senses to which "nakedness" and "clothing" refer, and how are these senses commonly metaphorized? In pursuit of answers to these questions I consider such matters as nakedness as material reality and practice — for example, the actual nakedness of radical Anabaptists during some sixteenth-century revolts, and the alleged nakedness of the "Adamians" who were supposed to disrobe for divine service, as well as the nakedness of the impoverished or insane. I also investigate the subject and the metaphors of nakedness and clothing in religious, political, social, and literary culture — for example, "the naked truth" of Christ that does away with all "shadows" or "figures" in Reformation polemics; the "courtly habiliments" of poetry that contrast with shamefully simple poetic apparel in George Puttenham's *Art of Poesie;* [5] "eloquence" as clothed — sometimes elegantly — and "truth" as naked or simply dressed in the iconography of rhetoric as well as in royal pageantry. My text as crux, *King Lear,* is one I regard as woven out of these strands of meaning — strands that also produce sumptuary legislation by proclamation, state-church-sponsored homilies and other complaints against "gorgeousness of apparel," sermons of the late sixteenth and early seventeenth centuries urging charitable distribution to "poor, naked wretches" (*Lear,* 3.4.28), and roughly contemporaneous morality plays and prose tracts dealing with necessity as opposed to luxury and allied themes.

The first two chapters of part 1, "Theory and Semantic Field," provide concrete examples, informed by my linguistic theory, of historical semiotics. They lay out areas of the semantic domain of nakedness and clothing in Reformation culture and in scholarly writing about Reformation culture. Chapter 1 concerns clothing metaphors used by conformists and nonconformists in controversy over matters of ceremony and government in the church, and by scholars writing about Anglican and Puritan positions; chapter 2 concerns clothing metaphors used by Catholics and Protestants in early Eucharistic controversy. My purpose in these chapters is to demonstrate concretely the sense in which language involves both relativity or flexibility and meaningful constraints or systematicity; thus, these examples undergird my reassessment, in chapter 3, of the linguistic model on which more loosely held ideas of indeterminacy and denial of reference, as well as of restrictive and closed systematicity have been based. Chapter 4, in preparation for the second part of the book, turns to the treatment of Renaissance or Reformation metaphors of nakedness and clothing in contemporary literary criticism, with a particular awareness, informed by the understanding of the shape and nature of the metaphor field, of the dangers of too precipitant a leap into the politics of metaphor.

The chapters in part 2, "Cultural Thematics," focus on semiotically resonant loci from *Lear* itself such as "so distribution shall undo excess" (4.1.70), or "Thorough tatter'd clothes [small] vices do appear: Robes, and furr'd gowns hide all" (4.6.164–65).[6] These loci and associated passages and scenes relate to "nakedness and clothing" and their possible linked and contrastive terms in the play and in Tudor and Stuart culture—for example, on the basis of the first scene: plainness, silence, the heart, "what we feel," as opposed to ceremony, speech, the tongue, "what we ought to say." (To consider the possible relevance of such analogies to a semiotic analysis is not necessarily to postulate a particular hierarchy of values; whether and in which cultural contexts one of the two terms in any particular pair is the preferred or primary one is precisely the question at issue.) The particular form that cultural potentials take in particular texts has to be worked out with an understanding of the operations of language in the semantic field we are examining and with the help of a wide body of relevant evidence. It is with the help of such evidence that chapters 5 through 8 describe the cultural semiotics of the concepts involved in the resonant locus and compare my approach and reading with specific political criticism of Shakespeare's play from various neo-Marxist, American new historicist, British "cultural materialist," and—less frequently—old historicist perspectives.[7]

In a manner not unrelated to the opposition between constraining system and possibly subversive subject, political criticism of Shakespeare has been structured by a right-left polarity; in fact, much of it, following on a long Marxist tradition of appropriating *King Lear*, regards that play as radical and anticipatory of revolution.[8] However, my purpose here—shaped by the results of my research—is very much *not* to enter the battlefield on which such lines have already been drawn, *not* to enlist in the cause of a Shakespeare analogically "conservative" or "radical" on all fronts. Rather, I want to reassess the evidence critics provide to link Shakespeare's language with the politics of one or another "side"—Anglican or Puritan, Tory or Whig, orthodox or sub-

versive, the ceremonious or the plain—and to provide compelling linguistic—and other—evidence for my own arguments, which make distinctions, when warranted, among social, economic, and political con-
servatisms, or radicalisms. It is not that a "radical" position, however
defined, is "unthinkable" in early modern England because "nonhegemonic or unusual." The first question is whether the evidence provided
in a particular case convincingly shows that the language at issue actually refers to a position that *is* radical in content—by some definition.[9]
If it were shown to be so, a second consideration would enter, for what
makes evidence convincing does include its "pervasiveness," precisely
its *usualness*.[10] Even an "unusual" position needs to be usual in some
subgroup for the reader to be convinced of its cultural meaningfulness.
Of course, it is true that one can never prove for certain that some position was not held by members of some past community if that position was so effectively suppressed that no clear evidence ever entered
the written record. However, a wide and thorough knowledge of what
was publicly said, where, and by whom—especially when what was
said may include ideas some critics claim as the very ones dangerous
enough for suppression—certainly influences one's sense of the proba-
bilities concerning what might have gone unsaid.

Theory

Such recent historicist movements as new historicism and cultural
materialism, as many critics note, have assimilated poststructuralist
theory, and with it, a taste for the "multicentric, shifting and provisional," and, as such, differ from the old historicism.[11] "Though recent
advocates of historicism dismiss dogmatic deconstruction because of
its divorce of cognition from the world, they nonetheless embrace
its rejection of apodictic knowledge, which they associate with 'mo-
nologism' or authoritarianism" (Horwitz, " 'I Can't Remember,' " 794).
Thus, consciously or not, these historicists are in some sense influenced
by Derrida's truly powerful—but, as I will argue in chapter 3—deeply
wrong misreading of Saussure's insights concerning sign-referent relations in language, on which rests, among other things, the whole idea
that there is *"nothing outside of the text."* [12] For Jean E. Howard, for
example, "Saussurian linguistics has challenged the premise that language functions referentially" and thus "the possibility of an historical

criticism" ("The New Historicism," 18–19). But a non-Derridean reading of Saussure challenges the very basis for such linkages. As we shall
see, there is no reason to accept the poststructuralist choice of language as *either* an "essentialist" "nomenclature" in which there is a
simple one-to-one relation of signs and referents, *or* a completely indeterminant entity, without any referential constraints. Similarly, there
is no reason to subscribe to the either/or of postmodern criticism
based on these alternative linguistic models; that is, we do not have
to choose either positivism or radical relativism, either authoritarian
totalization or polyvalency and free play. Yes, in theory, every individual, in isolation, completely unconstrained, could regard the same
term (for example, "naked") as having an infinite number of equally
plausible referents in each of an infinite number of situations. Or, every
individual could regard "naked" as a term opposed to an antinomous
term of his or her own unique choice (let us say, "curled"), thus giving
"naked" a virtually unique content by reasons of that contrast (that
is, as some variety of "straight"). Within cultures there certainly are
idiosyncracies of both these types. Nevertheless, the very nature of culture and language as social phenomena—dependent on shared and not
infinitely idiosyncratic responses—means that there do exist clusters
of cultural meaning, however complexly they may be structured. Un-
mysteriously, insofar as humans are comprised of overlapping—if not
perfectly congruent—subjectivities, insofar as there are biological, cultural, physical, material, and social circumstances (including texts, in
the narrow sense) that they share, their language will reflect and allow
them to express that sharing. As those circumstances—whether material or conceptual or both—shift or alter, language, too, will gradually shift or alter.

Whether stressing "the dominant ideologies and the radical countertendencies to these," or regarding literary works, in line with Greenblatt's early categorization, as "fields of force, places of dissension and
shifting interests, occasions for the jostling of orthodox and subversive impulses," new historicism and its cultural materialist counterpart
have rejected—as Greenblatt said when they first came on the scene—
an earlier "monological" historicism "concerned with discovering a
single political vision, usually identical to that said to be held by the
entire literate class or indeed the entire population."[13] This political
vision is held to have been "misrecognized" by that earlier criticism as
"a stable, coherent, and collective Elizabethan world picture," rather

than "the unreliable machinery of socio-political legitimation" (Montrose, "Professing," 18). In some formulations, this manner of thinking has meant valorizing the proliferation and/or rupture of meaning as ways of resisting ideological hegemony, as if meaning in itself were a form of political oppression, and freedom lay only with the "slippery signifier."[14]

However, such emphasis on "culture [as] not by any stretch of the imagination . . . a unity" (as the cultural materialist Jonathan Dollimore puts it in "Shakespeare, Cultural Materialism and the New Historicism," 6) may insufficiently address the "collective construction" that is language, even as used by disputants; as I shall also show, it may fail to take sufficient account of the particular shared understandings binding different parts of the Protestant culture of Tudor and Stuart England that were expressed in their particular shared language.[15] In its efforts to embrace models of polyvalency, poststructuralist historicism may fail to observe the degree to which both radical and conservative political possibilities are grounded in Reformation Protestant religious and social ideology as a whole, and thus may underestimate the degree to which change could emerge from within Tudor and Stuart culture, as opposed to only from "subversive" forces posed against it. The cultural situation of Reformation England may not be so much a matter of "dominant ideologies" and "radical countertendencies," establishment propaganda and unmasking subversion, as of shared salient contrasts reshaped—that is, given new referents and valuations—for local circumstances, by conservative and radical alike. Because culture as coded in language is shared, at any one moment, does not necessarily mean it is stable, harmonious, immutable, or universal!

The theory of meaning that underlies this attempt to describe the cultural semiotics of nakedness and clothing does make use of semantic relations of contrast, or "paradigmatic" opposition, but excludes neither referential relations nor the primacy of some shared sets of contrastive or opposed terms over others. It holds out the possibility that there do exist meanings that are more salient than others (that is, more likely to be foregrounded in people's thoughts) for certain cultures in certain contexts at specific historical moments, and it shows how a plausible case can be made for such salience.

Like the new historicists, then, I am interested in literature "as a part of the system of signs that constitutes a given culture" (Greenblatt, *Renaissance Self-Fashioning*, 4), in the "historicity of texts" (Montrose,

"Professing," 20), in the relation of literary and nonliterary texts to that system of signs, and even in dissolving the line between "literary foreground" and "political background" (Greenblatt, *Forms of Power*, 6)—insofar as that results from regarding literature as part of a cultural system of signs. However, I would stress that the "traditional" Protestant religious culture and ideology need fuller investigation as part of that historicity, part of the system of signs shared by Puritan and Anglican, nonconformist and conformist, to some degree even by superior and inferior—and not simply as concealed establishment propaganda.[16]

At the present moment, poststructuralist historicists interested in "the historicity of texts" may still be caught in an internal contradiction insofar as they also emphasize "the textuality of history" (Montrose, "Professing," 20). The "historicity of texts" means their "cultural specificity, their social embedment" (ibid.), and that cultural specificity presumably embraces the specific and never "disinterested" ideology or ideologies that shape those texts and to which they give shape—ideology being understood as the "network of beliefs and practices [through] which . . . historically constituted subjects . . . render intelligible the world around them."[17] However, the "textuality of history" means that "a full and authentic past" (Montrose, "Professing," 20) is not available to the scholar, who is herself constituted by ideology, especially when ideology is defined, in an Althusserian way, as "the very condition of our experience of the world, *unconscious* precisely in that it is unquestioned, taken for granted."[18] Poststructuralist historicists emphasize the social and linguistic construction of individuals as a bar to objective understanding of the past, yet also claim to be revealing something about that past that is not simply a projection of their present.[19] The both/and of Montrose's chiastic formulation is made problematic by the either/or binarism of determinism or autonomy, positivism or relativism.[20]

Particularly because new historicism on the early Greenblatt model is generally judged to make "totality the victor" (Holstun, "Ranting," 195), and to regard "apparent production of subversion" as "the very condition of power" (Greenblatt, *Shakespearean Negotiations*, 65), some critical new historicists do lament the binary opposition of structure and subject, "objectivist determinism" and "subjectivist free play," "structural determinism and post-structural contingency" (Montrose, "Professing," 20, 21). Montrose believes we should "resist the inevitably reductive tendency to constitute such terms [as hegemony and agency] as binary oppositions" (ibid., 21). Individuals are "endow[ed] . . . with *subjectivity* and . . . the capacity for agency"; they are also *"subject[ed] . . . to* social networks and cultural codes that . . . exceed their comprehension or control" (ibid.). Greenblatt himself—who may be said to have been acutely preoccupied with the "either/or" of cultural codes and individual autonomy from *Renaissance Self-Fashioning* on—has increasingly responded to criticism that he downplays human agency. In *Shakespearean Negotiations,* he agrees that "even those literary texts that sought most ardently to speak for a monolithic power could be shown to be the sites of institutional and ideological contestation" (3); more recently, he goes so far as to say "the belief that processes are at work in history that man can do little to alter" is one that his own new historicist work has "set itself resolutely against." [21]

Yet, although poststructuralist historicism largely addresses semiotic or signifying systems (or the semiotic aspect of economic or social systems), it crucially lacks a theory to explain the relation between semiotic code and individual message, limitation and multivalence of meaning, shared understandings and individual creativity. If we reassess postmodern criticism's dual inheritance of the presumed "implacable code" from "Saussurean" structuralism and the presumed "slippery signifier" from "Saussurean" poststructuralism, we *can* provide such an explanation; we can understand the precise sense in which— in Montrose's words—"collective structures . . . enable as well as constrain individual agency" ("Professing," 21). It is this that I seek to elucidate by means of my linguistic theory and its applications in the first part of this book.

Practice

A succession of critical paradigms including the new historical and cultural materialist has left us with a multitude of Shakespeares. The conservative Shakespeare of post–World War II Anglo-American New Criticism and "old" historicism, whose Elizabethan world picture was marshalled unproblematically in royalist, nationalist, and conformist Protestant causes, has long been superseded. This "essentialist" conservative Shakespeare has given way to a new historicist Shakespeare whose conservatism is much more problematically and paradoxically regarded as a function of "the production and containment of subversion and disorder" (Greenblatt, *Shakespearean Negotiations*, 40). Or to a newly topical Shakespeare whose work may be seen in "local" and contingent terms. If conservative, he may be so for topical and contingent reasons (e.g., because he flatters King James's plan for the Union of Scotland and England by negative example in *King Lear*); if radical, he may also be so for topical and contingent reasons (e.g., because he obliquely critiques—to avoid censorship of the 1608 Quarto—the Jacobean "justice" involved in the steps taken toward Union). And he may be regarded as both at the same time, thus valorizing "unresolved conflict and contradiction [more] than . . . integration" (Greenblatt, *Learning to Curse*, 168).[22] At roughly the same time, British cultural materialists seeking to dethrone the bard—who, in their estimate, has been used too long to bolster right-wing political views—either demystify Shakespearean traditionalism or read Shakespeare as himself a demystifier—as do recent (and not so recent) Marxists. Thus, in addition to the nonelitist, progressive liberal Shakespeare of some recent political criticism,[23] there are various newly radical Shakespeares—all encouraged by the critic's inclination to stress the continuities "From Lollards to Levellers"—as Christopher Hill's essay title puts it.[24] New historicist and cultural materialist radical Shakespeares, liberal progressive Shakespeares, and politically topical Shakespeares as well often have considerable clairvoyance about political and social events to come; they are very aware of "ideologically charged structures of authority and subjection" and "crises in power relations" that will lead directly to the civil wars.[25] Liberal, radical or conservative (or radical and conservative at the same time), these readings tend to emphasize and value societal polarization or fragmentation along religious and/or political lines, rather than to examine the possible shared values and concepts encoded even in the language of opponents.

Without wishing to return to a "universal" Shakespeare who automatically "transcends his historical moment,"[26] or to a simpler era of criticism—at the expense of the searching questions asked about the relation of literature to cultural codes in these various critical modes—one may raise a more rudimentary point. Whether postulating a conservative or radical Shakespeare, criticism loses credibility by removing the language of any play too far from contemporaneous usage, or by oversimplifying the relation of that language to contemporaneous or subsequent history. Nevertheless, in greater or lesser ways, this is what too many critics do. When insufficiently grounded evidence is supplied in political criticism, it may seriously mislead, encouraging far too hasty conclusions about what *is actually* subversive or orthodox, marginal or central.

Some political critics—viewing all history-making as political, and understandably concerned with promoting the right kind of current politics—seem to become impatient with the possible differences of past political philosophies (or other cultural practices) from our own, as well as with the historical research required to elucidate such complexities, and almost seem to regard attempts to recover them as false consciousness. The general suspicion of boundaries, closure, origins, and "universal" categories, and a reading of history that regards all ideology as repressive (and which also may regard historicist assertions of ideological difference between one age and another as repressing oppositional or marginal groups that existed then and still exist now)—all this has contributed to a postmodern approach to the Renaissance as "early modern" which may enshrine anachronism as a theorized practice, or attack its critique as inevitably serving a conservative agenda,[27] and preclude the benefits of a thorough search for evidence in a wide variety of cultural texts. In our critical moment, "a history or . . . a reading of literary texts" that "uncovers a [sixteenth- and seventeenth-century] world of violence, disorder and fragmentation" is applauded as "more radical."[28] Analyses are no longer convincing or implausible but "shrewd"; and "the test of a shrewd analysis is not whether it produces the truth, but whether it can recognize what is at stake in adopting one system of representation over another" (Kamps, "Ideology and Its Discontents," 10). Yet how—other than by fiat—is anyone who does not share the ideology of the critic to be persuaded about "what is at stake" in one or another "system of representation" if "the demand that a critique of ideology be objective" is abandoned? And if such a demand really "establishes an arbitrary hierarchy of knowledge that seeks to silence or dominate alternative modes of inquiry," how can one evaluate the results of those presumably valuable "alternate modes of inquiry" (ibid., 10, 8)?[29]

Part of my purpose, then, is to suggest a demystification of contemporary demystification—that is, to suggest how some contemporary readings of historical texts err—not by looking at political or economic motivations—but by too simplistically inscribing an ideology, politics, or language from our own cultural moment on another. Postmodern historicists certainly do "theorize their diverse practice as a hermeneutics of suspicion, a skepticism toward the status of evidence, interpretation, interpreter" (Horwitz, "I Can't Remember," 792). Yet "some forms of evidence are more verifiably objective than others" — as it is one of my major goals in this book to show.[30] There are alternatives "in speaking about our knowledge of the past . . . between complete self-confidence (all information is objective) and complete agnosticism (all information is projected or undifferentiated)" (ibid., 745). Even if "the questions [one] ask[s] of [one's] material and indeed the very nature of this material are shaped by the questions [one] asks of one's self" (Greenblatt, *Renaissance Self-Fashioning*, 5), even if one's ideological predispositions do lead one to foreground certain aspects of history, the answers one finds are not for that reason exempt from evaluation against as much relevant data as one can bring to bear.[31]

This, then, is an effort to map out the salient meanings of "nakedness" and "clothing" on a Renaissance-Reformation cultural grid; it is an attempt to give a large and full sense of what Shakespeare's clothing images "meant" in his time — and of what "meaning" itself is. Although of necessity not exhaustive, such an attempt neither reads those motifs in terms of the values of the critic's own culture, like some poststructuralist political criticism, nor in terms of the values of some corner of Renaissance culture held as a priori determinant, like some old historicism. The goal here has been to work out the functioning of a semantic system that fully and convincingly elucidates the relevant motifs in the play, and that exemplifies, in a particular and specific way, the general proposition that there are always practical constraints on theoretical indeterminacy.[32]

My investigation reveals the close connection of the language of Shakespeare's play to the common Christian culture of his time. In Reformation England there still existed a universe of discourse in terms of which even religious and political opponents could converse, if not agree, a universe of discourse that even the powerful and privileged and the lowly unfortunate could share. This universe of discourse encompasses the religiopolitical antipathies of "Puritans" and "Anglicans" — although its very language has been claimed, with little evidence (or none at all), as the exclusive hallmark of one side or another in a society held to be radically polarized by religious, political, and social differences. As such, this book also suggests — explicitly in its conclusion — that drama such as *King Lear* does not primarily engage its readers or viewers polemically, in terms of clearly opposed political or religious preferences or opinions, but sympathetically, in terms of shared moral

values. In a certain sense, then, one of the values of this book is a suspicion of "the hermeneutics of suspicion," which arose when the interests
of the discipline of English "shifted from literature as aesthetic artifact . . . to literature as cultural artifact whose aesthetic features often
mask political, racial, and sexual biases."[33]

One of the reasons for the salience of certain contrasts, referents,
and values in our case at hand is clearly the pervasiveness of Christian
culture; to ignore the sheer magnitude and weight of Christianity in
the Renaissance is to misrepresent that era.[34] If students of Shakespeare
have truly become interested in literature as "cultural artifact," they
will not shun such a connection. It is a misplaced assumption that a
"secular" drama that does not seek to save souls and is not a divine allegory has—for such reasons—no connection with the ubiquitous language of its time, in terms of which a full range of ideas, thoughts, and
feelings were expressed. As Rosalie Colie said a considerable while ago,
"Of course to deny *King Lear* its figural interpretation is by no means
to deny its reliance upon Christian imagery or its argument for conventional morality."[35] Or, as Debora K. Shuger cogently put it more
recently:

If it is not plausible to read Shakespeare's plays as Christian allegories,
neither is it likely that the popular drama of a religiously saturated culture could, by a secular miracle, have extricated itself from the theocentric
orientation informing the discussion of politics, gender, social order, and
history. The issue which has been ignored is not whether Shakespeare
teaches Christian doctrine . . . but how religious ideology, understood not
as a uniquely privileged "key" but as part of a cultural system, functions in
these plays.[36]

It is at the price of a full understanding of these plays as cultural artifacts that we regard that religious ideology and the language in which
it was expressed as merely part of "the unreliable machinery of sociopolitical legitimation" (Montrose, "Professing," 18).

Part I

Theory and Semantic

Field

∽ 1

Comely Apparel and the Naked Truth:

Metaphor and Common Christian Culture

"Clothing" is a convenient metaphor (in Lévi-Straussian terms, "good to think with") for working through some of the major oppositions in Western thought such as nature versus culture, wisdom versus eloquence, the literal versus the figurative, object versus sign. Such broad dichotomies are bipolar; as Derek Attridge observes, crediting Derrida, they "do not and cannot function as stable, given, mutually exclusive oppositions, of which one member is simply primary and self-sufficient and the other secondary, exterior, and dependent."[1] Indeed, the valences of such terms as "naked" or "natural" and the analogies built on them are always manipulable and relative — but always within certain cultural parameters. Each term *or* its opposite may be the "superior" one, depending on the particular paradigmatic contrast at issue (for example, "nakedness" may be better than "false" but worse than "decent" covering), and depending on the particular referents involved (for example, the "truth" — figured as a naked woman — is valued differently than an actual naked woman in Bedlam or on the street).[2] To take a major Renaissance and Christian instance: nature, when understood as the God-given, as God's handiwork (analogous to nakedness as primal innocence), is superior to culture or art, understood as human traditions or institutions (analogous to clothing as "polluted" or deceitful). On the other hand, nature, when understood as fallen, perverted, or weak (analogous to shameful nakedness) is inferior to culture, art, discipline, or grace, understood as the supplier, repairer, or rectifier of nature (and analogous to clothing as decent necessity, or essential protection).

Such terms as "naked" or "clothed" are indeed positively or negatively valenced in the mainstream and on the fringes of Judeo-Christian culture as a whole. To give a sense of that multivalence, we'll begin with a brief sketch of the "naked" and "clothed" within Jewish and Christian culture in Greco-Roman times, and glance, as well, at nakedness and clothing in certain fringe religious movements of the sixteenth century. Then we'll focus on a detailed examination of these terms in central Reformation religious controversy, illustrating not only their flexibility and relativity within cultural parameters, but their culturally meaningful systematicity as well.

In part because the Jews sought to distinguish themselves from the pagan world of license where nakedness was routine in gymnasia and baths,[3] there is "an enormous gap between Greek and Jewish attitudes towards the body," as Frank Bottomley indicates. In the Old Testament, after the Fall, nakedness is "related to poverty, destitution and exposure"; it is "a metaphor for complete vulnerability," "related to "subjective shame" and to "objective humiliation." In Leviticus, "the concept of nakedness seems to take on a special, almost technical, meaning" and "is particularly associated with incestuous and other unlawful sexual activity in the phrase 'to uncover his/her nakedness.'" In fact, "'nakedness' becomes almost synonymous with 'genitalia.'"[4] "Conversely, . . . clothes are related to status, honour and dignity," as well as associated with "protection and love."[5] In his allegory of Jerusalem as ultimately unfaithful wife, Ezekiel describes how God "spread [his] skirt over [her]" and "covered [her] nakedness" when she was "naked and bare" (Ezekiel 16:8; 16:7),[6] clothing her with "broidred work . . . fine linen . . . and silk" and decking her "with ornaments" — "bracelets," "a chain," "a frontlet," "earrings," and "a beautiful crown" (Ezekiel 16:10-12).

However, even in the Old Testament, clothing is not always a good; such glittering fineries may also be associated with the false allure of harlots and idols. "Thou didst take thy garments, and decked thine high places with divers colours, and played the harlot thereupon. . . . Thou hast also taken thy fair jewels made of my gold and of my silver, which I had given thee, and madst to thy self images of men, and didst commit whoredom with them" (Ezekiel 16:16-17). Somewhat rarer is the use of nakedness as a symbol of spiritually significant experience, or "religious ecstasy,"[7] as for example, when "the Spirit of God came upon [Saul]," and "he went prophesying. . . . And he stripped off his clothes, and he prophesied also before Samuel, and fell down naked all that day and all that night" (1 Samuel 19:23-24).

As Peter Brown shows in *The Body and Society: Men, Women and Sexual Renunciation in Early Christianity,* Christianity gradually brought about a new sensibility to nudity in the late classical world. "Nudity and sexual shame" had been "questions of social status." "The way people felt about being naked, or seeing others naked, depended to a large extent on their social situation." Social superiors were immune from "sexual shame" and could move about naked "without a trace of . . . shame in front of their inferiors," while those at the bottom of the social scale (such as the womenfolk of the poor), as "civic 'non-persons,'" had "no right to sexual shame." Early Christianity, in contrast, generally emphasized the "somber democracy of sexual shame," the "universal vulnerability of the body, to which all men and women were liable, independent of class and civic status."[8]

However, apart from the mainstream, in the early Christian ascetic movements, the positive symbolic signification of nudity as innocence and freedom from sin was exploited. Insofar as the participants regarded life "in a body endowed with sexual charactertistics," "all present notions of identity tied to sexual differences, all social roles based upon marriage, procreation, and childbirth," as "the last dark hour of a long night that would vanish with the dawn,"[9] they could even practice nudity because of their exemption from its temptations. The imagery of divesting oneself of old garments was already tied to baptism, the "rite of entry into the church," which enacted "an explicit stripping off of the distinguishing marks on which the hierarchy of ancient society depended," and emblematized the "primal, undifferentiated unity" of believers.[10] Thus, among the Encratites of the second and third centuries, who advocated strict continence for all the men and women of the Christian church, "baptism was presented as a rite of effective desexualization." When "the initiates stepped naked into the baptismal pool," they were understood "to have put off the sexualized 'garments' of their old body," and become "like little children." "The cold water cancelled out the hot fire that had given them birth. Into this water, the Holy Spirit descended, wrapping the person in a robe of glory."[11]

While there clearly were positive symbolic meanings of nakedness for the early sects, and in the church's rite of baptism, on the other hand, the charge of lewd nakedness, even from early times, often accompanied charges of gross immorality or sorcery (as it did much later on in the case of accusations against radical sixteenth- and seventeenth-century sects—about which we will hear more in chapter 4). The ascetic Priscillian, bishop of Avila, tortured and put to death by imperial order at Trier in 385 because of occult activities, confessed, "under judicial examination, . . . to his interest in magical studies, to having held nocturnal gatherings of (loose) women, and to having prayed naked [that is, to 'Adamianism']. The juxtaposition of the charges was surely intended to insinuate . . . that, in what was believed to be Manichee fashion, these activities had gone on at one and the same time and place." [12] As an anomalous state in a culture generally stressing sexual shame, nakedness clearly partakes of the potential of both the profane and the sacred.

The multivalence of voluntary nakedness and of fine clothing may be observed again in the stories of sixteenth-century messianic leaders like John of Leyden (Jan Bockelson), the messianic and militant ruler of Münster in the early sixteenth century. As Norman Cohn indicates, Bockelson's first religious and political act was to run "naked through the town in a frenzy and then [fall] into a silent ecstasy which lasted three days," but afterward he dressed in the magnificent clothes suitable to his special status as king of an egalitarian paradise on earth.[13] Bockelson "explained that pomp and luxury were permissible for him because he was wholly dead to the world and the flesh. At the same time he assured the common people that before long they too would be in the same situation, sitting on silver chairs and eating at silver tables, yet holding such things as cheap as mud and stones." [14] As Cohn also remarks, the "illiterate young slater of Antwerp called Loy Pruystinck," who was instrumental in spreading the doctrine of "Spiritual Liberty" — a messianic doctrine of the "Free Spirit" — over the Low Countries and France from about 1525 until it was suppressed in 1544, "as though to symbolize at once his vocation of poverty and his claim to a supreme dignity, dressed in robes cut as rags but also sewn with jewels." [15] Naked poverty is worthy and holy, yet gorgeous apparel is a symbol of dignity and worth.

Broadly speaking then, in the Judeo-Christian tradition as a whole, spiritual worth, innocence, or a state of grace may be powerfully symbolized by nakedness as well as by the wearing of fine clothing and adornments; shame and degradation may be powerfully signaled by nakedness as well as by excessive adornment. It does appear that the shamefulness of nakedness and the worth of appropriate or comely apparel is somewhat more stressed in Scripture and historical situation than the glory of "the naked truth" and evils of adornment — even if one allows for the New Testament imagery of, and Reformation Protestant emphasis on, various versions of "the naked truth." Nevertheless, the meanings and evaluations of nakedness and fine clothing do depend on what each contrasts with and refers to in particular texts and cultural situations. It is this relativity — which is really the intrinsic relativity of language per se—that allows people to agree on abstract issues and on values, and thus talk to one another, while concretely disagreeing. And it is with such abstract agreement and concrete disagreement that Reformation religiopolitical opponents discuss church ceremonies and doctrines pertinent to church ceremonies—in arguments in which clothing figures saliently as actuality and metaphor. Like any argument, those between Protestant conformists and nonconformists about "clothing" and "nakedness" in the church depend on those areas of agreement as well as of disagreement. Christian culture (especially because it is based on shared sacred texts, overlapping interpretive traditions, and shared values encoded in those texts) permits an abstract theoretic agreement on statements of the type "Everyone should be properly dressed." It may even permit agreement on the referents and paradigmatic contrasts of "properly dressed" when it is used outside the area of controversy. However, when that concept or term is metaphorically extended to the areas of clerical dress, or of "dressing" the church, or of church doctrine, there is disagreement on the meaning relations within which it functions; that is, with which opposed concepts "properly dressed" contrasts in some particular usage (for example, with "overdressed" or with "underdressed"). There is similar disagreement on the concrete reference of terms; that is, on which specific attire is to be seen as an actual instance of "properly dressed."

The Multivalence and Systematicity of Clothing Metaphors in Reformation Controversy

The metaphors of "the naked truth" and "decent and comely apparel" are used throughout the sixteenth and seventeenth centuries in religious controversy about ceremonies, and modern scholars themselves use these metaphors as analytic categories. Here, for example, is the contemporary author of a standard work on theology and worship, who identifies Puritan nonconformists with a preference for the naked truth:

Yet for [the Puritans] all these Anglican delights were compromises with Roman Catholicism, debilitating distractions . . . outward shows as pretty and irrelevant as carousels, the otiose gilding of the lily and the varnishing of sunlight. . . . When they came to build their own meeting houses, the houses were scrubbed, white, bare, as austerely naked as the soul should be in the sight of God, stripped of all its disguises and pretensions.[16]

The Elizabethan divine Richard Hooker describes the Puritan position in similar terms, although he takes issue with it. "Suppose we that God himself delighteth to dwell sumptuously, or taketh pleasure in charge able pomp? No, then was the Lord most acceptably served, when his temples were rooms borrowed within the houses of poor men. This was suitable unto the nakedness of Jesus Christ and the simplicity of his Gospel." [17] And roughly contemporary reformers or Puritans identify themselves with the metaphor of the naked truth.

The figurative priesthood as a shadow was perfected and ended in Christ, the one and only Priest. All they therefore that call again Aaron's apparel into the church dishonor Christ's priesthood, as though being the light itself he needed shadows. . . .

. . . Why do we not . . . in all things obey Christ, contenting ourselves with his naked and simple truth? [18]

For there are some which think Christ too base to be preached simply in himself, and therefore mingle with him too much the wisdom of man's eloquence, and think that Christ cometh nakedly, unless clothed with vain ostentation of words. Others esteem him too homely, simple and un-learned, unless he be beautified and blazed over with store of Greek or Latin sentences in the pulpits: some reckon of him as solitary, or as a pri-vate person without honor and pomp, unless he be brought forth of them very solemnly, accompanied and countenanced, with the ancient guard of the fathers and doctors of the Church to speak for him: or else must he be glozed out and painted with the froth of philosophy, poetry or such like. [19]

On the other hand, the Anglicans or conformists are commonly identified (and identify themselves) with the metaphor of decent and comely apparel. Hooker says "there is no necessity of stripping sacra-ments out of all such attire of ceremonies as man's wisdom hath at any time clothed them withal" (*LEP,* 5.65.3, in *Works,* 2:319). Donne argues in terms of apparel for the use of rich or set forms in religion: "Be-loved, outward things apparel God; and since God was content to take a *body,* let us not leave him naked, nor ragged." [20] He goes even further than such arguments, requiring for the church an "outward splendor," "a comeliness in the outward face, and habit thereof." "*Be the King's Daughter all glorious within;* Yet, all her glory is not within; for, *Her cloth-ing is of wrought gold,* says that text. Still may she glory in her internal glory, in the sincerity, and in the integrity of doctrinal truths, and glory too in her outward comeliness, and beauty" (*Sermons*, 8:165 [no. 6]). Hooker's comely apparel may also be quite sublime:

Touching God himself, hath he any where revealed that it is his delight to dwell beggarly? And that he taketh no pleasure to be worshipped saving only in poor cottages? Even then was the Lord as acceptably honoured of his people as ever, when the stateliest places and things in the whole world were sought out to adorn his temple. This most suitable, decent, and fit for the greatness of Jesus Christ, for the sublimity of his gospel. (*LEP*, 5.15.3, in *Works*, 2:53)

Yet, in spite of these apparent and clear differences with regard to the subject of proper "clothing" in the church, the clothing metaphor used by these opposed groups actually shares an underlying semantic structure. The usage of the metaphor is constrained in some shared, definable ways, even if the overall emphases differ: that is, even if each group tends to employ different contrast sets and referents—out of the implicitly accepted pool.

For now, then, let us consider what they share: certain ideas about proper clothing per se, if *not* about the proper "clothing" of the church. (After all, in a debate, each side is trying to win over members of a common audience.) Of all the possible positive functions of clothing, both sides recognize the function of a comely and protective covering for nakedness—which may mean a decent covering that avoids the shamefulness of immodesty, or a covering nice enough to avoid the shamefulness of beggarliness. (The meanings of "comely" include "decent" ["proper," "seemly," "sober," "decorous," or "appropriate"] as well as "nice" ["fair," "pretty"].)[21] Of all the possible negative functions of clothing, both sides recognize its potential uncomely use, when it is too inappropriately "mean," or too scant or immodest, or even wantonly superfluous, misleading, or deceitful, like the alluring "clothing" of prostitutes or idols—in which case the bare truth would indeed be preferable. The basis of the clothing metaphor, then, as employed in Reformation religious controversy, is an implicit agreement that clothing may be uncomely and that the absence of clothing would be indecent, and that both uncomely clothing and indecent nakedness are to be avoided. James I's description of the causes for God's invention of ordinary secular garments recognizes the exact same functions: "to hide our nakedness and shame; next and consequently to make us more comely, and thirdly, to preserve us from the injuries of heat and cold." James also warns of similar potential abuses: "If to hide our nakedness and shameful parts, then these natural parts ordained to be hid, should not be represented by any undecent forms in the clothes: and if they should help our comeliness, they should not then by their painted preened fashion, serve for baits to filthy lechery."[22]

It is because of such common bases, ultimately having to do with shared perceptions, values, and experiences, that metaphorical extensions from material clothing to "clothing" in the church are not really random, or accurately encompassed by the poststructuralist idea of the potentially infinite deferral of meaning. (There are hints of such common bases even in the passages supplied above to illustrate the *differences* in Anglican and Puritan uses of clothing metaphors. Hooker describes stately things as *"suitable, decent and fit"* for Jesus Christ. And the Puritan sermonizer says "some . . . think . . . Christ cometh nakedly, unless clothed with vain ostentation of words," thus implying that covering—though not superfluous or vain covering—is necessary.) It is this shared underlying structure, stemming, in fact, from attitudes toward actual, secular clothing, that allows opponents within religious culture to talk to each other at all. But such shared structures also allow opponents to hear each other as "saying the same thing" when it is convenient to do so, although they do not mean the same thing at all. For one side, "proper" clothing in the church may implicitly contrast with "foul and ragged clothes" (*LEP,* 5.29.2, in *Works,* 2:129), with a too undignified or too bare dress not showing sufficient reverence. For the other side, "proper" clothing may contrast with precious and emperor-like garments, with "glittering gear," with too theatrical or masque-like dress.[23]

While such paradigmatic contrasts as those just cited are more or less obvious, it is the different referents of "decently clothed" or "shamefully bare" that are extremely interesting in this particular case, because they reveal how both conformist and nonconformist Protestant share values within the general Christian culture that permit them to talk to one another. In fact, because their referents differ, both sides actually could make use of the *same* broad paradigmatic contrasts. Both sides use the "clothing metaphor" to make two general statements: (1) Clothing is a good if the alternative is a shameful or uncomely nakedness; (2) Clothing is not a good if the alternative is the naked truth—even if the Anglicans more often state the former and the Puritans the latter. However, the specific referents of the terms that take the positive or negative valence may greatly differ.

Let us first consider those occasions on which both sides assert that clothing is a good if the alternative is a shameful nakedness. The rabidly nonconformist *Marprelate Tracts* actually bewail the "poor, poor nakedness" of the present church government, and the author of "A Second Admonition to the Parliament" considers it necessary to "cover this shame with a right cover, that is, with a right reformation." [24] The government of the church must be clearly warranted and brought to perfection; to fail to provide such a reformation would be to settle for an inappropriate "nakedness." As the *Marprelate Tracts* put it, such failure to provide that "right cover" would be equivalent to agreeing with the false statement "A man is a man though he go naked; therefore, the Lord hath ordained no covering for his nakedness." [25] Similarly, and again in spite of our strong association of the Puritans with the theme of "the naked truth," the Presbyterian controversialist Thomas Cartwright can argue, in terms of a "dainty diet" and adorning jewels, the necessity of spelling out all aspects of church order. It is not true, he asserts, that there is "in the scriptures only [clothing enough] to cover [the church's] nakedness and not also chains and bracelets and rings and other jewels to adorn her and set her out; that, to conclude, there were sufficient to quench her thirst and kill her hunger, but not to minister unto her a more liberall and (as it were) a more delicious and dainty diet." [26] (Here Presbyterian discipline is justified by recourse to what might well appear a rather Anglican idea of shameful nakedness!) However, the very Scriptures that would provide the ordained covering for what the more radical consider a shameful nakedness, are for Richard Hooker, in themselves, bare and naked without the customs, traditions, and authority of men: "An earnest desire to draw all things under the determination of bare and naked Scripture hath caused here much pains to be taken in abating the estimation and credit of man" (*LEP,* 2.7.1, in *Works,* 1:318).

Significantly, both sides may also assert that clothing is not a good if the alternative is the necessary truth: a deceitful cover-up may obscure a truth that ought to be revealed, even a shameful one. The nonconformist Walter Travers disparages "the inventions of men, and of what men but even of such which have sought to paint and adorn with these colors the shame of their whorish idolatry and superstition." [27] But Hooker, too, can avail himself of the positive connotations of the metaphor of the naked truth: "It is not part of my secret meaning to draw you hereby into hatred, or to set upon the face of this cause any fairer glass than the naked truth doth afford" (*LEP,* Preface, 7.1, in

Works, 1:171). Even a famous statement of Milton's from *The Reason of Church Government*—a statement that begins with a clear celebration of a "naked Gospel"—amazingly goes on to use the clothing metaphor (with its implicit corroboration of the *need* for a covering) in order to argue, paradoxically, for a desirable "nakedness" in the church. Milton begins by asserting: "[A]ll corporeal resemblances of inward holiness and beauty are now past; he that will clothe the Gospel now, intimates plainly, that the Gospel is [when] naked, uncomely." On the one hand, indeed, for Milton, the true church itself has no need for "clothing." He asks: "Is our religion guilty of the first trespass, and hath need of clothing to cover her nakedness?" Yet, on the other hand, he goes on to say, "Christ is clothing upon our bareness with his righteous garment to make us acceptable in his father's sight"; that is, sinful man *does* require clothing, but the only clothing he requires is Christ. (Putting on Christ is a Protestant trope for justification to which I shall shortly return.) Thus, Milton's metaphoric language is based on culturally shared root ideas about inappropriate nakedness and the need for decent apparel, although this apparel, metaphorically extended—like the right reformation described in the "Second Admonition" and in the *Marprelate Tracts*—paradoxically may involve an absence of apparel in some of its literal or usual senses (for example, vestments and ceremonies). As well as commenting on the right clothing for religion, Milton, perhaps more in accordance with our expectations, explicitly recognizes the deceit involved in the wrong kind of apparel that obscures the naked truth of Christ (that is, "the polluted clothing of . . . ceremonies," the "gaudy glisterings" that "cover and hide [Christ's] righteous verity").[28]

The moderate Anglican Herbert Thorndike takes a position that contrasts with Milton's in a work written at about the same time. As clothing protects the vital heat or life of the body, so ceremonies protect the life of religion. Ceremonies are "the apparel of religion at the heart," though "some think, like the sun, [religion is] most beautiful when it is most naked." "As long as our bodily senses are managed to our soul's advantage, the heat within will starve without this apparel without."[29] Yet even Thorndike's comments illustrate my principle—that is, that opponents share a universe of discourse. Thorndike implicitly recognizes the danger of "mere" apparel by figuring ceremonies as the apparel of religion "at the heart"; he makes clear that the "clothing" of ceremony is functional (as opposed to merely showy, or decorative), by describing it in terms of protection of "internal heat," that is, of life itself.

If one is surprised by Cartwright's notion of proper (that is, Presbyterian) government as the church's adorning jewels, one will be even more surprised by Hooker's turning of Cartwrightian terms upside down once more against such as Cartwright—especially insofar as Cartwright's terms were already an attempt to turn Hookerian terms against such as Hooker. For Hooker, matters of government (*if* that government is Presbyterian) are "externals," equivalent to superfluous ornaments, which he in fact argues the church does *not* need:

> Let them which therefore think us blameable consider well their own words. Do they not plainly compare the one [things necessary unto salvation] unto garments which cover the body of the Church; the other [things accessory, things of external regiment in the Church] unto rings, bracelets, and jewels, that only adorn it; the one to that food which the Church doth live by, the other to that which maketh her diet liberal, dainty, and more delicious? Is dainty fare a thing necessary to the sustenance, or to the clothing of the body rich attire? If not, how can they urge the necessity of that which themselves resemble by things not necessary? (*LEP*, 3.3.4., in *Works*, 1:357)

In an effort to trap his opponents, Hooker here takes metaphor very literally as an indicator of "position"—like some modern critics, although, one suspects, more self-consciously. Thus, even Anglicans may metaphorically argue *against* rich attire, while using actual rich attire in the church. Puritans may use the metaphor of rich attire to argue for a church governed as they wish, and *without* actual rich attire. Hooker argues for a "modest" as opposed to an overly adorned church (that is, a church without superfluous Presbyterian "government"); on the other hand, if proper—even rich—adornment is a value, Cartwright agrees that his group has it, meaning, however, that very Presbyterian government.

I want briefly to turn from controversy about ceremonies and look a little more closely at the trope for justification in Christ referred to earlier, because it also makes both of the statements of value about actual and figurative clothing that we have seen are most likely within the framework of Renaissance Christian cultural expectations—that is, "Clothing is not a good if the alternative is the naked truth" and "Clothing is a good if the alternative is a shameful or uncomely nakedness." Christ is "the naked truth," before whom it is appropriate for the Christian to appear stripped of the polluted clothing of the old Adam, but he is also, in the common Protestant trope for justification, the new "clothing" that can cover the shameful nakedness of the old Adam. "The metaphor of being dressed in another's clothes . . . is one of the most ancient and standard ways of talking about imputed merit, as in Donne's 'So in his purple wrapped receive me Lord,' in Luther's talk of 'the righteousness [of Christ] with which God *clothes us* when he justifies us,' and in Ambrose's explication of Jacob being blessed in his brother's coat (highly approved by Calvin)."[30] Thus Christ embodies, at one and the same time, the values of appropriate nakedness and appropriate clothing. Not surprisingly, an Elizabethan private "Prayer at the putting on of our clothes," which alludes to justification, uses tropes both of being stripped out of polluted clothing and of being re-clothed in appropriate clothing:

Most gracious and merciful, Saviour, Jesus Christ, thou knowest how we be born, clothed and clogged with the grievous and heavy burthen of the first man, who fell away into fleshliness through disobedience. Vouchsafe, therefore, I beseech thee, to strip me out of the old corrupt Adam, . . . being soaked in sin. . . . Clothe me with thyself, O my redeemer and sanc-tifier, . . . which art the second man . . . . Be thou our clothing and apparel, to keep us warm from the cold of this world.[31]

To return to our controversialists then: the conformist and the non-conformist are both saying—in accordance with shared cultural postu-lates of the need for a covering and the need, at the same time, to avoid shameful or deceiving coverings (equivalent here to a basic or "core" concept of "proper clothing")—that the church they approve of is as naked as it should be and as clothed as it should be. These writers do not disagree on the core, nonmetaphoric meanings of their terms, al-though they sometimes disagree on the specific contrast sets to which their metaphorically extended terms most forcefully pertain, and they often disagree on the actual referents of those terms: What is decent but not deceitful apparel in the church? What is appropriate but not shameful nakedness? These clothing metaphors, then, remind us of the shared basis that allows dialogue or argument between opposed parties—and in a case where we may be surprised by such underlying similarities, having assumed that Puritans are committed to "the naked truth" per se and Anglicans to "decent and comely apparel" per se.

It should be noted that this "systematicity"—as I have called it—is nothing so self-conscious or technical as shared substantive theological principles or philosophical axioms. I am talking about a local linguis-tic systematicity that has to do with a particular semantic domain of a particular culture and time. As part of language this semantic domain is *coded* in certain ways; that is, certain concepts tend to enter into certain structural relations with certain other concepts. It is such coding Saussure talks about when he says, for example: "Modern French *mouton* can have the same signification as English *sheep* but not the same value," because "*sheep* has beside it a second term," "mutton," for "a piece of meat ready to be served on the table," "while the French word does not" (*Course in General Linguistics*, 115–16). This, in turn, is exactly the same thing Jonathan Culler is talking about when he imagines the change of value of "sheep" in English if the word "mutton" were to disappear from the language: "[T]he value of *sheep* would change radically; *beef, pork, veal*, etc. would become slightly more anomalous with the disappearance of one member of their paradigm class; sentences like *The sheep is too hot to eat* would become ambiguous." As he says, "Relations are important for what they can explain: meaningful contrasts and permitted or forbidden combinations."[32]

Thus, in choosing (from what is available in English Protestant language and culture) a particular contrast like "naked" versus "clothed"—over some other contrast—as the source for the vehicle of one's metaphor, one is also choosing what differences to assert or foreground on the level of the tenor, that is, the subject one is addressing. The assertions carried by "naked" as opposed to "clothed" (whichever side is taken as positive or negative) are clearly different from those carried by silk as opposed to wool—for example, "Taffata phrases, silken terms precise" versus "russet yeas and honest kersey noes" (*Love's Labor's Lost*, 5.2.406; 5.2.413). The "naked truth" is not the same as the "russet truth." "Systematicity" means that if "naked" (as part of the contrast set with "clothed") is "good," it is good in particular ways and not others, and what is good about it is presumed by the speakers who share the concept. Thus, for example, the positive value of "naked" is a value determined by its most common paradigmatic contrast, that is, being clothed in deceiving or corrupting clothing. Furthermore, the positive value of "nakedness" in the language and culture we've been examining is *not* the value of untrammeled free expression (or "letting it all hang out"), for example, as contrastive with repressive or constraining "clothing"—as it was in the America of the sixties, when one extolled "naked poetry." Our Renaissance example does show how and why certain contrasts—and not others—were basic to creating meaning with "clothing."

Since there are in fact many continuities (in addition to some discontinuities) of present-day language and culture with Renaissance Christian language and culture, it should not be surprising that these "meaningful contrasts" and "permitted or forbidden combinations" should seem obvious and familiar to us. We are talking about the root way we *mean* with language, the "core concepts" that have to do with very simple, basic shared experiences and values. Yet that very easy and obvious sense of familiarity can sometimes seriously mislead the critic when those contrasts and combinations relate to some aspect of culture and religion that has significantly changed. Russell Fraser equates Lear's presumed identification of "nakedness with lack of substance" with "the *mistake* of the medieval artist" who "clothes the higher principle [Reason] and leaves Nature, the lesser, unclothed."[33] He automatically sees the "naked Truth"—still of course, a resonant metaphor for us—as the positive term in the contrast. In doing so, he probably reveals our own contemporary defaults, our slant against markers of dignity or rank.

The use of clothing metaphors in Reformation controversy graphically illustrates the problems we may have in taking a writer's approval of the "decently clothed" or "ornamented," for example, as opposed to the "naked and plain" (or, of course, vice versa), as indicative of religiopolitical position, without a sufficient sense of the wider variety of oppositions in which shared terms or metaphors may participate and of incompatible referents to which shared terms may point. The metaphoric use of nakedness and plainness in a particular writer does not mean that his religiopolitical position follows analogously. The metaphoric use of "dress," even sumptuous dress, as we have seen, does not necessarily imply approval of actual rich dress (that is, vestments) in the church. The metaphoric use of stained-glass windows, as we shall see in chapter 3, does not necessarily imply that the writer's main purpose is a polemical apologia for actual stained-glass windows, and thus that the writer has the religious views the critic or historian regards as logically following from such a defense. For all these reasons the critic should not leap incautiously into the politics of metaphor.

Speakers use metaphors creatively, and that means differently in different situations, according to need, and by no means necessarily analogously or consistently—though, nevertheless, within the shared cultural frameworks (the very ones I am here trying to recover) that enable that use to be understood by cultural insiders. For example, Donne's use of the metaphor of glorious outward clothing suitable for a king's daughter (which we've already observed) in an argument for rich or set forms in religion, does not prevent him, on another occasion, from using Tertullian's work, *De Habitu Muliebri* (which "notes . . . excesses in women's dressing"), in order to dress down those preachers whose sermons are excessively "dressed." Donne castigates those who, "for pride," use "a superfluous diligence in their dressing" — that is, who mingle "too much human ornament, and secular learning in preaching" — and those who "*ad prostitutionem,* for a worse, for the worst purpose," mingle "human traditions, as of things of equal value, and obligation, with the commandments of God" (*Sermons,* 10:146–47 [no. 6]). Furthermore — in spite of his use of the metaphor of glorious outward clothing in his argument *for* set forms, and his use of the metaphor of superfluous dressing *against* secular learning in sermons — Donne may also use clothing metaphors completely in accordance with the values "*neither* superfluous and deceiving, *nor* too mean" on another occasion — as he does when he argues against the priests of Rome. These used their portions not for "sustentation," but for "their own splendor, and glory, and surfeit":

Christ . . . will be clothed in the poor that are naked, so he would be enriched in those poor ministers that serve at his altar; . . . when he would be so clothed, he desires not soft raiment fit for *King's houses,* nor embroideries, nor perfumes; . . . but yet, as he would not be . . . submitted to cold and unwholesome air in the naked, so neither would he be made contemptible, nor beggarly in the minister of his Church. (Ibid., 143).[34]

Comeliness and Secular Apparel

The extravagance of Elizabethan costume, especially in the court, has of course been noted by historians as well as contemporary observers. Such costume fully exemplifies Thorstein Veblen's categories (in his *Theory of the Leisure Class*) of conspicuous consumption, conspicuous leisure, and conspicuous waste, not to mention the fourth, added by Quentin Bell in *On Human Finery,* namely, conspicuous outrage.[35] For conspicuous consumption and conspicuous waste, consider the lavish amounts, the multitudinous layers of material used in contemporaneous costumes, as well as the complex workmanship with which the layers were treated. Doublets and other garments were stuffed and/or pinked and slashed ("This cloth of price, all cut in rags")[36] in order to show their lining or the embroidered shirt beneath; sleeves covered other sleeves whose material was pulled out decoratively; some sleeves were long enough to trail on the ground or be "cast over [the] shoulders, like cowtails";[37] breeches and hose were made of two different materials, elaborately patterned; huge ruffs could extend up to the ears or fall over on the shoulders. Phillip Stubbes's description of the latter is deservedly well known:

They have great and monstrous ruffs . . . of . . . the finest cloth that can be got for money, whereof some be a quarter of a yard deep, yea, some more . . . ; so that they stand a full quarter of a yard . . . from their necks, hanging over their shoulder points, instead of a veil. But if *Aeolus* with his blasts, or *Neptune* with his storms chance to hit upon the crazy bark of their bruised ruffs, then they go flip flap in the wind, like rags flying abroad, and lie upon their shoulders like the dishclout of a slut. (*Anatomy,* 51)

For conspicuous consumption, one may also consider the cost. A highly decorated hat band "composed entirely of pearls and valued at £30 was stolen from Sir Walter Raleigh's house in 1584."[38] "One imported ostrich feather, even before it went on sale in the shop, represented the approximate equivalent of a labourer's pay for five days' work."[39]

The Earl of Arundel . . . owed £1,023 to 42 mercers, silkmen, tailors, embroiderers and other tradesmen. The Earl of Essex owed his draper £736 and the Earl of Leicester owned seven doublets and two cloaks valued at £543. This was an extraordinarily high sum, in view of . . . the fact that the cost of the entire winter uniform for an officer serving in Ireland in 1599 totalled £4 0s. 10d.[40]

The sumptuousness of clothing at court stemmed in part from the standard Elizabeth herself set; she was reputed to have had more than two thousand dresses.[41] For conspicuous leisure, consider the difficulty of getting into these layers of clothing, the points (laces or cords) by which the privileged were trussed into their clothes by their servants, the pins that accomplished often temporary effects that would need to be redone. For conspicuous outrage, consider the jeweled ear pick "of gold enameled, garnished with sparks of rubies, blue sapphires and seed pearl" presented to Elizabeth in 1575.[42]

One might think that courtiers, noblemen, and others in the secular sphere would evince different attitudes toward secular clothing than churchmen, and that their clothing metaphors might also be significantly different from those we have been examining. To an extent

this is true. However, in spite of the lavishness of actual secular clothing, particularly in the Elizabethan court, and in spite of a growing
identification towards the mid-seventeenth century of the Puritan with
more sober clothing, the abstract injunctions concerning personal apparel for gentleman or prince — of which James I's *Basilikon Doron* provides an example we have already partially considered — do share that
middle term "comeliness" with arguments about too little and too
much "clothing" in the church. Thus, these injunctions do deplore extremes of defect *and* excess, as we shall further see.

Here is Thomas Elyot in his "mirror for princes," *The Governour*:

So is there apparel comely to every estate and degree, and that which
exceedeth or lacketh, procureth reproach, in a noble man specially. For apparel simple or scant, reproveth him of avarice. If it be alway exceeding
precious, and often times changed, as well in to charge as strange and new
fashions, it causeth him to be noted dissolute of manners.

The most noble emperors of Rome, Augustus, Trajan, Hadrian, An-
tonine, Severus, and Alexander, which were of all other incomparable in
honourable living, used a discreet moderation in their apparel, although
they were great emperors and gentles. How much more ought then Christian men, whose denomination is founded on humility, and they that be
not of the estate of princes, to show a moderation and constancy in ves-
ture, that they diminish no part of their majesty, either with newfangleness
or with oversumptuous expenses? And yet may this last be suffered where
there is a great assembly of strangers, for then some time it is expedient
that a nobleman in his apparel do advance himself to be both rich and honourable.[43]

Similarly, although in "The Steel Glas" George Gascoigne makes the
familiar attacks on greed (the pursuit of "sumptuous cloth of gold,"
"silks of strange devise," "pearls and precious stones," "mines of glis-
tering gold") as well as on the failure of hospitality, he also sees fit to
assert: "The sumptuous house, declares the prince's state, / But vain
excess, bewrays a prince's faults."[44]

King James's reign is commonly credited with a somewhat more
relaxed and less artificially flamboyant style than Elizabeth's.[45] And indeed *his* mean between extremes, in the context of his account, in
Basilikon Doron, of the functions of secular clothing as first instituted by
God, perhaps gives "comeliness" less leeway for extravagance, than do
some other "means":[46]

Be also moderate in your raiment, neither over superfluous, like a de-
boshed waster; nor yet over base, like a miserable wretch; not artificially
trimmed and decked, like a courtesan, nor yet over sluggishly clothed,
like a country clown, not over lightly like a candy soldier or a vain young
courtier; nor yet over gravely, like a minister: but in your garments be
proper, cleanly, comely and honest, wearing your clothes in a careless, yet
comely form: keeping in them a middle form . . . betwixt . . . gravity . . .
and lightness (*Basilikon Doron*, 45).

As we have already seen earlier in this chapter, of the positive functions
of clothing (aside from protection from the weather), James stresses
mainly a modest, and in *that* sense "comely" covering for a shameful
nakedness; he also stresses clothing's potential negative uses in immodest allurement.[47]

George Puttenham uses rather lavish *metaphors* of dress for a tenor
that understandably invites them, that is, in defense of a rich style "of
ornament poetical" that "may delight and allure as well the mind as the
ear of the hearers with a certain novelty and strange manner of con-
veyance, disguising it no little from the ordinary and accustomed." But
even he seems to be aware of the possibilities of excess. To begin with,
Puttenham does appear to equivocate by saying that such novelty and
strangeness, although raising the language from the "ordinary," will
make it "nothing the more unseemly or misbecoming, but rather de-
center and more agreeable to any civil ear and understanding." Now
certainly the examples he gives on the level of the vehicle of the metaphor suggest more than merely "plain and simple apparel." Puttenham
talks of "great Madames of honour" thinking themselves "more ami-
able in every man's eye when they be in their richest attire . . . of silks
or tissues and costly embroideries"; he talks similarly of Poesie showing itself "gorgeous" when no "limb be left naked and bare," but all
is ornamented with figures "that a poet setteth upon his language of
art," just as the "embroiderer doth his stone and pearl or passements of
gold upon the stuff of a princely garment." Nevertheless, in spite of this
clear stress on lavish ornament above the "ordinary" and the "vulgar,"
Puttenham, hedging, seems to slip in simple decency as a value—thus
muddying the line between necessary protection and lavish display—
when he speaks of the discomfitted "Madames of honour" as those
who "want their courtly habiliments" or "*at leastwise* [my emphasis]
such other apparel as custom and civility have ordained to cover their

naked bodies." Furthermore, and importantly, he is aware that there can be too much embroidery, too many colors:

[S]o nevertheless . . . if the same colours in our art of Poesie (as well as in those other mechanical arts) be not well tempered, or not well laid, or be used in excess, . . . they not only give it no manner of grace at all, but rather do disfigure the stuff and spill the whole workmanship . . . ; wherefore the chief praise and cunning of our Poet is in the discreet using of his figures, . . . by all measure and just proportion.[48]

All these pronouncements—including James's, then—suggest the ways in which a "middle form" or "comeliness" could be understood and, in some circumstances, even approved, by those who might in fact see different kinds of clothing as embodiments of it—from garb leaning toward the sober, to garb leaning toward the splendid. Of course, "comeliness" is a stretchable term; what that "decorous," "appropriate," and "proper"—that is, "comely"—"mean" might be is relative, insofar as what is "appropriate" is relative to rank and dignity. (The canonical definition of avarice in Aquinas allows for differences in style of life appropriate for different ranks; it is permissible for a person to "seek to possess material wealth to the degree that it is necessary for a life suited to his station.")[49] It is certainly possible that one man's "comely apparel" suitable to the occasion might be to another—who didn't think the occasion warranted it—an example of conspicuous consumption, leisure, waste, or outrage. Nevertheless, it is important to recognize that, even among Puritans, or those who sometimes deplore "excess" in apparel, evaluations of "comeliness" or due decorum *do* take into account what is fit or proper for rank, and what maintains social or civil hierarchy—even if Puritans do not think the surplice worn by bishops in their spiritual functions is "comely." One must be wary of leaping to the conclusion that radical Protestants or Puritans favored egalitarianism, and, consequently, an egalitarian simplicity of personal dress contrasting with the opulence favored by conservative hierarchists.[50]

In the later sixteenth and earlier seventeenth century, Puritans were not associated exclusively with plain or simple dress; Anglicans attacked them for both "excessively fine attire and overly simple clothing."[51] During this period and later, even Puritans recognized and approved of a certain sumptuousness of apparel as an appropriate marker of rank amongst the higher orders of society, or of position amongst magistrates, thus sharing in the virtually universal cultural respect accorded the maintenance of the visible signs of difference in degree. Philoponus, the traveler who has been to Ailgna in Stubbes' *Anatomy*, finds "the execrable sin of Pride, and excess in apparel" the "greatest abuse" there, and wishes, along with Spudeus, the other interlocutor, that "a decency, a comely order . . . a *decorum* were observed"; he spends the greater part of the discussion of clothing lambasting its outrageous excesses (27, 30). Nevertheless, he makes considerable allowances for the use of "silks, velvets, taffeties, and other such rich attire" that Spudeus asks him about:

> It is lawful for the potentates, the nobility, the gentry, yeomanry, and for every private subject else to wear attire every one in his degree, according as his calling and condition of life requireth; yet a mean is to be kept, for . . . every extreme is turned into vice. The nobility . . . and the gentry . . . may use a rich and precious kind of apparel . . . to ennoble, garnish, and set forth their births, dignities, functions, and callings. . . . The magistrates also and officers in the weal public . . . may wear (if the Prince or Superintendent do godly command) costly ornaments and rich attire, to dignify their callings, and to . . . show forth the excellency and worthiness of their offices and functions, thereby to strike a terror and fear into the hearts of the people to offend against the majesty of their callings. (Ibid., 33, 34) [52]

Yes, Puritans were thought identifiable—especially by their mockers, perhaps, and especially towards mid-century—by their short hair and narrow, plain bands (that is, collars). A 1602 play describes the courtship of a Puritan lady (whose pretentions to virtue it mocks) by a suitor who gains entry to her house after he has changed his style of dress:

> I parted for that time, and came again,
> Seeming to be conformed in look and speech,
> My shoes were sharp toed, and my band was plain,
> Close to my thigh my metamorphiz'd breech:
> My cloak was narrow capped, my hair cut shorter,
> Off went my scarf, thus marched I to the porter. [53]

A song making fun of Civil War–period Puritan fashions is almost identical:

> For ever something did offend her there,
> Either my broad beard, hat, or my long hair.
>> My band was broad, my 'parel was not plain,
>> My points and girdle made the greatest show;

My sword was odious, and my belt was vain,
>   My Spanish shoes were cut too broad at toe!
My stockings light, my garters tied too long,
My gloves perfumed, and had a scent too strong.[54]

Nevertheless, even at the time of the Commonwealth—according to students of costume—"plainness and severity in dress was less a distinction of religion than of social class" and therefore could be forsaken by the leaders of society, whatever side they were on.[55] The well-born parliamentarian, Colonel John Hutchinson, son of a knight, and the parvenu Puritan, General Thomas Harrison, son of a butcher or grazier, both dressed as lavishly as they thought they should, although they were both regicide Independents, as a story Mrs. Lucy Hutchinson tells in her *Memoirs* wonderfully reveals:

A great ambassador from the King of Spain was to have public audience in the house, and was the first who had addressed them, owning them as a republic. . . . The colonel himself had on that day a habit which was pretty rich but grave, and no other than he usually wore. Harrison addressing himself particularly to him, admonished them all, that now the nations sent to them, they should labour to shine before them in wisdom, piety, righteousness, and justice, and not in gold and silver and worldly bravery, which did not become saints; and that the next day when the ambassadors came, they should not set themselves out in gorgeous habits, which were unsuitable to holy professions. The colonel, although he was not convinced of any misbecoming bravery in the suit he wore that day, which was but of sad-coloured cloth trimmed with gold, and silver points and buttons; yet because he would not appear offensive in the eyes of religious persons, the next day he went in a plain black suit, and so did all the other gentlemen; but Harrison came that day in a scarlet coat and cloak, both laden with gold and silver lace, and the coat so covered with clinquant (foil), that one scarcely could discern the ground, and in this glittering habit he set himself just under the speaker's chair; which made the other gentlemen think that his godly speeches, the day before, were but made that he alone might appear in the eyes of strangers.[56]

Conversely, at an earlier date, William Laud, as bishop of London, could rebuke a too gallantly dressed minister and point to his own plainer apparel as exemplary.[57]

Because of the cultural importance of visible signs of degree, gentlemen seem to have felt it more desirable to recommend or legislate

appropriate dress for their social inferiors than to have their own dress
regulated. Joan Kent points out that although some more radical Protestant members of the House of Commons introduced apparel bills in
the early seventeenth century on the grounds that excess in apparel
was a sin "which occasioned the disapproval of God, who had dressed
men first in skin," opposition to such legislation was sometimes based
on the feeling that such bills were "a threat to the very social distinctions which earlier [Elizabethan] bills had been designed to mirror and
reinforce."⁵⁸ "The . . . apparel bill of 1621, which would have coupled
the gentry with servants and apprentices and legislated them all into
cloth . . . encountered opposition from at least one gentleman." John
Jephson, "knight for Hampshire," felt that " 'there was no reason there
should be so much [difference between the nobility and gentry] as is
between silk and cloth and so little left betwixt us and our servants as
betwixt October and May a gentleman should not know his wife from
his chamber-maid.' " When, in 1622, "a committee on trade, composed
of privy councillors, proposed similar regulations for the wearing of
cloth they suggested that the nobility and gentry be persuaded to wear
cloth in winter 'by example rather than by command' and that only
'the meaner sort of people' be obliged by proclamation to do so."⁵⁹

It is because of the discrepancy between the singularity of some expression such as "comeliness" and the variety of different oppositions
or referents it may pertain to that we as critics, and indeed Reformation controversialists as well, can make the same texts serve so many
different arguments. In fact, religious partisans themselves sometimes
indicate their awareness of the pliability of such terms as "comeliness," whether applied to actual clothing or to church "clothing," that
is, to ceremonies. For example, one of the interlocutors in the Puritan
Arthur Dent's *The Plaine Man's Pathway to Heaven* very understandably
asks, "But, who shall judge what is comely, sober, handsome, modest,
etc.? For every man and woman will say, their apparel is but decent and
cleanly; how gallant, brave, and flaunting soever it be."⁶⁰ William Bradshaw, a moderate Puritan, writing at the beginning of James's reign
against "the Ceremonies Imposed upon the Ministers of the Gospel . . .
by Our Prelates" (such as the still annoying surplice), shows his awareness of the pliability of "comeliness" in the way he puts and answers
the argument of the opposition.

It is necessary to salvation, that men should not only worship God, but
worship him in a comely, decent, and orderly manner, it being a matter of

damnation to worship God in a confused, unseemly, and disordered manner, but by the doctrine of our prelates, comeliness, decency, and order, consists in the use of these ceremonies; ergo, in their judgement they are necessary to salvation.

Answ. . . . What if the Synod should decree that the King should hold the Archbishop's stirrup, and the Prince and the nobles kiss his toe, once or twice a year? and withal they should protest, that they do not require this as a worship, or honor to the Archbishop, but only for comeliness, order, and edification? were not this a shamefull shift, as bad as the thing it self?[61]

In fact, Bradshaw himself, in the course of trying to show that those ceremonies termed "indifferent" by the bishops are in fact an evil, makes a point crucial to the argument of this chapter, namely, that such terms as "shamefully bare," "comely and decent," "whorishly decked out"—while tapping shared systems of value—are perceived as being appropriately embodied or avoided only in the choices of one's *own* group.[62]

A thing indifferent (in the largest extent of sense) is any *mean* between two extremes. . . . To be a *mean* between two *extremes,* is to be so seated between them, as that it stand equally affected to either, inclining no more to the one than to the other. . . . By all this it may appear that things indifferent, are not such simply in themselves and of themselves considered, but as they are compared and have relation to the said opposite extremes. . . . The very essence therefore of a thing indifferent, consists in that equal and indifferent reference and relation that it hath to some two opposite terms or extremes, unto which either in sense or reason it is compared, and by which only it is measured. . . . So nothing is in and of it self indifferent, but only in relation and reference to some opposite extremes: *And those things which in some such respect may be indifferent, in some other respect may be extremes.*[63]

For all the slipperiness of linguistic signs, however, there is a clear difference between such relative meaning and either the absence of meaning or an uninterpretable plethora of possible meanings. It is the culturally *shared* paradigms that such terms do enter into—the *common* contrasts, and even the *common* referents—that permit a variety of contemporaneous readers or hearers of literature to participate in its values and therein find their own.[64] And these paradigms do demarcate some semantic ground. The "comely," for example, is definitely not the extravagantly decorated or overdecorated (one does not find public spokesmen for anything admittedly lavish, in the sense of *indecorous*), nor is it the too bare, mean, or immodest. As we have seen, both Elyot in *The Governour* and the Puritan Stubbes, as well as King James, share, with others, the idea of a mean between vain, newfangled, or preposterous excess, and unseemly baseness, even if—once concrete referents are chosen for each of these anchoring extremes—it might turn out that their "means" are somewhat different.

Nakedness and Clothing in Controversy about the

Eucharist: Anxiety about Representation?

Before leaving the issue of the multivalence and systematicity of metaphors of nakedness and clothing in Reformation controversy, I want to
turn to the use of such metaphors in early Reformation controversy—
this time between Protestants and Catholics—about the Eucharist. My
purpose is to suggest how a general cultural potential—that is, the
use of clothing metaphors within Christian culture as a whole to embody and manipulate culturally significant oppositions of nature (or
grace) and culture, object and sign, and the like—may take particular
local forms tied to and constrained by particular historical, textual, and
theological traditions. At the same time, because Reformation concern
with the nature of the Eucharist has been read in a very modern—or
postmodern—manner by contemporary critics, this chapter will also
suggest what care must be taken in reading the metaphors of a previous culture and historical moment, lest we misleadingly impose our
own metaphysics and epistemologies.

Representation and Real Presences

Metaphors having to do with theatrical dress or costume are used by
Protestants to disparage the "theatrical habits,"[1] the "glittering gear"[2]
of Catholic ritual. The mass itself is described as a vain spectacle, or
mere illusion, a mumming, a dumb-show, a "stage play" that feeds
men's eyes with "mad gazings and foolish gauds."[3] At the same time
Protestants defend *themselves* against the charge that their own religious
representations are no more than "nude and bare" signs. Perhaps it is
this sort of language that encourages some critics, such as Jonas Barish
and James R. Siemon, to attribute to the Renaissance what sounds like
a very postmodern understanding of—and anxiety about—the "representations" or signs involved in religious ritual. If the reformers tried
to strip all magical and theatrical properties from religious rites, to

make them closer to signs, *mere* signs, Jonas Barish suspects "the ultimate effect . . . was to downgrade the idea of incarnation, and to
make even the original Incarnation look uncomfortably theatrical."[4]
In *Shakespearean Iconoclasm*, James R. Siemon seems to regard Lear's
dramatic trajectory as analogous to the historical shift from a Catholic
view of the Eucharist, which sees "symbol and referent" as "essentially
unified," to a Reformation Protestant position, which "insists upon the
distance between [them]"; Lear at first believes in "an absolute conflation of the symbol with the reality it signifies," "a magical valuation
of representation," but moves from such an "idolatrous relationship to
his representations" to "the final iconoclastic destruction of imagery."[5]
As Siemon argues, "the reformers viewed ecclesiastical observances as
dangerous insofar as they 'had come to replace, rather than merely signify invisible realities' " (61, n. 45).[6]

In fact, Siemon asserts "there is no better index to the uneasy status
of likeness during the post-Reformation period than the debates over
the nature of the Eucharist" (57), and David Bevington, in his review
of Siemon's book, seems to concur: "The holy Sacrament is central to
the debate between symbolic and essential truth of representation."[7]
When Bevington speaks of "essential truth of representation," he appears to be invoking the idea that signs (linguistic or other) are linked
to things in some motivated way, as words were felt to be connected
to their referents in the pre-Saussurean "nomenclature" view of language; when he speaks of "symbolic representation," he appears to
be referring to the contrastive idea that signs are linked to things in
an arbitrary or nonmotivated—or perhaps only partially motivated—
way. Siemon indicates he is writing in terms of two traditions (plausibly
parallel to Bevington's two kinds of representation), a neo-Platonist
tradition in which "there is a substantial relation of image to prototype," and an opposed way of thinking in which images are "only
images, mere signifying elements . . . dependent on arbitrary convention"—and he attributes that new way of thinking to the reformers
(53–54). Siemon emphasizes that for them "the sacraments are bodies
of stories *only*."

So the Eucharist reminds one of the unique historical event—Christ's sacrifice of body and blood—and its elements are bread and wine only because
Christ has named them as representations. Without that act of naming, of
inscribing a likeness between the elements and his flesh, there would be
no relationship between this symbol and that referent. . . . Without the be-

liever's subjective consciousness of the particular story in which that meaning originated, the arbitrary physical element is without value. (60–61)

He asserts that the reformers thought ritual "became an idol" without that "active consciousness of [its] historically instituted meaning" (60, 59–60).

Certainly, questions having to do with the nature of representation, that is, with the nature of signs, are in some sense involved in theological discussion of the Eucharist. And indeed, the language used by Reformation controversialists does tease the contemporary reader with its resemblance to particularly postmodern concerns about absence and presence, emptiness and fullness. For example, the Marian martyr, Nicholas Ridley, arguing against transubstantiation says: "If therefore [Christ] be now really present in the body of his flesh then must the supper cease, for a remembrance is not of a thing present but of a thing absent. And there is a difference between remembrance and presence, and as one of the fathers saith: 'A figure is in vain where the thing figured is present.'"[8] Nevertheless, as we shall see, postmodern distinctions do not fully elucidate or account for the use of metaphors of clothing and nakedness in Reformation Eucharistic controversy. The postmodern emphasis on signs as mere signs (in binary opposition to signs intrinsically linked to essences) does *not* map fully or convincingly onto the conceptions of Reformation Protestants, such as Ridley or Thomas Cranmer, seeking to situate themselves between Catholics, on the one hand, and more theologically radical Protestants, such as Zwinglian memorialists, on the other. Such distinctions don't fully explain Cranmer's insistence, for example, that there is "a warrant for the *apparel* of bread and wine, that they shall not go altogether naked, and be nude and bare tokens."[9] Nor do they account for Ridley's statements defending antitransubstantiation. According to Ridley, the papists "belie the preachers of the Gospel" and "bear the simple people in hand," when they accuse those preachers of making

the holy sacrament, ordained by Christ himself, a thing no better than a piece of common baken bread . . . [or of making] the holy sacrament of the blessed body and blood of Christ nothing else, but a bare sign, or a figure, to represent Christ, none otherwise than the ivy bush doth represent the wine in a tavern; or as a vile person gorgeously apparelled may represent a king or a prince in a play.[10]

Before one attributes the nuances of "mere" symbolic representation — and its attendant anxieties — to the Renaissance, one needs to examine more closely actual debate over the Eucharist, particularly by Protestants opposed to transubstantiation, but insistent, like Ridley and Cranmer, that the sacraments were not "vain, nude, and bare tokens" (Cranmer, *Answer*, 17).

It is indeed true that Protestants stress the historical event as giving the eucharistic signs their meaning. It is also true that they emphasize the need for active faith and understanding, as opposed to mere physical reception of sacramental signs.[11] However, most English Protestants, from Ridley to Hooker and beyond, are vigilant in protesting that the eucharistic signs are not "empty tokens," or "mere" signs. This is a position they attribute to others, such as Zwingli—who may actually have approached it, since he has almost a Durkheimian view of the ratification of the community of believers in the sacrament.

Discussions of the nature of the Eucharist by Calvin, Cranmer, Ridley, and Hooker share a denial of transubstantiation or the corporeal eating of Christ's body present under the "accidents" of the bread and wine. On the one hand, these *are* figures or signs; the corporeal body of Christ is not present but absent. To take the words of institution ("This is my body," etc.) literally, is, of course, to subscribe to transubstantiation. These Protestants thus agree, using Augustine's distinction, that there is a difference between the figurative visible sign or outward part of the sacrament perceived by the physical senses (*sacramentum*), and the spiritual reality that can only be spiritually understood (*res*).[12]

However, at the same time, these discussions deny that the sacraments involve *mere* signs that contain what they signify *only* in the sense that "a thing is present in that which signifieth it" (Cranmer, *Answer*, 11).[13] They deny that these signs are "vain or bare tokens"—"which betokeneth only and giveth nothing, as a painted fire, which giveth neither light nor heat" (ibid.);[14] thus, they deny that these are signs presented to the memory only as a reminder, and not spiritually effective in some manner. These Protestants stress that these signs are not mere signs; there is a thing conveyed, the spiritual presence of Christ. Yet they allow or even insist that the outward sacrament is figurative. Rather than emphasizing "symbolic" representation at the expense of "essential," they emphasize that *both* "symbolic" and "essential" representation occur in the sacrament.

Thus, most English Protestants hold the doctrine of the real spiritual presence—a doctrine arrayed against the specter of an extreme memorialism attributed to Zwingli and others. Hooker comments that "some did exceedingly fear, lest Zwinglius and Oecolampadius would bring to pass, that men should account of this sacrament but only as of a shadow, destitute, empty and void of Christ" (*LEP,* 5.67.2, in *Works,* 2:349). Calvin is a bit more generous when he speaks of the same Swiss reformers: "[Zwinglius and Oecolampadius] forgot to define what is the presence of Christ in the Supper in which one ought to believe, and what communication of his body and blood one there received. So Luther thought that they intended to leave nothing else but bare signs without any corresponding spiritual substance. Hence he began to resist and oppose them, even to the extent of denouncing them as heretics." [15] At one and the same time, then, Calvin insists on the "reality" and the "symbolic" nature of the sacrament: "We declare then that in the Supper we eat the same body as was crucified, although the expression refers to the bread by metonymy, so that it may be *truly said to be symbolically the real body of Christ,* by whose sacrifice we have been reconciled to God." [16] That is, the sacrament conveys the real (spiritual) body of Christ, but it is also symbolic in that it is not the real (corporeal) body of Christ. Calvin says, "We hold that in this ordinance the Lord does not promise or set forth by signs, anything which he does not exhibit in reality. . . . Nor do we thus teach that the bread and wine are symbols, without immediately adding that they truth they represent is conjoined with them." [17]

B. A. Gerrish explains that both Zwingli and Calvin "were careful to make a distinction between sign and thing signified, and for the same reason: to avoid the virtual identity of sign and reality in Roman Catholicism and Lutheranism"; nevertheless, "Calvin's position is still, in effect, the exact opposite of Zwingli's." "In Calvin's view it is the nature of the sacraments [as "divinely appointed signs"] to cause and communicate . . . what they signify." Thus, once again, "the thing signified is inseparably bound up with the sacramental sign," which is both "not empty" and without "any intrinsic power." [18]

Similarly, for Hooker, "we are not to doubt but that [sacraments] really give what they promise, and are what they signify." They are "means effectual whereby God . . . delivereth into our hands that grace available unto eternal life, which grace the sacraments represent or signify" (*LEP,* 5.57.5, in *Works,* 2:258). What should be emphasized—even if there is some tension in the denial of Christ's corporeal presence and the affirmation of his spiritual presence—is that the spiritual presence is still, for these Reformation Protestants, a real presence. The emphasis on the bread and wine as "mere signs" is only half the story; to remove the "theatrical magic" of transubstantiation from the priest's consecration certainly does not necessarily "downgrade the original Incarnation."[19]

Clothing Metaphors in the Discussion of the Eucharist

Metaphors of clothing or theatrical apparel, so handy for encoding relations of object and sign, the literal and the figurative, easily enter the discussion of the nature of the Eucharist because of that discussion's grounding in the Augustinian definition of outward sign (*sacramentum*) and inward thing (*res*). Protestants accuse Catholics of taking the sign for the thing, that is, acting toward the sign as if it were the thing, and thus being guilty of idolatry.[20] But although Catholics, in Protestant eyes, may take signs for realities, Protestants also stress, that for *them* the signs in themselves are indeed more than theatrical make-believe *because* of the spiritual presence of Christ. Calvin says, "[W]e must then *really* receive in the Supper the body and blood of Jesus Christ, since the Lord there *represents* to us the communion of both."[21]

And although I distinguish between the sign and the thing signified, I do not teach that there is only a bare and shadowy figure, but distinctly declare that the bread is a sure pledge of that communion with the flesh and blood of Christ which it figures. For Christ is neither a painter, nor an actor, nor a kind of Archimedes who presents an empty image to amuse the eye; but he truly and in reality performs what by external symbol he promises.[22]

The sacramental sign itself may be figured as the clothing of Christ, who is its *res* (i.e., the thing); as far back as Wycliffe it was argued that "the priest, in celebrating the mass, did not make or consecrate the body of Christ but the sacrament, as the sign or garment of Christ."[23] However, these "garments" are not—for Protestants, including Nicholas Ridley—mere signs *in the way that theatrical costumes are*. As we have seen, Ridley defends his position against those papists who, he says, accuse "the preachers of the Gospel" of reducing the holy sacrament to "a bare sign, or a figure," comparable to a theatrical illusion, as when "a vile person gorgeously apparelled . . . represent[s] a king or a prince in a play." His metaphor recognizes the inherent emptiness of signs divorced from the things they represent, but, like Calvin, Ridley insists that Protestant sacramental representation is inherently different from theatrical representation because the sacramental signs are conjoined to the truth they represent.

Thus the idea that "clothing" may be a *bare* sign is used by these Protestants both to attack Catholic ritual and to explain why Protestant rites are not subject to the charge. "Bare" means "mere" in the sense in which the shadowy image Calvin contrasts with the eucharistic reality is "mere"—an "empty image to amuse the eye." But is it possible that the meaning of the word "bare" in Ridley's passage is at least in part a function of its opposition to "gorgeously apparelled"? If so, Ridley is asserting, in the same breath in which he says the Protestant sacrament is not like deceiving clothing (and in that sense a mere sign), that it is also not bare, in the sense of not without clothing. It may seem that this latter meaning is unlikely. However, as we shall shortly see, the history of—and the contemporaneous use of—"bare" in relation to the sacrament suggest that the force of "unclothed" is at least residually present in Ridley's phrasing. Yet if so, and if costume is a deceiving outer garment, would not the *approved* thing be the naked truth, the naked thing itself? How can both nakedness and clothing (albeit false clothing) be negatively judged, and indeed exemplify the same thing—a mere sign or image?

The use of phrases like "nude and bare" in reference to the sacrament can be traced at least to the First Helvetic Confession of 1536, expressing the beliefs of the Reformed Church of Switzerland.[24] Hooker cites this Confession when he explains that "[i]n writing and speaking of the blessed sacraments we use for the most part under the name of their Substance not only to comprise that whereof they outwardly and sensibly consist, but also that secret grace which they signify and exhibit" (*LEP*, 5.58.2, in *Works*, 2:259–60). His note reads: "Arcanarum rerum symbola non nudis signis, sed signis simul et rebus constant" (2:259 n. 95). This may be translated as "The symbols of secret things consist not of naked or nude signs, but of signs and things at the same time." And indeed, shortly before the passage quoted, Hooker asserts: "[W]e are not to doubt that they really give what they promise, and are what they signify. For we take not baptism nor the eucharist for bare *resemblances* or memorials of things absent, neither for *naked signs* and testimonies assuring us of grace received before, but (as they are in deed and in verity) for means effectual" (*LEP*, 5.57.5, in *Works*, 2:258). An English translation, *The Confescion of the Fayth of the Sweserlandes* (1548), gives the passage as follows:

There is twain which are named in the church of God sacraments, bap-tyme [*sic*] and hosting, these be tokens of secret things, that is of godly and spiritual things, of which things they take the name, are not of naked signs, but they are of signs and verities together. . . . In the hosting and thanks giving the bread and the wine are signs, but the thing and verity is the communion of the body of our lord, health and salvation found and remis sion of sins, the which are received by faith even as the signs and tokens are received by the bodily mouth.[25]

Now the Latin word "nudus," used in the Helvetic Confession — lit-erally meaning "naked," "unclothed," "bare" — of course may be figu-ratively used for "bare" in the sense of "empty," "uncovered," "deprived of," "unadorned," and, nonphysically, in the sense of "mere," "alone," "only." As we have seen, the many instances of denial, in Reforma-tion literature, that the eucharistic signs are "nude" or "naked" signs carry a strong sense of "bare" as "mere." Yet, it is hard to imagine that the literal meaning of "naked" as "unclothed" is completely absent from the minds of controversialists. That meaning certainly is explicit in Thomas Cranmer's disputation about the Eucharist with Bishop Stephen Gardiner, later Queen Mary's chancellor. Cranmer's argument explicitly involves both metaphoric "nakedness" and metaphoric "ap-parel," and nakedness, as in the Ridley passage, is not a positive term — although a certain kind of apparel at least implicitly is. The use of cloth-ing metaphors in this dispute suggests a theological alternative to both "bare signs" and "deceiving clothing" — an alternative that resolves the apparent contradiction that results when both being naked and being clothed seem to be presented as unacceptable.

Gardiner admits that Cranmer calls the bread and wine "holy tokens," not "bare tokens." Yet Gardiner believes that for Cranmer "Christ [is] not . . . spiritually present in them, but only as a thing is present in that which signifieth it." This, to Gardiner, "is the nature of a bare token." Thus, according to Gardiner, Cranmer believes that "there is nothing to be worshipped, for there is nothing present but in figure and in a sign: which whosoever saith, calleth the thing in deed absent" (*Answer*, 11).

Cranmer, on the other hand, argues "they be no vain or bare tokens, as you would persuade, (for a bare token is that which betokeneth only and giveth nothing, as a painted fire, which giveth neither light nor heat;) but in the due ministration of the sacraments God is present, working with his word and sacraments" (ibid.). Cranmer's subsequent language perhaps begins to suggest that "bare" (as well as "nude") mean precisely "unclothed," because he conjoins both words with "naked": "Is therefore the whole use of the bread in the whole action and ministration of the Lord's holy supper but a naked or nude and bare token?" he asks (ibid., 16). But it is when they both come to talk of "apparel" that it seems inescapable that they are both aware of the force of "nude" as "unclothed." Gardiner says

And albeit this author [i.e., Cranmer] would not have them bare tokens, yet, and [i.e., if] they be only tokens, they have no warrant signed by scripture for any apparel at all. . . . Wherefore, if the very body of Christ be not in the supper delivered in deed, the eating there hath no special promise, but only commandment to do it in remembrance. After which doctrine why should it be noted absolutely for a sacrament and special mystery?

Cranmer's response includes: "For so might we as well say, that the water in baptism is a bare token, and hath no warrant signed by scripture for any apparel at all: for the scripture speaketh not of any promise made to the receiving of a token or figure only" (ibid., 16, 17). Furthermore, at one point, Cranmer, speaking as if he has caught Gardiner arguing in his favor, says: "And now I am glad that here yourself have found out a warrant for the *apparel* of bread and wine, that they shall not go altogether naked, and be nude and bare tokens, but have promises of effectual signification" (ibid., 36). Thus, for these controversialists, tokens (the English "token," as well as "representation," is often used for Latin "symbolum") are "bare" if they are only signs. As such, they are pitifully incomplete, unclothed. But, if they involve "effectual grace and operation" (ibid., 17), they have "apparel." A necessary "apparel" seems to be used as a metaphor for the "effectual signification" itself, which clothes the otherwise shamefully bare signs; "nakedness" is the absence of the effective grace or spiritual presence of Christ. The inner spiritual *res* can clothe the bare external sign.

Thus the wearing of deceiving external apparel—like the gorgeous kingly costume of the "vile" actor in Ridley's metaphor—*and* the state of nakedness, nudity, or bareness may be used to describe the same thing *seen from different perspectives*. That is, the metaphor of mere costume and the metaphor of the naked body may each be used to describe empty signs, without the "thing" of the sacrament, which is Christ or grace. In the one case, bread and wine are not the garment of Christ but a deceiving theatrical costume cloaking his absence, and an actual vileness. In the other case, the bread and wine are shamefully "naked . . . nude and bare tokens" if they have no apparel, no "effectual grace and operation," and do not give what they promise.

An emphasis like Ridley's on the lie of gorgeous apparel might be understood as paying implicit homage to the idea that Christ's truth *is* appropriately "naked" in contrast to the glittering costumes of an idolatrous religion — that is, to mere apparel. Usually it is the Protestant who charges the Catholic with the sins of false costume and the Catholic who charges the Protestant with inefficacious nakedness. But it is characteristic of the use of the "clothing metaphor," as we have seen, that both parties may make both claims (although, as we have also seen, on any given occasion, they tend to make only one or the other). In this case, the Protestants Cranmer and Ridley associate clothing with a mere outward show, a "sign" or "token" cut off from an actual thing, but they also claim that Christ's truth is not "vain, nude, and bare" since Christ's real presence clothes or dresses the otherwise naked signs. Although Protestant imagery may sometimes focus on Christ's naked truth, which is, as Calvin says, "the body" that allows us to dispense with "shadows" or "figurations,"[26] the statement that "nakedness" is lacking in dignity, is shameful or incomplete — an idea bolstered by so many biblical uses of "naked" — is also frequent in the Protestant cultural universe. This latter statement is one encouraged by the traditional trope for justification: one is invested or dressed in Christ by imputation of his merit and thus does not appear before God shamefully and sinfully naked.[27]

The fact that Ridley stresses at one and the same time the *two* negatives — that is, that the Protestant sacrament wears neither false clothing nor no clothing, but, implicitly, only the right clothing — may underscore, if in a small way, the importance of clothing and the shamefulness of nakedness, even in a religious culture that can fetishize "the naked truth." The emphasis is on what true religion wears, not on what it doesn't. The stress does not fall on the idea that *they* have false clothing, and *we* have none. Rather, what is implied is their clothing is false or inappropriate, ours isn't. Of course we have clothing; we are neither immodestly without it, nor dressed in the wrong deceitful kind; what we are wearing is fit and proper.

Like all users of metaphor, the Reformation controversialists use it to affirm what they wish; it is not that they don't have positions, but that they may describe those positions with apparently conflicting terms, contrast them with different implicit terms, or use the same terms for different referents, or different terms for the same referents. A historically based semiotics of such metaphors as "clothing and nakedness" will map out the referents and paradigmatic contrasts of key terms in a wide variety of usages in order to understand what semantic resources "they" had available and the systematic basis that permitted their creative (but effective) positing of new referents. Thus it will enable us to come closer to understanding what "they" understood when they chose these metaphors to embody and discuss issues of concern, and what their actual positions were on these issues. In the absence of such an understanding, we may, quite unconsciously, provide our own referents and contrastive terms, and argue in terms of them, becoming trapped in our own metaphors; we may also expect consistent analogies (e.g., that a Puritan or Presbyterian or radical Protestant position will always side with the "naked" and its apparent analogues).

Early Protestant reformers like Bullinger and Tyndale may insist on the naked truth as opposed to shadows when they are advocating the abrogation of ceremonies. Yet Bullinger, for example, uses the language of shadows and nakedness in a different way when talking of rhetorically effective similitudes: "[M]en do more easily conceive and understand the doctrine of heavenly things, when it is shadowed out under some dark and covert sign of earthly things, than when it is nakedly and spiritually indeed delivered." [28]

This is important because a religion that opposes pictorial or plastic images of the holy does not necessarily, for that reason, oppose verbal or poetic images; thus the leap from Protestant iconoclasm to a radical "Shakespearean iconoclasm," understood as undermining "essentialist" modes of representation, may be cast in doubt. From the Elizabethan homily "Against Perill of Idolatry" to George Herbert's "Notes on Valdesso's *Considerations,*" a relevant distinction is drawn. Sculpture or painting has an intrinsic appeal to the senses and easily permits treating the image as if it were what it represents; verbal figures appeal to the mind and require the mediation of the understanding. And pictorial emblems might even do the same; Huston Diehl has shown that Protestants who disparaged images nevertheless used emblems to show why images should be disparaged. [29]

Siemon reads Shakespearean drama as "refracting the struggles over imagery and likeness that vexed post-Reformation England and found

their most obvious expression in the various phenomena of iconoclasm" (*Shakespearean Iconoclasm*, 30), and he reads *Lear* itself as evinc-
ing a "fundamental iconoclasm" (251). "Men killed one another over
the *dissimilarity* between the "visual image" and "transcendent reality"
(10). As we have seen, he believes "there is no better index to the uneasy status of likeness during the post-Reformation period than the
debates over the nature of the Eucharist" (57), and he tends to draw a
fairly sharp line between a neo-Platonic or Catholic "essentialist" conception of the relation of sign and reality and a post-Reformation "arbitrary" one — conceptions he apparently sees implicated in the respec-
tive Catholic and Reformist understandings of the Eucharist (57–58).
But this binarism simply doesn't map onto the Calvinist understanding
of the relation of the eucharistic signs to the real "spiritual presence"
they conjoin; nor does it map onto the Calvinist eucharistic doctrine
itself, which affirms neither transubstantiation nor memorialism.

∼ 3

Constraints and Freedom: Extensionist Semantics

and Its Implications for Criticism

Different oppositions and referents, as well as shared core concepts and contrast sets based on shared experience and values, clearly explain the apparently cross-cutting—even contradictory—use of the metaphors of the "naked truth" and "decent and comely apparel" in Reformation controversy, as we have seen. Importantly, this examination of clothing metaphors reveals the systematicity—as well as the creative malleability—with which Renaissance Christian culture thought "with" clothing, and as such provides a specific illustration of how a semantic domain may be shaped by culture and yet enable novel creations. My post-Saussurean extensionist linguistic theory that has informed this approach may now be more explicitly—if still only briefly—addressed, and its significance and applications better understood.

Extensionist Semantics

At first glance, one might be tempted to solve the problem of opposed labels ("cup" or "glass," "naked" or "clothed," "Anglican" or "Puritan") being used for the "same" entities by insisting on more inclusive and/or fine-grained definitions of such terms. A definition of "cup," or "Anglican," then, would enumerate the set of distinctive features that would apply absolutely to the whole membership of the category, with the result that any one application of the term would on principle be made exactly on the same basis as any other. However, this approach to meaning—the "nomenclature" view, according to which we merely name entities that already have a clear, demarcated existence in the world—is one that Saussure very correctly discredited, and that poststructuralists, who also don't believe language is "transparent," reject as well.[1] Indeed, for Saussure, such terms as "cup" and "glass" (like "naked" and "clothed" or "Puritan" and "Anglican") are descriptions not of objects in the world, but of concepts—concepts that are applied to the world of things in creative but not random ways. Our names are of a piece with, or come into existence along with, our concepts, and therefore our use of them is understandable only in terms of the relations of these concepts to other concepts. Thus, the often heard injunction to "define one's terms" is not a solution because such definitions do not account for the full range of actual uses of words/concepts. When we try to account for the use of particular terms, or to justify a particular use of our own, we are dealing with the conceptual universe of speakers of the language at a particular time and place, and/or our own conceptual universes, and neither we nor they use words in "total-category" ways.[2] Thus, for example, even though there do exist situations in which it is useful or necessary to think of a drinking glass as made of glass, cylindrical, used for cold drinks, and so on (for example, when contrasting "glasses" with "cups"—made of china, hemispherical, and used for hot drinks—for someone learning English), we would almost immediately be faced with the problem of the more ambiguous items (for example, the tall cylindrical drinking vessel made of plastic and sometimes called a "cup," sometimes a "glass"), which give rise to the need for "defining our terms" in the first place.[3]

Does this mean, then, that one person's "cup" only minimally overlaps with, or bears only a Wittgensteinian "family resemblance" to another's, just as some members of a family "have the same nose, others the same eyebrows, and others again the same way of walking"?[4] This would be equivalent to saying that one person thinks of a cup as cylindrical, another as made of china, and so on, and any one such idea of "cup," though perhaps sharing some feature(s)—a handle, perhaps?—with some other idea of cup, is no more focal or primary than any other. Neither literary criticism nor any other discourse could make any determinate statements at all in such a situation. Therefore, it is best first to consider the possibility that speakers within a culture at a particular time do share rich prototypes for some given term (and the term with which it contrasts), but may on occasion use that very term to talk past one another, because each fastens on a different attribute of a multifeatured entity in a particular situation of implicit contrast.

We can see that cross-cutting assignments to some particular category need not mean that the labelers have entirely different conceptions of the prototypical or "core" members of the category (or have no such focal or primary categories at all) by further following the cup/glass example. If we ask our child to get the glasses for the dinner table and he goes to the cupboard and finds cylindrical drinking vessels made of plastic, as well as hemispherical drinking vessels with handles, he will not return empty-handed, but with the plastic vessels. In this context, shape (and perhaps function, that is "for cold drinks") are the deciding factors; what has been called an "extension" from the prototype has been made on one (or two) dimensions.[5] But if we ask the child to bring the cups for the party buffet and he goes to a cupboard containing glass glasses and paper or plastic drinking vessels, he will as easily return with the latter. In this case, an extension from the prototype is also involved, but interestingly enough it is a negative one; the paper or plastic "cup" has been labeled on the basis of what it is not made of, in contrast to "glass" glasses. "Cup" is not simply redefined to apply to a new object; rather the overall paradigmatic contrast "cup versus glass" is adjusted to the local situation, and in this case only "not made of glass" versus "made of glass" is relevant. Whether a particular label is used depends less on the totality of the match of the object's features to all the features that define the particular category than on the match of the specific features involved in the relevant opposition. In the first situation the child reasons: If it's a glass, it must be tall and cylindrical versus short and hemispherical, and for cold drinks; in the second, he reasons: If it's a cup it must be not made of glass versus made of glass. But, of course, it is easy to see that my use of the label "glass" for a plastic drinking vessel in a situation where the relevant opposition is "for cold drinks" versus "for hot drinks" and your use of the label "cup" for the same vessel in a situation where the relevant opposition is "made of glass" versus "not made of glass" does not imply that we have different understandings of the "meanings" of the words. Were there no prototypes on which the child sent to the cupboard might base his selection in the given situation of contrast (and no features central to that situation), he might return with a green plate when we asked for a cup because he had previously encountered a green cup.

This extensionist semantic theory, then, helps us grasp the slipperiness of language, but also points toward the role played by shared understandings grounded in culture and experience. It emphasizes relations of contrast or opposition ("paradigmatic contrast"), but does not exclude referential relations or the greater primacy of some culturally available contrasts and referents over others. In such domains as kinship systems and color terminology—just as in the domain of cups and glasses—we find culturally and experientially grounded limits to the "deferral of meaning," limits encompassed and explained by means of such a semantics.[6]

As we've already seen in chapter 1, this extensionist approach may also shed some light on disagreements among Reformation controversialists in the complex realm of religious values coded in clothing metaphors. Indeed, foregrounding the role of semantic relations of contrast or opposition may clarify the far from self-evident dynamics underlying specific critical disagreements, when critics, like the Anglican and Puritan users of clothing metaphors discussed in chapter 1, interpret the same situation or evidence in a way that serves different arguments. This is what happens, for example, when W. H. Auden labels George Herbert's poem "The Windows," "Anglican," and Sheridan Blau labels it "Puritan" on the basis of Herbert's apparent disparaging of the preacher's "speech alone."

Paradigmatic Opposition and Opposite Conclusions from the Same Evidence

> Lord, how can man preach thy eternal word?
>   He is a brittle crazy glass:
> Yet in thy temple thou dost him afford
>   This glorious and transcendent place,
>   To be a window, through thy grace.
>
> But when thou dost anneal in glass thy story,
>   Making thy life to shine within
> The holy Preachers; then the light and glory
>   More rev'rend grows, and more doth win:
>   Which else shows watrish, bleak, and thin.
>
> Doctrine and life, colours and light, in one
>   When they combine and mingle, bring
> A strong regard and awe: but speech alone
>   Doth vanish like a flaring thing,
> And in the ear, not conscience ring.[7]

Herbert's poem pertains to religiopolitical issues of outer sign and inner faith, ornamentation and plainness—issues often addressed in the "clothing" metaphors with which we have been concerned. W. H. Auden focuses on the *vehicle* of the poem's central metaphor. He regards "The Windows"—on the basis of its apparent subject—as a justification of certain "externals" in the Anglican church.[8] He writes, "The Reformers, for instance, disapproved of all religious images, but Herbert thought that, on occasion, a stained-glass window could be of more spiritual help than a sermon."[9] As evidence, he gives the last stanza. Thus, for Auden, "speech alone" refers to sermons and is the negative pole of a weighted contrast between the limited ear and the responsive eye—caught up in apprehension of such beautiful "visible signs" as stained-glass windows. Auden is operating in terms of an old pedagogical tradition that Hooker uses too when he says—with regard to the "outward form of . . . religious actions"—that "not only speech but sundry sensible means besides have always been thought necessary, and especially those means . . . which [are] object to the eye, the liveliest and the most apprehensive sense of all other" (*LEP,* 4.1.3, in *Works,* 1:418). On the other hand, Sheridan Blau focuses on the *tenor* of the poem's central metaphor, the preacher, and sees Herbert as advocating "a homely style of preaching" which "resemble[s] that of the preachers of the Puritan opposition."[10] "Herbert thought of himself in the pulpit as a nearly unobtrusive medium through which God's messages might pass. Serving such a function, the priest would aspire to the condition of transparency, or more precisely, translucency" (Blau, "Homiletic Theory," 21). For Blau, then, "speech alone" refers to "mere eloquence" and is the negative pole of a disjunctive contrast between the plain or undecorated and the falsely decorated, between a nakedly holy life and intrinsically false adornments or "colors." "The parson's holy life [is] the most eloquent adornment of his sermon" (22).

Thus each critic is bringing a "historical" construct involving a particular contrast set to the poem. Both focus on "speech" as a negative term, but each has a slightly different referent for "speech," seeing it as contrastive with different opposed terms; Auden regards speech as sermons contrasting with "visible signs," while Blau sees it as rhetorical eloquence or mere words contrasting with actual deeds. Oddly, Blau's contrast set does not take account of the poem's clearly colored windows (in which the story of God has been "anneal[ed]" [*Works of Herbert,* 67]), instead forcing them to be as colorless, transparent, or translucent as clear glass, which they cannot be. Auden's emphasis on the inefficacy of sermons (in a poem which starts by asking "Lord, how can man preach thy eternal word?") hardly accounts for the role of the *tenor* of the metaphor—the preacher. It would appear that Herbert's use of colored windows as a metaphor is not easily assimilable either to the "clear glass versus decorated glass" contrast often associated with the Puritans,[11] or to the "visible signs versus mere speech" contrast associated with Anglicans. In this case any contrast set ascribed to Herbert—if it is to be plausible—must explain the role of the preacher *and* of specifically colored windows in the poem.

Indeed, for Herbert, it is the preacher's desired union of doctrine and life, speaking and doing (symbolized by the indissoluble union of color and light in the annealed windows) that contrasts with "mere colors," which are analogous to "speech alone." According to Renaissance sacred rhetoric, "one must be moved to move others"; "the affective power of rhetoric . . . results from grace." In true preaching, "art and feeling" are as indissolubly joined as are colors and light in the annealed windows of Herbert's poem.[12] The glow of inner divine presence that appears in the pathos or coloration of his words makes the preacher akin to stained-glass windows, not to a pane of transparent glass. The stained glass annealed with God's story makes light glow that otherwise might "show[] watrish, bleak and thin"; the preacher, imbued with God's living spirit, may win the congregation who read the story of the living God in his own holiness and zeal. Thus, in "The Windows," Herbert uses the very target of contemporary iconoclasm as a metaphor—not to vindicate the actual object as a "visible sign" in the church—but to fervently describe, and beseech God for, the inner dynamic faith that permits ardent and holy preaching.[13] This poem does not speak to the question of Herbert's religous position in terms of the dichotomy Anglicans/"externals" versus Puritans/"inner" faith.

The malleability of semantic domains with terms like "naked" and "clothed" or indeed "inner" and "external" remains cautionary for any one who would casually identify features in the work of a religious poet such as George Herbert, or of a "secular" playwright such as Shakespeare, as on the "side" of "the plain" or "the ornamented," the "naked truth" or "comely apparel," and, consequently, as on the side of one or another of the presumed political analogues of such terms, such as "radical Puritan" or "conservative Anglican." Yet, at the same time, the meaningful cultural systematicity with which such terms operate holds out at least the possibility that one might make determinate arguments in particular instances.

The case is not dissimilar when biblical texts with a wide range of possible referents are used as evidence for particular religious or political positions. Sheridan Blau regards Herbert's citation—in his *A Priest to the Temple*—of the Pauline injunctions, "Let all things be done unto edifying," "Let all things be done decently and in order" (*Works of Herbert*, 246), as linking him with the Puritans on the basis of concern for decorum—that is, the suiting of style to an unlearned audience ("Homiletic Theory," 26–28). Leah S. Marcus, on the other hand, uses these passages as evidence that he believes in a style that "like the liturgy, must reflect an ideal of beauty and order," and thus links him with the Anglican advocacy of set forms.[14]

"Defining one's terms" is no more a solution to the problem of the critical use of different labels for the same texts than it is a solution to the problem of the use of both "cup" and "glass" for the same object. Certainly few of the writers whom one might want to label as "Puritan" or "Anglican" will embody all features that might define a prototypical "Puritan" or "Anglican." It would be very difficult to "place" anyone at all if we insisted that anyone we call "Puritan," for example, must embody all of them. In fact, the critic—or Reformation Englishman—using the term "Puritan" has in mind some specific features out of a prototypic set that do definitively contrast with the corresponding features of an opposed concept such as "Anglican" in a particular context. For example, he might contrast Puritan asceticism with Anglican "cakes and ale" in the context of Sabbath-keeping. But other possible attributes of Puritanism (e.g., industry, the habit of examining one's conscience regularly, iconoclasm) would not be at issue in a particular application of the label. Nevertheless, even in such cases of more complex domains than the relatively concrete "cups and glasses," such uses of the labels do not automatically rule out the possibility that critics have significantly overlapping core concepts.[15]

Even in the muddier area of conflicting critical use of terms, it is worth bringing to consciousness those implicit paradigmatic contrasts that encourage critics to focus narrowly on some single feature of a category. Thus, in the case of "The Windows," the culture of criticism leads Auden and Blau to consider Herbert's lines about "speech alone" as "Anglican" or "Puritan." Auden reasons: If the poem is "Anglican," "speech alone" must refer to sermons that fall on deaf ears and contrast with "visible signs"; Blau reasons: If the poem is "Puritan," "speech alone" must refer to merely speaking well (with rhetorical effectiveness), and contrast with doing well. The critics don't disagree that a taste for "visible signs" characterizes Anglicanism, not Puritanism; they of course share the overall opposition between the concepts. They don't even disagree that aspects of church services or furnishings can be obtrusive or effective, and that "speech alone" is obtrusive and/or ineffective for both Anglican and Puritan. What they disagree on is whether, in this poem, "speech alone" signifies sermons themselves or rhetorically ostentatious sermons.

In cases such as Marcus's and Blau's use of the Pauline text as evidence for a more or less "Anglican" or "Puritan" Herbert, we need to remind ourselves that the same feature, for example, "plainness" — however defined — may constitute evidence of membership in either one of two opposed categories. The term "Anglican" is ambiguous because it refers to an institution that is more or less "plain" or reformed, depending on whether that institution is contrasted to Catholicism or to Puritan ideals.

The same ambiguity may explain such conflicting categorizations of Herbert as Heather Asals's "Anglican, and even what we now call 'high' Anglican,"[16] as compared to Leah Marcus's categorization of him as someone who "may well not have considered himself a high churchman at all" ("Anglican Plain Style," 184). And the explanation does not preclude the possibility that Asals and Marcus share a significant conceptual cluster or "core" for Anglicanism, which includes such features as an emphasis on set formal order and due ceremony. Asals assigns Herbert to the category "high Anglican" on the basis of his sacramentalism (belief in the "real presence").[17] Marcus, on the other hand, assigns Herbert to a non-high church category on the basis of his desire for "a beautiful plainness" in "the language and liturgical dress" of the British church, as well as in religious poetry ("Anglican Plain Style," 188). She certainly contrasts this style of worship and poetry with Catholicism's "gaudy Roman excess," or what "might be called Roman poetry: a poetry of decorative externals that shadow or paint the truth rather than reveal it in its simple clarity" (ibid., 189). Nevertheless, Marcus — who rightly emphasizes that the plain style had a wider currency than scholarly polarities about Anglican ceremonialism and Puritan simplicity allow — does recognize that such "beautiful plainness" was used to persuade people to accept the established forms and ceremonies of the Anglican Church (ibid., 182–83). Thus her "core concept" of Anglican does overlap with that of Asals, who stresses "ceremony, gesture and vestment" (*Equivocal Predication,* 4). Marcus sees Herbert as favoring heartfelt, simple forms over Catholic "decorative externals"; he is not Catholic and therefore firmly Protestant. Asals sees Herbert as favoring outward forms and ceremonies and a high church sacramentalism; he is not Protestant and therefore high Anglican. The established English church being less ceremonious in some senses than the Catholic and more ceremonious than those who would purify it further wished, it lends itself to such cross-cutting assignments to category.[18]

Post-Saussurean Semantics: Reference without Regress

Thus, Reformation controversialists—as we have seen in the first two chapters—and contemporary critics as well, don't really use signs in endlessly differing implicit contrast sets, sharing nothing more than names such as "clothed" and "naked," "Anglican" and "Puritan."[19] There is a difference between the theoretical possibility of a multitude of referents and paradigmatic contrasts for a sign such as "naked" and the practical reality of likely referents and contrasts in a particular cultural situation.

Indeed, there is no reason to ground the idea of the infinite regress of meaning in Saussure, even if Derrida's reading of him encourages the view that he "implicitly put in question the 'metaphysics of presence' which had dominated western philosophy" (Belsey, *Critical Practice,* 136),[20] and even though critics following Derrida borrow Saussurean terms for an "absurdist gesture,"[21] and take the role of opposition in language all the way to indeterminacy, where what "X" means is "not Y" and what "Y" means is "not Z" and what "Z" means is "not A," and so on into the regress of infinite intertextuality.[22] The Derridean misunderstanding of Saussurean linguistics lies at the heart of deconstruction, and deconstructive understandings of language and its relation to the world have been and continue to be enormously influential— not the least in shaping some aspects of new historicism and cultural materialism.[23] On the one hand, because, in Saussure, language is not a "transparent" window to the world, poststructuralist thought may regard it as completely unconstrained by referential relations, and emphasize linguistic "constructivism," the view that the world is simply "representation" or construct—and the number of such constructs theoretically legion.[24] On the other hand, an incomplete idea of Saussurean *langue* as an always already existent "implacable code" may contribute to the idea that the social construction of individuals in language utterly constrains their linguistic creativity or freedom. Thus, rereading Saussure may also help us to meaningfully re-assess (and mediate in a new way) the opposition between hegemonic semiotic systems and individual subjects in various poststructuralist movements such as new historicism, cultural materialism, and neo-Marxism, whether the emphasis there is on the constraining and containing Saussurean "implacable code," or on the post-Saussurean "slippery signifier" always in play and subject to radical appropriations.[25]

It is Derrida's misreading of sign-referent relations in Saussure that is the basis of the very idea that there is nothing *but* misreading, *"nothing outside of the text,"* no "referent (a reality that is metaphysical, historical, psychobiographical, etc.) or . . . signified outside the text whose content . . . could have taken place outside of language" (*Of Grammatology*, 158). And new historicists such as Jean E. Howard inherit a Derridean Saussure:

Saussurian linguistics has challenged the premise that language functions referentially. . . . If literature refers to no ground extrinsic to itself, what can be the nature of its relationship to an historical context of material reality? In fact, if one accepts tendencies in poststructuralist thought, is the possibility of an historical criticism even conceivable? ("New Historicism in Renaissance Studies," 18–19)

Yet, the radically arbitrary relation of *signs* to the *world* that deconstructionists frequently proclaim is not logically entailed in the Saussurean concept of the arbitrariness of the link between *signifier* and *signified*, which together make up the sign. In Saussure, the relation of signifier to signified is radically arbitrary, that is, there is no substantive — as opposed to historically grounded social — reason why the particular sound-image "tree" should refer to the concept "tree."[26] However, nothing in Saussure's thought requires that we assume that speakers using the same words share only the mere names and use concepts without significant relation to others' use of them or to the world.[27]

First of all, in Saussure's groundbreaking *Course in General Linguistics*, the signifier or "sound-image" is "not the material sound, a purely physical thing, but the psychological imprint of the sound, the impression that it makes on our senses" (66), albeit the signifier is confused by contemporary critics with the physical sounds that make up a word, or with their representation in written or printed letters.[28] In the *General Linguistics*, furthermore, the signified is equally "psychological" (65) and is a "concept" (67)—the concept by which we encompass a thing or a class of things—albeit the signified is confused by contemporary critics with external reality, that is, with actual referents, or objects in the world to which the already misunderstood signifier is supposed to refer. For Saussure signifer and signified together make up the sign. They mutually demarcate each other, coming into existence at the same time; they are "united in the brain by an associative bond" (66). It is the signified component of Saussure's sign (the sign's internal referent) that points out of the sign to actually existent phenomena—even if in an arbitrarily segmented or clumped form.

However, poststructuralists focus on signifier and signified, and, splitting them apart and moving them out of the mind, treat the signifier's sounds as if they were the sign, and the signified as if it were an external reality or existent thing.[29] Once again, the relationship between signifier and signified, between *"sound-image"* and *"concept"* (67) is indeed arbitrary, but poststructuralist thought all too easily confuses the sign with its signifier and its referent with its signified; thus it confounds the radical arbitrariness of the signifier/signified link with the modest arbitrariness by which the signified merely imposes a segmentation on the continua of the external phenomenal world.[30] Admittedly, this is a confusion encouraged by the diagram in Bally and Sechehaye's compilation of the *General Linguistics* (67), which pictures a tree over the signifier "arbor" without indicating that the tree is a concept and not a thing, and it is a confusion shared by others, such as Ogden and Richards.[31] Thus, the recognizably arbitrary nature of the relationship between the parts of the sign leads to the assumption that the relationship between sign and referent (taken as the word and the thing in the world to which it points, respectively) is radically arbitrary, and from there to the notion that reference can not exist, or to the Whorfian idea that language in itself completely determines perception.[32]

For Saussure, language (*langue* versus *parole*) is inevitably social, collective: "the social side of speech, outside the individual who can never create nor modify it by himself; it exists only by virtue of a sort of contract signed by the members of a community" (14). Of course, this is as true among those who radically qualify its powers of meaning as among those who celebrate them. *Langue* depends on a "community of

speakers," and never exists "apart from the social fact." It is "the whole
set of linguistic habits which allow an individual to understand and
to be understood" (77).[33] Thus, unless we want to assume a community of speakers sharing only names, language must depend on socially
shared systems of signs that include salient shared sets of contrastive or
opposed terms (that is, paradigmatic contrasts). The salience is an important limitation on the infinite regress. Although, for Derrida, "the
centrifugal movement of any single word ultimately spreads out across
every other word in the whole language,"[34] in fact words do not exist
in potential contrast sets with all the other words of the language, except in the most abstract of senses. Jonathan Culler's example of the
hypothetical disappearance of the word "mutton" illustrated just this
concept: "Certain local modifications would ensue . . . but vast areas of
the language would not be affected in discernible ways. The example
of linguistics need not lead one to expect the complete solidarity of
every system" (*Structuralist Poetics*, 14). John M. Ellis more recently explains why there is no "limitless . . . play of differences"; what he says
pinpoints the rationale for my own emphasis in this book on shared
"uniquely relevant contrast[s]," such as false clothing versus the naked
truth, or modest apparel versus unseemly nakedness:

If terms can play (a) indiscriminately against all other terms and (b) endlessly and indeterminately rather than specifically, the result would be
nothing—no specific contrasts that generate meaning, no significant differences forming systems, nothing identifiable or recognizable to anyone,
hence no communication and no meaning at all. . . . If anyone takes *black*
as playing against every other word in English, indiscriminately, then he
does not understand its meaning. It is when he knows that a uniquely relevant contrast is with *white* and also knows how that linguistic contrast is
relevant to the corresponding contrasts in visual experience, that we are
sure he understands it. (*Against Deconstruction*, 54)

Nothing in Saussure, furthermore, prevents one from positing that
there are referential understandings (also culturally shared) that inform
the contrasts that operate within *langue*. That the meanings of signs are
relational rather than absolute—the great contribution of structuralism—does not mean they have no referential meaning (or some purely
solipsistic reference), that is, no ability to refer, in given contexts, to the
physical, psychological, and so on world. Yet many literary theorists
seem to assume that because Saussure emphasized paradigmatic mean-

ing, he simply excluded referential meaning. "The Saussurean view on this matter is that words take their meanings from their paradigmatic structure: their relationships to other words in language so that reference is arbitrary or accidental, and in any case outside the province of semiotics. The extreme of this position is that there is no such thing as reference."[35] Nor should the fact of this relational meaning lead to the conclusion that there *is* no physical world—though, without batting an (imaginary) eye, some literary critics and theorists interpret Saussurean structuralism to mean just this, that language entirely creates and shapes reality.[36] In fact, there is no necessary implication in Saussure that the world itself or things in the world have no shape or natural groupings, or that linguistic phenomena in themselves have no shape or constraints, or, finally, that there is no "systematic relationship of linguistic concepts ('signifieds') to the world."[37] "It should not be forgotten that most of the phenomenal world, as we perceive it, is not an undifferentiated continuum; and the way in which it is categorized conceptually and linguistically might very well depend upon our recognition of certain focal types of colour, shape, biological and social function, etc."[38]

Language, as we have noted, is an intrinsically social phenomenon. However, the sharing of the tool does not mean that originality in its use is impossible. Saussure foregrounded passive, shared, preexistent *langue*, because *langue* was the new conceptualization he was elaborating; however, he fully recognized the existence of active, individual, continually created *parole*, the role it plays as the vehicle of individual expression, and the role it plays in shaping future *langue*. The notion that language (or culture, or ideology) is coded, and that, as a code of (syntagmatic and paradigmatic) relations, it always already exists, should not lead us to the idea that language "constructs the subject" in the sense of removing all possibility of human agency, of authorship, or intention, or originality. The fact that language is coded at all levels is the very condition of its being meaningful—not a determinant or restricter of its meaning in use. The codes of human language are always changing in response to human experience in the world— whether that experience is of material or physical conditions or of the vagaries of intellectual fashion; at any one time, these codes permit an infinity of messages. Speakers and writers are free to create new variants of old codes or new messages out of old codes just as Thomas Cartwright does when he calls Presbyterian discipline the "chains and bracelets and rings and other jewels [that] adorn [the church] and set her out."[39] Speakers and writers are free to overlap alternative codes — just as, for example, e. e. cummings, writers of "concrete poetry," and some "language poets" overlap the codes of graphics with the codes of verbal or written language.[40] In contrast with deconstruction's emphasis on the endless chain of signifiers, and with the emphasis, in some new historicisms, on the plethora of "subject positions" by which individuals construct the world, the emphasis in this book is on the shared understandings that enable meaning in language. Yet it should not be forgotten that those very understandings, rather than being simply constraints — like the "implacable code" of ideology in some other new historicisms — are also what make possible new, creative, or changed understandings.

～ 4

The Perils of Taking Sides: Literary Interpretation

of the Naked and the Clothed

As we have seen, injunctions about "proper clothing" are slippery, because the same terms may be used by controversialists when they actually have in mind different referents, different opposed concepts, and different referents of those opposed concepts. Thus, in order to understand the precise religiopolitical positions such terms and metaphors encode, we need, where possible, to unmask apparent similarities. Yet such injunctions also have a certain systematicity that is equally part of cultural reality; the terms and metaphors used also encode some shared concepts, values, and oppositions. We now turn to consider some of the general implications of these understandings for criticism seeking to identify the religious and/or political position of texts within Renaissance Christian culture, as well as for *Lear* criticism that tries to account for the play's representations of nakedness and clothing.

General Implications for Political Criticism

The Reformation controversialists we have examined all claim, in effect, to be as clothed and as naked as they ought to be. In general, no one ever believes one's own religion (or oneself) is indecently clothed, or dressed in merely ostentatious clothing unrelated to the essence within. So, too, when the issue and/or language of "mere externals" as opposed to "inner essence" comes up in the Reformation discussion of ceremonies, there is no one in the religious sphere who would claim to be a believer in "mere externals," that is, no one who claims to be an idolater. In fact everyone knows he or she is not a believer in "mere externals." As we have seen, shared contrasts and abstractions concerning appropriate and inappropriate uses of clothing permit controversialists to "talk the same language," even though they may not mean the same things at all; similarly, terms such as "externals of worship," "idolatry," and even *"via media"* are used in ways that suggest common abstract definitions. But what differs, nevertheless, are the answers to such questions as "Is *this* idolatry?"—that is, the identification of particular acts as examples of "innapropriate worship," or of particular church ceremonies as "externals," "middle ways," or "extremes."

What is especially interesting about such terms as "idolatry" and "externals" is that they are always used to define negative attributes in implicit contrast with positive attributes that each group always claims for itself. No insiders justify externals *qua* externals; it is only "other people," seen from the outside, who are idolaters.[1] "The Papists adore the element of bread as the very person of the Son of God," says an Anglican bishop.[2] For that papist, however, insofar as he believes that "the natural body and blood of our Saviour Jesus Christ" is "present really, under the form of bread and wine," and that "after the consecration there remaineth no substance of bread and wine, nor any other substance but the substance of Christ, God and man," he is not, by definition, worshipping an idol when he is reverent.[3] Consequently, a person's avowal that he is not an idolater, or even that he adopts a position between the extremes of concern with "externals" and the complete rejection of "visible signs," or the imputation of such a position to a person, are not informative statements about that individual's religion—or politics—however much they may tell us about the salience of these issues in his mind. It is important to be wary of the dangers of leaping to specific conclusions from such general descriptions, which may describe the position of all "reasonable insiders," seen from the inside.

In fact, there is much agreement among radical and conformist Protestants, and even among Catholics and Protestants, that idolatry is the adoration of religious signs as opposed to the mysteries symbolized and that such signs are not to be adored.[4] All groups make distinctions between the proper use and the abuse of images and their equivalents. Furthermore, as John Phillips says: "At no time was it possible in practice to *prove* that idolatry was taking place, since the worship of a created thing in place of God occurs in the mind of the worshipper rather than in the image addressed."[5] With regard to the sacrament, for example, even the most "high Anglican" defender would insist it is the thing referred to that is adored and not the image or sign that refers. Thus, William Laud: "I say adoring at the Sacrament, not adoring the Sacrament."[6] Calvin strikes what sounds like a somewhat similar balanced note—concordant with the doctrine of the spiritual presence we looked at in chapter 2—in his discussion of sign and mystery in the sacred supper: "By the corporeal objects which are presented in the sacrament, we are conducted, by a kind of analogy, to those which are spiritual. . . . Here it behoves us to guard against two errors; that . . . we may not, by undervaluing the signs, disjoin them from the mysteries with which they are connected; nor, . . . by extolling them beyond measure, obscure the glories of the mysteries themselves" (*Institutes*, 4.17.3, 4.17.5; 2:643, 645).

This is not to say that no distinctions can be made: it is useful to consider the frequency with which writers turn to or ignore particular arguments. High Anglicans and/or Catholics may discriminate, more often than nonconformist or radical Protestants, between appropriately and inappropriately used images or between honor and worship. Calvin, although distinguishing between the sign and the mystery to which it refers in a manner suggesting that homage is due to each (in his discussion of the sacred supper just quoted), also refuses at times to even consider making distinctions. "Nor is it of any importance," Calvin says, "whether they worship simply the idol, or God in the idol; it is always idolatry, when Divine honors are paid to any idol, under any pretense whatsoever" (*Institutes*, 1.11.9, 1:124). He irately comments that "these ingenious men deny that the honor which they pay to images is worship, as if, when compared with ancient idolatry, it were possible to see any difference." He typically insists on God as what is *not* present to the senses: "The invisible image of God is not in that which is seen, but precisely in that which is not seen."[7]

Like the term "idolatry," the term *"via media"* may be less meaningful than it appears to be when used, as it often is by critics, to describe a religiopolitical position, because it too is relative—although it may not sound that way—and therefore requires further elucidation, comparison, and contrast. The *via media* argument about a writer's religiopolitical position is convenient for critics for the same reason it was convenient for polemicists: different particular "extremes" and "means" may be thought of as defining a *via media*, or middle way; one may have in mind a new extreme that makes a former extreme a mean—as the moderate Puritan William Bradshaw saw.[8] This might not be worth saying if it weren't for a perhaps inevitable tendency in critical thought to equate all mean-between-the-extremes positions, rather than to attempt to make the necessary distinctions among them. Agreement on a general statement may mask disagreement on the referents to which it applies; obviously, one man's extreme may be another man's midpoint. What the Anglican Laud would call naked may or may not be what the Anglican Herbert would call naked. Thus, John Phillips comments on Laud: "Despite these adjustments to the service, which had not been seen for some time in England, Laud claimed he walked a middle path between 'overburdening the service of God,' and leaving it 'naked.'"[9] Similarly, the argument that a religious poet or a theologian favors neither mere externals nor formlessness, but a meaningful union of externals wedded to internals and indistinguishable from them, may be used to describe Herbert as well as Laud, and is so used.[10] Such an argument will not distinguish between Herbert and Laud; it merely asserts the ideal uniformly held by "reasonable insiders," who may well each hold different practices to be exemplifications of it. Indeed, Richard Strier's interpretation of the *via media* position often ascribed to George Herbert—on the basis of his obviously relevant poem—"The British Church"[11] is both a welcome attempt to particularize the general and an illustration of the difficulties involved. Herbert describes his church as liturgically neither proudly painted nor undressed, neither "too gay" nor "too mean." According to Strier, however, he sees it as "not . . . midway between [Rome and Geneva]," as opposed to "roughly equidistant" from each of them. Genevan practice is less culpable than Roman, a matter of "folly rather than sin," and thus Herbert's middle way is not really in the middle.[12]

In contrast, Joseph Summers uses Herbert's gloss on the Pauline text ("Let all things be done unto edifying," "Let all things be done decently and in order" [1 Corinthians 14:26, 40]) to argue for what in effect is a rather high Anglican Herbert. This ubiquitous text—the latter part of which was often used to justify actual vestments as well as metaphorical attire (i.e., ceremonies) in the church—does itself suggest the need to balance concerns. It clearly says that both edification and decency and order are necessary; certainly Reformation controversialists and other writers, as well as contemporary critics of religious poetry read it as implying that both superfluous ceremonies and inappropriate nakedness should be avoided. It is for this reason that Herbert's citation of Paul's injunctions in *A Priest to the Temple*—in parallel, it would appear, with his own "the middle way between superstition, and slovenliness" (*Works*, 246)—invites the labeling of Herbert as a *via media* Anglican. Yet Summer's argument involves a logical error that is easy to overlook; the reason it is easy to overlook is that the appearance of a middle way is easily constructed from *any* two terms set in opposition.

In the Christian's life, as well as in the Church, all things must be done both "decently" and "to edification." Whether it was in administering the sacraments, sweeping a floor, serving as a Justice of the Peace, or writing poetry, the dual "object of our duty," God and man, must always be perceived and order and rational "edification" were inevitably the proper expressions of love. It was this emphasis on the value and significant inseparability of contemplation and action, of faith and reason, of God's creation on this earth and in heaven, which enabled Herbert to avoid the "superstitious" rejection of the material and the "slovenly" rejection of form. (Summers, *Herbert*, 65)

Noting that Herbert advocates a " 'middle way between superstition, and slovenliness,' " Summers says Herbert would "avoid the 'superstitious' rejection of the material and the 'slovenly' rejection of form," this antinomy fitting neatly into his other inseparable opposing terms ("decently" and "to edification," "God and man," "contemplation and action," "faith and reason"). But, what does the avoidance of the superstitious rejection of the material mean? Summers has Herbert avoiding both too great a fear of material things and too great a disregard for formal order. This tends to put the emphasis on the exoneration of the material *and* the formal. If this is a *via media* at all, it is one very different from other possible, and indeed in this case, plausible ones, for example, that between the purely material and the purely spiritual. I should think "superstitiousness" is historically more often a charge levied by those who think they themselves have no material idols against those they think are idolaters, than it is a charge levied by any group against others they accuse of being too afraid to make use of the material. Indeed, in the passage in question, Herbert says the parson does all he lists—seeing that the books are clean, and so on—"not as out of necessity, or as putting a holiness in the things" (*Works*, 246), and later Herbert uses "superstition" (286) to refer to overvaluing the priest's holy water in the time of popery, that is, to refer to too great a regard for the material, not to too great a fear of using it. Thus Herbert's "middle way" in this particular case plausibly mediates between the extremes of "slovenliness" or sheer disorder or unkemptness, and "superstition," or the undue veneration of material signs and objects, that is, between a deficiency of "decency and order" and an excessive regard for ritual at the expense of "edification."

It should now be clear in what senses so multivalent and contested a text as "Let all things be done unto edifying," "Let all things be done decently and in order" does not in itself "explain" a writer's position. As was the case with the related concept of "proper clothing," many could and did agree on this text as a precept, but the issues they argued about were what was comely or decent, what was edification, and what edified. Hence, the famous words in the "Admonition to the Parliament" of 1572: "And as for the apparel, though we have been long borne in hand, and yet are, that it is for order and decency commanded, yet we know and have proved that there is neither order, nor comeliness, nor obedience in using it. There is no order in it, but confusion: No comeliness, but deformities: No obedience, but disobedience, both against God and the Prince."[13] These words do not take issue with the need for comeliness or order, but with whether the prescribed apparel is comely or contributes to order.

Let us consider some aspects of the arguments about edification as a final example providing the kind of awareness necessary to avoid taking such malleable terms in less than their full and slippery contexts. The Pauline precepts are ones, as suggested, that everyone agreed with in theory; yet here is a case where we can specify the differing metaphysical assumptions that led to divergent interpretation.

Archbishop Whitgift regards the Pauline rule about edification as applying strictly only to some things in the church, but regards the rule about order and decency as applying to everything: "This sentence [1 Corinthians 14:26] cannot be applied generally to all things used in the church, if we truly interpret the meaning of the apostle, but to the gift 'of tongues, to prayers, and to prophecies,' whereof he hath made mention before. Neither can I perceive that any learned interpreter doth take it as a general rule for all rites and ceremonies" (*Works of Whitgift*, 1:197). Thus, as Whitgift understands the sentence contextually, when Paul says "all," he at one time means "everything," but at another time means only everything in a subcategory of "all." "For of things used in the church, some pertain to instruction, and some to order and comeliness. For the first he giveth this rule, 'Let all things be done to edifying.' For both the first and the second he giveth this . . . 'Let all things be done decently and in order' " (ibid., 1:197–98). However, Whitgift does not go quite as far as to say that ceremonies performed for decency and order "do not edify at all." Rather, "those ceremonies and rites, which are appointed by the church for order and comeliness, do edify as ceremonies, that is, not of themselves, but *per accidens*, 'accidentally.' " They "tend to edifying, as other ceremonies and things used in the church (as pulpit, . . . kneeling, singing, and such like) do" (ibid., 2:56, 1:198, 2:56).[14] Thus, Whitgift considers that one may be edified by a white surplice because it functions as an instructive symbol. Edification as he defines it is closely connected with signification. White garments signify the office of ministers, who are as angels of God in the church (ibid., 2:63, 65). Their wearers may be imperfect, but "man, being impure, may have external instruments to bid him (as it were) remember what he ought to be" (ibid., 2:65).

Among the many causes of Thomas Cartwright's inability to accept the idea that the surplice is edifying is his insistent feeling that its signification is inappropriate. For Cartwright, purity belongs wholly and only to the heavenly state; if whiteness refers to heavenly purity, it is unfitting for earthly ministers:

And, if it be meet that the ministers should represent the angels in their apparel, it is much more meet that they should have a pair of wings . . . to put them in remembrance of their readiness and quickness to execute their office . . . than to wear white apparel, which is a token of pureness from sin and infection, and of a glory, which neither they have nor can have, as long as they be in this world. (Ibid., 2:64)

Cartwright's distaste for any argument that suggests the spiritual efficacy of such external signs makes him rise to exasperated and sardonically comic heights:

And then also, if there be a virtue in a white garment, and the signification thereof be so strong to work godliness, it were meet that the order were taken that the whitest cloth should be bought, that should be often (at the very least every week once) washed by a very good launder, and with soap; for if the white help, more white helpeth more, and that which is most white helpeth most of all to godliness. (Ibid.)

Cartwright's definition of edification was a "far more precise and demanding one" than Whitgift's; it involved the spiritual growth and inward purity, "in the midst of a corrupt and corrupting world, of a community of true believers."[15] Edification as such was tied intrinsically to the particular Presbyterian church discipline that could keep consciences pure, and was inconsistent with the offence given to the godly by vestiges of popish ceremonies.[16]

Hooker's view of edification—like Whitgift's, one that justifies "visible signs"—also clearly contrasts with Cartwright's. Hooker's edification encompasses what appeals to the understanding or involves knowledge, and "visible signs" used "in performance of holy actions" are instructive, making men "the better informed to what effect such duties serve" (*LEP,* 4.1.3, in *Works,* 1:418). But Hooker's view of edification also includes what appeals to the emotions, fosters reverence, or inculcates an appropriate frame of mind. By his definition, ceremonies, which "work by commonness of use much" (*LEP,* 5.65.4, in *Works,* 2:319)—and which the nonconformist sought to remove from the church as distinctly not edifying—seem to edify almost inevitably: "[M]en are edified . . . when their hearts are moved with any affection suitable thereunto; when their minds . . . are stirred up unto . . . reverence, devotion, attention and due regard" (*LEP,* 4.1.3, in *Works,* 1:418).[17]

Because of the leeway for interpretation that such justifying texts as this Pauline one clearly have, as well as the universality of the insider's view that the externals he or she approves of always serve inner faith, one must take care, when using such texts or ideas to locate writers' particular religious or religiopolitical "positions." It is crucial to attend to the referents of the terms and to the paradigmatic contrasts in which those terms participated. Thus, for example, there may be differences in the discussion of "externals" between religious writers who focus on the avoidance of profanation and those who focus on the avoidance of idolatry.[18] There may also be differences, even among conformists, between that attitude toward "externals" that presumes that where there is weeping and kneeling, there are likely to be the internal emotions that should accompany such shows, and that attitude that asserts that such signs are not necessary for, nor the cause, nor the result of, an internal repentance.[19] In any case, it is assuredly on such distinctions that any convincing attribution of religious (or political) "position" must rest.

Clothing and King Lear

Most of the critical discussions that focus on "clothing" in *King Lear* do attempt to locate the values of the play in "nakedness" and its apparent or presumed textual analogues—silence, the heart, "what we feel," plainness—and do tend to seek a univalent "meaning" for "nakedness." The authors of these discussions—like most critics—hear the text speak in terms of values that are still recognizable as values or overlap with their own, and at the same time, are values that may be ascribed to the playwright's culture. Although the topic ("imagery") of most of these discussions connects them with a prior moment in criticism, their limitations are in essence little different from the limitations of more recent political readings linking nakedness or plainness to political or religious position—which the second part of this book will address. Both these formal and these political readings tap into only a small part of the rich meaningfulness of concepts of clothing and nakedness; they would benefit from a more complete and more precise account of the relations of contiguity or contrast in which various types of "clothing"—decent, ragged, whorish, and so forth—appear, as well as of the referents to which such terms point in actual Renaissance use.

Russell Fraser is perhaps the critic most insistent on only one available cultural value, one that takes no account of the strong valences on the shamefulness of nakedness—and the necessity for clothing to hide it—still obtaining in Renaissance Christianity. He makes use of absolutely valenced categories of "show" and "substance" to talk about *Lear*. "Nakedness is not the badge of inferiority but Truth," and "Truth, . . . as the Renaissance bodies her forth, is unapparelled," he states. In fact, he is so sure that the superior principle must be unclothed, that (as mentioned in chapter 1) he equates Lear's "perversely blind" identification of "nakedness with lack of substance" with

the *mistake* of the medieval artist who, depicting a contest between Nature and Reason, clothes the higher principle and leaves Nature, the lesser, unclothed. Mantegna also, painting the two Venuses, indicates by her nakedness the inferiority of Aphrodite to Urania. But the right reading is otherwise. . . . Conversely, Man the hero, in Henry Medwall's *Nature*, as he puts on those mufflings, is diminished.[20]

Emily W. Leider is concerned with the contrast of the " 'robes and furr'd gowns'—the superfluities—of language," in *Lear*'s opening scene, to the "verbal nakedness" of the final scenes; she explores the way in which Lear himself moves from grandiloquent language with long periods, using the first person plural royal "we" (1.1), to the plainness and simplicity of "I am a very foolish fond old man" in the reconciliation scene with Cordelia (4.7.59) and the unstudied spontaneous feeling of "Never, never, never, never, never" at the terrible denouement (5.3.309).[21] For Cordelia, Kent, and ultimately, for Lear, fewer and sharper words (more "specific, monosyllabic, fricative, choppy, repetitive" or "native" ones), or silence, or actions—as opposed to loquacious flattering speeches—are what express truth, true feeling, or essence.[22] Sheldon P. Zitner, reacting to the denouement, likewise comes down hard against words, form, decorum, stating that "the demands of form and decorum in language may lead to untruths."[23]

Thelma Greenfield's commentary specifically on clothing in *Lear* does recognize that the symbolic value of nudity and its analogues may be ambivalent ("Especially in the Middle Ages, nudity could symbolize either the superior or the inferior quality"); she cites the four symbolic meanings of nakedness distinguished in medieval moral theology and also mentioned by Erwin Panofsky in his discussion of Titian's *Sacred and Profane Love*—to which I shall shortly return—as evidence of this ambivalence.[24] However, not unlike the other critics mentioned, she does tend to see Lear's divesting of himself rather unambiguously as a matter of his finding himself; she does tend to equate the "essence of man" with the " 'thing itself,' " "stripped" of the "external trappings of worm's silk and cat's perfume."[25] Thus Greenfield, like Fraser, argues that Henry Medwall's morality play *Nature* (printed 1530?) shows Man's degeneration in "a simple and consistent pattern of meanings" through the symbolism of the putting on of clothing; Man's acceptance of the "gift of garments" is "the first step in the typical long series of evil practices and companions which he affects throughout the play." She implies that Man misuses his freedom of choice in accepting "World's arguments in favor of the garments [which] are eminently practical and specious."[26] The astute and careful Robert Heilman, whose language frequently captures multivalent meanings in *Lear*—the way in which disguise is both a good and an evil and nakedness a symbol of defenselessness and yet a defense—nevertheless also mainly embraces the Christian value of nakedness at the expense of the Christian value of proper clothing, in a position not so much "wrong" as incomplete. Heilman stresses that "in Lear's situation, nakedness alone is meaningful and clothes are a 'sophistication,' " and that Lear finally "gives up prerogative and protection, throws away clothes which have no meaning." "The gorgeous are doomed," he concludes. "In proud array, Lear failed; uncrowned, half-naked, he is saved."[27]

Among more recent political critics of the play, Richard Strier finds in plainness—"plain speech and conscientious breaches of decorum," "plain style" (and their presumed politically radical Protestant analogues)—a clear "locus of value." He therefore also finds that "the moral moorings of the play threaten to come loose" when Cornwall "offers a brilliant . . . parody of affected plainness" in response to Kent's "'tis my occupation to be plain" (2.2.92). But Strier concludes: "As is the case with Lear's association of plainness with pride in scene 1 (line 128), the play does not support the possible critique. The plain style remains a locus of value."[28] Walter Cohen finds a positive connection of "Lear's periodic undressing" and "the Ranter and early Quaker tendency to go 'naked for a sign,' to 'go naked as . . . [Adam] did, and live above sin and shame,'" and he also asserts that "Edgar's concluding preference for feeling over platitude surely belongs in the radical Protestant tradition."[29]

However, the "superior quality" is not so clearly nude, even in the Renaissance, and a reduction to being uncrowned and half-naked not so unambiguous a victory, even in a Christian culture. Critical comments that focus on the spiritual superiority that the absence of material possessions might confer may underplay the negative connotations—also part of a Christian culture, and of human experience in that culture—of shameful or helpless and unprotected nakedness, connotations that also must have been highly significant in shaping audience reaction to *Lear.*

Although Erwin Panofsky argues that the clothed lady is the inferior principle in Titian's *Sacred and Profane Love,* he emphasizes "the ambivalence of nudity as an iconographical motif."[30] In fact, the overall stress appears to be on the shamefulness of nudity, rather than on its naked truth, in the group of "four symbolical meanings of nudity" distinguished by "medieval moral theology." The first of these, *"nuditas naturalis,"* is "the natural state of man." "Natural" nakedness represents nature as fallen, perverted, or weak, in a shameful or helpless state "conducive to humility"—that is, requiring grace, culture, art, or discipline to repair or rectify it. *"Nuditas virtualis"* is described as a "symbol of innocence," "preferably innocence acquired through confession." Such symbolic nudity employs the Christian trope of divestment of polluted "clothing" to figure the recovery of an original innocence, and, as such, uses body to stand for soul. However, because confession repairs man's "natural," fallen state, the innocence of *nuditas virtualis* is an achieved innocence. Thus, even if *nuditas virtualis,* and *nuditas naturalis* as well, are in some degree good, these symbolic categories also suggest the limitations of the natural or naked. *"Nuditas criminalis,"* the third category, is "a sign of lust, vanity, and the absence of all virtues"; it is a category exemplifying perverted or fallen nature, and one that assumes that rationality requires being clothed (Panofsky, *Studies in Iconology*, 156). It was used "in representations of pagan divinities, devils, vices, and sinful humans" (ibid., n. 95). Perhaps only "*nuditas temporalis*," "the lack of earthly goods, which can be voluntary (as in [the practice of] the Apostles or monks) or necessitated by poverty" (ibid., 156), invokes nudity as a simply positive symbol of a "natural" state superior to human traditions or institutions, which are analogous to "polluted" clothing. Of course, even so, a life of voluntary poverty would involve an achieved innocence, a disciplining of the natural self.

Panofsky summarizes:

> Not only in the Bible but also in Roman literature actual nudity was often thought objectionable, because it indicated either poverty, or shamelessness. In a figurative sense, however, it was mostly identified with simplicity, sincerity and the true essence of a thing as opposed to circumlocution, deceit and external appearances. All things are 'naked and open unto the eyes' of God [Hebrews 14:3]. . . . *Nuda virtus* is the real virtue appreciated in the good old days when wealth and social distinction did not count, and Horace speaks already of *nuda Veritas*, though the Greek writers, characteristically enough, rather imagined Truth as dressed in simple garments.
>
> When, at the end of the classical period, actual nudity had become so unusual in public life, that it had to be 'explained' like any other 'iconographical' feature, the explanation could thus be both damaging and favourable. (Ibid., 155)

Although Titian may make nudity the superior principle, medieval artists did the reverse. In the type of composition that Panofsky labels "debating-picture," where "the debating partners stand for such notions as 'Nature' and 'Reason,' or 'Nature' and 'Grace,'" the "loftier principle" is draped and the inferior nude. In fact, "wherever mediaeval art established a deliberate contrast between a nude figure and a draped one the lack of clothes designates the inferior principle" (ibid., 154, 156).

The symbolism of clothing, then, need not be simple, as it is not, indeed, in *Nature* and later sixteenth-century morality plays which, like Reformation controversy, shape and are shaped by a cultural semiotics.

It is true that World, who gives Man the garments brought in by Worldly Affection, belongs to the triumvirate of "World, Flesh, Devil," the traditional enemies of mankind; Reason, at the beginning of the Second Part—when Man has already fallen into temptation—describes World as such:

And for to show you what wise they us impugn,
First doth the World give us an allective
To covet riches and worldly renown,
With other vanities that be used in this life.[31]

It is also true that World introduces Man to Worldly Affection, and, after that, to Pride and the Seven Deadly Sins. However, it must also be said that the entire process of Man's accepting the robe, cap, and girdle brought in by Worldly Affection and given to him by World is approved by Reason and ultimately condoned by Innocency. Reason, having heard Man's vow of innocence, of having "Of sinful deed and thought all innocent, / Subdued to Reason as is obedient" (ll. 384-85), in fact does "hold it well done and right expedient / That ye were brough[t] unto the World's presence" (ll. 391-92). Reason thus addresses World:

Sir World, it is the mind and also pleasure
Of lady Nature, as she bade us to you tell,
That ye accept and receive this her creature
With you for a season here to dwell,
Desiring you heartily to entreat him well
With all the favour that ye can devise,
Wherin ye shall do her great pleasure and service.
(ll. 400-6)

When World accepts Man, "ordained to reign here in this empry" (l. 422), he seems to echo Nature's words about how God gave to man "the emprise / Of all this world, and feoffed [him] with all / As chief possessioner of things mortual" (ll. 82-84).[32]

Admittedly, even as one begins to make a case for the garments World gives Man as by no means intrinsically corrupt, one is not sure how to take Man's avowal that he is clothed sufficiently by Nature, and protected by Innocencye ("as a maiden pure, / I wear on me the garment of Innocency" [ll. 437-38]) in response to World's "Ye be all naked! Alas Man, why thus, / I make you sure, it is right perilous!" (ll. 433-34) Nevertheless, whatever these ambiguities—and there are not a few—it does seem quite clear that Man, *wearing* the garments given by World and sitting in World's throne, still speaks in a humble and righteous manner, thus suggesting that there may be use or abuse of natural gifts, stewardship or prodigality. World says:

I give you here authority and power
Over all thing that conceived is in the space

> Of all the earth that round is in compass,
> To be as lord of every region,
> And thereof I give you peaceable possession.
>
> (ll. 472–76)

And Man, wearing the garments, thanks God for his gifts in a humble manner, and promises that he will live in a manner concordant with God, even if at the expense of suffering pain in the *world:*

> Blessed be thou my lord most bounteous,
> That of thy great abundant charity
> Me thy wretched creature hast honoured thus
> With natural gifts and worldly dignity.
>
> .   .   .   .
>
> For certes, it is mine heart's desire
> So to demean me in this life present
> As may be most unto thy pleasure
> And unto Nature not disconvenient.
> This is my will and my chief intent,
> This will I observe — thy grace to borrow —
> Though I therefore suffer much worldly sorrow.
>
> (ll. 477–80; 484–490)

Reason approves this vow "thou here openly to God dost promise" (l. 497). Thus, even if wordly dignity *tends* to corrupt, these garments are not unambiguously the first step in a downward progression.

Although the play's modern editor describes World as at first seeming "morally neutral, but in fact sid[ing] completely with the vices," and regards the action of Man's being brought into the presence of World as symbolizing "the inevitablility of man's coming into contact with the world and consequently falling into sin" (199, note to ll. 390–91), T. W. Craik argues that World should be understood differently, and that Man's degradation is not marked until he allows Pride to make a fashionable costume for him.

There is no indication that Man has as yet become worldly in any bad sense; Reason and Innocency both offer advice, but this is merely advice to avoid sin in his now responsible position, not to abandon a sin already committed. It is only in ordering him to associate with merry companions, "be they never so vicious or abominable," and in replacing Innocency with Worldly Affection, that the World becomes sinister. Worldly Affection assists Sensuality in gaining Man's ear, and sends in Pride, who devises for Man a "gallant" costume more extravagant than his own. It consists of a gown freely adorned with broad lace, an open-backed and sleeveless doublet, a white silk shirt, velvet striped breeches, and multi-coloured hose.... The point of the play is clearly that there are degrees of worldliness, the first equivalent to experience and the second to sin.[33]

The World may be dangerous; its gifts entail a responsibility that they be used appropriately. However, to accept them is not automatically to forfeit innocence.

Decent or even fine apparel may be a value, as much as plainness or nakedness is. In the later morality plays, although fine apparel may be presented in negative contrast to plainness (for example, in *The Trial of Treasure*, where Treasure is "a woman finely appareled" and Trust "a woman plainly [appareled])," [34] it is not necessarily presented this way. "Truth" might often wear "her traditional, distinctive white robe," [35] but magnificent costume, as well as white robes, may be appropriate for Christ, or for virtues. And indeed, the *same* costume of "purple, cloth of gold and ermine," with "crown, orb, and sceptre" might be used for Christ (or Wisdom), for God, and also for the "World, who bestows wealth and power on Man—worldly gifts which bring temptations," as in *Nature*.[36] Decent apparel, or apparel standing for material possessions well used, may also mediate between excessive clothing and some form of nakedness or poverty, just as Man's earlier costume of robe, cap, and girdle perhaps mediates between his "nakedness" and the "staring" scarlet of Pride's headdress and the extravagant gown with "wide sleeves that hang adown" that "would make some lad in this town / A doublet and a coat" (*Nature*, ll. 748, 768–70). It is clear that clothing may disfigure, for example, when Usury, in *The Three Lords and Three Ladies of London* (1590), "covers Conscience with Fraud's cloak very cunningly"—a cloak that contrasts with the white robes she wears when she is her unobscured self.[37] But, on the other hand, clothing may also appropriately attire, for example, when, in the same play, Lucre—meant now as appropriate reward—is decked out by Honest Industry, or Love is decked out by Pure Zeal.[38] Even magnificent costume may be appropriate, as when Lord Pomp in the same play is described by his page Wealth as rightly representing "the stately magnificence and sumptuous estate, without pride or vainglory, to London accomodate." [39]

The negative implications of fine apparel are also not an issue when it is clear that an appropriate use of material riches is involved. Thus the rich apparel of "Learning with money" in *All for Money* [1578] — as compared to the rich apparel and moneybags (reminiscent of the usurer) of the churl, "Money without learning" — does not send a negative signal. "Learning with money" — and here "Learning" seems to refer to theology and the philosophy or "science" that serves it — unlike the uncharitable "Money without learning," uses his learning to rule his riches and indeed supports the poor scholar, "Learning without money"; thus his rich apparel is in some sense deserved, or a true mark of his charitable stewardship of wealth.[40] As the Prologue says, "[T]he creature of God is not evil of him self."

> Money ill used is the devil's snare and hook,
> Whereby many are brought to endless damnation:
> But the godly do bestow it to their salvation.[41]

While figurative nakedness might be a good in metaphors of the "naked truth," it is crucial for the resonance of nakedness in *Lear* that most situations in which actual nakedness — or even "vile and ragged apparel" — was likely to occur were humiliating or shameful. Like Lear, the mad might be found naked or nearly naked. Geoffrey Goodman, writing of the corruption of nature in *The Fall of Man*, says, "I will therefore go from [man's] naked bed to Bedlam, where you shall find men naked out of their beds. . . . The irons enter into their flesh, they are used in the nature of wild beasts, but their greatest misery is, that they have no feeling of their own misery."[42] Like Poor Tom, the destitute might be naked; and when they were found outside of their own parishes, the punishment inflicted on them might include the humiliation of nakedness. Actual nakedness was more likely linked with the disorder of social life, the failure of the family and of charity, with debasement and shame, than with any glorious truth.

When "Adamians" or "Adamites" — or Anabaptists — chose to literalize the metaphor of the naked truth by going naked, or when such extreme sects came up in discussion, the response was scorn or opprobrium, or violent suppression. Bishop Nicholas Ridley provides an example of such contempt. He is replying to Bishop John Hooper's refusal, during the early vestiarian controversy, to wear the bishop's vestments. Hooper's grounds were that "the Aaronic priests used vestments in their ministry, because the truth of their priesthood, Christ himself, had not come: but Christ, when himself was to be sacrificed, was divested of all his vestments, showing his priesthood by this, that, because he was the truth itself, he now no longer had need of any veils or shadows." [43] Ridley's reply alludes to the Adamian practice of nakedness at divine service as the *reductio ad absurdam* of a position requiring scriptural warrant for all "things indifferent," all differences from a primitive "purity":

Where it is said, 'The naked hanging of Christ upon the cross lacketh not his mystery,' surely no more lacketh the purple wherein he was clad, nor the white garment wherewith Herod mocked him, in the time of his passion. Oh! this were a jolly argument for the sect of the Adamians, of which Epiphanius saith that they assembled themselves, both men and women, naked, in the time of their divine service, to resemble the innocency of Adam and Eve in paradise.[44]

The Renaissance response to actual instances of such ideological nakedness was often more than mere contempt. "Early in 1535 an incident occurred that was often reported to the discredit of the Anabaptist movement as a whole. Seven men and five women stripped off their clothes, as a sign, they said, that they spoke the naked truth, and ran through the streets of Amsterdam crying, 'Woe! woe! woe! the Wrath of God.' They were set upon and killed, and persecution rose to a new crescendo of intensity." [45] The revulsion with which such enactments of radical innocence were met may be heard in Ephraim Pagitt's mid-seventeenth-century *Heresiography*. Pagitt, a royalist who wished to establish Presbyterianism (as preferable to Independency), characterizes fourteen heretical groups; among these are the Adamites, "a kind of Anabaptists, who think clothes to be cursed, and given to man for a punishment of sin, whereas they think themselves to be innocent and without sin." (The Anabaptist pictured along with other exemplary types on the title page is naked.) Pagitt adds an additional description of a sixteenth-century Anabaptist sect he read about in Bullinger (the marginal note reads *Pueres similes*):

Mr. *Bullinger* in his first book against *Anabaptists*, nameth others; as some of them under pretence of childish innocency, played many odd pranks: one having kept his excrements in store many days, poured them out in the street, and turned himself naked into them, saying, *unless we be made like little children, we cannot enter into the kingdom of heaven*. Others for the same reason would ride upon sticks and hobby-horses (like children) in great companies, and women would run naked with them, and then in pure innocency they lay together, and so in the end it proved children's play indeed.[46]

Like Nicholas Ridley, other ministers insist on the necessary use of apparel in a post-Edenic context (although they may also dwell on the inappropriateness of the excessive use of such a marker of shame):

For most true it is that apparel, whereof we now pride so much, was and is the accuser of sin, for our first parents were naked before they sinned, and *were not ashamed,* because nothing gave cause to blush, they free from sin, and being made to the image of God. But having transgressed his commandment, they saw their nakedness and sinful bodies by eating of the apple, and did blush, for shame, blushing and confusion are the fruits of sin, to whom now some coverture was necessary, as well to keep the less honorable parts secret, as to defend them from the parching sun and winter's cold. Wherefore our good God, gave to either of them a coat of pelts or skins. This simple sufficient attire condemneth two sorts of persons, the *Adamites* which run naked, to counterfeit *Adam* and *Hevah,* which thing if God would to have had in use, he had not given these naked creatures these needy coats. The other are our lusty gallants of either sex, that too too much do glory in their apparel, which is and ought to be to them, a preacher of their father's shame.[47]

Clearly for such ministers this shamefulness of the naked body is intrinsic and unavoidable. Similarly, Calvin asserts in his commentary on Genesis that "we can not see a man naked without shame: the like shame is not in the sight of an ass, or a dog, or a bull. Moreover, every man is ashamed of his nakedness, though he be not seen of others."[48] Even man's spiritual reformation does not change this shame, as Henry Holland explains: "Now his deformity is such, that not withstanding he be received to grace, and reformed in some measure in Christ, yet till he be refined in the resurrection he cannot well think of, much less look upon his own nakedness without shame, as we see in our first Parents."[49] Indeed, in a kind of back-formation, Gervase Babington stresses exclusively the *metaphorical* implications of the nakedness of Adam and Eve. He asserts that the placing of them naked in Paradise "showeth us how God would have us walk before him, verily naked, without cloaks and covers, masks and shadows of any coloured craft," but it is a "nakedness and nudity *not of body but of mind,* of counsels, and actions" that "the Lord ever loved, and the contrary cloaking he as heartily hateth."[50] Of course, a literal nakedness or seminakedness may figure a symbolic nakedness of mind; but, at the same time, the symbolic possibilities of nakedness are tinged and constrained by the negative attitude toward literal nakedness.

Thus, while there is no question that the positive image of the naked truth does occur in both literary and visual Renaissance texts,[51] the pressure of the idea of actual nakedness as shameful appears to be strong, especially in the English Renaissance. The medieval category of nakedness as *nuditas criminalis* persists; for all the use of nude figures and naked gods and goddesses in European Renaissance visual art, the Reformation rejection of the pagan gods involves the rejection of their diabolical nudity. A work such as Stephen Batman's *The Golden Booke of the Leaden Gods* (the animus of which is evident in its title) interprets Venus who is "figured . . . naked with a garland of flowers and roses on her head" as follows: "Her garland of roses doth signify the superfluity which wantons require, and being naked, the shameless care of virginity."[52]

In visual and in literary contexts, simple clothing often seem to modify the "nakedness" that exemplifies Truth—making it only a near-nakedness. The traditions of a simply dressed and a naked Truth co-exist. In the 1630 edition of Cesare Ripa's *Iconologia*, Truth is both a "golden-haired woman dressed in white, who holds a mirror and a pair of golden scales," and, in another example, "naked but adorned with a few white veils."[53] Where actual nakedness was clearly not acceptable, as in pageants making use of such motifs as "Truth the daughter of Time," simple clothing would have to stand for the truth.[54] Even in traditions or situations where there is a particularly strong figurative association of nakedness (which is opposed to deceitful clothing) and the truth, such as Protestantism's emphasis on the naked truth of Christ (as opposed to the pollution of Catholic ceremonies), the figure of "the true church" is very likely to be clothed, because of the strongly felt shamefulness of actual nakedness—perhaps particularly in a woman. The figure set in opposition to the bedecked whore of Babylon (as well as to saints decked out as if they were "some Princes of *Persia* land with their proud apparel") in the Elizabethan "Homilie against Perill of Idolatrie, and Superfluous Decking of Churches" is a chaste matron, and hardly naked. The homilist is resistant to the possibility, as we can see in the quotation below; in fact he does not want to imagine either the false church or the true as "naked." He asserts that the true ugliness of the bedecked false church would be revealed were she stripped of her merely outward adornments, and seen "(I will not say naked) but in simple apparel," like that worn by the true church; on the other hand, the true church—clearly also not naked but dressed in that simple apparel—requires nothing more elaborate because she is inwardly beautiful.

For she being in deed . . . a foul, filthy, old withered harlot . . . and under-standing her lack of nature and true beauty, and great loathsomeness . . . doth . . . paint herself, and deck and tire her self with gold, pearl, stone, and all kind of precious jewels, that she shining with the outward beauty and glory of them, may please the foolish fantasy of fond lovers, and so entice them to spiritual fornication with her. Who, if they saw her (I will not say naked), but in simple apparel, would abhor her, as the foulest and filthiest harlot that ever was seen. . . . Whereas . . . the true Church of God, as a chaste matron, espoused (as the Scripture teacheth) to one husband, . . . is content with her natural ornaments, not doubting, by such sincere sim-plicity, best to please him, who can well skill of the difference between a painted visage, and true natural beauty.[55]

A practice that attests to the shamefulness of nakedness or near nakedness, even in a Protestant culture that values the figurative "naked truth," is the "divestment" of clothing in actual acts of "degradation," which Shakespeare's audience might semiotically link with Lear's tear-ing off of his "lendings" (3.4.108). As Margaret Ranald shows: "Accounts of chivalric, military and ecclesiastical degradations were readily avail-able to Shakespeare and his contemporaries." "Degraded knights and soldiers lost any privileged position they might have in law to be tried by their peers . . . and instead became liable to the penalties of the civil law," as also happened in the case of ecclesiastical degradation.[56] The shameful aspects of loss of rank in a ranked society with highly visible—often showy—insignia of rank including clothing are under-lined by such ceremonies. Of course, when degradation is suffered by the saints of Christ, and the garments they are divested of are the fool-ish and abominable gear of Antichrist, their beggarliness is also the badge of the elect. Yet, in spite of the Protestant potential to celebrate the "naked truth" of the martyrs—stripped of ecclesiastical dignities by their Catholic persecutors—Foxe's descriptions also invoke pity and lamentation for such "unaccomodated m[e]n" (3.4.106-7) who have fallen to a ragged and vile estate.

Consider, for example, of the six degradations that took place during Queen Mary's reign as reported by Foxe, the degradation of Thomas Cranmer, according to the pope's "Pontificale," on February 14, 1556.[57] First, Cranmer was invested in the special vestments of a subdeacon, a deacon, a priest, a bishop, and an archbishop, not "most rich and costly," as "at his installing," but all made "of canvas and old clouts, with a mitre and a pall of the same suit done upon him in mockery" (Foxe, *Acts and Monuments*, 8:72). Then he was divested of all these; Foxe's emphasis is on the magnitude of the change and the pity of Cranmer's "bare" and "ragged" apparel.

And so they did [take his pall], and so proceeding took every thing in order from him, as it was put on. Then a barber clipped his hair round about and the bishop scraped the tops of his fingers where he had been anointed. . . . Last of all they stripped him out of his gown into his jacket, and put upon him a poor yeoman-beadle's gown, full bare and nearly worn, and as evil favouredly made, as one might lightly see, and a townsman's cap on his head; and so delivered him to the secular power.

After this pageant of degradation, and all was finished, then spake lord Bonner, saying to him, "Now are you no lord any more." . . . And thus, with great compassion and pity of every man, in this evil favoured gown was he carried to prison. (8:79–80)

Foxe's emphasis in the description of Cranmer's martyrdom on March 21 is similar:

The lamentable case and sight of that man gave a sorrowful spectacle to all christian eyes that beheld him. He that late was archbishop, metropolitan, and primate of England, and the king's privy councillor, being now in a bare and ragged gown, and ill favouredly clothed, with an old square cap, exposed to the contempt of all men, did admonish men not only of his own calamity, but also of their state and fortune. For who would not pity his case, and bewail his fortune, and might not fear his own chance, to see such a prelate, so grave a councillor, and of so long continued honour, after so many dignities, in his old years to be deprived of his estate, adjudged to die, and in so painful a death to end his life, and now presently from such fresh ornaments, to descend to such vile and ragged apparel? (8:84)

Indeed, the "how the mighty have fallen" theme—clearly the cultural property of both Catholics and Protestants—was a motif of the sermon preached by the Catholic Dr. Cole at the burning, as well as by

Cranmer himself, who made himself his own text. Cole spoke of how "a man of so high degree, . . . the second person in the realm of long time, a man thought in greatest assurance, having a king on his side; notwithstanding all his authority and defence" has been "debased from high estate to a low degree, of a councillor to become a caitiff" (8:86). And Cranmer exhorted the people to contempt of the world, particularly of riches, and to brotherly love:

The third [exhortation] is of St. James, who speaketh to the covetous rich man after this manner: 'Weep you and howl for the misery that shall come upon you: your riches do rot, your clothes be moth-eaten, your gold and silver doth canker and rust; and their rust shall bear witness against you, and consume you like fire. You gather a hoard or treasure of God's indignation against the last day.' Let them that be rich, ponder well these . . . sentences; for if they ever had occasion to show their charity, they have it now at this present, the poor people being so many, and victuals so dear. (8:88)

The pity and humiliation of a fall from high to low estate, from reverence and dignity to scorn and misery, from gorgeous or fresh to vile and ragged apparel sounds strongly in these descriptions, even if, at the same time, one recognizes the martyr's implicit glory in his service to God, and in his emblematizing the truth about the frailty of worldly pomp.

There are more overt hints of that glorious heroism as well. Such Protestant martyrs as Cranmer almost mock the mockeries put on them, degrade their own degradations. When Nicholas Ridley was degraded in 1555, as Foxe reports, "they put upon the said Dr. Ridley a surplice, with all the trinkets appertaining to the mass. And as they were putting on the same, Dr. Ridley did vehemently inveigh against the Romish bishop, and all that foolish apparel, calling him Antichrist, and the apparel foolish and abominable, yea too fond for a Vice in a play" (7:544). Since Ridley, like many others, rejected the wearing of the surplice, he can mock those who would take it away: "Lord God, what power be you of, that you can take from a man that which he never had!" (ibid.). Similarly, Archbishop Cranmer could mock his degraders while they were taking off what Protestants made fun of as "glittering gear" and the like: "All this," quoth the archbishop, "needed not; I had myself done with this gear long ago" (Foxe, 8:79).[58] Foxe certainly does lament the poor clothes in which the martyrs come to the stake; Latimer wore "a poor Bristol frieze frock all worn, with his buttoned cap, and a kerchief on his head, all ready to the fire, a new long shroud hanging over his hose, down to the feet, which at the first sight stirred men's hearts to rue upon them, beholding on the one side, the honour they sometime had, and on the other, the calamity whereunto they were fallen" (7:547-48). But there also creeps in a note celebrating the dignity of that martyr reduced to his bare shirt, without any accoutrements at all. "Whereas in his clothes [Latimer] appeared a withered and crooked silly old man, he now stood bolt upright, as comely a father as one might lightly behold" (7:549).

The movement out into the green world, shepherd's world, pastoral oasis, or wilderness (even threatening wilderness) without one's normal accoutrements of rank or status, in formally comic narrative structures like that of pastoral romance—even if a forced movement, and even if in lowly disguise necessitated by external threat—taps into these positive Christian meanings of divestment of "worldly" externals, resonates with a little of the Christian penitent's move into the wilderness, and his subsequent trial of soul. In such narratives, when the garments of worldly position or wealth are stripped off, important truths are revealed. Pastoral romance—which lies behind *Lear* in an inverse way—tests its heroes who turn shepherd or foresters with a courtesy book test of true nobility.[59] "So that if we will effectually comprehend the true essence of man, and with a right eye consider his qualities, he should cast off all his hability, deprive himself of honour, forsake the goods of fortune, lay aside his costly apparel, and so we ought to behold naked, not his body, but his mind."[60] Yet the value of such figurative "nakedness" is very conditional. Such "naked truth" is, after all, only a temporary extremity in these narratives which end with the restitution of true—and always noble, or at least gentlemanly—status; the truths nakedness reveals are actually those which legitimate that status. Whatever form the test of the hero takes, his proven virtue reaffirms his entitlement to noble rank and its insignia and accoutrements—which thus become true outward symbols of an inner essence. Under such circumstances, where good princes are involved, it turns out that their "gold mean[s] . . . outstanding wisdom," "the sparkle of [their] gems . . . extraordinary virtue as different as possible from the common run," their "warm rich purple . . . the essence of love for the state"—as Erasmus has it—whereas, as he goes on to say, "if you strip [bad princes] of their royal ornaments and inherited goods, and reduce them to themselves alone, you will find nothing except . . . a creature steeped in perjury, sacrilege, perfidy, and every other kind of crime." [61] Thus such pastoral romance reaffirms the idea that the existing social order has its rationale in nature itself, not mere convention. An intrinsically temporary nakedness revealing qualities of mind is followed by a reinvestement that assures the reader that these noble or royal ornaments are no mere gaudy shells, no equivalent of the "gorgeous apparel" of the "vile person . . . represent[ing] a king or a prince in a play" (to use once again Ridley's words, examined in chapter 2), but an external sign of an internal worthiness. However, in *Lear*, of course—which has been called "pastoral tragedy" [62]—the wilderness is not ultimately restorative, and the suffering mind cracks.

Whether "nakedness" is seen positively, or negatively (as appears to be more often the case, on balance), an awareness of the paradoxical malleability of such categories as "naked" and "clothed," "plain" and "elaborate," was built into the culture. The unreliability of these features as signals is a virtual commonplace, within and outside of the sphere of religious controversy. Lawrence Humfrey comments that "even in base apparel, the mind may be no less haughty, than in gorgeous." [63] John Woolton writes: "Under a frieze coat oftentimes there lurketh a purple mind: and again, under purple and silk, an humble and gentle nature." [64] Similarly, for Hooker: "[A] foul scar may be covered with a fair cloth, and as proud as Lucifer may be in outward appearance lowly." [65] Perhaps such comments as these were ranged against a Puritan pride in lowliness. Yet even radical religious controversialists could comment on the ways in which plainness could be used as a mask; the separatist Henry Barrow, speaking with biblical precedent, recognizes both possibilities: "As for their apparel, it is either too nice and curious, or else too affected and framed as the rough garment to deceive." [66]

Most of the critics of *King Lear*, then, read that text's dichotomies largely in accordance with what appears to be our own cultural dichotomy between the falsely artful and the nakedly true (and the reasons why that dichotomy is salient for us may have something to do with the historical ascendancy of Protestantism in part, as well as with our living in a post-Romantic age). As such, these critics may downplay Lear's serious concern with affronts to the deference and dignity marked by such symbols as retinues and "gorgeous" apparel (2.4.268), his need for "ceremonious affection" (1.4.59), his need to "reason not the need" for the "superfluous" too strictly (2.4.264–65). [67] They may fail to notice that Edgar who goes naked as Poor Tom, or speaks like a peasant, can also appear "fair and warlike" (5.3.143) in full military regalia, to defend his right and contest his brother Edmund's in the eloquent language of formal challenge (5.3.126–42). They may also fail to notice that the plain-spoken Cordelia is described by the Gentleman who attends on her in the most courtly and elegant language:

> You have seen
> Sunshine and rain at once; her smiles and tears
> Were like, a better way; those happy smilets
> That play'd on her ripe lip seem'd not to know
> What guests were in her eyes: which parted thence,
> As pearls from diamonds dropp'd.[68]
> (4.3.17–22)

Here again, the point may be that the subject in question is as "naked" and as "clothed" as he or she ought to be, and that the culture values both "nakedness" and "proper clothing." Attempts to identify religious and political positions exclusively with one or the other may well be ill advised. When looking for the locus of values of a play by Shakespeare—a writer so long and reasonably credited with dealing with "mighty opposites," or "contrarieties," or "both sides of the question" [69]—we should not deny him an awareness of the paradoxical malleability of such categories as "naked" and "clothed," "plain" and "elaborate" so clearly available in his culture. As we shall see more fully in the second part of this book, the "values" of *Lear* do not inhere in a simple series of contrasted attributes (plainness, silence, the heart, what we feel, nakedness; ceremony, speech, the tongue, what we ought to say, gorgeous array) rigidly embodied in its characters and easily analogous to religious and political positions in Shakespeare's world. Pervasive evidence shows that the very hallmarks claimed for one or the other side—the establishment or the subversives, the orthodox or the nonconformists—belong exclusively to neither. Thus, the idea of a seriously polarized early seventeenth century society is put in doubt, and the need to consider more fully the common Christian culture of the time forcefully reemerges.

Part II

Cultural Thematics

꩜ 5

The Plain Heart according to Her Bond: Sociopolitical

Readings and Family Relationships

The first scene of *Lear* has elicited sometimes contradictory sociopoliti-cal readings. These characterize Cordelia and her "bond" in terms of large-scale changes in society and social organization—for example, the change from "feudalism" to "capitalism"—or, in terms of large-scale changes in political or social ideals—for example, the change from hierarchical, "patriarchal" to more egalitarian "contractual" mod-els. Cordelia may be identified with the old system or the new. Some critics link her with hierarchical feudal duties and rights, on the basis of her "care and duty" (1.1.102), the obligations of her "bond." Other critics link her with the radical Protestant (i.e., more "contractual") side of a presumably splitting society—on the basis of the "plainness" (129), or "heart" (92), and the promise to act (rather than merely speak with "oily art" [224]) with which she proclaims her daughterly bond, or on the basis of the supposed legalism of her words ("according to my bond, no more nor less" [93]).[1] Should we read Cordelia's assertion of fidelity to her "bond" in 1.1 as evidence of the politics of the scene or of the play?

According to My Bond

The nature of the "bond" itself and Cordelia's attitude toward it are often read in terms of the transition, in England, from traditional to modern, feudal to capitalistic, kinship-based to individualistic society. The Althusserian-Marxist reading given by James H. Kavanagh, in his essay "Shakespeare in Ideology," the neo-Marxist reading of Walter Cohen in *Drama of a Nation*, the new historicist reading given by Franco Moretti, in " 'A Huge Eclipse': Tragic Form and the Deconsecration of Sovereignty," and the more traditional historicist reading given by Jonas A. Barish and Marshall Waingrow in their much older essay,

" 'Service' in *King Lear*," all identify Cordelia's "bond" as more feudal than individualist, and value it as such. For Kavanagh, "In the face of Lear's confusion of self-aggrandizement with respect for natural/social Order, Cordelia quietly asserts her love." In the play as a whole, a "hierarchical ideology of fealty, faith and restraint, which lives the world as a field of reciprocal obligation" is juxtaposed to an "individualist ideology that lives the world as a field of calculation, self-gratification and perverse desire." [2] For Cohen, "Cordelia's evocation of her 'bond' and her 'duty' draw on the contractual heritage of feudalism" (*Drama of a Nation*, 329).[3] For Moretti, "Cordelia still inhabits a world of reciprocal obligation, of feudal rights and duties, whereas Lear aspires to absolute omnipotence." [4] For Barish and Waingrow, also, Cordelia's bond is "feudal," involving "rights as well as duties, on each side," "privileges . . . granted" and "duties . . . imposed"; it is "expressive of mutual love and responsibility." As such, it contrasts with a colder "legal transaction, a *quid pro quo*," a "document negotiable by a bond salesman," in which the "reciprocity" becomes "contingent." An example of this legalistic bond is provided when Lear takes Kent into his service (after Kent trips Oswald): "I thank thee, fellow. Thou serv'st me, and I'll love thee" (1.4.87–88).[5]

For Kathleen McLuskie, in contrast, it is Cordelia's language that is legalistic and delimiting: "Her legal language suggests a preference for a limited, contractual relationship: 'I love your majesty / According to my bond, no more nor less.'" And the personal and the political are related: "The conflict between the contractual model and the patriarchal model of subjects' obligations to their king was at issue in contemporary political theory and Cordelia's words here introduce a similar conflict into the question of obligations within the family."[6] McLuskie is thinking in terms of the abandonment of the "ideal of 'fidelity' for that of 'interest'" and the transformation "of the social bond from a feudal 'oath' to the 'contract' of natural right philosophy," to use the words of Moretti.[7] Our sense that Puritanism had a significant role to play in such shifts has been fostered by work on Puritan covenantal or contractual thinking: "Through the covenant men became the 'bondsmen' of God—not the children—and the image implied the voluntary recognition of an existing debt, a legal or commercial obligation." Furthermore, "a contract, for the first time, was clearly seen as an agreement between equals, unmarked by deference or humility on either side, fully voluntary and unforced on both sides and a matter not of personal loyalty or fear, but of conscience. . . . Even the covenant between God and fallen men, thought John Preston, 'implies a kind of equality between us.' "[8]

The old historicist critic John F. Danby seems to hear *both* a faithful feudal and a colder legal meaning of "bond" at this moment in the play. While he argues that Cordelia definitely does not mean it as such, "for . . . the sixteenth century," he says, "a 'bond' is a potentially frigid thing," and not something "holy" or "binding." "For Lear . . . as for the critics after Johnson, 'bond' rings with a dead note. . . . [Shakespeare] made Shylock a stickler for his 'bond.' "[9] Indeed, some commentators hear Cordelia's words as evidence of her being proud in a rather stiff-necked Puritan way. The historian Conrad Russell comments, for example, that Cordelia is "perhaps the most sympathetic stage portrait of a Puritan, . . . but . . . less sympathetically portrayed than modern audiences sometimes suppose: after all, her obstinately literal-minded rejection of a harmless ceremony did lead to a great deal of unhappiness."[10] Finally, in his essay, "The Cultivation of Anxiety: King Lear and His Heirs," Stephen Greenblatt poses an "older contractual bond between parents and children" against Lear's "demand for unbounded love," but *also* links that "reciprocal and limited" bond with legal contracts, in a positive way; he gives a richer and more convincing historical description of Cordelia's "ethos" than most of the critics we have surveyed, but, nevertheless, one that only partially overlaps with my own—as will shortly be seen.

A contract in English law implied bargain consideration, that is, the reciprocity inherent in a set of shared obligations and limits, and this understanding that a gift could be only be given with the expectation of receiving something in return is incompatible with Lear's sense of his royal prerogative, just as it is incompatible with the period's absolutist conception of paternal power and divine power.[11]

When we dichotomize hierarchical/feudal versus individualist, are our categories consistent with the announced or implicit perceptions and feelings of Jacobeans, as far as we can ascertain those? If Jacobean society *is* beginning to polarize, and along these particular lines, would Cordelia have been an emblem of resistance to "patriarchal kingship" and desire for a more contractual relationship between king and subject, or an emblem of the patriarchal and feudal relationships threatened from within by the king's own behavior? Or not necessarily either? Might it be that opposed or purportedly opposed "sides" could find their values emblematized in the same figures? It is this aspect of "common Christian culture"—the existence of which is perhaps more tenable before the Laudian era—that I wish to address in connection with Cordelia and her "bond."

Shakespeare's characters and their conflicts often do seem to be made from the same cultural materials as those used by moralists and biblical exegetes. Even if we have rightly abandoned a view of such work as "sources," we nevertheless need to consider its full range in order to address the issue of how Shakespeare's plays might have struck his audience or audiences. The range is important because it is so easy to take a single example and use it to illustrate whatever point of view one might hold. Thus, John F. Danby quotes Thomas Becon's *Catechism*, with its "strong Protestant" view that superiors are " 'not to be obeyed' " " 'if they command anything contrary to the word of God,' " as evidence that "in effect . . . parents must first be sensible before filial obedience can be expected at all" (*Shakespeare's Doctrine of Nature*, 116). Becon is offered as support for the justness of Cordelia's self-assertion against her father's demands for public flattery. Nevertheless, Danby is picking and choosing what suits his purpose: preventing us from accusing Cordelia of an inappropriate rebelliousness, while at the same time linking her with "strong Protestant" restiveness. He is perhaps too readily confounding the serious matter of parental violation of God's will with the lesser matter—implied by his word "sensible"—of parental foolish behavior. One should not conclude too quickly that "strong Protestantism" permits children to judge their parents, and to withold obedience if they are found wanting.

In fact, many "strong" Protestants may easily be found who assert that even parents who are not sensible must be reverenced. Robert Cleaver's book on household government, for example, speaks of "what ingratitude" it is "not to love those of whom, next after God, [children] have their life and being"; the "love that parents do bear to their children, besides so many their labors, sorrows, troubles, and vexations," is what "should *bind* [children] reciprocally to love them." Moreover, he emphasizes "this *band* of the love of children towards their parents, should take such place, not only toward such parents as are loving and gentle, but also . . . even toward such as be rigorous." [12] Another writer on the subject asserts that even "simple . . . crabbed and very wayward" parents, even "decrepit and doting parents are . . . to be

honored and reverenced." This writer urges: "[W]here the father commandeth that which is not against God, he is to be obeyed even as God,
because he [i.e., God] hath commanded thee to obey thy parents." [13]
Just what is it that children owe parents is conveyed in this literature in
words and images shared with *Lear*. For Matthew Griffith, when a child
sees his parents' "infirmities," he must "go backward (with Noah's two
sons) and cover their nakedness before men." [14] For Dod and Cleaver,
expounding the fifth commandment,

If the parent be blind, the child must be an eye unto him; If he be lame,
he must be a staff to uphold him. . . . And this duty, indeed, the very law
of nature doth require. For, the father hath paid for it before hand, and it
is but due debt. For, when the child was born naked into the world, and
could not help himself, and was without all friends, and could not so much
as put one morsel of meat into his own mouth, nor hang one rag upon his
back, to keep him warm, who pitied him? who relieved him? [15]

Thus, at the moment when Lear violently exclaims, disowning Cordelia, that "the barbarous Scythian / . . . shall to my bosom / Be as
well neighbor'd, pitied, and reliev'd, / As thou my sometime daughter"
(1.1.116–20), he is invoking that very parent-child "bond"—brazenly
violated, to his mind, by Cordelia's behavior. Perhaps the Scythians
are in his thoughts for the very reason they are mentioned by another
moralist, Peter Barker: "The Scytes a barbarous people, yet held the
very sepulchres of their fathers in great reverence." [16]

Even the well-attested Protestant point that children must leave
father and mother and cleave to their spouses, a point which might be
offered as further evidence of the unreasonableness of Lear's demand
for total love, is countered by Geffray Fenton's *A Forme of Christian Pollicie*:

It is a question of many, whether a man is more *bound* to nourish and
succour his father and mother, or his proper wife: whereunto may be an-
swered, that in the case of obedience and subvention, there is more *bound*
of duty to parents, but not touching cohabitation. And to prove the *bond*
of duty to parents, it is certain by treble right, natural, divine, and human,
which including an immutable and inviolable *bond*, can not be weakened
or abolished by marriage, as well for that it is the first, most authentic, and
hath a treble *bond*, . . . as also for that it *binds* marriage with a new subjection, that the wife with her husband, ought to strain all their power and
means to relieve such as by marriage are made their father and mother. [17]

Indeed, Cordelia's implicit promise to reserve "half [her] love," "half [her] care and duty" (102) for her father is notably generous, befitting the most idealized familial morality—although of course in the immediate dramatic context her emphasis is on the "half" due her plighted lord, as well as on the hypocrisy of her sisters who "say / they love [their father] all" (99–100).

Even if Puritan covenantal thinking *had* begun to refigure the relationship of men to God as a "bond" in a more contractual sense, the relationship between children and parents hardly is an agreement "between equals, unmarked by deference and humility." [18] The relationship remains asymmetrical. In Renaissance moral commentary, the proper behavior of parents to children gets less attention than that of children to parents; proper parenting mainly means rearing children so that they are duly deferent, and the parent may avoid the self-recrimination that comes too late—like Lear's: "Judicious punishment! 'twas this flesh begot / Those pelican daughters" (3.4.74–75). "That ill sap that doth appear in the bud, came first from the root," as Dod and Cleaver assure us (*Ten Commaundements*, 196). Parental negligence or parental bad example produces the wayward child. [19]

Thus "bond" is a positive term used in this "strong" Protestant literature, which stresses the "due debt" a child owes his parent. This debt seems to be a binding obligation under all circumstances; it is certainly not a matter of a freely chosen contractual relation, legalistic or not. The division between feudal and bourgeois bonds—whether seen as a division between the old-fashioned authoritarian and the new individualist, or as a division between the charitable and the calculating—does not necessarily map onto late Renaissance uses of the term. Cordelia, in scanting the "ceremonious affection" Lear desires (1.4.59) may fall slightly short (Lear later calls her fault "most small" [1.4.266]) of that complete fidelity to the child's bond required even when the parent is "wayward." However, hers is not a fault for one "side" of a polarized culture, and a virtue for the other, but a fault—however mitigated by the circumstances—recognizable by the culture as a whole.

To Plainness Honor's Bound

Lear's accusation, "Let pride, which she calls plainness, marry her" (129) associates Cordelia with plainness, as does Kent's description of his own — and, implicitly, Cordelia's — manner of speech: "To plainness honor's bound / When majesty falls to folly" (148-49).[20] Deeds are opposed to words when Kent turns to Regan and Goneril with "And your large speeches may your deeds approve / That good effects may spring from words of love" (184-85), as well as when Cordelia says "[S]ince what I [well] intend / I'll do't before I speak" (225-26).[21] The deep heart is opposed to the glib tongue when Cordelia speaks aside, "I am sure my love's / More ponderous than my tongue" (77-78),[22] and when she addresses Lear soon after with "I cannot heave / My heart into my mouth" (91-92), as well as when she speaks of wanting "that glib and oily art / To speak and purpose not" (224-25). We have seen that Cordelia's assertion of fidelity to her "bond" per se is very slim evidence for determining the sociopolitical resonances of the scene. But does her "plainness" more definitively link her with a particular religious position that would help us read the politics of the scene as a whole? Cohen, for example, suggests that Cordelia's " 'plainness,' a commitment not to a verbal style but to the language of truth," belongs to "the same norm" as Edgar's closing words ("Speak what we feel, not what we ought to say") which he later characterizes as a "preference for feeling over platitude [that] surely belongs to the radical Protestant tradition" (*Drama of a Nation,* 337, 355).

Certainly Puritan writers describe themselves as "plain" and certainly critics have plausibly identified Puritanism and radical Protestantism generally with plainness of many kinds, including material plainness. And yet, such assertions as Cohen's are based on palpably partial evidence. *The Office of Christian Parents,* an anonymous guide to household and family management (a genre particularly favored by Puritans), printed in 1616 by a Cambridge printer associated with Puritan writings, certainly valorizes the plain truth as opposed to oily deceit; the subject is proper companions:

And lastly, their manner is to utter truth without counterfeiting, and therefore they are described, *to have . . . a pure heart, . . .* that is, their deeds, words, and heart going alway together, they never deceive any person whatsoever. Therefore it is said of them, *The lips of truth shall be stable,* meaning thereby, that an honest man will be found by experience, to speak the truth simply without all dissimulation. If then you find the manner of a Christian's behaviour to be thus plain, open, and true, you may boldly associate your selves unto him. . . . But wicked men will use smooth words to please, and as the Psalmist saith, *Softer than butter, and more gentle than oil:* but it is to deceive.[23]

However, the high church Lancelot Andrewes also disclaims against "they that speak fair and mean mischievously; all false brethren, that have their lips swim with butter and oil, and in their hearts carry a sword to stab a man."[24]

Puritans evidently favored plain speech over elaboration; the "Second Admonition to Parliament" casts aspersions on "profane and heathenish orators, that think all the grace of preaching lieth in affected eloquence, in fond fables to make their hearers laugh, or in ostentation of learning."[25] But King James—no lover of Puritans—also extols plainness, and indeed a tongue united to the heart:

It becometh a king, in my opinion, to use no other eloquence than plainness and sincerity. By plainness I mean, that his speeches should be so clear and void of all ambiguity, that they may not be thrown, nor rent asunder in contrary senses like the old oracles of the pagan gods. And by sincerity, I understand that uprightness and honesty which ought to be in a king's whole speeches and actions: That as far as a king is in honour erected above any of his subjects, so far should he strive in sincerity to be above them all, and that his tongue should be ever the true messenger of his heart.[26]

Similarly, in a later speech to Parliament, King James asserts he is "only to deliver now unto you matter without curious form, substance without ceremony, truth in all sincerity," it being "better to utter matter, rather than words." Here, furthermore, he makes his own use of the figure of the simply clothed chaste woman, beautiful by virtue of her own natural ornaments as compared to the bedecked harlot—an ancient Christian contrast we have already observed used in the Elizabethan *Homilies* to exemplify the true, Anglican Church as opposed to the false, Catholic one:

Studied orations and much eloquence upon little matter is fit for the universities, where not the subject which is spoken of, but the trial of his wit that speaketh, is most commendable: but . . . in all great counsels of parliaments, fewest words with most matter doth become best, where the dispatch of the great errands in hand, and not the praise of the person is most to be looked unto: like the garment of a chaste woman, who is only set forth by her natural beauty, which is properly her own; other deckings are but ensigns of an harlot that flies with borrowed feathers.[27]

We must take care not to become victims of our own dichotomies; plainness of heart or speech, preference for actual deeds over mere words are clearly values with a broad Christian—and human—base; and *of course* not even the greatest celebrator of eloquence would claim the virtues of oil and butter used simply to deceive, in short, of "a glib and oily art."

Perhaps even more than they are connected with plainness, Puritans or strong Protestants are connected by modern critics with the "inward" reverence of the mind and the true feelings of the heart as opposed to "outward shows," or "platitudes." This "inner-outer" distinction, often applied to church ceremony in Reformation controversy, is also applied by strong Protestants themselves to the behavior of children toward their parents. In *The Christian Man's Closet: Wherein Is Conteined a Large Discourse of the Godly Training Up of Children,* an English translation of *De Oeconomia Christiana* (Antwerp, 1558) written by Bartholomaeus Battus, a Flemish Protestant persecuted by the Inquisition,[28] the speakers inform us:

Theodidactus.
This word *honour,* doth signify a true reverence and lowliness of heart, for this outward show in vailing of the bonnet, and bowing of the knee or body, is nothing worth, except there be joined therewithal the inward reverence of the mind, wherein godly children do testify, that they esteem nothing more precious and dear unto them than the love and honour of their parents.

Theophilus.
Our unlearned youth have always supposed and thought, that true honour hath consisted in the putting off their cap, and making of curtsey, and there is none other thing due unto parents: Wherefore we would be right glad to hear further of you, what it is to honour parents. (63r)

Yet even this very strong Protestant tract recognizes the need for *both* inward honor and outward ceremony—ceremony clearly not regarded pejoratively—at least in the matter of children's behavior toward parents. "Ceremony," even if theologically inadmissable in the church to some Protestants, is not automatically seen as analogously so in the home. If our dichotomies are risky, the analogies easily built on them are even more so.

Theodidactus.

. . . Therefore to honour parents is not only to salute them humbly, to speak to them lovingly, and to use them courteously, to put off the cap before them, to give them the way and upper hand in every place: But also the holy Scriptures do teach children to obey their parents, to serve them, to fear, love, honour, and reverence them, not only in words and outward show, but in their hearts and minds also. . . . Nay rather there is double honour due to our parents and elders, that is to say, both an outward and inward honour: the outward which consisteth in ceremonies, and outward behaviour, which we attribute unto them, with our loving words, gentleness, and servicableness: [and] the inward honour, whereby we love and embrace them with all our hearts and minds, and the law of God doth require both these of children. (63v–62r)[29]

Protestants do differ on the nature of the ceremonies appropriate in the church; they differ, as well, on the relationship of "ceremonies" to "inward honour." Yet there seem also to be broadly shared values of sincerity and integrity within Christian culture as a whole, even shared values about decorous or comely outward behavior, which, for no one, *of course,* is a matter of mere externals. Everyone is likely to have agreed that both some form of "outward behaviour," or "ceremonies," and of "inward honour" were requisite—perhaps especially in some areas of life, such as the household or family; certainly the division of the honor due parents (and superiors generally) into "inward" and "outward" is a conventional one used by the high church Lancelot Andrewes in his *Catechistical Doctrine* as well as by Puritans.[30]

Moreover, everyone acknowledged that the internal, the heart, is ultimately more important than externals; when the question is of mere outward shows (and "externals" easily become mere), everyone derogates them in favor of inner truth. Thus, Cordelia might have been scripted, so to speak, by someone like the Puritan nonconformist Samuel Clarke, writing of "The Life and Death of Mrs. Jane Ratcliffe":

She *loved not in word, or in tongue only, but in deed, and in truth,* 1 Joh.3.18. and this appeared in that she made her deeds of charity and good will always better than her words, whereof she was so chary, that some blamed her for want of affability, which being objected to her, she said, *I like not the lavish language of some, who have their mouths full of complemental courtesy to every one, though their hearts be shut and contracted.*[31]

Or, Cordelia might have been scripted by someone like William Gouge —a moderate Puritan (but on the royalist side during the Civil War) who similarly describes the duties of children to parents in his important manual *Of Domesticall Duties*: "Actions are better signs of the disposition of the heart than words. . . . Fair words joined with contrary deeds, cannot but be accounted merely complemental and hypocritical. Where there is a contrariety betwixt words and deeds, the one will be a witness against the other, and that man's condemnation the greater."[32] However, not only Puritans, but conformists as well, disdain mere outward shows, civil or religious; the Anglican defense of "visible solemnity" in "public actions . . . of weight, whether they be civil and temporal or else spiritual and sacred" (Hooker, *LEP*, 4.1.3, in *Works*, 1:418–19), of course does not apply to hypocritical or inappropriate shows. Cordelia also might have been scripted by someone like Francis Bunny, a conforming Calvinist. In *A Guide unto Godlinesse; or, A Plaine and Familiar Explanation of the Ten Commandements* (1617), he argues: "For honour is a reverent affection imprinted in our hearts toward others, without forcing or constraint; without which affection of the mind, the outward show is scarce a shadow of honour, and is many times done by cap and courtesy, or such outward reverence, to them who are contemned and scorned of them that do it."[33] Finally, we may turn to the high church Andrewes, who does not fail to make his own assertions that God "must have not only the outward but the inward man, the heart" (*Catechistical Doctrine*, 120). "Inward charity is of greater esteem than outward, because it cureth the more principal part of man," he affirms, quoting Augustine (ibid., 164). Rituals alone will not do: "Neither will outward abstinence serve the turn, without inward sorrow" (167).

In fact, Christian commentators of all persuasions writing on the fifth commandment—which they all treat as about obedience to superiors—make a distinction between mere external "eye service" serving men and true internal "heart service" serving God. Children and servants may curry favor with parents and masters by their observable actions, but inner loyalty is what really counts. The Puritan *Christian Man's Closet* speaks of obedience "in the simpleness of your hearts, as to Christ himself, not with the eye service as pleasing men" (65v). Lancelot Andrewes speaks of "eye service, deceitful diligence, only at their own pleasure, and before their master's face . . . whereas they should do it with singleness of heart, lest the chief master be displeased" (*Catechistical Doctrine*, 189).

When the choice is between "ponderous" (1.1.78) shows that "purpose not" (225) and the inner truth of the heart—and this is certainly the way Cordelia sees her own choice in 1.1—everyone agrees that the heart takes precedence. "Fair words joined with contrary deeds cannot but be . . . hypocritical," as Gouge says, and Cordelia shares Kent's suspicion that the "large speeches" or "words of love" of her sisters will not be validated by "deeds" and "good effects" (184–85). Her love almost forces her into silence ("What shall Cordelia speak? Love, and be silent" [62]); in this context, her defense of that silence ("I cannot heave / My heart into my mouth" [91–92]) taps into shared values that elevate heart over tongue, heart service over eye service. Indeed, Cordelia says she lacks "a still-soliciting eye" (231), that is, it is not in her nature to continually solicit her father before his face with mere outward shows; true as opposed to "professed bosoms" (272) require no "glib and oily" (224) speeches.

Insofar as Cordelia comes across particularly as a daughter who would give heartfelt love and obedience as opposed to a mere ceremony of love and obedience, perhaps *some* Puritans in Shakespeare's time could have seen her as a positive exemplar of their own emphasis on the inner truth. Alternatively, insofar as such insistence on the superiority of inner to outer, deed to word, plainness to eloquence is heard as "pride, which she calls plainness" (129)—that is, as a form of that hypocritical pride or "singularity" often associated with Puritans by their enemies—perhaps *some* anti-Puritans could have seen Cordelia, at least momentarily, as a negative exemplar of that group.

While these are possibilities, it seems to me much more likely that, in 1.1, everyone would recognize his or her own value of true "inward" feeling (stressing the avoidance of "glib and oily" flattery) *as well as* his or her own value of "outward" "ceremonious affection" (stressing deferent obedience even to the somewhat unreasonable parent). These values *are* in tension; tragedy is not set in motion by easily avoidable mistakes. These opposed values, however, should not be linked with Puritan or Anglican, potential Roundhead or potential Cavalier, because it is clear that both values or "sides" are present in the common Christian culture as a whole. Everyone agrees that parents require respect and obedience; everyone agrees that heart service is better than lip service. Thus everyone can see that Cordelia slightly scants the outward honor due parents, and everyone can also see that her heart leans in the right direction.

Described by Lear as a "little seeming substance" (198), and by France as someone "dismantle[d]" of "so many folds of favor" (217–18), the disowned Cordelia exits with "Time shall unfold what plighted cunning hides" (280).[34] France's description of her emphasizes her unprotected nakedness in contrast to the grace of parental favor she formerly enjoyed—in accordance with the biblical use of clothing and nakedness to figure protective love and destitution, respectively. However, by using the words she uses as she exits, Cordelia obliquely and more positively associates herself with the naked truth that is the daughter of time, and associates her sisters with the corruption and menace hidden behind voluminous or many-folded garments such as are worn by the Whore of Babylon, or the bedecked harlot exemplifying the false church.[35] As suggested in previous chapters, the idea of the "naked truth" is not the exclusive property of Protestant or Catholic, Puritan or Anglican. Both Mary Tudor and Elizabeth thus use the motto "Veritas filia Temporis," Truth the daughter of Time, a motto—connected with the naked truth—that contributes to the resonance of Cordelia's exit line.

When Cardinal Pole returned from exile he greeted his queen, Mary: "'Numbers conspired against her, and policies were devised to disherit her, and armed power prepared to destroy her, yet *she being a virgin, helpless, naked, and unarmed,* prevailed.'"[36] In greeting Mary this way, the cardinal alluded to the same Latin motto, "Veritas filia Temporis," that she in fact chose for "her personal device . . . the legend on her crest . . . the State seal of her reign, [and] her coins."[37] But such symbolism could be appropriated by either side. On the day before her coronation in 1558, Elizabeth's procession passed by an "allegorical sideshow of Time and Truth" in which Time led forth "'a personage . . . all clad in white silk, and directly over her head was set her name and title . . . *"Temporis filia,* The daughter of Time.". . . And on her breast was written her proper name, which was "Veritas", Truth, who held a book in her hand, upon the which was written *Verbum Veritatis,* the Word of Truth.'"[38] Once again, Truth held a book, the *Verbum Dei*—as she did at an allegorical performance at Mary's wedding—but the book Truth presented to the queen this time was the Bible in English—the very book Mary had banned.[39]

One should not, then, equate Cordelia's "plainness" and "truth" with antiauthoritarianism of a singularly "Puritan" sort. While these terms have the potential to become politically charged in specific contexts, they also participate in broadly shared frameworks that permit non-partisan readings, or at least not overtly ideological ones. Up to a point, such shared frameworks would permit both sides of a diverging audience to find their "own" values within a literary work.[40]

Raiment, Bed, and Food

The very distinction between a feudal past seen as ideal and charitable, and a bourgeois present seen as cold and calculating in its "quid pro quo" arithmetic—a distinction found in both old historicist and neo-Marxist criticism—may be a somewhat inappropriate or overdrawn one for our period; political readings of the play based on such assumptions may have serious weaknesses—whichever "side" Cordelia is connected with. Social history and the contemporaneous biblical commentary and guides to household management we have been concerned with—in which, as we shall see, an idealized social morality seems to coexist with a realistic sense of the quid pro quo nature of human relationships—suggest that such sharply drawn lines need rethinking.[41]

Even if kings were not supposed to abdicate, the ordinary parent's exchange of "premortem" inheritance for "raiment, bed, and food" (1.4.156) is a common European pattern,[42] and one for which there is much English evidence, particularly in the late Middle Ages.[43] What is particularly interesting is that these contractual arrangements were set forth in detail, that this was indeed a form of "bargaining . . . for sustenance in old age," specifically for "food and drink," "clothing," and "a cottage or at least a room in which to spend the rest of their days." [44] The quid pro quo aspect of the arrangements sounds in a passage from Robert Mannyng of Brunne's *Handlyng Synne* (about 1303) about a man who gave his son

> alle hys land and hous,
> And al hys catel in toune and felde,
> Þat he shulde kepe hym wel yn hys elde.[45]

And the sense that the parent truly moved into a new category once he had taken this step is chillingly clear in the example of one Anseline in 1227, who

agreed to give his daughter to Hugh, with half of his land. Furthermore the father-in-law and the married couple were to live together in one house. . . . First, the arrangements to be made were agreed upon between the father and his prospective son-in-law. . . . A marriage bargain was made. . . . Second . . . there was a ceremony. Anseline went out of the house, handed over to the married couple the door by the hasp, and then begged lodging out of charity. The ceremony must have been meant to symbolize that Anseline gave the couple the house and that he was to be no more than their lodger.[46]

Although Peter Laslett's work has demonstrated "the overwhelming preponderance of nuclear family households in England since at least the later sixteenth century,"[47] other historians provide evidence for the presence of "the old folks at home," and their "being provided with bed, board, and access to the fire." Margaret Spufford has found such examples in "Staffordshire and Warwickshire in the fifteenth century . . . and in Cambridgeshire wills of the sixteenth century." Spufford suggests that the status of such old folks at home underwent a fundamental change once they had given up their property. "In seventeenth-century Cambridgeshire, once a man retired and had given up all his land, he was a sojourner, although he might live in the house that had once been his own. There he had, by right, no abiding place."[48] It is in fact just these sorts of contractual maintenance agreements that Greenblatt links with Cordelia's "ethos" ("Cultivation of Anxiety," 97); unlike the critics who link her with Puritan legalism, however, he does not regard that ethos as a newly calculating, explicitly bourgeois, or individualist one.

Thus a contract between a parent and his child providing "raiment, bed, and food" in exchange for an endowment or inheritance — if not a dominant pattern in the sixteenth and seventeenth centuries — hardly entailed Puritanism or capitalism. Even Lear's arithmetical frame of mind ("Thy fifty yet doth double five and twenty, / And thou art twice her love" [2.4.258–59]) may not mark a change from holy feudal relationships to colder bourgeois ones, but remind his audience of a long imaginable social practice. The strong sense that art, after all, does imitate life certainly strikes the reader of *Lear* who learns, for example:

The question of maintenance of the old is dealt with very specifically in Scandinavian law, which resembled that of Normandy in its emphasis on equality. . . . Equality of rights meant equality of obligations. When a man divided his property among his children, the law permitted him to make a circuit, known as *flaetfoering,* spending the number of days with each heir in exact proportion to the quantity of goods he had received.[49]

Furthermore, in the common law, partition or division of property —
as opposed to unigeniture — was the general rule for nonroyalty where
daughters were involved.[50] And it was common for landowners to settle
all or part of their inheritance on daughters in the form of dowry at the
time of their marriages.[51]

While the English moralists and biblical expositors of the sixteenth
and seventeenth century stress the ideal duties of children toward their
parents, they also exhibit a realistic sense of the actual mercenary, calculating, and cold relationships that could obtain between humans
including parent and child; the *cri de coeur* they evince about the mistreatment of parents by children suggests the idyllic picture may be
urged *because* it is so far from the truth. When threatened at retirement
with "drastic loss of their status and authority," the old might well
fear, as Greenblatt suggests, that — despite the "gerontological bias"
and "marks of deference" in their society — "age's claim to authority
was pathetically vulnerable to the ruthless ambitions of the young"
("Cultivation of Anxiety," 95, 93, 94, 93). The belief Edmund attributes
to Edgar to discredit him in his father's eyes — "sons at perfect age, and
fathers declined, the father should be as ward to the son, and the son
manage his revenue" (1.2.72–74)[52] — was a possible if rare economic arrangement. Cordell Annesley's sister Grace did try to "get her father
judged lunatic because he was senile and 'altogether unfit to govern
himself or his estate,'" and economic considerations were likely in the
case, since the father did in fact leave most of his property to Cordell.[53]

On the one hand, the ideal solicitude of child for parent, the kindest
of "kind nurser[ies]" (1.1.123), is figured in the quite frequent allusion to
the daughter who, in an extreme situation, actually nurses her parent.
"Now what so rare to be seen, as the child to give the mother suck? A
man would think that it were against nature; were it not the first law of
nature, to love our parents. And therefore none of our breasts should
want this milk of piety towards our decrepit parents" (Griffith, *Bethel*,
374–75).[54] On the other hand, there is a sense of inevitable discrepancy
between the love of parents and the love of children; the idea that "love
descends and does not ascend" is a commonplace.[55]

Love descendeth and goeth downward, it doth not ascend and go upward:
parents then love their children, but children divers times love not their
parents. . . . *Torquatus* driven out of his father's house, pined away with
sorrow: nowadays children pine that they cannot drive their parents out of
their houses.[56]

These boiling hearts not bearing just reproof, undutifully have oft, if we could remember it, repined at their authority, impatiently fretted at their due correction, . . . if we have not openly thrown out a curse, yet have our hearts included a wish. . . . We laugh to see our parents' shame, we smile at their wants, we publish their infirmities, we disdain their ignorance, we loathe their age.[57]

Some children will honour their parents (as the harlot doth her paramour) whilst they are *Nouns Substantives,* able to stand of themselves, and in the *Dative case;* but if once they decline so far as to come to the *Ablative absolute,* then these *Participles* will be governed no longer by them: their obedience is *mercenary;* and *no penny, no Pater noster.* (Griffith, *Bethel,* 272–73)

It is the nature and property of dogs not to acknowledge our parents. And if it be a dogged nature not to acknowledge them, it is much more brutish to offend them, to hurt, beat, and offer injury unto them. (Battus, *Christian Man's Closet,* 70)

No wonder certain writers, sometimes clearly Puritan, criticize primogeniture, which might give wastrels an undeserved patrimony, and insist that "those be used best which are best, and those have most goods given them, that have most grace in their hearts."[58] Indeed, *The Younger Brother His Apologie: or, A Father's Free Power Disputed, for the Disposition of His Lands* argues: Why pass on an estate to someone who "consumes the womb of his family (*viper-like*) wherein he was born," someone who "devours in some sort, them of his own *species,* society and blood"? "Some of these *furious fiends* have brought their *all-tenderhearted parents* to the greatest of all woes, *beggary in their old age.*"[59] The fairy-tale preference for the youngest and most virtuous in *King Lear* seems to echo the emphasis—often Puritan—on the right of the parent to decide on the basis of desert, to prefer the youngest child, "[F]or grace maketh the younger to be the elder, and sin maketh the elder, the younger" (Dod and Cleaver, *Ten Commaundements,* 203).

The picture Shakespeare gives of Goneril and Regan's mistreatment of Lear—even if Lear takes the steps that permit that mistreatment—is notably like that of "unnatural" children in Christian moralistic literature as a whole; both that literature and Shakespeare are probably responding to some degree to the circumstances of social life. Warnings like the Fool's ("Fathers that wear rags / Do make their children blind, / But fathers that bear bags / Shall see their children kind" [2.4.49–51])[60] are articulated numerous times; their language may remind us of Goneril and Regan's about-face from their initial oiliness and their sudden concern with overexpenditure and efficiency:

The unnatural disposition of many ungracious children [is such] that so long as the parents have any thing to give, and something may be gotten by them, all that while they will be so kind, and so loving, and there is such striving and catching, that well is he that can get the old parent to him: but when once he is drawn dry, and they have sucked all from him, then he is neglected of all, then every day is a year till he be dead; then he is a burden and a clog, then they exclaim, that he doth nothing but spend, and troubles the family. Such cruel and bitter words are heard oft-times from the mouths of wicked and unnatural children. (Dod and Cleaver, *Ten Commaundements*, 192–93)

Although, as the sixteenth- and seventeenth-century biblical expositors and moralists never tire of pointing out, honor and reverence are owed even to decripit and foolish parents, they at the same time frequently sound such notes of pragmatic wariness, suggesting little confidence in those duties being paid, suggesting, indeed, that filial love has a strong economic component. "Honor and worship toward God" may be "always too short and failing," [61] but no such infinities seem to be connected with the love of child for parent—sometimes even of parent for child. Thus, a pragmatic and psychologically down-to-earth attitude toward familial relationships is not uncommon in these works; warnings not to put one's self into one's children's hands, not to become dependent on them, occur in quite a few.[62]

But yet more foolishly and unadvisedly do they which through too much affection and love being yet alive, do yield and deliver up into the hands of their children, their goods, coin and all their inheritance, wholly persuading themselves to live more easily of the benevolence and love of their children. . . . For better it is thy children to pray and entreat thee, than that thou shouldest be fain to look into their hands. (Battus, *Christian Man's Closet*, 77–77v)

Behind these discussions then, as well as behind those contracts in which inheritance or endowment was exchanged for maintenance, is an understanding that human relationships, even within the supposedly sacred bounds of the nuclear family, do depend on a quid pro quo. That exchange may indeed be understood as at bottom, economic or mercenary. But, it may also be understood psychologically, as the return of affection or decent treatment that can be involved in any close human relations. In such terms a concerned-sounding Gervase Babington, bishop of Exeter, speculates about the underlying causes of mistreatment of parents by children: "The very unnatural and unkind dealing of parents with their children in their youth, denying them relief, and comfortable help, maketh them often (though it should not) when they have attained to any estate, to deal as undutifully with their needy parents again."[63] If one hears any legalism in

> You have begot me, bred me, lov'd me: I
> Return those duties back as are right fit,
> Obey you, love you, and most honor you
> (96–98)

one might well say it is a culturally sanctioned legalism with a broader base than that provided by law, or legal ideas of contract per se. For these are the terms—with all their quid pro quo enumeration of "due debts"—of filial duty straightforwardly described in the moral commentaries we have surveyed.

Such "legalistic" attitudes, then, are not necessarily "new" in the sixteenth and seventeenth centuries, nor, certainly, the result of a change from feudal bonds to contractual bonds. Indeed, taking as "indices of the development of capitalism: the establishment of the concept of private, fully alienable property; the widespread use of monetary values and the dominance of market forces; the wide-scale presence of wage labour," all of which "can be traced back to the thirteenth century at least," Alan Macfarlane argues "that there does not seem ever, in recorded history, to have been a sudden revolution at all in England." Macfarlane points out that children in England were "separate economic individuals" from the thirteenth century, having "protected property rights—in what they were given and in what they earned—even against their parents"; "children did not automatically invest their wealth back into a family fund from which they automatically inherited." Thus, "parents could disinherit children, while children could, in a sense, disinherit their parents, by refusing to maintain them." The Poor Law Act of 1601 required only that children support those parents unable to work, and even this requirement was less likely to be enforced than the requirement that parents support children, or husbands support wives. Perhaps then, as Macfarlane also suggests, children understood that they were burdens or costs, and "they reciprocally turn[ed] their old people into burdens, problems and costs." However difficult it is to generalize about family affection, we may note the "element of *reluctance,* of bargaining and negotiation between the generations, reflecting a conflict of interests," in the making of maintenance contracts, in the moralists' advice, and in *King Lear* itself.[64]

When Majesty Falls to Folly

Several recent critics regard *King Lear* as a political play with "an intense Stuart topicality" (Marcus, *Puzzling Shakespeare,* 151) pertaining to the conflict "between the contractual model and the patriarchal model of subjects' obligations to their king."[65] Annabel Patterson asserts that the December 1606 performance of the play (following James's November 1606 opening of the third session of Parliament "with a long speech in which he urged a final resolution" of the issue of the Union of England and Scotland) "offered unmistakably to its royal spectator . . . a very different view of the relationship between fathers and children than that which his speech took for granted, a vision not of fatherly blessings but of patriarchal injustice and folly, in which echoes of his own propaganda could be heard, but strangely maladjusted." For Patterson, "in Lear's authoritarian rhetoric . . . there is an implicit critique of James's public pronouncements"; Kent, in contrast, is "a figure of responsible public service and counsel" —if not necessarily an allegorization of "the reformist party in the Commons" (*Censorship,* 70, 71). Leah Marcus hears in *Lear* the echo of a king who attempted "to work his will upon recalcitrant subjects who committed . . . minor . . . infractions" in "the matter of Great Britain and on numerous other occasions" (*Puzzling Shakespeare,* 151), a king whose Project for Union was an aspect of a "broad encroachment upon traditional 'liberties' " (149), a king who had "already encountered severe opposition to his highhanded notions about the power of royal prerogative" (150).[66] For these critics—more or less explicitly—because the division of the kingdom is presumably the unwise political act of an "authoritarian" King Lear, it alludes to the equally unwise but opposite political act (the plan for Union) of an authoritarian King James.[67] The "insistent Stuart referentiality" (Marcus, *Puzzling Shakespeare,* 151) such critics perceive in the play is based on the assumption that James's behavior was vainglorious, as well as overbearing and authoritarian, that constitutional issues opposing the royal prerogative to the liberties of Englishmen were in clear focus in early Stuart England, and that English politics were already polarized into royalists and an opposition or reformist party as early as 1606. For these critics, then, Shakespeare has performed an authorial "analysis of a particular style and ideology of monarchy," with the result that King Lear is negatively judged by his Jacobean audience as authoritarian, patriarchal, and absolutist; for them, the play "evidently . . . includes a critique of the authoritarian, patriarchal and constitutionally absolutist *theories* of James himself" (Patterson, *Shakespeare and the Popular Voice*, 106, 107).

The complexities of the Union issue itself are not so reductively seen by some historians. Both R. C. Munden and Bruce Galloway argue that the plan for Union was not inherently irrational, that James did not present it in a purely theatrical or mystical manner, and that he was neither peremptory nor browbeating, but rather, cautious and slow in his attempts to begin its implementation.[68]

The reading of the Union issue that substantiates Marcus's and Patterson's picture of an authoritarian, vainglorious, and browbeating James I is of course one that follows the general lines of "Whig" history,

emphasizing the importance of parliament, of the Lower House within parliament, and of those in the Commons who spoke against 'royal interests.' Politics was thus seen as a battleground between a 'Court Party' of dependents and a relatively well-organized, fixed-membership 'Opposition' seeking to rectify grievances, secure parliamentary privileges, and expand the scope and effectiveness of the House. (Galloway, *Union*, 18–19)

However, as Galloway asserts, "attempts to define a single opposition 'policy' on union are . . . doomed" (168). Rather than there existing a clear *"party* of 'opposition,'" resistance came "from a range of individuals," some of whom supported James on other issues, individuals "differing greatly in their method of opposition" (168). He concludes that Union was defeated, not by an already formed parliamentary faction opposed on political principles, but because, on this "specific issue," there was a "general revolt," fed by the less noble motivations of "prejudice," concern for "nationhood," "self-interest and conservatism" (169, 170). There was as yet no organized factionalism, albeit no reason why such a faction could not come to exist (169).[69]

The difficulty with the Whig (and to some degree Marxist) view of seventeenth-century history, which stresses political causation and progress toward democracy,[70] is, as Barry Coward suggests, that "histo-

rians have been too willing to assume that contemporaries, like themselves, knew of the impending constitutional crisis of 1640–1 and that
they were preparing for it for many years beforehand." Indeed, "one
of the mistakes of analysing historical development is to assume that
events proceed evenly along an unbroken line." It is useful to distinguish "between the problem of explaining the reasons for the political
conflicts of the late sixteenth and early seventeenth centuries . . . and
that of explaining why the . . . crisis of 1640 developed and escalated
in a radical direction."[71] Of course "revisionist" history, which stresses
greater complexity of motivation, fragmented, rather than more clearly
opposed parties, and the more accidental or random nature of out-
comes, must itself meet the latter challenge.[72] Yet, it is worth noting
that even those who have critically assessed revisionism feel that future
scholarship must incorporate its insights, if not fully accept its conclusions:

Clearly some of the most straightforward 'Whig' assumptions are no
longer tenable. There was no simple split between the 'government' and
the 'opposition' in early Stuart England; revisionist historians have usefully
highlighted the divisions inside the court and the council under James and
Charles as well as undermining the notion of the House of Commons as
the sole and coherent site of opposition. Neither do we accept the picture
of MPs as premature American patriots, defending recognizably modern
liberal notions of liberty. . . . [T]here were long-term ideological and social
tensions in England but we do not thereby assume that these led inevitably
to the type of conflict that emerged in 1642; the moves to war were complex, hesitant and contradictory.

　　The potential for conflict was there, however. It has become commonplace to emphasize those elements in early Stuart political culture which
stressed order, harmony and consensus.[73]

Even Johann Sommerville, who writes to "challenge the claim that
broad unity on constitutional questions prevailed in early Stuart England," and who argues that there were at least "two markedly different
consitutional theories"[74] then available, says:

Of course, the mere existence of divergences of opinion on matters of
political theory does not entail any sort of political conflict, far less Civil
War. It would be wrong to suppose that serried ranks of absolutists, armed
to the teeth, stood ready to fight their ideological opponents in 1603,

though it is clear that ideas which were familiar in 1603 had by 1642 acquired the greatest and most immediate political importance.[75]

Having come this far in our survey of the history relevant to political criticism, we can conclude, at least, that a fuller and more balanced examination of the relation between opposition to the Union issue and king-Parliament relations than that governing these narratives is required—if literary arguments about *King Lear* are really going to take account of history.

King James and the Destabilization of Patriarchal Kingship?

Such recent critics as McLuskie and Patterson, then, suggest that *King Lear*, by giving what they see as a picture of "patriarchal injustice and folly" (Patterson, *Censorship*, 70), destabilizes the very analogy between father and king—who is, in James's own words, "*parens patriae*, the politic father of his people"[76]—and provides a critique of patriarchal kingship directed at James, who might be said, perhaps, to have "confused" his subjects with his children.[77] One might get the impression that the father-king analogy already belongs *exclusively* to a royalist or absolutist line of thought, as opposed to a parliamentarian one emphasizing government by contract; one might also think that the concept of "patriarchy" had already become suspect. But does the father-king analogy as it appears in English Renaissance culture support readings of *Lear*'s first scene that foreground the implicit wish of child or subject, for a more "contractual," and less patriarchal, relationship?

The analogy between father and king itself clearly favors absolute monarchy insofar as a child is just as unable to cast off his or her father as a subject is to depose a divinely appointed king. If originally "fathers had been kings," if "political and kingly power were essentially the same thing," and if "the king's power was derived from God alone" (Sommerville, *Politics and Ideology*, 27, 29), it could be shown that "the earliest political societies had not been self-governing democracies, but absolute monarchies ruled over by a king and father" (ibid., 29). Such "patriarchalist ideas were common in early Stuart England" and, Sommerville asserts, helped form "the basis of absolutist thinking" (27). King James himself argued that government by kings descended directly from the first patriarchal power—that of Adam over his family.[78]

Similarly, the Canons of the Convocation first called in 1603, which were set out in *Bishop Overall's Convocation Book* of 1606 (but not published until 1690, and, in fact, never officially approved), give an account "of the descent of patriarchal power from Adam to the crowned heads of Europe,"[79] and explicitly deny any originary contract:

If any man shall therefore affirm, that men at the first . . . ran up and down in the woods, and fields, as wild creatures, . . . acknowledging no superiority one over another, until they were taught by experience the necessity of government; and that thereupon they chose some amongst themselves to order and rule the rest . . . ; and that consequently all civil power, jurisdiction, and authority was first derived from the people, and disordered multitude; . . . and is not God's ordinance originally descending from him, and depending upon him, he doth greatly err.[80]

When Robert Filmer, in his *Patriarchia,* codifying these long available traditions of political thought, explains the king's relationship to the laws, he emphasizes the kindly rule of the father that King James also emphasizes in his own political works; he also shows, as does James, that just as the kindliness stems from fatherly solicitude, so too, all judgments of *what* is kindly and necessary for children or subjects are the prerogative of the father-king. For Filmer, "[t]he father of a family governs by no other law than by his own will. . . . There is no nation that allows children any action or remedy for being unjustly governed. And yet for all that every father is bound by the law of nature to do his best for the preservation of his family."[81] In "The Trew Law of Free Monarchies," James writes: "The king is above the law, as both the author and giver of strength thereto; yet a good king will not only delight to rule his subjects by the law, but even will conform himself in his own actions thereunto, always keeping that ground, that the health of the commonwealth be his chief law." Yet he is "not bound thereto but of his good will, and for good example-giving to his subjects."[82]

Nevertheless, for all the ease with which the father-king analogy lends itself to absolutist political thought, it was *not* the unique property of absolutists. The fatherhood of kings could support absolute power, but it could also argue for tender solicitude and appropriate care of all children, and it could argue against tyranny and unrighteous wrath. Thus Hooker, for example, who was no absolutist, describes the king as the "common parent" of all estates "whose care is presumed to extend most indifferently over all" (*LEP,* 8.6.8, in *Works,* 3:405). And even radical Protestant political thinking did not deny the father-king analogy, though it sometimes used it for ends different from James's. The Marian martyr John Hooper certainly uses the analogy in a way that appears to parallel James's: "Whosoever will govern a commonwealth aright, must love it and the members thereof, as the father his children: as Xenophon saith, 'a good prince differeth nothing from a good father.' "[83] However, for Hooper, a good father must support true religion. Just as for the later Puritans, the only *true* king is God (therefore because God is a king does not mean that kings are gods), so, for Hooper, the only true exemplar of a father is God; those who require their subjects to disobey him are not worthy of being called fathers metaphorically. "We must obey neither them, neither their laws: they be not then our fathers, but rather strangers, that would draw us from the obedience of God, which is our very Father."[84] It is a qualification even made by the royalist Lancelot Andrewes in his discussion of "higher and lower place," of God's having "given such excellency to some that He styled them gods" (*Catechistical Doctrine*, 174): "Now as Chrysostom saith, they must first be fathers, before they be honoured as fathers," that is, they must be the " 'cause of our well being' " (175). In Psalm 82 "is set down, how 'God standeth in the congregation of princes,' and seeth how they use their honour" (181). "Though He calls them gods, yet they be but men; they have rule committed to them, but Christ hath power to dispossess and punish them" (ibid.). Although "the wickedness of a man cannot take away the force of God's commandment [to honor superiors]" (182), yet "absolute obedience is due to God only, and kings are to be obeyed so far as their commandments are not repugnant to God's commandments" (183). "This honour must be . . . 'for God's sake.' . . . As Hierome saith . . . 'our father must be loved, but our Father and Creator must be preferred before him' " (184).

Thus, while it was generally held by "political thinkers of all persuasions" that government was essential, superiority and subjection were inherent in the law of nature, and the best government was monarchical, not democratic (Sommerville, *Politics and Ideology*, 63, 17, 18, 63), it was also understood that tyranny was not a good; it was, in fact, *unfatherly*. The Puritan Robert Allen's terms are not intrinsically different from the high church Andrewes's: "All superiors also should so live and govern, as they may be worthy honour, as is hereupon plainly to be gathered that the Lord forbiddeth on the one hand all anarchy or want of government, and disordered confusion, together with all tyrannous, overstately, proud, and rigorous lordliness and dominion, yea every un-kind and *unparent-like* abuse thereof." [85]

The father-king analogy can also simply emphasize the downward flow of unstinting love from a good prince to his people. Like so many Protestant commentators, in his "Trew Law of Free Monarchies," James says: "[W]e see by the course of nature, that love useth to de-scend more than to ascend." (In his vulnerable dotage, what Lear asks is that such "unbounded love" ascend.)

And as the father of his fatherly duty is bound to care for the nourishing, education, and vertuous government of his children; even so is the king bound to care for all his subjects. As all the toil and pain that the father can take for his children, will be thought light and well bestowed by him, so that the effect therof redound to their profit and weal; so ought the prince to do towards his people. As the kindly father ought to forsee all inconve-nience and dangers that may arise towards his children, and though with the hazard of his own person press to prevent the same; so ought the king towards his people. And as the father's wrath and correction upon any of his children that offendeth, ought to be by a fatherly chastisement sea-soned with pity, as long as there is any hope of amendment in them; so ought the king towards any of his lieges that offend in that measure. And shortly, as the father's chief joy ought to be in procuring his children's wel-fare, . . . to think that his earthly felicity and life standeth and liveth more in them, nor in himself; so ought a good prince think of his people.[86]

If for James, kings should exhibit the kindness of good fathers, for the strong Protestant *Christian Man's Closet,* fathers should take care not to exhibit the faults of erring kings. Fathers should not be among those "that have been moved with such wrath, cruelty, or rather madness, which have exceeded the bounds and limits of their function and duty in chastening, and have used themselves like tyrants: towards their chil-dren" (Battus, *Christian Man's Closet,* 24).[87] Tyranny, or even anger un-seasoned with true correction, makes one a bad father as well as a bad king—in fact one who may lose the names of father or king—even if ultimately what constitutes tyranny may be defined differently by King James and by radical Protestants.

Not everything that is true of fathers, then—for example, their rule without the consent of their children—is involved in every use of the father-king analogy. Elizabethans and Jacobeans rarely thought along absolutely rigid analogical lines. Strong Protestants certainly denied reverence for their "forefathers" in the church:

It is a common argument nowadays, what are you better than your fore-fathers? Did not they go to mass, worship images, run on pilgrimage, fall down before the holy sacrament of the altar? . . . *Walk ye not in the ordinances of your fathers, neither observe their manners, nor defile yourselves with their idols.* . . . Oh that our Papists . . . should . . . not be so blinded with their vain shadows of fathers, times, and customs, but would measure the truth of religion by the square of the word.[88]

But a denial of reverence for custom in the church was not equivalent to a denial of reverence for fathers in the family.[89] It was possible to keep the spheres of family, church, and state protected from glib analogy. In fact, rigid analogical thinking was criticized from within English Protestantism itself. Hooker points out that "diversity of things is usual to be understood, even when of words there is no diversity. . . . If I term Christ and Caesar lords, yet this is no equalling of Caesar with Christ" (*LEP*, 7.4.3, in *Works*, 3:370). The moderate Puritan William Gouge warns: "A child may kneel to his parent, and to the king. Yet it followeth not that he maketh his parent a king. Neither will it follow that by kneeling to his parent he maketh him a God because men kneel to God" (*Of Domesticall Duties*, 439).

Thus, if act 1, scene 1 of *Lear* levies a critique, that critique may have been read by a contemporaneous audience, and especially by the king in power, as a critique of failures of fatherly, kindly, and temperate kingship, rather than as a critique of those aspects of the father-king analogy that lend themselves to the defense of patriarchal absolutism. Indeed, as Debora K. Shuger suggests, the "belief (or wish) [coming from theology] that love has the power to overcome the beloved and hence to instill uncoerced obedience reappears in patriarchal politics. The ruler should care for the subject and the subject cheerfully, willingly, and lovingly obey the ruler."[90] Such a mixture of loving care and authority appears in Geffray Fenton's ideal picture of the reciprocities of kindly paternalist kingship and subjects' willing humility. Political society, he says,

is . . . as a general family or household wherein good governors do put on the same careful affection to the advancement of their subjects which wise and dear fathers use to their entirely beloved children . . . . Let then wisdom, love and zeal of magistrates . . . surmount their authority in commanding . . . . And let humility, frank obedience and perfect love be greater in the subjects than their civil subjection.[91]

Clearly, the bases for the analogy of the paternal, monarchal, and divine are not all negative for Jacobeans.

Finally, then, "fault" in 1.1. is necessarily ambiguous. Without predicating a major political and religious polarization in early Jacobean society, or suggesting that kingship was already subjected to a radical critique, we may recognize that there is tension in the cultural values this opening scene invokes. There is tension between authority in fathers—and perhaps in kings—and their wisdom and love, and there is tension between obedience and humility in daughters—and perhaps in subjects—and their resistance to "crabbed" and overly "rigorous" authority in their superiors. But tensions within a shared culture are not the same as polarizations that threaten incipient revolution.

Even if different constitutional theories were available in various forms for the using as the provoking situations occurred, "the political nation was not yet ideologically divided," and "the political landscape was not polarized into two clearly marked camps," royalists and parliamentarians, supporters and opponents of James I.[92] "In the early seventeenth century the Crown could draw upon substantial reserves of loyalty, which not even the events of Charles's reign entirely exhausted." Even plays "about corrupt courts and evil rulers" were not necessarily "perceived as indictments of the reigning monarch or the prevailing political system" in such an era, but instead might be criticism coming from within a position of loyalty to, support of, or acceptance of existing institutions.[93] The moves to civil war were indeed "complex, hesitant and contradictory."[94]

I'll Teach You Differences:

Hierarchy, Pomp, Service, Authority

King Lear is a play with an agonizing concern about "differences," that is, about deference and dignity in a hierarchical society—as marked by such symbols as retinues and "gorgeous apparel." It is a play full of questions of subordination and insubordination. A king invests his sons-in-law with his "power / Pre-eminence, and all the large effects / That troop with majesty" (1.1.130–32), and then attempts to use the shock value of kneeling in ironic deference before one daughter in order to get the "ceremonious affection" (1.4.59) denied him by another, who "abated [him] of half [his] train" (2.4.159). An insolent servant—putting on the "weary negligence" (1.3.12) urged by his mistress, the king's daughter—ignores the king's commands, identifying him merely as "my lady's father" (1.4.79). A loyal servant, the king's own banished retainer—in disguise—defends his diminished master's threatened dignity by tripping the negligent servant and roundly admonishing him: "I'll teach you differences" (1.4.89). For that "service" (1.4.87–88) the loyal retainer earns the king's money reward and promise of love.

Yet *Lear* is also a play in which the king himself appears to criticize the rank-marking "gorgeous apparel" of the daughter who would entirely strip him of his retinue, when he says "Why, nature needs not what thou gorgeous wear'st / which scarcely keeps thee warm" (2.4.269–70). And it is also a play in which a king preaches a sermon to himself on pomp taking physic (3.4.33), urges himself to "shake the superflux" (3.4.35) to "poor naked wretches" (3.4.28), and, shouting "Off, off, you lendings" (3.4.108), strips off his own "gorgeous apparel."

Recent political critics commonly read *Lear*'s treatment of rank and the dignities of rank as socially and, often, politically radical, foreshadowing mid-seventeenth-century social and political upheavals. For Annabel Patterson, the play's "positions on rank, though presented dialectically,"

lead inevitably to Lear's great speech of social inversion ["handy-dandy, which is the justice, which is the thief?" (4.6.153–54)],[1] which the Folio accentuates by adding the injunction, 'Change places', the heart of a radical theory of economic change and exchange. . . . Social mobility, expressed earlier in the upstart Oswald and the humiliation of Kent, in the yeoman whose ambitious son . . . leaves him behind in his climb towards gentrification, implies its own extreme conclusion. If men can change places on the social hierarchy, then those places have no absolute value, and complete inversion becomes, to the seeing ear of madness, utterly thinkable. (*Shakespeare and the Popular Voice*, 111)

Patterson believes that Shakespeare is performing in the play "a radical analysis . . . on the economic structure of his own society" (ibid., 115). "Lear begins the analysis out of self-interest with a critique of Regan's invocation of 'need' as a principle to deny him his retinue" (112). At first his "abstract conception of need" is a "mere strategy in his argument with Regan" (113); he still harbors the misconception that basic needs *are* satisfied in beggars, and that "to introduce the principle, 'to each according to his need', would require them to turn in their 'superfluous' goods" (112). But his belief is "shattered" on the heath "by contact with Poor Tom" and the Fool (ibid.). His "abstract conception of need" is "rendered concrete (and its meanness admonished) by empirical evidence" when he learns "the art of our necessities is strange, / and can make vild things precious" (3.2.70–71);[2] he now accepts "need as the source of value (if what we most need is shelter from the elements, the worst kind of shelter will outvalue the most precious clothing)" (113). Patterson's not fully articulated assumption—hinted at in her allusion to the Marxist principle " 'to each according to his need' "—seems to be that what Lear achieves is a materialist conception of need philosophically compatible with a classless society.

For Walter Cohen, in *King Lear*, "Shakespeare's outcasts and lower-class characters articulate a thoroughgoing critique of hierarchy," albeit "without discovering a political vehicle for their beliefs" (*Drama of a Nation*, 327). Lear himself is credited with an "absolute rejection of hierarchy" and the play as a whole with a "subversive egalitarianism" (ibid., 336) that links it with the radical seventeenth-century sects (Levellers, Diggers, and Ranters).

Whatever the direct influence of the play on the Revolution, *King Lear* takes its place in a tradition of popular radicalism . . . that may extend without a break from the Peasants' Revolt of 1381 to the present. And just as the radical sects have increasingly proved the present age's most valued predecessors among seventeenth-century Protestants, so too the corresponding revolutionary dimension of such works as *King Lear* . . . may come to seem the most precious legacy from Renaissance theater. (Ibid., 356)

Margot Heinemann also comments on the "reversal of degree," the "rôle reversal of riches and poverty, power and powerlessness," "king and clown," that is part of the targeting of "an unjust and unequal society" in *King Lear;* she connects

the deriding of accepted categories of sin, . . . property and officially enforced law . . . [with] Utopian ideas which survived, . . . more or less underground, in late-Elizabethan and Jacobean times, among radical religious sects such as the Family of Love, and were to surface again forty to fifty years later in the revolutionary years, first with the Levellers, and after their defeat with Ranters and Seekers.[3]

And for Richard Strier, in *King Lear,* Shakespeare "consistently dramatized and espoused the most radical . . . ideas" about "how superior powers ought to be obeyed" ("Faithful Servants," 111).[4]

If for these critics the play is incipiently or ultimately radical in its presumed inversions of social and political hierarchy, for James H. Kavanagh, writing quite persuasively from an Althusserian Marxist perspective, it is not radical enough. In Lear's address to Regan, "O reason not the need!" the apparently antihierarchical sentiment really serves the hierarchical:

The 'basest beggar's' 'need' for more than bread becomes an image of, and thus a discursive 'production' of Lear's 'need' to retain his royal perquisites. The quite specific address to Regan as an aristocratic subject — 'Thou art a lady', where 'lady' means a woman of a certain *class* — is conflated with the universalized address to 'everyman' who wants a life better than the beast's.[5]

For Kavanagh, this kind of discourse "effaces the . . . real inequality of place that it assumes and confirms" ("Shakespeare in Ideology," 159). He judges the antihierarchical and hierarchy-validating aspects of the speech as necessarily contradictory: "But of course, one has *either* a universal concept of need tied to the satisfaction of all human subjects, or a variable concept of need tied to specific classes within a natural hierarchy. These discourses are really incompatible" (ibid.).[6]

Is *Lear* hierarchy-validating or antihierarchical, or both? What are its politics with regard to social "differences" and the gorgeous markers of those differences, to masters and servants, social and political superiors and inferiors? If the play does stress both human need and the privileges (and duties) of specific classes, is it historically persuasive to say that such discourses were ideologically incompatible in the early seventeenth century—however incompatible they appear to us in the late twentieth century? This chapter as a whole will show the many senses in which a strong belief in "spiritual equality" or Christian egalitarianism clearly coexisted with a recognition of "politic inequality"— not at all "efface[d]"—that is, of the social hierarchy and paternalism felt to be utterly necessary to the stable functioning of society.[7] Lear's great speech does simultaneously reason against the need for gorgeous apparel and retinues *and* argue against such niggling reasoning. In an effort to comprehend such dualities historically, the first part of this chapter examines this speech in the contexts of the anti-*luxuria* tradition, contemporaneous official commentary on "excess of apparel," the general Protestant division between the spiritual and political realms, and, finally, nonconformist commentary on "monstrous and vain apparel."

As has been indicated, some political critics regard the play's social concerns and values as generally "revolutionary," best explained in terms of the antihierarchical ideas of radical religious sects at the time of the English Revolution. The second half of this chapter specifically examines the relation between the spiritual and political realms in the works of Reformation religious conformists and nonconformists close to the time of the play. The nature of the relationship between the hierarchical and antihierarchical strands of *Lear* is well illuminated by reference to these works; the Christian egalitarianism or "spiritual equality" exemplified in the social concerns of *Lear* certainly coexisted with political inequality in the thought of *contemporaneous* nonconformists. Christian egalitarianism appears in more radical forms in the revolutionary sects, but *Lear*'s social politics cannot be linked exclusively to theirs.

*O, Reason Not the Need and the Anti-*luxuria *Tradition.*

O, reason not the need! our basest beggars
Are in the poorest things superfluous.

Allow not nature more than nature needs,
Man's life is cheap as beast's. Thou art a lady;
If only to go warm were gorgeous,
Why, nature needs not what thou gorgeous wear'st,
Which scarcely keeps thee warm.[8]
(2.4.264-70)

On the one hand, Lear's speech resembles the anti-*luxuria* arguments of Seneca in his ninetieth epistle to Lucilius, and of the church fathers Clement and Tertullian, in their doctrinal treatises: human nature needs very little and all else is superfluous. This is an argument that could be used against "unnecessary" wealth—like the "promotions and benefices . . . curious building, sumptuous and delicate fare, well appareled servants, trim decked horses" that bishops have, which are attacked by the author of an early antiprelatical tract, "A Supplycacion to Our Moste Soveraigne Lorde Kinge Henry the Eyght" [1544]: "Do not these things faintly agree with the saying of their predecessor, Paul the Apostle, which sayeth: 'When we have food and raiment we must be contented?' "[9] On the other hand, Lear's speech also makes an argument rather like that portion of the Elizabethan "Homilie against Excesse of Apparrell" which argues against those persons "altogether past the limits of humanity, who, yielding, only to necessity, forbid the lawful fruition of God's benefits" (102-3), an argument akin to Hooker's lenient interpretation of the same Pauline sentiment.

The Apostle, in exhorting men to contentment although they have in this world no more than very bare food and raiment, giveth us thereby to understand that those are even the lowest of things necessary; that if we should be stripped of all those things without which we might possibly be, yet these must be left; that destitution in these is such an impediment, as till it be removed suffereth not the mind of man to admit any other care. . . . Unto life many implements are necessary; more, if we seek (as all men naturally do) such a life as hath in it joy, comfort, delight, and pleasure. (*LEP*, 1.10.2, in *Works*, 1:240)

Lear's speech both demarcates a strict line between the necessary and the superfluous and argues against too strict a conception of necessity. Not unlike the "Homilie against Excesse of Apparrell" as a whole, it suggests that those who "forbid the lawful fruition of God's benefits," even for the basest beggars, are "past the limits of humanity," *and* that neither Lear nor the playwright ultimately speak "against convenient apparel for every state agreeable" (108).

The dividing line between the necessary and the superfluous, the functional and the luxurious appears to be very clear in such church fathers as Clement of Alexandria and Tertullian, and in such moralists as Seneca. For Tertullian, in *The Apparel of Women*—an essential treatise in the long Christian antifeminist tradition that associates luxurious and superfluous clothing with women in particular and requires that they study *not* to be alluring—"superfluous elegance" can be avoided by using only those things that "come from God, who is the Author of nature," and not from "the Devil, who is the corrupter of nature."[10] Had God wished us to wear colored garments, for example, he would have produced sheep "with purple or sky-blue fleeces" (126). Craftsmanly and artistic skills involved in the manufacture of elaborate cloth and the mining and manufacture of jewels are, for Tertullian, attributable to the fallen angels. All of these things, about which God knows, were "placed . . . on earth for a test" (144).

Similarly, Clement of Alexandria, in *Christ the Educator*, a *locus classicus* on the question of gorgeousness of apparel, insists on the utter worthlessness of rare and precious metals and stones which nature has not made easily available and which create invidious distinctions among men. Clement, like Tertullian (and like Seneca, as we shall see), is certain that "no-one is destitute when it comes to the necessities of life, nor does any man need to look far for these."[11] Since "the universe is made for the sake of self-sufficiency, which anyone can acquire by a few things" (128), "metals dug out of the earth" (127) and other luxuries may easily be eliminated as serving no "practical purpose" (126).[12]

For Seneca, writing in his ninetieth epistle on the question of necessity and luxury, the principle of distinction between the two was a normative nature. "Nature has laid upon us no stern and difficult law when she tells us that we can live without the marble-cutter and the engineer, that we can clothe ourselves without traffic in silk fabrics, that we can have everything that is indispensable to our use, provided only that we are content with what the earth has placed on its surface." Seneca urges us to live like the lilies of the field: "The things that are indispensable require no elaborate pains for their acquisition; it is only the luxuries that call for labour."[13] Like Clement—who abhors "these flimsy and luxurious things . . . with the scanty protection they afford, [which] do nothing more than disgrace the body, inviting prostitution" (*Christ the Educator*, 182)—but with less moral disgust, Seneca comments on nonfunctional clothing "that will conceal nothing, the clothing which affords—I will not say no protection to the body, but none even to modesty!" (*Ad Lucilium*, 411). As we have seen, King James somewhat similarly deplores "unnecessary" nonfunctional uses of clothing, for example, the representing of the "natural parts ordained to be hid . . . by any undecent forms in the clothes" (*Basilikon Doron*, 45). A similar eye anatomizes Regan, whose "gorgeous" apparel "scarcely keeps [her] warm."

Like the Reformation controversialists examined in chapter 1, Clement, Tertullian, and Seneca agree that clothing per se may be deceitful and that the absence of clothing would be shameful, and that both deceitful clothing and immodest nakedness are to be avoided. However, these thinkers stress the deceitful and immoral uses of superfluous and unnecessary clothing over and above any appropriate uses of gorgeous apparel as a marker of status, honor, or dignity. As "hard primitivists," they value nature, or the God-given, over culture or art.

Even for these thinkers, however, the strict division of the functional and the nonfunctional, the necessary and the superfluous, the natural and the unnatural is hard to maintain. In the Golden Age men followed that normative nature, says Seneca, but, finally, he also says, "nature does not bestow virtue; it is an art to become good" (*Ad Lucilium*, 429). Indeed, in part because Scripture—as well as describing gold and silver negatively as the false allure of idols—equates precious metals and jewels literally or metaphorically with worth or dignity (as we saw in chapter 1), even so austere a Christian text as Clement's cannot escape some ambivalence. In the following passage Clement clearly allegorizes, but, of course, the basis of his metaphor is the worth of actual gold or jewels.

The Word says about the Lord, in David's psalm: "The daughters of the king have delighted thee in thy glory; the queen stood on thy right hand, clothed in a garment interwoven with gold and in a golden-fringed tunic," referring not to a garment of luxury, but to the ornament the Church wears, woven out of faith, undefiled, composed of those who have obtained mercy. In that Church, the sinless Jesus "shines out as gold," and the elect as golden fringes. (*Christ the Educator*, 185)

Clement similarly comments: "To say that the city of the saints is built of . . . jewels, even though it is a spiritual edifice, is a cogent symbol. . . .

By the incomparable brilliance of the gems is understood the spotless and holy brilliance of the substance of the spirit" (191).

The Elizabethan "Homilie against Excesse of Apparrell" is similar to the treatises of Clement and Tertullian, and even to Seneca's epistle, in its concern with luxury, especially in women's clothing, and in specific shared motifs: the division between the unnatural, which belongs to the devil, and the natural, which belongs to God, the greater hardiness of the more ascetic. On the one hand, like the treatises of the Fathers, it argues a strict separation between "all things natural" that are "the work of God," and "things disguised or unnatural" that are "the works of the Devil," between the "inward garnishing of [the] mind" and "outward blasings"—those "smells and savours" which cannot hide "beastliness" and which "do rather deform and misshape . . . than beautify" (106–7). The homily is devoted to the subject of pomp taking physic, to warning us to "make not provision for the flesh, to accomplish the lusts thereof, with costly apparel" (103). On the other hand—not completely unlike the church fathers—the homily also allows for "the moderate use of apparel"—apparel permitted by God, "not only for necessity's sake, but also for an honest comeliness" (102); and that "moderate use" of clothing, as the homilist explains, is like the permitted "honest and moderate recreation" from herbs, oils, and wine, which "refresh[es] our senses," although it is not strictly "necessary."

Even as in herbs, trees, and sundry fruits, we have not only divers necessary uses, but also the pleasant sight and sweet smell, to delight us withal, wherein we may behold the singular love of God towards mankind, in that he hath provided both to relieve our necessities, and also to refresh our senses with an honest and moderate recreation. Therefore David in the hundred and fourth psalm . . . showeth that God not only provideth things necessary for men, as herbs and other meats, but also such things as may rejoice and comfort, as wine to make glad the heart, oils and ointments to make the face to shine. So that they are altogether past the limits of humanity, who yielding only to necessity, forbid the lawful fruition of God's benefits. (102–3)

This argument for the lawfulness of "moderate recreation" and against a stricter accounting, although more permissive, is not completely unlike Clement's (which, in its turn, is a little more moderate than Tertullian's). Clement says: "These flowers and herbs have been created for our needs, not to be misused as luxuries. We concede room for some little indulgence, but it is sufficient if we enjoy their fragrance; we need not be decked out with them" (*Christ the Educator,* 159).[14] For Clement, "natural desires have a limit set to them by self-sufficiency," and "all that avoids dire need" is "a mean" (108), yet he also would not have us develop a fear of perfumes (150), and seems to be an early advocate of aroma therapy.[15]

However, not surprisingly, exactly what is necessary, or a little more (that is, exactly what is "moderate" or "comely") in this English Renaissance text, is relative to rank, as it is in the sumptuary laws of the time; not everyone is entitled to the *same* "moderate" and "comely" use of apparel beyond mere necessity. The homilist speaks of that "very good provision made against . . . abuses, by divers good and wholesome laws," which if obeyed might "in some part serve to diminish this raging and riotous excess in apparel" ("Homilie," 105); he tells us he speaks "not against convenient apparel for every state agreeable: but against the superfluity" (108). (Thus, of course, "superfluity" becomes a term as relative as "appropriate," "comely," or " 'convenient.' ") Every man must "behold and consider his own vocation, in as much as God hath appointed every man his degree and office, within the limits whereof it behoveth him to keep himself" (103). The homilies themselves are related to governmental economic policy which encouraged dressing down the wealthy for their pursuit of "superfluous" apparel, though certainly not to the point of egalitarian bareness. Increasingly, merchants were exchanging English wool and hides for foreign silks and velvets and other manufactured goods that wealthier English consumers demanded; sixteenth-century statesmen wanted to keep such precious raw materials within England to encourage national productivity in dressing, working, and creating manufactured goods from them, and to encourage English self-sufficiency. Avarice—even channeled toward English goods—could not be recognized as economically productive quite yet, but the desire for "superfluous luxuries" could be condemned.[16]

Can a recognition of universal *human* need—perhaps even for more than is "strictly" necessary—really coexist with "a variable concept of need" (Kavanagh, "Shakespeare in Ideology," 159), which assumes that hierarchical superiors *need* more? The dualism central to Reformation Protestant theology goes far toward explaining the coexistence—even in far less propagandistic works than the "Homilie"—of such purportedly "contradictory" values.

Protestant Dualism

Although it undoubtedly has some roots in Augustine's "two cities," this dualism derives from Luther's distinction between "two governments": "the spiritual, which by the Holy Spirit under Christ makes Christians and pious people, and the secular, which restrains the unchristian and wicked so that they must needs keep the peace outwardly, even against their will." The one government exists "to produce piety, the other to bring about external peace and prevent evil deeds; neither is sufficient in the world without the other."[17] Similarly, the Puritan divine William Perkins asserts:

There be two states or regiments in the world: the kingdom of heaven which is the regiment of the gospel, and the regiment of the world which is the temporal kingdom. In the first estate, there is neither father nor mother, neither master, mistress, maid nor servant, nor husband nor wife, nor lord nor subject nor inferior, but Christ is all and each to other is Christ himself. There is none better than other, but all alike good, all brethren and Christ only is lord over all. . . .

. . . In the first regiment I am a person of mine own self, under Christ . . . [and] must after the example of Christ humble myself . . . and let every man go over me. . . .

In the temporal regiment, thou art a person in respect of another. Thou art husband, father, mother, daughter, wife, lord, subject and there thou must do according to thine office. If thou be a father, thou must do the office of a father and rule, or else thou damnedest thyself.[18]

Calvin explains that the two governments — "one spiritual, by which the conscience is formed to piety and the service of God; the other political, by which a man is instructed in the duties of humanity and civility" — must be understood in order to avoid misunderstanding Christian liberty. "This distinction will prevent what the gospel inculcates concerning spiritual liberty from being misapplied to political regulations; as though Christians were less subject to the external government of human laws, because their consciences have been set at liberty before God; as though their freedom of spirit necessarily exempted them from all carnal servitude" (Calvin, *Institutes*, 3.19.15, 2:89–90).

This dualism of governments parallels the dualism of the "inward" and the "outward" person, as expounded by royalist divine and strict Puritan alike. Matthew Griffith, later a royal chaplain and Cavalier, asserts:

Indeed it is true that in Christ we are all one, both in respect of the inner man; there being neither Jew, nor Grecian, barbarian, nor Scythian, bond, nor free. . . . And also in respect of the means of happiness: yet in respect of the outward man, there are masters and servants still; Prince and people; bond and free. . . . When therefore the Apostle saith, Be not the servants of men; he speaks in respect of the inner man, which in servants is as free as masters. (*Bethel*, 385)

William Gouge, known as an "arch-Puritan" for his strictness of life — in response to the "objection" "If master and servant be both Christians, they are brothers: but brothers are equals, and neither subject to other" — similarly asserts:

Rule and subjection are matters of outward policy, they tend to the outward preservation of church, commonwealth, and family, in this world: but faith, piety, and such graces are inward matters of the soul, tending to a better life.

These being thus different, one that is more excellent in the one, may be inferior in the other. Yea though there be an equality in the one, namely, in spiritual things, yet there may be a disparity in the other, namely in civil and temporal matters. And though Saints may be far inferior to infidels in outward estate, yet they are not a whit the less glorious before God. The honour proper and peculiar to Saints is inward, not visible to the carnal eye of a natural man. (*Of Domesticall Duties*, 593)

In answer to the objection "It is the prerogative of Christians to be all one: but subjection of servants to masters is against that prerogative," Gouge says:

That prerogative is merely spiritually: for in Christ all are one, as they are members of Christ, which is a spiritual body: not as they are members of a politic body. A politic inequality is not against a spiritual equality. . . . [Christian] liberty is from the curse and rigor of the moral law: from the ceremonial law and the rites thereof: from Satan, sin, death, and damnation: but not from those degrees which God hath established betwixt man and man, for the good of mankind. (Ibid.)[19]

Accordingly, both Puritans and conformist Protestants dolefully comment on the contemporary confusion of degrees, and the difficulty of telling master from servant. William Perkins complains that "the meaner sort nowadays spend that they get in fine apparel and good cheer . . . and it is very hard . . . to discern the master from the servant: and there is such excess in all degrees that now for daily attire the noblest are the plainest."[20] Confusion of attire is threatening to good civil order; it is clear that—even for staunch Puritans—fine apparel, as a marker of rank or dignity, has a role in the preservation of order in a gentry-ruled society. Although Phillip Stubbes's interlocutor Philoponus lambasts outrageous excess in apparel, as we have seen, he also makes considerable allowances for the nobility and gentry to "use a rich and precious kind of apparel . . . to ennoble, garnish, and set forth their births, dignities, functions, and callings," as well as for the civil magistracy "to wear . . . costly ornaments and rich attire, . . . to strike a terror and fear into the hearts of the people to offend against the majesty of their callings" (*Anatomy*, 33–34).

Thus there is much precedent for the coexistence of values or attitudes that may seem outright contradictory to us, that is, Christian concern for spiritual brothers, however lowly, and "politic" concern with "lord and subject," "Prince and people"—with rank and dignity and their markers, which order and uphold civil society.

O, Reason Not the Need: What Politics?

How do Lear's particular words frame and address these issues of necessity and superfluity, "spiritual equality" and "politic inequality"? Are they consistent with the broad outlines of Protestant thought and the dualism therein contained, or do they point, in some sense, to that dualism's precariousness?

Lear's first lines imply that those who "reason the need" would find "our basest beggars / . . . in the poorest things superfluous" (2.4.264–65). With these words—which I hear as self-consciously ironic—he suggests the concept of "necessity," as used by the privileged, works only to benefit them, since it is applied to the "superfluous" beggar, but not to the superfluous noblewoman. Lear's irony recognizes that the relativity ought to work in the beggar's favor as well; the beggar, too, needs more than merely what is necessary. But, as Lear's language suggests, in spite of their need, for "basest beggar[s]" there is in fact no comfortingly "worst" state such as Edgar briefly deludes himself with ("To be worst, / The lowest and most dejected thing of fortune, / Stands still in esperance, lives not in fear." [4.1.2–4]),[21] or such as the homilist praises in his hard primitivistic way, when he speaks of "the poor labouring man," who "can abide in the field all the day long, when the North wind blows, with a few beggarly clouts about him" ("Homilie," 104). Their betters—talking of "necessity"—might chose to deprive "basest beggar[s]" further, to deprive them of even "the poorest things"; that ambiguous term, "necessity," might serve to strip the impoverished of what is less than barely sufficient. Thus, Lear's lines about the "basest beggar" imply that arguments based on "need" are slippery indeed, because such arguments pretend there is an absolute division between the necessary and the superfluous, but such arguments apply that division only relatively—that is, to the case of social inferiors.

Yet Lear's speech also has recourse to the concept of "need": "Why nature needs not what thou gorgeous wear'st, / Which scarcely keeps thee warm" (269-70). Such a concept is necessary, if the vicious and privileged are to be shown just how unnecessary their own "necessities" are. Like the works of Seneca and the church fathers, and parts of the "Homilie against Excesse of Apparrell," Lear's speech also does demarcate a strict line between necessity and luxury or waste in order to preach physic to his daughter's pomp, to trim the selfish excesses of wealth and power. Similarly, the homily asserts: "[O]ne man spendeth that which might serve a multitude, and no man distributeth of the abundance which he hath received, and all men excessively waste that which should serve to supply the necessities of other" (105). Regan's excessive apparel subverts the very functions of clothing, which are, thus far—in this strict view—only modesty and protection, by accomplishing neither, and that apparel marks her, as well, as a shameless woman who gives in to the lusts of the flesh. Her excessive apparel also suggests she is one of those with "millions of sundry sorts of apparel lying rotting by them," while "the poor members of Jesus Christ die at their doors for want of clothing" (Stubbes, *Anatomy*, 59), or, as the "Homilie" has it, quoting Isaiah 17:7, one of those who "in abundance and plenty of apparel hideth his face from him that is naked," and therefore "despiseth his own flesh" (106).

Thus Lear does apply a moral caustic to Regan—the concept of strict "need"—quite seriously. But, of course he applies the concept to her at the same time as he wants to suggest—without total fairness— that it is viciously and falsely applied to himself. He expects that she can no more readily part with the garments that mark and dignify her rank than he can part with his retinue, and so she can understand his loss. However, the need can only not be reasoned in his case—as he asks—if it also should not be in hers. To summarize, then: this speech clearly connects the dignities of rank with the need of the basest for some dignity. The speech's implicit support for "allow[ing] nature more than nature needs"—which implies there is an *absolute* requirement for something more than mere necessity—is a support that neverthe-less preserves the *relative* difference in that supplement or "addition" for beggar and king. Lear's speech clearly foregrounds both genuine Christian concern with the lowly, whose need must not be reasoned too closely, and secular concern with the indicators of rank and dignity seen as symbolic—hardly material—necessities, in accordance with the overall dualism of Protestant thought. Intense sympathy for the in-tensely needy can coexist with "a variable concept of need." Concern for the mistreatment of other humans can coexist with a firm sense of hierarchy; it is the sinfully proud who "use their servants as if they were beasts, their inferiors as servants, their equals as inferiors, and as for superiors, acknowledge none" (Hooker, "A Learned Sermon on the Nature of Pride," in *Works*, 3:606). We need neither eliminate the hierarchy-validating discourse on the way to a more universal concept of need, as does Patterson, nor regard it as ideologically incompatible with the discourse recognizing human need, as does Kavanagh.

Yet certainly these "discourses" coexist differently in *Lear* than in the "Homilie." In the "Homilie" concern for giving pomp physic and the frank acknowledgement of a social order that differentiates the degree of pomp suitable for every rank appear to coexist without overt ten-sion. The homilist targets the excesses of those who have risen from one estate to another and of the poor who don't accept their degree or vocation more than he targets the excesses of the wealthy or privi-leged by birth. Like many contemporaries looking for security in fixity of social rank in the face of social mobility, the homilist is against all change in status, against conspicuous consumption in those on the rise: "[M]any one doubtless should be compelled to wear a russet coat, which now ruffleth in silks and velvets, spending more by the year in sumptuous apparel, than their fathers received for the whole revenue of their lands" (103–4).[22] "He that is ashamed of base and simple at-tire, will be proud of gorgeous apparel, if he may get it" (103). There is as well in the "Homilie" an unacknowledged tension between the ab-stract allowance of those pleasures surpassing "divers necessary uses," of "convenient apparel for every state agreeable," and the apparently stricter standard of necessity particularly applied to, and praised in, those of low degree: "the poor labouring man . . . can abide in the field all the day long, when the North wind blows, with a few beggarly clouts about him," while "he that ruffleth in his sables, in his fine furred gown, corked slippers, trim buskins, and warm mittens, is more ready to chill for cold" (104). This "hard primitivistic" note is also struck by the church fathers; Clement, for example, suggests that those "who live on simpler foods are stronger and healthier and more alert, as servants are, for example, in comparison with their masters, or farmer-tenants in comparison with their landlords" (*Christ the Educator,* 97). It is hard to avoid a sense—ironic for present-day readers, and not entirely outside the range of irony for the Renaissance—that the poor have greater opportunities for comfort and health than the rich. In Lear's speech, on the other hand, the notion that any hierarchical social system must be ambiguous about the dividing line between the "necessary" or "natural" and the "superfluous" or "unnatural"—insofar as what is necessary for one man is superfluous for another lower down the scale—*is* ironically foregrounded: in a hierarchichal social system, where what is "necessary" or "natural" is relative to one's station, one man's necessity is inevitably another man's superfluity.

Is such awareness of the relativity of necessity particularly radical, or unusual among contemporaneous political positions? A quotation from the radical nonconformist Henry Barrow, which also foregrounds the relativity of necessity, may help us.

Well now if these noble or rich men be given to riot and gluttony, with all manner of delicate fare, pampering up the flesh, . . . that in them is but good housekeeping: if they and their retinue exceed in monstrous and vain apparel, it is but raiment fit to their degree, age, or sex. . . . As for most insatiable and greedy covetousness in joining not field unto field, but town unto town, until they be lords of a whole country, that is but good husbandry, wise foresight, and allowable providence for them and their posterity.[23]

The class antagonism of these sentiments is certainly clear, albeit the grounds of criticism are traditional and Christian, and a case could certainly be made for Barrow's accusing the privileged of extreme false consciousness—or, if such "noble or rich men" don't really have self-deluding beliefs, of arrant hypocrisy. However, in the play, it is a royal father who accuses his royal daughter of "vain apparel"; it is a royal daughter who trumps up charges against her royal father of "riot," and that royal father is on his way to learning — if in some sense too late — that his retinue and raiment are first of all symbols of his steward-ship. Shakespeare's "demystification" of the relativity of necessity is not as destructive of paternalist solutions as Henry Barrow's — or Kava-nagh's — might be.

To summarize: in Shakespeare's world, those who are privileged with the dignities of rank, at their best, will understand the need of the basest for some dignity. The variable concept of need that Kavanagh condemns, which assumes that hierarchical superiors *need* more, also permits them greater means to render their sympathy concrete in acts of charity. The values that emerge from the speech are commensu-rate neither with a frankly exploitative and heartless political and social conservatism, nor with a radical egalitarianism (opposites which may be more artifacts of political criticism than of historical study), but with a species of Christian paternalism — and they are values consistent with those that emerge from the play's language, taken in its full historical context — on the subject of charity as well (as we shall see in chapter 7).

But Doesn't Spiritual Equality Threaten Politic Inequality?

For Patterson, as we have seen, Lear's "thinking about the ways in which wealth is distributed" (*Shakespeare and the Popular Voice*, 112) is part of Shakespeare's "lifelong meditation on the structure of English society" which produced "a mature radicalism" (10). For Cohen and Heinemann, as we saw, Lear's social concerns make the play a "power-ful critique of neofeudal values," "subversive[ly] egalitarian," indeed "revolutionary" (Cohen, *Drama of a Nation*, 332, 336, 352), and link it with the radical antihierarchical thinking that emerged in the period of the civil wars in extreme religious sects such as the Levellers, Diggers, and Ranters. In Cohen's view, "[T]he radicals of the period systemati-cally reformulate and extend Lear's revolutionary insights" (352) which include his "absolute rejection of hierarchy" (336); Lear becomes "at last fully worthy of Cordelia" when, "ironically conjur[ing] up 'The great image of Authority,' . . . he rejects all hierarchy, insisting instead on his common humanity" (334).[24] Heinemann locates the politics of the play in an attack on "an unjust and unequal society" ("Demystify-ing the Mystery of State," 79) where "all the difference" between "the rich and poor . . . the powerful and powerless" "lies in clothes and ceremony" (78); that attack takes shape in a "reversal of degree," an "'upside-down' dimension" (80). Such reversals are said to draw on popular traditions such as those associated with the "iconoclastic, egalitarian" (81) and "anti-clerical" (82) foolery of the Renaissance Fool;[25] they also draw on ideas — such as the "deriding of accepted categories of property" — of "radical religious sects," ideas "which survived in a serious and organized form, more or less underground, in late-Elizabethan and Jacobean times," were "attacked by King James as . . . *dangerous* Puritanism," and "were to surface again forty to fifty years later in the revolutionary years" (82).

In such minority sects as the Diggers and Ranters, and to a lesser degree among Levellers, a demand for social and political equality of Christians may accompany the emphasis on their spiritual equality and need for better treatment.[26] However, because *Lear* shares some concerns about social problems with such Christian movements does not mean it shares all — or shares the solutions proposed. The matter of interest here is the assumption that *Lear's* social criticism must link it exclusively with the most radical groups — as opposed to with more widespread and available tendencies — as well as the assumption that religious radicalism is likely to involve social — or political — radicalism. A case may certainly be made for consistent notes of protest, even for "a line of cleavage which will lead straight from the origins of the church to the decisive rift of revolution in 1640."[27] However, our goal is not to understand, by means of hindsight, the continuity of lines of protest that may be said to culminate, in some sense, in revolution — when the extreme sects, in any case, had only a small role — but rather to understand whether there was any substantial connection of religious radicalism with political and social radicalism in 1606. The major issue for nonconformists at the time of *Lear* was still hierarchy and its markers of "clothes and ceremony" (to borrow Heinemann's words) *in the church*. The demand for spiritual equality in the church can *sound* a lot like a demand for political or social equality in society; nevertheless, nonconformists could fervently believe in spiritual equality without having an analogous regard for social and political equality. Those who rejected the "gorgeous apparel" of priestly vestments, the marks of dignity and rank in the church, or who rejected prelacy itself did not necessarily carry such attitudes over into the civil sphere, radically critiquing the supremacy and dignity of kings, as well as the social superiority of nobles and gentry. As we shall see, for nonconformists, it was perfectly possible—even characteristic—for a belief in social and political hierarchy, and even an acceptance of the pomp and splendor that were its signs, to coexist with a strong distaste for ecclesiastical hierarchy and a fervent desire to reform the church; certainly, religious radicalism—and social criticism—did not necessarily entail antihierarchical social attitudes *in* 1606. Indeed, even Puritan political radicals wary of James's behavior toward Parliament in the 1620s, and revolutionaries and regicides after 1649, were not *socially* radical. Let us fully consider the evidence, in order to understand how *Lear*'s concerns with "differences," with deference and dignity, retinues and gorgeous apparel, were likely to have been heard by contemporaneous audiences.

From early in the sixteenth century, the antipathy of the more religiously radical (whether Erasmians, Protestants, Puritans, or separatists) toward ecclesiastical lords and their gorgeous apparel and showy retinues sounds strongly, and threateningly. Their indignation at displays of episcopal wealth and haughtiness, and their disdain for marks of "superiority" in the church, as well as for ceremony and ceremoniousness generally, certainly were perceived often as threats to political hierarchy itself; and the perception persisted, even when opponents of episcopacy denied they were making such a connection. The virulently antiepiscopal strain in Reformation Protestant thought encapsulated and focused a hatred of oppression that often does seem hard to separate logically from hatred of "lordliness" *simpliciter*—as in the derisive antipathy of a reforming spirit like Martin Marprelate: "The said John Whitgift, with the rest of his brethren, doth spend and waste the patrimony of the Church . . . in . . . persecuting the true members of Christ, her Majesty's most trusty and loving subjects; and also upon their own pomp and ambitious pride, in maintaining a rude ungodly train of vile men." [28] The very esteem with which the world regards symbols of superior status fueled the ire of reformers like the authors of the "Second Admonition to Parliament," who condemned any distinguishing marks worn by the ministers of the church: "rochets, hoods, caps, cloaks, tippets and gowns, or such like implements used by the Pharisees which claimed high rooms, and made large borders on their garments, and loved to be greeted, and to be called Rabbi, which things by our saviour are forbidden his ministers." [29] The "Second Admonition" disdains the ceremonies of courtly courtesy, the lordly retinues, the office of domestic chaplain to the nobility in tones that bear what sounds like unmistakable class hostility—suggesting once again that criticism of ecclesiastical pomp voices considerable hostility to social hierarchy. While the desired church government allows "only painful and true preachers," the current one allows

ignorant asses, loitering and idle bellied epicures. . . . Such a fellow must have the benefices, the prebends, the archdeaconries, and such like loiterers' preferments, especially if he can make low curtsey to my Lords, and know his manners to every degree of them, or can creep into some noble man's favour to bear the name of his chaplain, this is he shall bear the preferments away from all other, and to flaunt it out in his long large gown, and his tippet, and his little fine square cap, with his tawny coats after him, fisking over the city to show himself, none can have that he may have, except some certain fat fellows, with long bags at their girdles, and some in their sleeves.[30]

The figure the writer ends with is the traditional personification of Avarice, wearing a version of the "robes and furr'd gowns" that "hide all" (4.6.165).

Thus, the discrepancy or tension between clerical/prelatical privilege and the spiritual equality of Christian brothers is salient from early Reformation times in strong Protestant literature. The tension between royal privilege and Christian equality may certainly be heard as well. The early Reformation "Supplication of the Poore Commons" (1546) sounds a note repeated over and over again when churchmen, in the role of spiritual advisors, address their sovereigns—advice rejected by such sovereigns as James when he disdains "proud Puritans, claiming to their parity, and crying, We are all but vile worms, and yet will judge and give law to their King, but will be judged nor controlled by none."[31]

Oh gracious Prince, here are we, your natural, and most obeisant liege people, constrained to forget . . . that we are of nature and by the ordinance of God your most bounded subjects, and to call to remembrance that by our second birth we are your brothers and fellow servants . . . in the household of the Lord our God. . . . We beseek you . . . that you call to remembrance that dreadful day, when your Highness shall stand before the judgment seat of God in no more reputation then one of those miserable creatures which do now daily die in the streets for lack of their due portion.[32]

The threat to political and social supremacy from the idea of spiritual equality was particularly alive to conformists, who emphasized the inevitability of the analogy between spiritual and secular hierarchies in the minds of their nonconformist enemies. "It was just because the bishops represented . . . royal control" of the church, "that the Puritans could be called seditious and accused of saying . . . 'No bishop, no king,' " as James I thought, and as Elizabeth undoubtedly suspected as well.[33] Richard Bancroft believed that monarchy and Presbyterianism could not coexist, and also feared that Presbyterian elders would spy on the nobility and gentry. He wondered what the people would say, "when they should see these noblemen and gentlemen come to the pastors with their caps in their hands." And he warned: "But you must remember always that they hate superiority. Equality, that is it, which pleaseth them."[34] Bancroft's class prejudices are clear; he derides English Presbyterians: "As though Christ's sovereignty, kingdom, and lordship were no where acknowledged, or to be found, but where half a dozen artisans, shoemakers, tinkers, and tailors, with their preacher and reader . . . do rule the whole parish."[35] Like Bancroft, Hooker questioned whether the nobility would submit to Presbyterian courts where they would be judged by "mean persons . . . from whom no appeal may be made unto any one of higher power";[36] he was sympathetic to the nobility's keeping of chaplains because he understood that the rich might not want to go to church with the poor.[37]

The ideology of Calvinist Protestantism itself, with its ambiguously conditional allegiance to constituted authority contributed to conformist fears. As Peter Lake and many other historians point out, "The whole cult of the godly prince and magistrate, to which nearly all Calvinists subscribed, was deeply ambiguous," emphasizing the authority of magistrates (who, after all protect the true religion), but with the proviso that that authority be used in the manner the godly think fit.[38] On the one hand, Calvin asserts:

It behoves us to use the greatest caution, that we do not despise or violate that authority of magistrates, . . . which God has established by the most solemn commands, even though it reside in those who are most unworthy of it, and who . . . pollute it by their iniquity. For though the correction of tyrannical domination is the vengeance of God, we are not, therefore, to conclude that it is committed to us, who have received no other command than to obey and suffer. This observation I always apply to private persons. (*Institutes*, 4.20.31, 2:804)

On the other hand, there is that famous doctrine of the "inferior magistrate":

[I]f there be, in the present day, any magistrates appointed for the protection of the people and the moderation of the power of kings . . . or with power such as perhaps is now possessed by the three estates in every kingdom where they are assembled; I am so far from prohibiting them, in the discharge of their duty, to oppose the violence or cruelty of kings, that I affirm, that if they connive at kings in their oppression of their people, such forbearance involves the most nefarious perfidy, because they fraudulently betray the liberty of the people, of which they know that they have been appointed protectors by the ordination of God. (Ibid.)

Because two of Calvin's English disciples, Christopher Goodman and John Ponet, had written in defense of rebellion against ungodly rulers during the reign of the Catholic Mary, and because Calvinist parties in Scotland, France, and the Netherlands also justified rebellion, it is not surprising that "ever since Queen Elizabeth's time, the Puritans' enemies had warned that their attacks on the church would lead to revolution. Whitgift, Bancroft, and Laud all considered them potential rebels who, as Laud said . . . 'do but begin with the Church, that they might after have freer access to the State.' "[39] Bishop Richard Bancroft warned in 1593 that since Genevans overthrew their bishop,

it hath been a principle, with some of the chief ministers of Geneva, (but contrary to the judgement of all other reformed churches, for aught I know, which have not addicted themselves to follow Geneva) that if kings and princes refused to reform religion, the inferior magistrates or people, by direction of the ministry, might lawfully and ought (if need required) even by force and arms, to reform it themselves.[40]

Even at this moment when English Puritanism was at least outwardly crushed, for Bancroft, the entire history of Protestantism on the Continent and in Scotland kept its threat to all "superiority," civil as well as ecclesiastical, very much alive.[41] Bancroft warns that "the Anabaptists in Germany began with the bishops and clergy, but they ended with the civil magistrate." He is particularly disturbed by the precedent established nearer home in Scotland. As Bancroft indicates, "[T]he . . . King and Queen [Mary Stuart and her husband Francis II of France] denied, to confirm, or to ratify the acts" of the Parliament of 1560; this Parliament, held with their consent but in their absence (after the death of the regent, Mary's French mother) adopted the *Confession* of John Knox, abolished the authority of the pope, and prohibited the say-

ing of Mass. Nevertheless the reformers made light of the idea that—
as Bancroft puts it—"it could not be a lawful Parliament, where there
was neither scepter, crown, nor sword borne," and they claimed that
"those were rather, but pompous and glorious vain ceremonies, than
any substantial points, of necessity required to a lawful Parliament." In
a passage that might be heard as extraordinarily resonant for *King Lear,*
Bancroft goes on to ask us to consider whether the Scots Reformer
George Buchanan (in his *De Jure Regni*) "maketh not the like assault
against Princes, that his companions did against Bishops,"

as in deriding their titles, misliking their pomp, and in glancing at their
revenues. He termeth the honorable phrases of Majesty, Highness, and
Lordship . . . unlawful and corrupt kinds of speech, which are used in
court, and do proceed . . . from flattery. He gibeth at the state which
Princes take upon them, when they show themselves to the people, com-
paring them to children's puppets, which are garishly attired.

After also, he insinuateth that a good Prince should appear and come
abroad, only defended with his innocency, . . . not with a proud company of guarders, and of pensioners, and of silken knaves. He would have
kings to content themselves with less revenues and service, commending
the discipline of Laconia, where it was strange to have one man pull off
another man's socks, at his going to bed.[42]

If such a firmly antagonistic attitude toward the supremacy of princes
and all their pomp was credited to Scottish Presbyterian reformers,
readings of *Lear* in the context of continued English reformist discontent as—at least obliquely—a radical play seem very plausible. Bancroft
sees the Scots reformer as contemptuous of those "honorable phrases
of Majesty, Highness, and Lordship," that "ceremonious affection"
whose loss Lear's party deplores. According to Bancroft, Buchanan also
jibes at a king's "state" (which Kent warns Lear to reserve [1.1.149]), and
compares his public appearance to that of puppets, lending support to
those who—like David Kastan—argue that kingship itself was beginning to be perceived as a sort of theatrical illusion.[43] Bancroft's reformer
is also scornful, as are Goneril and Regan, of those retinues with which
both secular princes and ecclesiastical lords showed themselves in public and which are of such concern to Lear himself. Finally, Bancroft's
Buchanan evinces a negative attitude toward the very idea of "service"
itself, and specifically mentions the pulling off of socks—as an unnecessary service or indulgence; we might be reminded of that moment

when Lear, having anatomized justice, asks for the service of having his boots pulled off—once again divesting himself of some of the clothes that mark status and privilege (4.6.173)—but with the help of another's labor. Here is grist for the mill of any politicizing critic indeed.

Politic Inequality and Spiritual Equality Again

Nevertheless, such tantalizing "echoes" may well mislead. We need now to make the case for English nonconformity that mitigates against reading it—or *King Lear*—as protorevolutionary.

One must not forget that the doctrine of the godly prince required that there be a prince, that he wield significant authority, and that he forcefully defend the church against the very papists rebels had resisted in France, the Netherlands, and Scotland; most English Protestants did hope for such a godly prince in Elizabeth.[44] One should not underestimate even the Puritan allegiance to Elizabeth, encouraged by that growing English nationalism which took some of its incentive from virulent anti-Catholicism. As Peter Lake convincingly argues: "Since the Protestant analysis of popish anti-Christianity proceeded through a series of binary oppositions, every negative characteristic imputed to Rome implied a positive cultural, political, or religious value which Protestants claimed as their own exclusive property." Popery was the Protestant model of tyranny, illusion, and trickery; kings or queens inimical to true religion got assimilated into the model.[45] Certainly, "[I]f the Prince failed to live up to his divinely appointed role as the champion of the gospel and the hammer of the papists," as Peter Lake puts it, resistance was ultimately possible.[46] But it was by no means immediate.

From the beginning, the English Reformation stressed the "seditious and anti-monarchical character of [Roman Catholic] political doctrines" (Sommerville, *Politics and Ideology*, 44). From around the time of the first Presbyterian manifesto, John Field and Thomas Wilcox's "An Admonition to the Parliament" (1572), to the early Milton in 1641, Puritan dissenters insist that their criticism of the superiority of bishops stems from concern to protect the true superiority of the prince in the state. "An Exhortation to the Bishops to Deale Brotherly with Their Brethren" (1572) asks: to "say there ought to be no lordliness in the ministry: bishops' livings ought to be abated . . . and themselves made equal to their brethren; is this to overthrow a whole state?" The "Exhortation" scoffs at the idea that "to honor the almighty, were to dishonor the Prince." [47] One of the Marprelate tracts, "The Just Censure and Reproofe of Martin Junior" (1589) professes wonder that " 'humbly and dutifully to entreat' " for redress of the church's miseries is interpreted by "John Canterbury" [Archbishop Whitgift] as " 'to threaten that the lawful magistrate should be thrust out of the Commonwealth,' " and " 'to rebel against her Majesty, to pull the crown off of her head, to make a faction to wrest the sceptre out of her hand, and to shake off all authority.' " [48]

Importantly, Perez Zagorin says that no doctrine advocating rebellion, even against ungodly rulers, "was ever maintained by any Puritan advocate" after Elizabeth came to the throne. "For more than seventy-five years the non-conformists remained at one with English Protestantism in upholding the duty of obedience and non-resistance to princes." [49] Sommerville indicates that ideas about resistance were "infrequently" expressed in the years before 1640, and mentions only one Elizabethan Puritan who advocated "deposition of tyrannical rulers. . . by inferior magistrates or by a representative assembly" (*Politics and Ideology*, 73). Even Charles I was given many warnings; such radicals as Henry Burton as late as 1631 and John Lilburne as late as 1639 held that while the magistrate may be denied active obedience if he commands any act against God's laws, actual rebellion was unlawful. [50] The question of when resistance was legitimate was clearly a vexed one even for radicals.

As doubts about the religious reliability of Charles I grew during the 1620s even relatively radical spirits like Henry Burton responded by simply increasing the stakes and assuring Charles that, of course, he must and would fulfill his role as a godly prince in the final struggle between Christ and Antichrist. . . . Yet by 1628 Burton was warning Charles not to slide from godly rule into its opposite, tyranny, and by 1636 he was expressing the sarcastic hope that the people would not conclude from Charles' actions that "this king hath no regard to his sacred vows." The logical culmination of this train of thought was reached in 1641 when Richard Baxter, convinced that Charles was implicated in the Irish rebellion, concluded that in effect the king had abdicated and thus become subject to legitimate resistance. Of course in the second and third decades of the century such ultimate decisions were a long way off. Yet . . . the role of the godly prince, at least as defined by many of his subjects, placed very considerable constraints on James' freedom of movement. [51]

As late as 1641, in his first antiprelatical tract, *Of Reformation*, John Milton was making the standard argument that monarchy could exist without prelacy. "We may infallibly assure ourselves," Milton says, that the Presbyterian church discipline "will . . . agree with monarchy, though all the tribe of Aphorismers, and Politicasters would persuade us there be secret, and mysterious reasons against it."[52]

King Lear was performed on December 26, 1606, not too long after the Hampton Court conference (January 1604) so disappointing to the moderate Puritan cause—a conference understood by some historians as contributing to the radicalization of Puritanism.[53] Yet, if we look at a Puritan such as William Bradshaw, who published many tracts around the time of Hampton Court, we can see how far we still are from 1640 or 1649. This is because Bradshaw, "one of the intellectual fathers of independency,"[54] was also a staunch defender of royal supremacy, and of social hierarchy. Among Bradshaw's tracts are those that strongly object to ceremonies ordered by the bishops, such as "A Treatise of Divine Worship, Tending to Prove the Ceremonies, Imposed on the Ministers of the Gospel in England, in Present Controversie, Are in Their Use Unlawful" (1604). On the other hand, among these tracts as well, is "A Protestation of the King's Supremacy, Made in the Name of the Afflicted Ministers, and Opposed to the Shamefull Calumniations of the Prelates" (1605), which staunchly supports submission to civil authority.

Bradshaw's tracts are evidence of a firm monarchist position among Puritans still incensed about surplices and the sign of the cross in baptism, issues still rankling after Hampton Court. For Bradshaw (who does seem to advocate parity in the church, or, at least, considerable reduction in the authority of bishops), there is no contradiction between parity in the ministry and monarchy in the state: disapproval of bishops does not mean disloyalty to kings.

Equality in ecclesiastical jurisdiction and authority, of churches and church-ministers, is no more derogatory and repugnant to the state and glory of a monarch, then the parity or equality of school-masters of several schools, . . . shepherds of several flocks of sheep, or masters of several camps, families, yea [Puritans] hold the clean contrary, that inequality of churches, and church-officers . . . was that principally that advanced Antichrist unto his throne, and brought the kings . . . of the earth unto such vassalage under him: and that the civil authority and glory of secular princes and states hath ever decayed, . . . the more that the ecclesiastical officers of the church have been advanced and lifted up in authority, beyond the limits and confines that Christ in his word hath prescribed unto them.[55]

The argument Bradshaw makes about the desirable control of the church by the secular prince is very much part of that central Protestant tradition of the "godly magistrate." The Puritans Bradshaw defends hold "that those civil magistrates are the greatest enemies to their own supremacy, that in whole or in part, communicate the virtue and power thereof to any ecclesiastical officers."[56] In his treatise on the "Kings Supremacy," he asserts, "We are so far from making claim of any supremacy unto ourselves (and those ecclesiastical officers which we desire) that we exclude from ourselves and them (as that of which we are utterly uncapable) all princely and lordly state, pomp and power whatsoever."[57]

The critique of ecclesiastical hierarchy in no way implies for Bradshaw any diminishment of royal "state" and dignity. Bradshaw's work makes clear that—apparently unlike many conformist critics of Puritanism—he does not regard ceremonies in the civil and the religious sphere as analogous. He has no quarrel with civil ceremonies: "The right use [of these] is called civility, and the contempt rudeness: the end of civil ceremonies is to signify and shadow those inward affections that one man desireth to shew to another: In the due use of these ceremonies consists humanity, lowliness, courtesy, good manners, civil state, and pomp."[58] Some ceremonies, furthermore, may even be "common," that is, "equally used in civil and religious matters," without detriment to the latter because of their use in the former. For example, "bowing the knee used in prayer, is a religous ceremony, signifying in that action a divine reverence of God." Yet it "is a ceremony that is and may be used to the magistrate, to shadow forth also civil worship due unto him."[59] Furthermore, Bradshaw has no problem with civil decency as appropriate, if not essential, to religious worship; thus, we should "come to the assembly clothed, and that in seemly and usual apparel, according to our civil callings in the world," and we ought "to give as much as may be, upper place to our civil superiors."[60]

Indeed, Bradshaw tries to maintain the separateness and sanctity of the spiritual realm—so easily compromised in a state church—by actually ceding a great deal to the civil realm, even *within* the place of worship. Thus, insofar "as . . . persons in civil respects excel, so in the excercises of religion in civil matters they may excel others' assemblies." While the congregations "of which kings and nobles make themselves members, ought to have the same ecclesiastical officers, ministry, worship, sacraments, ceremonies, and form of divine worship, that the basest congregation in the country hath," they may differ quite remarkably in other respects. As long as "inferior congregations" do not have to "maintain the silken and velvet suits, and lordly retinue of the ministers, and ecclesiastical officers of princes and nobles" by means of "ecclesiastical tithes and oblations," royal and noble "chapels and seats may be gorgeously set forth, with rich arras and tapestry, their fonts may be of silver, their communion tables of ivory, and if they will covered with gold; the cup out of which they drink the sacramental blood of Christ may be of beaten gold set about with diamonds; their ministers may be clothed in silk and velvet, so themselves will maintain them in that manner."[61] In a Martin Marprelate such a comment might well be ironic, but that is not clearly the case here. Even if there is a touch of irony about what such congregations might want to *do* with their money, that irony does not undercut Bradshaw's point about the permissibility of "civil" differences, as long as inferior congregations don't have to pay for them. Bradshaw even attempts to answer the concerns of previous writers such as Hooker and Bancroft, who, as we have seen, objected to Presbyterian discipline because it might subject political or social superiors to ministers who were their social inferiors. The Puritans hold, according to Bradshaw,

that if the party offending be their civil superior, . . . they are to use, . . . throughout the whole carriage of their censure, all civil compliments, offices and reverence due unto him; that they are not to presume to convent him before them, but are themselves to go in all civil and humble manner unto him, to stand bare before him, to bow unto him, to give him all civil titles belonging unto him; and if it be a king and supreme ruler, they are to kneel down before him, and in the humblest manner to censure his faults, so that he may see apparently that they are not carried with the least spice of malice against his person, but only with zeal of the health and salvation of his soul.[62]

However problematic such a relationship between sovereign and minister of God might be from the political point of view, Bradshaw surely does not describe it to prove its impossibility. Indeed, the conformity (of "ecclesiastical officers, ministry, worship, sacraments, ceremonies, and form of divine worship") that Bradshaw wants *requires* the godly magistrate to secure and enforce it.

It is clear that, for Bradshaw, equality in the spiritual realm does not invalidate hierarchy in the civil realm. It is even perfectly possible to give bishops civil honor as *civil* lords. But—in accordance with his strict separation of the civil and the religious spheres, even within the place of worship—Bradshaw rejects the analogy that the vestments ordered by the bishops were merely the prince's livery, not established "for any holiness' sake or religion, but only for a civil order and comeliness." [63] To allow the surplice would be to give bishops spiritual homage, and that is not possible.

A servingman, being a civil person, upon the bishop's pleasure wearing a tawny coat, and a chain of gold, holding up his train, going bare-headed before him, holding a trencher at his table, lighting him to the house of office . . . doth by these actions, as it were by solemn signs, acknowledge civil homage to him, being a civil lord and master: So a minister of the gospel, and a pastor of a particular congregation, being by his office a meet spiritual man; being commanded by the bishop, as he is a spiritual lord and master over the church of God, to wear a tippet, a square cap, a priest's gown and cloak, a surplice; to make crosses upon children's faces . . . ; I say a minister doth thereby give solemn signs and tokens of spiritual homage to their spiritual lordships. . . .

. . . There is none of us that stand out in these matters, but have ever been content to yield unto their lordships all civil honor, such as is given to barons, earls, dukes, and princes; yet, except they were Gods and Christs: we have no reason to give spiritual homage unto them. [64]

In fact, Bradshaw even bolsters his argument against the detested signs of spiritual homage with metaphors from social and political hierarchy! "If any apparel do deform God's true worship, it is that apparel that doth most beautify and grace the false and idolatrous worship of God: as that apparel must needs most deform a wise man that doth adorn a fool, and that apparel must needs be most unbeseeming a king, that is seemly and decent for a beggar." [65] His similitude is based on a sentiment shared by Cordelia's Gentleman who, seeing the mad weed-crowned Lear run off, cries out, "A sight most pitiful in the meanest wretch, / Past speaking of in a king!" (4.6.204–5). Both Bradshaw and the gentleman certainly find the need for dignity-marking apparel in civil superiors reasonable.

Especially with the benefit of hindsight we may see that Bradshaw's position and ones like it were ultimately unworkable; we may also see that the mix of "politic inequality" and "spiritual equality" is always likely to be a tense one. Nevertheless, at the turn of the century, commitment to "politic inequality" and "spiritual equality" certainly could coexist. And even Puritans could accept the legitimacy of "gorgeous apparel" in the civil sphere, as a matter of propriety or decorum, *and* as a marker of social status, dignity, and civil authority.

Nonconformism and Social Order

The late Tudor and early Stuart period was an age threatened by "profound social dislocations," rapid urbanization, increasing endemic poverty of a new kind, and an increasing population of vagabonds— swelled by peasants uprooted by changes in the landed elite's management of estates, retainers discharged from service in noble households, and disbanded soldiers.[66] In a traditionally hierarchical society threatened with disorder, the great question is "Who will reverence or obey him whom he taketh to be his equal?" as William Gouge asks (*Of Domesticall Duties*, 591). Puritanism itself may have been in part a response to a specter of complete social disorder; it was in many ways a socially conservative movement, concerned with order and stability, and increasingly having leaders among the elite of towns. "It is apparent that urban magistrates, gentlemen, and noblemen too, perceived no conflict between evangelical protestantism and the social status and public responsibilities of magnates and notables." The desire of Puritan members of Parliament for religious reform, while it could be represented as hostile to authority, "was not part of a wider interest in political reform, . . . an expression of social anomy, [or] . . . in any proper sense of the term revolutionary."[67]

Even if the structure of the church was profoundly disordered according to the most radical Puritans, "the social hierarchy of degrees and the distinction of callings was exactly as it ought to be, requiring only that order should be preserved by each member respecting his proper place."[68] Pre-Jacobean Puritans such as William Perkins attest to such concerns with good order:

Persons are distinguished by order, whereby God hath appointed that in every society one person should be above or under another. . . . And by reason of this distinction of men, partly in respect of gifts, partly in respect of order, come personal callings. . . .

... When we begin to mislike the wise disposition of God and to think other men's callings better for us than our own, then follows confusion and disorder in every society.[69]

Puritan "callings" may not be completely congruent with social ranks as determined by birth, but the respect for the existing order of inferior and superior, master and servant remains; religious zeal and social conservatism may coexist. In a famous sermon of 1584, Laurence Chaderton—the first master of Emmanuel College—"attributed the cause of all disorder . . . in commonwealth and church . . . to neglect and transgression of 'this general law and commandment of God' in respect of order"; Chaderton "gave a central place in his catalogue of disorders to 'disobedience to superiors' and 'contempt to inferiors.' "[70] Even Christopher Hill notes that the "social implications" of "patriarchal theory," with its emphasis on the authority of the father over the family and the master over the servant, "were accepted no less by Puritans" such as Udall, Perkins, and Bownde, than by monarchists. As late as 1644, "Rutherford in his *Lex, Rex* attacked only the conservative monarchical application of the theory."[71] The asymmetries of master-servant relations were not yet systematically attackable as violations of "the rights of man" in an Enlightenment spirit. As A. L. Beier indicates, "Legally, both service and apprenticeship were forms of servitude."[72] For the Puritan Gouge, a master is in the family what a magistrate is in the Commonwealth and masters bear Christ's image; therefore "in rebelling against their master [the servants] rebel against Christ" (641). Gouge comforts the outwardly unequal servant with his inner spiritual equality: "[T]hough servants cannot be admitted into the courts of men to make their complaint, yet heaven is open to them" (692). Francis Dillingham reminds "Christian servants [who] might think that by Christ they were freed and set at liberty, from all outward service: and therefore it was unequall and unjust, that they should serve any masters" that "Christ came not to take away the government of commonwealths and families."[73]

In fact, Gouge attributes to the Anabaptists the argument "against the authority of masters, and subjection of servants" and the teaching "that all are alike, and there is no difference betwixt masters and servants"; he asserts that those "who are rebellious, and disdain to be under the authority of another, and are ready to say of their master, *We will not have this man to reign over us*, are fitter to live among Anabaptists than [among] orthodoxal Christians" (Gouge, *Of Domesticall Duties*,

592, 604). Other extreme dissenters like the Brownists were feared by the more moderate for "alluring servants from their masters, children from their parents, wives from their husbands, with whom they had smitten covenant, although to their bodies' hurt and affliction."[74]

The holiness of the church *was* felt to be compromised by its incorporation into the state; to be told that the surplice is the livery that the bishops — as the queen's servants — wear,[75] or that priestly garments work only for "a *civil* order and comeliness" (my emphasis) — as the mayor of London explained to a group of 1567 separatists — certainly fueled nonconformist ire.

Mayor: The Queen hath not established these garments . . . for any holiness' sake or religion, but only for a civil order and comeliness; because she would have the ministers known from other men, as the aldermen are known by their tippets, and the judges by their red gowns; . . . and likewise lords' servants are known by their badges. I will tell you an example. There was an alderman . . . that went in the street, and a boisterous fellow met him and went between him and the wall and put him toward the channel, and some that were about him said to him, "Knowest thou not what thou doest? He is an alderman." And he said, "I knew him not, he might have worn his tippet." Even so, when the ministers began to be despised, the Queen's grace did ordain this priests' apparel, but the people cannot be content and like it.[76]

Nevertheless, it is interesting that the mayor's appeal to the dissenters implies that even this "boisterous fellow" would easily have yielded place had the alderman "worn his tippet." Lawrence Stone indicates that the matter of who took the wall and who yielded it was a cause of street quarrels until perhaps the early eighteenth century.[77] The mayor argues "reasonably," in a way that implies the social acceptance of the role of marks of deference in a policeless but hierarchical society. His principle is the same stressed in similarly anecdotal remarks by the rank-respecting author of *A Health to the Gentlemanly Profession of Serving-Men* (1598): the marks of dignity are meant to inspire civil deference to one's social betters and, by preventing the confusion of superior and inferior, master and man, to avoid civil disorder.

But if a nobleman or gentleman nowadays, could not otherwise be known but by his liberality, I fear me, if I should tread the Strand, I should often (for want of knowledge) undutifully justle some of them, and scarce lend my cap, to whom a low leg should belong. For trust me, I met (not long

since) a gentleman in Fleetstreet, whose living is better worth than 2000.
marks yearly, attended with only one man, whose apparel was much better
than his master's, though he was a Justice of Peace [in] his country.[78]

Thus, while it might seem inevitable that rejecters of rank and its insignia in the church would reject the same in the state (especially insofar
as a state church already conflated the civil and spiritual realms, making
its bishops lords in Parliament), this was not necessarily the case. Even
if ultimately the idea of "spiritual equality" may be said to have had a
role in the establishment of a greater degree of "politic equality," this
was a long, slow process. And in a society dependent on masters and
servants, it was not a process that would begin by undoing their unequal and asymmetrical relationship.

Hierarchical thinking and arguments against the abuses of kings coexisted. We may find in the Puritan William Gouge, something like
that paradox of "filial freedom"—the concept of freedom within service or subjection—which Milton exemplified in the unfallen Adam
and Eve in book IV of *Paradise Lost*.[79] "For we may call service under
unconscionable masters *servitude*, and . . . service under religious masters, *liberty*" (*Of Domesticall Duties*, 640). "As God is the master of servants, so he is the master of masters also. As servants are the Lord's
freeman, so masters are the Lord's servants" (691).

Even the regicide John Hutchinson—freely described in his wife's
memoirs, published long after the Civil War, as led "by a right enlightened conscience . . . that it was his duty to act as he did" in signing
"the sentence against the king," believing he could not refuse, "without giving up the people of God . . . into the hands of God's . . . enemies" (*Memoirs*, 336)—in no way seems to have abandoned his respect
for gentility, or to have become socially egalitarian during the Inter-
regnum. While Hutchinson agreed with a group of men described as
desiring that "common justice . . . would . . . equally . . . belong to the
poorest as well as to the mighty"—a group opposed to "the ambition
of the grandees of both [the Parliament and the army]" in 1648—and
"for this and such other honest declarations . . . nicknamed levellers,"
he did not agree with another group "who rose up afterwards with that
name," and who "endeavoured the levelling of all estates and qualities"
(316). Indeed, Hutchinson's relationship as lord to his tenants, master
to his servants, perfectly fulfills that asymmetrical ideal this chapter has
outlined. Hutchinson is described as attending so well to "the government of his own house and town"

that there was never any man more feared and loved than he by all his domestics, tenants, and hired workmen. He was loved with such a fear and reverence as restrained all rude familiarity and insolent presumptions in those who were near him, and he was feared with so much love that they all delighted to do his pleasure.

As he maintained his authority in all relations, so he endeavoured to make their subjection pleasant to them, and rather to convince them by reason than compel them to obedience, and would give way even to the lowest of his family to make them enjoy their lives in sober cheerfulness, and not to find their duties burdensome. (368–69)

Mrs. Hutchinson's negative remarks about particular nobles actually reinforce an ideal of nobility. For example, she says, "The lords, as if it were the chief interest of nobility to be licensed in vice, claimed many prerogatives" (316). After speaking of Cromwell's making of "lords and knights" ("[He] wanted not many fools, both of the army and gentry, to accept of, and strut in, his mock titles"), she continues: "Then the Earl of Warwick's grandchild and the Lord Falconbridge married his two daughters; such pitiful slaves were the nobles of those days" (371). In fact, Mrs. Hutchinson's prejudice is really against the parvenu, even a parvenu like the regicide Thomas Harrison: "For at that time the major-general, who was but a mean man's son, and of a mean education, and of no estate before the war, had gathered an estate of two thousand a year, besides engrossing great offices, and encroaching upon his under-officers; and maintained his coach and family, at a height as if they had been born to a principality" (348). She definitely bristles when her own husband replaces his suit "of sad-coloured cloth trimmed with gold, and silver points and buttons," with a "plain black suit," only to find that this very parvenu who urged that "gorgeous habits . . . were unsuitable to holy professions" has arrayed himself in a dazzling costume "so covered with clinquant (foil) that one scarcely could discern the ground." [80] Clearly, gorgeous apparel is still a marker of social status and civil authority.

There is certainly also no sign of social leveling in the politically highly critical diaries written in cipher by the staunchly Puritan Sir Simonds D'Ewes between 1622 and 1624, and only recently deciphered.[81] A frequent sermon-goer given to self-examination before taking communion, and a man preoccupied with efficient use of his time studying the law, D'Ewes is disgusted with James's sodomy (*Diary*, 93) and generally scandalous public behavior with Buckingham (57,

87), as well as with his constant breaking of the Sabbath. He worries about James's religious coolness, feels somewhat better when James is reassuring about not tolerating Catholics,[82] agitates about the Spanish match that increases "the misery of a discontented and almost daring people" (135). He is highly disturbed by James's treatment of Parliament, criticizing him for "his intention to break up the parliament" on January 2, 1622 (56) and for "showing himself more unjust towards the parliament than ever any king had done" a few days later (57): the king's reasons for dissolving Parliament "gave little satisfaction to any and therefore, if the English had not altogether lost their spirits, some rebellion was expected" (ibid.) Yet, as his editor notes, from his early childhood D'Ewes "was fascinated by his paternal ancestry and his greatest desire was to be thought a gentleman"; he "spent a lifetime proving the nobility of his ancestors" (introduction, 40). Furthermore, although he disparages the "vanities" of the Christmas season and money spent on the Spanish exploits, he seems to have a certain respect for truly lavish appearance and to be prepared to notice when princes or others fail to achieve quite the proper splendor. He understands the difference between surface dazzle and true wealth, as well as the game of understatement.

This blessed Lord's day that should have been spent in God's service was past over in jollity and feasting, besides the pomp at court and desire to see it, made thousand others to break the sabbath. . . . In the morning, . . . the two Spanish Ambassadors went towards the court . . . . Their clothes were alike very beautiful to the eye but not rich, being but of the thicker sort of tinsel cloth. Their followers no way brave. . . . The Marquess of Inoioza was of a mean stature, an imperfect countenance, by the miss of part of his nose and lips and to make himself the rather noted, his carriage was careless and no way stately, as if he should persuade men to imagine that all that he had was within. (147)

He also knows how understatement may be balanced by a discrete display of extraordinary dazzle—or perhaps his comments on the king's not quite so gorgeous apparel suggest he thinks a true king *would* be a little more "awful."

His majesty was appareled in plain satin, of a violet or sad purple colour, with cloak outside; of the same colour a velvet kind with fur rather fitting the state of an aged king, than any way to express a striving to seem more awful or to be reverenced by his apparel. Yet to show that he retained the decorum of a prince in these outward respects, he had a most rich and transparent diamond in his hat, which he wore with more regard and a better grace than usually. (147–48)

In the pre–Civil War period, and later, the ideas of differences between man and man, of superiority and subordination were deeply ingrained, even among Puritans zealous for reform in the church. Thus there is no widespread seventeenth-century revolutionary egalitarian ethic contesting the hierarchical social system marked and served by differences in apparel, or the ideals of "service" that bind inferior and superior, and even the supremacy of princes that these ideas often serve; however, dissatisfaction with a prince's failure to champion the gospel and hammer the papists as the godly saw fit was certainly one potential cause of political dissatisfaction.

Of course, it is difficult to prove what the lowly and not so lowly serving in rich men's houses — or worse — thought of their servitude. But Ian Archer does suggest that the values of service and subordination were internalized by at least some servants:

It would seem that the reciprocity of the master-servant relationship served to contain tensions, and that the household functioned rather well in identifying its members with the prevailing value system. The contribution of this process to the maintenance of order is suggested by the readiness with which the "better sort of apprentices" revealed conspiracies to riot to their masters, calling into question the notion of a homogeneous apprentice culture.[83]

This is not to say one cannot perceive the tensions, the discrepancies between ideal solutions and the intractability of the very problems the ideals were meant to obviate, contain, or resolve. Ian Archer describes the many complaints in Renaissance London about severe correction on the part of masters, as well as about their failure to provide necessities; he concludes that "although the relationship between masters and servants weakened the solidarity of the young because of the way some apprentices came to identify with their masters . . . the control of householders and, indeed, the examples they set were never adequate to ensure the full internalisation of the values of order among the young" (*Pursuit of Stability*, 218). Tensions and discrepancies peer through moralists' works on household management such as Gouge's

Of Domesticall Duties (as they peer through *King Lear*), attesting to the realities of insolence and grumbling of servants, to the general instability of "living-in" in the unsettled world of the sixteenth and seventeenth centuries.[84] If servants, wrongly given the upper hand, "come to this high pitch to rule, rather than to be ruled, they will quickly prove intolerable. . . . It falleth out in this case betwixt servants and masters as betwixt scales, or balances; if the weights that use to lie in one balance to keep it down be taken away, it will suddenly fly up, and so the other balance will be kept down" (652). The terrible irritations of insolent servants come across so powerfully in Gouge's treatise that Beier calls it "a catalogue of discord."[85] Yet, in the absence of any other fully developed and widespread social philosophy, the very instabilities of "living-in" could certainly make the ideology of proper service—whether based on conscience and/or personal loyalty or fear—that much more compelling as a way to cope.[86]

Fear and Love in a Patronage Society

Gouge is capable of pragmatic advice based on a cold look at human nature; he urges that "masters keep their servants in awe and fear. Children must be kept in subjection: much more servants" (650). Yet, he also stresses that "masters ought so to carry themselves as their servants may rather reverence, than dread them" (653). William Wentworth's 1607 advice to his son Thomas, future earl of Strafford, is even more cynical about the possibility of genuine trust and love between superiors and inferiors. "In matters that concern men's private respects and their profit they are not much to be trusted." It is only to "some old servant that hath all his living and credit under you" that Wentworth instructs his son to talk openly. Tenants, "notwithstanding all their fawning and flattery . . . seldom love their landslord in their hearts." "He that will be honoured and feared in his country must bear countenance and authority: for people are servile, not generous and do reverence men for fear, not for love of their virtues which they apprehend not."[87]

Although Shakespeare gives us nightmare inversions of "service" as rendered by Oswald and Edmund, he does not portray a world like Wentworth's, in which there can be no generosity or trust. In addition to Oswald's and Edmund's "service," he gives us the ideal loyalty Kent and the Fool bear Lear, and the loyalty the Old Man, who was "[his] tenant, and [his] father's tenant / These fourscore years" (4.1.13–14), bears Gloucester.[88] The Fool echoes the pragmatically opportunistic advice Wentworth gives his son when he says: "Let go thy hold when a great wheel runs down a hill, lest it break thy neck with following; but the great one that goes upward, let him draw thee after" (2.4.71–74), but it is not advice he follows:[89]

> That sir which serves and seeks for gain
> > And follows but for form,
> Will pack when it begins to rain,
> > And leave thee in the storm.
> But I will tarry, the Fool will stay,
> > And let the wise man fly.
>
> (78–83)

Such loyalties are not unlike the love and regard Gervase Markham describes during the golden age of service in *A Health to the Gentlemanly Profession of Serving-Men:* "For in these days what greater love could almost be found, than betwixt the master and the servant: it was in manner equal with the husband's to the wife, and the child's to the parent" (C2v).

The emphasis on due hierarchy and service was one part propaganda; it did benefit the patriarchal, landed elite. But it also expressed the ethos of those who cast their lot with gentlemen—or even aspired to gentlemanly status themselves—in a society of patrons and those who benefited from patronage—a society in which the major division was between gentlemen and nongentlemen.[90] For serving-men displaced from a fairly comfortable job, like those for whom Markham speaks, it was virtually a paradise when lords kept hospitality and many servants; he's not one to lament " 'Twas never so merry a world since gentlemen came in." George Buchanan—as reported by Bishop Bancroft—may say kings should content themselves with less service (when he commends "the discipline of Laconia, where it was strange to have one man pull off another man's socks, at his going to bed"). Martin Marprelate Senior may mock that sort of service when he puts imagined words into the mouth of "John Canterbury" ("[F]or, poor men, you have nothing but what you get in our service").[91] Yet, one must note, it is this very service Markham sorely laments:

> When Country's causes did require
> Each nobleman to keep his house,

Then bluecoats had what they desire,
Good cheer, with many a full carouse.
(E2v)

According to Elizabethan and Jacobean conformists such as Bancroft, Puritan political radicals derided ceremonies, retinues, and the very service that one man does another; their assault on princes and nobles parallels their assault on bishops. Yet such opinions are more often attributed to nonconformists by their enemies than claimed or carried out by the nonconformists themselves. Particular caution might be required, then, in making arguments that the social politics of *Lear* involve an "absolute rejection of hierarchy," and are "subversive[ly] egalitarian (Cohen, *Drama of a Nation*, 336) on the model of protorevolutionary or revolutionary radical sects (or even of purportedly radical contemporary nonconformism). One should not even conclude that "places [on the social hierarchy] have no absolute value" for Shakespeare (Patterson, *Shakespeare and the Popular Voice*, 111), because *King Lear* calls attention to the possibility that superiors misuse, or are unworthy of, their dignities, and records as well a decline in deferential and ceremonious service, and threats to the dignities (and retinues) of royal and noble. As we have seen, broad Protestant tradition, *including* its strong Puritan or nonconformist strands, embraces political and social inequality as the mainstay of social order, at the same time as it emphasizes spiritual equality. Protestant and Puritan tradition in no way precludes criticism of masters, lords and princes (as well as of servants, tenants, and subjects) for failure to carry out their proper roles, or criticism of the lordly for failure to merit the pomp that distinguishes them. However, to be aware of such failures was not in itself an incentive to revolution, but often a motive for restressing the values of true stewardship within a paternalist system.

A Peasant Stand up Thus?

Nor is it clear that the condemnation of "contempt to inferiors," or the treatment of one's servants as beasts, is the same as the approval of leveling. Certainly, in the scene (4.6.226) in which Edgar prevents Oswald from killing his "proclaim'd prize," Gloucester, Edgar responds to Oswald's "lofty" manner with a peasant dialect "intended as . . . specifically lower class." However, it need not follow that "the effect is to reinforce the image of this sort of *peasant rebellion* as a paradigm of moral action," as Strier asserts ("Faithful Servants," 122, my emphasis). The nobleman, Edgar, rather than standing for the "peasant," incorporates into himself the values of true speech and honesty for which the peasant stands. Like the noble heroes of pastoral romance who take on the guise of humble characters, in effect he has "deprive[d] himself of honour, forsake[n] the goods of fortune, [laid] aside his costly apparel," so that we may "behold naked, not his body, but his mind."[92] He thus proves he merits the status misfortune has stripped him of.

Nevertheless, the nameless servant's defiance of Cornwall's authority in 3.7—just as Cornwall goes to put out the second eye of Gloucester—may well seem a "radical political act." For Strier, the servant who fatally wounds Cornwall is involved in "the *most radical possible* sociopolitical act" (119, my emphasis). Strier reads *Lear* in light of the writings of "the Marian exiles John Ponet and Christopher Goodman, [and] . . . the Scots John Knox and George Buchanan, . . . the most radical political theorists of the century" (108). We have already examined the senses in which an emphasis on honest and loyal service of inferior to social superior in the secular sphere is inconsistent neither with Puritanism nor with the exemplary master-servant relationships in Shakespeare's play—all of which weaken Strier's larger claim "that in *Lear* Shakespeare consistently dramatized and espoused the most radical . . . ideas" about " 'how superior powers ought to be obeyed' " (111). But let us look at the possibly significant exception of Cornwall's servant; here the good servant cannot be both loyal and honest. In what senses is Cornwall's servant's a radical act?

Cornwall, along with Albany, is the reigning power, and he is punishing Gloucester as a traitor to the state. Certainly, as already mentioned, active resistance was virtually universally censured in the Elizabethan period, even in the case of evil rulers who performed repugnant or unjust acts. The "Homilie against Disobedience and Wilfull Rebellion" asks:

What shall subjects do then? shall they obey valiant, stout, wise, and good princes, and contemn, disobey, and rebel against . . . undiscreet and evil governors? God forbid. . . .

. . . A rebel is worse than the worst prince, and rebellion worse than the worst government of the worst prince that hitherto hath been. . . .

. . . God . . . maketh a wicked man to reign for the sins of the people. (*Certaine Sermons*, 279–80)

Launcelot Andrewes argues similarly, in *A Pattern of Catechistical Doctrine*, that "the wickedness of a man cannot take away the force of God's commandment," and therefore "inferiors owe . . . honour to superiors that are evil and wicked."[93] "The doctrine that subjects could never justifiably use force against the king was the most commonly expressed political principle in early Stuart England," even by "those who wished to limit his power most stringently" (Sommerville, *Politics and Ideology*, 35, 71). Moreover, those few theorists—almost always Catholic until the Civil War—who "did admit the legitimacy of resistance" said "it had to take place on public, not private authority" (ibid., 71, 75).[94] As Strier notes, certainly Cornwall's servant is "not a 'public person,'" and "his action is one of outright interference rather than mere nonobedience" ("Faithful Servants," 119). Tyrannicide by a private person is justified only by a radical writer like Ponet (who comes close to outright advocacy of rebellion against an ungodly prince during Mary's reign).

Yet, Cicero's *De Officiis*, a standard Renaissance school text by a writer beloved of the humanists—a text recommended by Sir Thomas Elyot in *The Governour*—is even more radical on this issue. It *does* justify tyrannicide, even by individuals, in certain cases—cases that seem less cautiously defined than Ponet's "exceptions."[95] In the Stoic "category of duties in particular (i.e. exceptional) circumstances"—as M. T. Griffin and E. M. Atkins assert—Cicero "found his justification for tyrannicide and, in particular, for the murder of Caesar by men who had been his friends." For Renaissance readers, tyrannicide in the case of a Caesar—no lawful king—might well not have been in the same category as regicide, yet Cicero's arguments do seem to apply broadly to de facto rulers of whatever stripe. Individuals and states may be prohibited "from benefitting at another's expense," but "citizens who have a duty to their country, their friends, and mankind in general [are not prohibited] from injuring someone who harms his community and places himself outside the pale of human society by his subhuman behavior" (xxvi). Cicero alludes to Caesar's murder to illustrate the exceptional situation "when something that is generally and customarily considered to be dishonourable is found not to be so." In this instance, "Did the beneficial . . . overcome honourableness? No indeed; for honourableness followed upon what benefitted" (3.19, 107). "The neglect of the common benefit is . . . contrary to nature; for it is unjust" (3.30, 111). Tyrants' strategies of instilling fear make men hate them, and often result in their deaths (2.23, 71). Cicero even deplores such physical acts as maiming by those in power, for "nothing cruel is in fact beneficial" (3.46, 117).[96]

> There can be no fellowship between us and tyrants. . . . Indeed, the whole pestilential and irreverent class ought to be expelled from the community of mankind. For just as some limbs are amputated, if they begin to lose their blood and their life, as it were, and are harming the other parts of the body, similarly if the wildness and monstrousness of a beast appears in human form, it must be removed from the common humanity, so to speak, of the body. (3.32, 111)

Cornwall's self-description *before* the blinding of Gloucester prepares for our understanding of the servant's act as tyrannicide provoked by emotional pain at witnessing unjust cruelty. Thus, when the servant "thrill'd with remorse, / Oppos'd against the act" (4.2.73–74), he wrought vengeance on a self-admitted tyrant who used his bald power to give vent to his personal anger under the mere appearance of justice:

> Though well we may not pass upon his life
> Without the form of justice, yet our power
> Shall do a court'sy to our wrath, which men
> May blame, but not control.[97]
> (3.7.24–27)

Although the servant pays with death—a legal death—for his act, he is clearly regarded as the instrument of God's vengeance by Albany:

> This shows you are above,
> You [justicers], that these our nether crimes
> So speedily can venge![98]
> (4.2.78–80)

Furthermore, Cornwall and Regan's acts, performed with "cruel nails" (3.7.56), may be understood as contributing to the reputation for cruelty that their state seems to earn—a cruelty that must spark opposition, according to Albany. Even while he is steeling for the invasion by France and Cordelia (accompanied by the king), Albany notes that they come "With others whom *the rigor* of our state / Forc'd to cry out" (5.1.22–23, my emphasis). "If . . . the heavens do not their visible spirits / Send quickly down to tame [these] vild offenses"—to use

Albany's words on another occasion—"Humanity must perforce prey on itself, / Like monsters of the deep (5.2.46–50).[99] Such cruelty turns humans into monsters altogether outside moral order. As one of the servants says about Regan, as she leads out the bleeding Cornwall, "If she live long, / And in the end meet the old course of death, / Women will all turn monsters" (3.7.100–2).[100]

Tyrannicide, even if condoned by Cicero in a commonly read book, would certainly still qualify as radical in most senses of the term.[101] However, given the general availability of *De Officiis*, perhaps the act of Cornwall's servant is not quite properly identified as "the most radical possible sociopolitical act," as justified by "the most radical political theorists of the century." (Certainly there is no particular reason to make an argument concerning Shakespeare's thinking about social and political hierarchy as a whole on the basis of it.)

Another reason for caution in connecting the act of Cornwall's servant with the radical or revolutionary politics of a Ponet or a Goodman is the very ambiguousness and contradictoriness—which Strier himself mentions—of the Reformation discussion of the question "whether there were limits to the obedience that inferiors owed their social and political superiors." As Strier says: "On the one hand, the Reformers extolled (over against the papacy) the God-given legitimacy of secular rulers; on the other, they insisted on the God-given legitimacy and inviolability of individual conscience" ("Faithful Servants," 106). "Over against the papacy" is the crucial phrase. Ponet, Goodman, Knox, and Buchanan were writing against *Catholic* rulers. The decisive test of tyranny was the attempt of the ruler to subvert the true religion. Calvinism in opposition and Calvinism entrenched were different matters. The Protestant potential for resistance to constituted authority increased where the ruler was Catholic and decreased where the ruler was Protestant; the Protestant emphasis on obedience to constituted authority increased where the ruler was Protestant and decreased where the ruler was Catholic. Bancroft, whom we encountered earlier fulminating against Buchanan, the Scots resistance theorist, attributed similar doctrines to Elizabethan nonconformists. According to Sommerville, "Doubtless he exaggerated the influence of Buchanan and like-minded authors," though "they plainly exercised some influence" (*Politics and Ideology*, 72). A telling attestation to the strength of belief in the godliness of monarchy and the necessity for obedience *when the monarch is Protestant* is the fact that Buchanan—although a

Protestant urging resistance to a Catholic ruler—was condemned by English political writers for putting forth popish views![102]

Even when the subversive aspect of Protestantism comes to the fore, "radicals" do not take rebellion lightly, needing always to preserve the authority of the authorities *they* think just and appropriate. After the Civil War, the regicide Hutchinson, who did feel his conscience was free to relieve his country from "any tyrant or invader of the people's rights" (*Memoirs*, 383), and who "thought [the protectors] greater usurpers on the people's liberties than the former kings" (ibid., 382–83), nevertheless did not hear "a manifest call from God" "to rise up against them"; he felt he must "suffer patiently that yoke which God submits him to, until the Lord shall take it off" (ibid.). On the other hand, even when Protestants under a Protestant monarch or "conservative" writers emphasize obedience to constituted authority, resistance is not quite utterly *unthinkable* on the basis of what they say—or fail to say— about obeying one's conscience. Both the more "radical" and the more "conservative" texts have ambiguities that lean in the opposite directions.

Ponet himself does not approve rebellion against tyrants without caveats. In his chapter "Whether it be lawful to depose an evil governor, and kill a tyrant," he does stress the role of representative bodies in a republican-sounding way: "As God hath ordained magistrates to hear and determine private men's matters, and to punish their vices: so also will he, that the magistrate's doings be called to account and reckoning, and their vices corrected and punished by the body of the whole congregation or commonwealth."[103] But whether "private men" can redress grievances when kings put themselves above the laws is a question Ponet, more than Cicero, actually seems to hedge. Ponet's discussion of the "ethnics" and those "Christian regions" who hold that they can, seems both to judge them negatively *and* almost to justify what they do. On the one hand, though the "ethnics . . . think it lawful for every private man (without respect of order and time) to punish evil," and "the laws of many Christian regions do permit, that private men may kill malefactors, yea though they were magistrates, in some cases" (G8r), "forasmuch as all things in every Christian commonwealth ought to be done decently and according to order and charity: I think it can not be maintained by God's word, that any private man may kill. . . ." On the other hand, Ponet immediately lists a number of general exceptions, which he supports with specific biblical examples from God's word—examples involving God's inward commandment to the killer. A private man may not kill, he says,

except (where execution of just punishment upon tyrants, idolaters, and traitorous governors is either by the whole state utterly neglected, or the prince with the nobility and council conspire the subversion or alteration of their country and people) any private man have some special inward commandment or surely proved motion of God: as Moses had to kill the Egyptian, Phineas the lecherers, and Ahud king Eglon, with such like: or be otherwise commanded or permitted by common authority upon just occasion and common necessity to kill. (G8r–G8v)

The case of the deliverer "Ahud" (Ehud) who killed Eglon, the king of Moab (who had enslaved the people of Israel [Judges 3:12–26]) is one in which, as Ponet describes it, the "whole state" did seem to "utterly neglect[]" the problem; the case of the Maccabean leader Matathias (1 Maccabees 2:17–28), who refused to commit idolatry as ordered by King Antiochus, slew a Jew who did, and slew the commissioners sent with the order, is another one where the whole state was useless, being all idolaters, and where, indeed, the killer was a representative of his people. Ponet considers these examples of those obeying an inner command of God to be somehow "lawful," for he says: "But if neither the whole state nor the minister of God's word would do their common duty, nor any other *lawful* shift before mentioned can be had, nor dare be attempted . . ." (my emphasis). Nevertheless, he concludes this sentence with extreme praise of the efficacy of *passive* means in the combat of evil: "[Y]et are not the poor people destitute altogether of remedy, but God has left unto them two weapons, able to conquer and destroy the greatest tyrant that ever was, that is *Penance* and *Prayer*" (*Short Treatise*, H6v).

While, in the overwhelming majority of cases, Elizabethans and Jacobeans, nonconformist or conformist, condemn rebellion (and even more assuredly condemn any private man's redress of grievances against the magistrate), the mainstream Protestant idea that God's strictures and values are ultimately more important than man's, that one must, if *forced* to choose, obey God rather than man, is part of Christian culture, and not the exclusive property of radicals or Puritans. And that Protestant *potential* for resistance to authority may be heard in injunctions against excessive servitude to humans, or against obeying those who transgress God's laws, and, especially, in assertions that those who command the transgression of God's laws forfeit—in some sense—their rightful authority. Of course nonresistant Christians who are killed by a tyrant because of their passive disobedience may win martyrs' crowns in heaven. But it is hard not to imagine *active* disobedience in those cases where simply not obeying the tyrant's positive command—that is, practicing passive disobedience—still clearly permits the transgression of God's commands to occur. In any case, at the least, the very same example of what Strier calls "service through resistance" to unlawful commands is given both by the radical Ponet and the more conservative Puritan Gouge, as well as by the royalist divine, Matthew Griffith—albeit neither Gouge nor Griffith gives overt sanction to any form of active resistance. The example they all choose is the refusal of Saul's servants to kill Ahimelech and the priests in 1 Samuel 22:17. For Gouge,

[i]t is the property of a parasite to say what a master will have him say, and deny what he will have him deny, and so to do what he will have him to do. Doeg that fawning dog at Saul's word slew all the Lord's priests. . . . So prone are servants to soothe their masters, as there is no sin so horrible which at their master's command they will not be ready to do. . . . Servants are bound to obey in all things which are not *against God,* and must obey in nothing but what *is in the Lord. (Of Domesticall Duties,* 638–39)

Matthew Griffith says, "But know that his command, or his profit is no warrant for thee, that art his servant, to say or do what is unjust" (*Bethel,* 387).[104] How *does* one avoid soothing a master in his horrible sin, or doing what is unjust, if even one's passive disobedience permits one's master to carry out an unjust act?

Thus the actions of Cornwall's servant also do not feel like any clear endorsement of *"the most radical possible sociopolitical act"* (Strier, "Faithful Servants," 119, my emphasis) because the language of Protestants less radical or republican than Ponet comes so close to an endorsement of the servant's action—even if it does not explicitly condone it. The Marian martyr Hooper voices the strong Protestant sentiment that "in case [superior powers] instigate their subjects to the transgression of God's laws, we must obey neither them, neither their laws: they be not then our fathers, but rather strangers, that would draw us from the obedience of God, which is our very Father."[105] It is a sentiment also voiced by the Puritan monarchist Gouge: "For when masters command and forbid anything against God, they go beyond their commission, and therein their authority ceaseth" (Gouge, *Of Domesticall Duties*, 639). The reverence due age or authority may be forfeited by those who commit such acts as the blinding Cornwall performs. Cornwall's servant does seem to question the respect due Regan's authority (as well whether her behavior is gender-appropriate) when he says:

> If you did wear a beard upon your chin,
> I'd shake it on this quarrel. What do you mean?
> (3.7.76–77)

Indeed, radical interpretations are *potentially* present not only in the texts of Puritans who approved monarchy, but even in the texts of high churchmen. Lancelot Andrewes, for whom "the wickedness of a man cannot take away the force of God's commandment [to honor superiors]," nevertheless also puts a limit on obedience, as we saw in the last chapter ("absolute obedience is due to God only, and kings are to be obeyed so far as their commandments are not repugnant to God's commandments" [183]); albeit less strongly than Hooper, Andrewes also asserts that "they must first be fathers, before they be honoured as fathers," that is, they must be " 'the cause of our well being' " (175). The Protestant idea that one must, if forced to choose, obey God rather than man is always available for radical action, always has the potential to be used to legitimate resistance against "ungodly" princes, but was not always so used. These *are* ambiguous doctrines.

Even if a case can be made for the servant's as a *politically* radical act—albeit one justified in a common school text, as well as in one of "the most radical political theorists of the century" (Strier, "Faithful Servants," 108)—it does not follow that "in *Lear* Shakespeare consistently dramatized and espoused the most radical . . . ideas" about " 'how superior powers ought to be obeyed' " (ibid., 111). To be against overly rigorous, ungodly, or tyrannical behavior in the civil superior power is not necessarily to object to patriarchal principles or social hierarchy.[106] Such principles as Gouge's ("Servants are bound to obey in all things which are not *against God*, and must obey in nothing but what *is in the Lord*. . . ." [*Of Domesticall Duties*, 639]), it is important to note, may and do clearly coexist with social conservatism, acceptance of social hieararchy, and respectful awareness of the need for obedience to rulers. Like William Bradshaw, Gouge combines staunch Puritanism in religious matters with monarchical principles. Furthermore, because violent resistance was only very rarely advocated—usually in a hedged form and against Catholic rulers—does not mean there was no discussion of kingly rule or its limitations or its relation to the law. Respect for sovereignty does not require acceptance of exploitation and injustice; Christian ideals of kingship that insist on kingly concern for the unfortunate, as well as Christian and English ideas of justice that insist it be more than a "form"—about both of which more will be said in chapters 7 and 8—can go along with such respect.

∿ 7

So Distribution Should Undo Excess, and Each Man
Have Enough: Anabaptist Egalitarianism,
Anglican Charity, Both, Neither?

This chapter will focus on two passages: first the words Gloucester utters when he gives a purse to the "naked fellow" we know to be Edgar. He invokes the heavens:

> Let the superfluous and lust-dieted man,
> that slaves your ordinance, that will not see
> Because he does not feel, feel your pow'r quickly;
> So distribution should undo excess,
> And each man have enough.[1]
> (4.1.69–73)

The second passage is Lear's parallel moment of recognition, in his "poor naked wretches" speech:

>   Take physic, pomp,
> Expose thyself to feel what wretches feel,
> That thou mayst shake the superflux to them
> And show the heavens more just.
> (3.4.33–36)

John F. Danby links these passages with radical Anabaptism, as does Walter Cohen (like other Marxist or neo-Marxist critics finding a critique of property in the play); Jonathan Dollimore links Gloucester's words in particular with a demystification of Christian charity.

Danby regards Gloucester's prayer, like Lear's, as expressing "the sentiment of Christian 'communism'" (*Shakespeare's Doctrine of Nature*, 186). Indeed, Danby says:

It is a Christian levelling of society—the logical and full expression of charity—which is pointed to. The 'superflux' of the 'superfluous' man is all that which he has in excess of his needs, not merely those crumbs which he can afford to do without. Such a distribution as will undo excess will obviously lead to an equalitarian society. (187)

According to Danby this is the sentiment of "primitive communism" that comes from that Christian tradition expressed in Lollards, Anabaptists, and those "splinter parties of religious eccentrics" who kept "extremer traditions alive," such as Familists, Seekers, Ranters, and ultimately, Levellers and Diggers (187–88).

For Cohen, Lear's "poor naked wretches" soliloquy, like Gloucester's speech, "is ultimately a radical version of noblesse oblige, still viewing the misery of the poor, as it does, from the perspective of the ruling class." However, "where the helpless earl relies on divine intervention to ensure social equity, the more defiant king reverses the relationship" in a "secular, materialist inversion of religion" (*Drama of a Nation*, 334). "Lear in his madness eventually gains an even more revolutionary understanding of his position in society" and "rejects all hierarchy" (ibid.) Popular and radical Protestant communism are the sources of his insights. "An important historical precedent for Lear's social insight was the 'backward-looking and idealized communism' that, according to Christopher Hill, the lower classes of Tudor and Stuart England opposed to feudalism and capitalism alike" (334–35).[2] "The subversive egalitarianism, the rejection of authority, the possible advocacy of utopian communism . . . of *King Lear* look back to Anabaptism" (336). Cohen also links these ideas with the "radicals of the [Civil War] period," who "at the level of ideology . . . systematically reformulate and extend Lear's revolutionary insights" (352). Thus, for example, "the Ranter Abiezer Coppe's demand that men of power 'Bow before those poor, nasty, lousy, ragged wretches' recalls Lear's invocation to 'Poor naked wretches' " (353).[3]

Arnold Kettle, like Cohen, reads the play as "a devastating critique of capitalism" (Cohen, *Drama of a Nation*, 332). Commenting on "Poor naked wretches," Kettle says:

[Lear] is forced to recognize the pervasive helplessness of the poor in the face of the power of the rich, those who have property. Thus his direct personal contact with ruling-class inhumanity leads him to question the validity of property itself and the authority and exemption from elementary human moral values it confers. In this, Lear's development is not at all unlike that of later seventeenth-century radicals like Winstanley.[4]

Terry Eagleton, quoting both Lear's and Gloucester's words, interprets similarly: "If one could truly *feel* that wretchedness, register it sharply on the senses, then one would be moved to share one's surplus with the poor in a fundamental, irreversible *redistribution* of wealth."[5] Annabel Patterson finds in the play a "critique of the socioeconomic system of Jacobean England" (*Shakespeare and the Popular Voice*, 108); "the central scenes on the heath . . . situate gibes" at James's granting of monopolies or knighthoods, made earlier in the play, "in a far more radical argument, showing them not to be casual throwaways, but the building blocks of an emergent structural analysis of power and class relations" (112). "Poor naked wretches" is a "radical text" (114).[6]

Jonathan Dollimore argues that Shakespearean tragedy is "subversive," providing "a critique of ideology" and "the demystification of political and power relations" (*Radical Tragedy*, 4). In his view, *Lear* exposes pity or empathy—which actually maintains the existing power structure—as ineffectual; "Justice, we might say, is too important to be trusted to empathy" (ibid., 192). For Dollimore, while the mad Lear's pity is "mainly . . . an inseparable aspect of his own grief" (ibid.), it is Gloucester—expressing "more than compassion"—who is the demystifier; he "perceives, crucially, the limitation of a society that depends on empathy alone for its justice."

> Thus [Gloucester] equates his earlier self with the 'lust-dieted man . . . that will *not see/Because he does not feel*.'. . . . Moreover he is led to a conception of social justice (albeit dubiously administered by the 'Heavens' . . .) whereby 'distribution should undo excess,/And each man have enough.' (Ibid.)

For Dollimore, presumably, Gloucester understands that the privileged life essentially precludes the perception of injustice, and it is this, as well as his "conception of social justice" involving "distribution" that make his the more demystifying and radical vision.

In spite of all these claims, in fact, "distribution," "excess," "enough," "superflux"—the terms of Lear's and Gloucester's speeches, which these critics view as radical or subversive—are all terms that belong to the traditional and authoritative, not to say authoritarian, discourse of charity, a discourse used by Elizabethan and Jacobean legislators and administrators—city and town aldermen, justices of the peace, churchwardens, and overseers of the poor—and by Anglican and Puritan ministers. The sentiments these words express are not radically egalitarian, but entirely compatible with homiletic exhortations to private and public charity, with the poor laws and other governmental mechanisms of charity, and with Protestant social thought as a whole. All of these were perfectly accordant with—indeed, dependent on—the existence of a hierarchical social order, and plausibly had at least the partial motive of reinforcing it.

There is, of course, a tradition of Christian communism, taking its inspiration in part from the Acts of the Apostles (2:44–45; 4:32–35) or Luke (18:22), practiced in monastic communities, and among some Anabaptists. But Gloucester's words on "distribution" quite clearly point away from such possibilities.[7]

King Lear relates to the outpouring of homiletic literature that came at a time when there was both an increase in poverty and/or concern about the poor, and an increase in governmental response to poverty.[8] Crucial to the play's visual imagery and woven through its textual fabric, are the same biblical themes that dominate the homiletic literature.[9] According to "An Homilie of Almes Deedes,"

Christ in the Gospel avoucheth . . . that the alms bestowed upon the poor was bestowed upon him. . . . In relieving their hunger, ye relieved mine, in quenching their thirst, ye quenched mine, in clothing them, ye clothed me, and when ye harboured them, ye lodged me also, when ye visited them being sick in prison, ye visited me. . . .

. . . And again, To do good to the poor, and to distribute alms gladly, see that thou do not forget, for with such sacrifices God is pleased. Esay the Prophet teacheth on this wise, Deal thy bread to the hungry, and bring the poor wandering, home to thy house. When thou seest the naked, see thou clothe him, and hide not thy face from thy poor neighbour, neither despise thou thine own flesh. (*Certaine Sermons*, 155–56)

The human being's radical lack of accommodation, born, as he is, a "poor, bare, fork'd animal" (3.4.107–08) dependent on his "own flesh," underscores his need for charity. As Hooker says, we enter the world "as naked in mind as we are in body. Both which necessities of man had at the first no other helps and supplies, than only domestical; such as that which the Prophet implieth, saying 'Can a mother forget her child?' such as that which the Apostle mentioneth, saying 'He that careth not for his own is worse than an infidel' " (*LEP*, 1.10.2, in *Works*, 1:241). To owe "the worm no silk, the beast no hide, the sheep no wool, the cat no perfume," as Lear ironically asserts while tearing off his clothes (3.4.104–5), is to be reduced to piteous extremity, not to achieve a desirable lack of "sophistication." [10] Pitiably naked humankind is radically dependent on the "lendings" we can and must provide for each other, as members of a family, first, and then as members of society, lendings withheld by the wicked children in the play whose "flesh and blood . . . is grown so vild," as Gloucester says, "That it doth hate what gets it" (3.4.145–46). [11]

The neglect of charity in the world of the play is extreme, as Cordelia's words suggest when she says "Mine enemy's dog, / Though he had bit me, should have stood that night / Against my fire" (4.7.35–37). [12] She is actually, of course, describing the domestic charity denied in the play by noble family member to needy noble family member, though the point may well be that if charity—a "duty in this frozen age of the world . . . much neglected," as John Downame says—is dead, its demise will first be apparent at the level of the immediate family. [13] The extremity of the need Cordelia describes and the severity of the neglect of charity in the world of the play are best gauged by the prioritized lists of appropriate recipients of charity in the homiletic literature, for example, in John Downame, William Gouge, and Caleb Dalechamp: "immediate family . . . spiritual kindred . . . wider kin . . . neighbours and friends . . . strangers and finally . . . enemies"; outside the pale, of course, are those dogs and wolves the play's imagery evokes. [14] Ironic references to pampered dogs in *Lear,* such as "the Lady Brach [who] may stand by the fire and stink" (1.4.112–13), recur in this literature. [15] Men are said to "lay the lash of oppression on their poor brethren, exhibiting less care for the needs of poor men than they do for their own dogs"; [16] the dogs of the well-off (most likely hunting dogs) are said to be better fed than the poor members of Jesus Christ. Men's hearts, Downame complains, "seem frozen unto such an icy, if not flinty hardness, that the deep sighs and scalding tears of the distressed poor cannot thaw or supple them" (45). Men who oppress the poor are "the mighty hunters of the earth, that hunt the poor people as the wild beasts do their prey," says Charles Richardson, giving his version of humanity "[preying] on itself / Like monsters of the deep" (4.2.149–50). [17] It is "the coat of the naked that thou lockest in thy wardrobe," says Henry Bedel in his *Sermon Exhortyng to Pitie the Poore;* "The pride of apparel maketh us forget the patched poor, and our dainty soft lodging their hard couches and straw." [18] In London, says Stubbes, "[T]he poor lie in the streets upon pallets of straw, . . . or else in the mire and dirt, . . . having neither house to put in their heads, covering to keep them from the cold, nor yet to hide their shame withal, . . . but are permitted to die in the streets like dogs, or beasts, without any mercy or compassion shewed to them" (*Anatomy*, 59–60). In the context of such literature as a whole—so clearly linked in concept and image to the world of *Lear*— we may best evaluate the meanings of "distribution," "excess," the "superflux," and "enough."

Distribution and the Superflux

Let us begin with the obvious. "Distribution" is the actual word for private almsgiving, as well as for nationally or locally legislated charity (that is, the poor rate), as it is in the homily quoted above; the Geneva Bible has for Hebrews 13:16 "To do good, and to distribute forget not: for with such sacrifices God is pleased." Downame says that the right end of giving alms is so that "God might be glorified by this bountiful distribution" (59). "Distribution" is the word used in civic documents in connection with the poor rate; a 1574 London "precept for the collection for the poor" notes that there are those "ready to be famished for lack of relief" and authorizes churchwardens to

collect and gather the devotion and charitable alms of well-disposed people towards the relief and maintenance of the said poor to be distributed in such parishes of this city as hath most need thereof and as shall be appointed by such persons as shall be named by the lord mayor of this city for the distribution of the same.[19]

Robert Allen, in his *Treatise of Christian Beneficence*, written after the Poor Law of 1598, said that care for those unknown to the individual householder "could now be left to 'the charge of the public distribution.'" (He also noted that the "'public ordinance of God doth not take away and suppress the particular disposing of men's private benevolence,' but rather augmented it," that is, the charitable could continue to make private donations to supplement the parish poor rates.)[20]

We also find that the Tudor authorities made actual redistributions of goods, though certainly not along egalitarian lines (see note 34). In times of bad harvests or of severe unemployment, when food riots threatened or occurred, the government reissued the Book of Orders— first issued in 1587—for circulation to all justices of the peace. "The main target was hoarding, engrossing and regrating, and nonessential use of grain," for example, in the making of starch; "[A]s much food as possible was to reach market, and, once there, was to be sold first to the poor at low prices and in quantities sufficient to satisfy their needs." [21] For example, in November 1597, after several years of harvest failure, the London livery companies, which sold grain purchased by the corporation of London for the sake of the poor, "were instructed to sell their meal to the 'poorer sort' at 4d. per bushel below the prices prevailing in the markets . . . probably just within [their] range" (Archer, *Pursuit of Stability*, 201). In some places the poor themselves were distributed; "Devon householders in 1597 were assigned one or more poor persons for whom they provided two meals a day on pain of a fine of 18d. per week." [22]

The immediate context of Gloucester's giving of a purse to Poor Tom also supports reading Gloucester's "distribution" as paternalism: Gloucester has been led in by the Old Man who has been "[his] tenant and [his] father's tenant / These fourscore years" (4.1.12–13) whom he has asked, "for ancient love," to "bring some covering for this naked soul" (4.1.43–44).[23] Thus, in 4.1 Gloucester enters supported by an old man who announces himself a loyal subordinate, and then in his turn Gloucester extends charity to someone in

> the basest and most poorest shape
> That ever penury, in contempt of man,
> Brought near to beast.
> (2.3.7–9)

The language of gesture here does indeed say something about the traditional contract between rich and poor, powerful and powerless. As he is served *by* his subordinates, so he serves or is generous *to* his subordinates. Paternalism may be something we disapprove of, and "ancient love" may seem small protection against injustice. Nevertheless, such ideas of "customary obligation" are deeply embedded in the social and political thought of the time, and such obligations are widely regarded as essential for smooth social relations.[24]

So much, then, for the word "distribution." On to the "excess" of the "superfluous" man and "the superflux."

The "enough" that each man ought to have was understood to be relative to his rank, and the "excess" or "superflux" that he ought to give was understood not to prevent him from maintaining that rank. Christian commonplaces on these issues do assume—however urgently charity is exhorted—that social ranks will not be affected. Downame, urging the necessity of alms, explains: "God hath so ordained that there shall always be poor . . . for the exercise of their faith and patience, and of rich men's bounty and obedience, that so both being approved, both may also be richly rewarded" (44). The poor need the rich for benefits of body, but the rich need the poor for benefits to their souls. The rich have material advantages but moral vulnerability; the poor must endure deprivation, but have a moral edge.[25] Riches are not in themselves sinful. It is only if stewardship is abused, if the rich go beyond the differences suited for their rank, that their expenditure becomes "excess."

Numerous texts use the concepts of "distribution" and "excess" in a manner entirely concordant with Gloucester's use of them. The "Homilie against Excesse of Apparrell" asserts: "one man spendeth that which might serve a multitude, and no man distributeth of the abundance which he hath received, and all men excessively waste that which should serve to supply the necessities of other" (*Certaine Sermons*, 105). Bedel in a sermon preached in 1571 at Christ's Church in London where he was vicar, urges his listeners

not to be unmindful of our brethren the poor members of Christ, seeing that . . . even our excess would content their need, and our waste serve their lacks. . . . Watch us waste in superfluity, that should be the portion of the poor. . . . Ye I say that live in this excess with superfluity, have some remorse to the poor in their misery.[26]

During periods of great scarcity of grain and threatened starvation as well as threatened disorder or rebellion, civil and ecclesiastical authorities quite literally urged a shaking of the "superflux," a "distribution" to "undo excess." In 1596, "the Archbishops of York and Canterbury issued letters to the bishops of their provinces" urging the wealthy " 'to use a greater moderation than heretofore in their diet,' " and to fast not only on Fridays, but "to do without their suppers on Wednesdays also. . . . The ministers and churchwardens were to send monthly certificates of the observance of these orders with the names of any who were negligent."[27] In March of 1598, after four years of harvest failure, the lord mayor of London

required the aldermen to prescribe some fit time of day for the parish poor to receive relief from the houses of the richer sort. The corporation, privy

council, and ecclesiastical authorities joined forces in pressing the duty of
fasting. Companies were enjoined to forbear their election feasts and use
the money saved for the relief of the poor. The corporation's Wednesday
and Friday fast, introduced in August 1596, received backing from the privy
council and archbishop of Canterbury in December, and the ecclesiastical
authorities mobilised their machinery to enforce it. Householders were instructed to hand over the monies saved by forbearing Wednesday suppers
to parish collectors, and the parish authorities required to make monthly
presentments to the archdeacon of those infringing on the fast. (Archer,
Pursuit of Stability, 198–99)

Provision for the Poore (London, 1597), by Henry Arthington, further
demonstrates how commonplace and nonrevolutionary this language
of distribution and excess is. In the spirit of the traditional emphasis
on each estate having its advantages and liabilities, Arthington mentions the sins both of the poor ("idleness, wasting, impatience") and
the "poor makers": "The very overplus of prodigal persons, [that] mis-
spent so much in bibbling and bellycheer." "All other sorts of excessive
persons" should be "drawn to due moderation, and their overplus con-
verted to the use of the poor: it would appear by computation that
maintenance enough might be had for almost innumerable poor persons, if corn should bear the double price in all markets."[28]

Neither Puritan nor Anglican commentators confuse this necessary
"shaking of the superflux" or "distribution" of "excess" with egalitarianism or leveling. For one thing, giving is not usually a matter of reducing
oneself to one coat, if one has only two, but of observing the ubiquitous mean between the extremes of "lavish prodigality" and "base
niggardliness" (Downame, *Plea of the Poore,* 24).[29] Moreover, it is often
quite clear that, contra Danby, the poor are *supposed* to get just those
very crumbs from the rich man's table, to be satisfied with considerably less than their betters: "When Dives hath dined, let Lazarus have
the crumbs."[30] Thomas Drant, in *A Fruitfull and Necessary Sermon, Specially Concerning Almesgeving* (1572), while forcefully—if traditionally—
attacking the greed of all estates or ranks, including lawyers and lords,
also says: "Bread will serve beggars. Beggars may not be choosers.
They are bold beggars that in Stangatehole take men's horses by the
heads, and ask money, beggars may not be of the opinion of the Anabaptists that every man's goods are common."[31] In the case of great
need, charity may diminish one's estate.[32] But generally, while the poor

should be given wholesome food, not that "base and sluttish food as [the givers] would scarce offer unto their dogs," they do not require "superfluous dainties" (Downame, *Plea of the Poore*, 72 [*sic,* after 91]). Downame quotes with approval Saint Augustine's dicta: "Austine saith . . . Let the rich enjoy their superfluities, and let them relieve the poor with necessaries: let them use those things which are bought at high rates, and give the poor such as are good cheap" (93). William Vaughan says the rich who "clothe themselves sumptuously, *without* reserving means to furnish the poor members of Christ" will be divinely punished, but he also says that "noblemen may gorgeously attire themselves, so long as they clothe the needy and distressed members of Christ." [33] "Our basest beggars" might well be adjudged "in the poorest things superfluous" (2.4.264–65) since, for both Puritans and Anglicans, need was entirely relative to rank. "[W]e must remember not to make one rule for all men, that things sufficient for one should be sufficient for all, but every man must be measured according to his condition and degree." [34] As we have already seen, when Lear himself cries "Reason not the need," he both powerfully admonishes the potential meanness of a rank-based charity — which may reserve only "sluttish food" for "the poor members of Christ" — and argues the need of the highest for the dignities of rank.

Off, off, You Lendings

In divesting himself of the silk of the worm, the wool of the sheep, the hide of the beast and the perfume of the cat, however, Lear may be seen as performing an extreme penitential — as well as lunatic — act. After observing the "poor, bare, fork'd animal" (3.4.107–8) that is Edgar — who, he says, "wert better in a grave than to answer with [his] uncover'd body this extremity of the skies" (3.4.101–2) — Lear totally divests himself of the "superflux," the privileged silk and perfume that stand in the way of Christian fellow feeling. His is an act of contrition for his failures of stewardship that follows thematically and emotionally from his recognition "O, I have ta'en / Too little care of this!" (3.4.32–33), an act that is a sort of spiritual humiliation or penance in the *memento mori* tradition. Tearing off his own clothes, Lear makes himself *see* by making his own flesh *feel* (unlike Gloucester's "superfluous and lust-dieted man, / . . . that will not see / Because he does not feel" [4.1.67–68]) what pathetically vulnerable humans—without even the barest replacement for the covering nature provides other species—must endure.[35] At the same time Lear's divestment of his own gorgeous apparel is of course a deranged act, an ironic and despairing overcompensation, an act of uncontrollable despair and grief stemming from self-pity as well as self-loathing.

The particular term "lendings," while literally applicable to what is borrowed of worm, beast, sheep, and cat, also sounds the note of "stewardship"; the accoutrements of power and possessions themselves are only lent on the condition that one behave in a manner worthy of their dignity, that is, that one use them responsibly, as a prayer from King Edward's time eloquently says.

The earth is thine, (O Lord), and all that is contained therein; notwithstanding thou hast given the possession therof unto the children of men. . . . We heartily pray thee, to send thy holy Spirit into the hearts of them that possess the grounds, pastures, and dwelling places of the earth, that they, remembering themselves to be thy tenants, may not rack and stretch out the rents of their houses and lands . . . after the manner of covetous worldings . . . that they, remembering the short continuance of their life, may be content with that that is sufficient, and not join house to house, nor couple land to land. . . that after this life they may be received into everlasting dwelling places.[36]

Too much silk and perfume may easily qualify as "superflux," especially in an economy thought of as a "zero-sum game," in which one can only win what someone else loses; what the rich overspend further deprives the dependent poor.[37] It is the absence of silk or perfume that marks the idealized hospitable lord.

> He hath a great deal rather for to see:
> Than silk on back, good victuals on his board,
> And spend his rent his hospitality.[38]

At the turn of the century, the parliamentarian George More—one of those who worked on the poor law—compared England to decadent secular Rome: "When waxing proud, she wasted her wealth, in sumptuous buildings, superfluous feasts, and rich attire, wantoness was in her streets, vice possessed her houses, and misery soon after overtook her self. . . . For the common wealth much better it is that good hospitality be kept, than that fair houses be built." [39]

The issue of "superfluous" apparel, insofar as it is foregrounded in Lear's self-divestment, links that self-divestment with central Christian themes—the fall of the mighty from their seats, the inevitable loss of rich "lendings" in egalitarian death. Both the Protestant martyr Thomas Cranmer and his Catholic persecutor Dr. Cole knew that "riches do rot, . . . clothes be moth-eaten, . . . gold and silver do canker and rust." [40] Even kings and courtiers might agree, for example, with Lawrence Humfrey, whose language is reminisicent of Lear's in his divestment:

Costly robes . . . are the tokens and signs of virtue. . . . Beware also they must, lest shining outwards, perfuming the air with sweetest odours, inwards they be found unclean and stinking. For gold, silver, velvet, nought else renoumeth [sic], than man's fond estimation. The first, being only fruits of the earth, the basest element: the last, the seed of a simple worm. [41]

In fact, even sermons delivered at court could lambast luxury in clothing in these broad Christian terms. Thomas Drant, Grindal's chaplain—although ultimately directing more of his criticism toward courtiers than toward kings—dares to talk about the abuse of apparel in the strongest such terms at Windsor in 1569:

Rich men are rich dust, wise men wise dust, worshipful men worshipful dust, honorable men honorable dust, majesties dust, excellent majesties excellent dust. . . . From him that weareth purple, and beareth the crown down to him that is clad with meanest apparel, there is nothing but garboil, and ruffle, and hoisting, and lingering wrath, and fear of death, and death it self, and hunger, and many a whip of God. [42]

One of Drant's texts is Matthew 11:8, "They that wear soft clothing, are in kings' houses" (K5r); he says the text does not mean "*ergo,* they may wear soft apparel," for "many things have been done in kings' houses, that might not be done" (K5v). Here Drant does have a somewhat more specific political point. His argument is that "courtiers in kings' houses [who] do wear soft and delicate apparel," "tender courtlings" who wear "soft raiment"—and not the "hard apparel" that John the Baptist wore —are "milksops . . . likely enough to prove reeds, (if they come under duress) and not hard rocks in religion" (K5v). Soft apparel is associated with an 'effeminate' softmindedness in matters of religion; as often in the English Reformation, the preacher implicitly advises the potentate that the backbones of Protestants must be stiffened against Catholic threats at home and abroad.[43] Diatribes against soft and luxurious apparel as "superfluous" possessions, then, might, on occasion have political teeth, but in general they are so clearly within the Christian mainstream that it would be difficult to claim them as peculiarly incendiary.

Thus, Gloucester's "distribution," "excess," and "enough," like Lear's "superflux" that would show the heavens "more just," are well accounted for by traditional Protestant rank-respecting exhortations to compassion and charity—without any need for recourse to Anabaptist communism, the "rejection of all hierarchy," or indeed the postulation of something "more than compassion" which issues in something other than *charitable* distribution.[44]

As we saw in chapter 5, even to assume that *Lear* is about the transition from the feudal to the bourgeois, the moral to the market economy, the patriarchal to the materialist—as the critical commonplace has it—may be to overidealize the past and demonize the "bourgeois Puritan" contemporary moment. To practice—or exhort to practice—the Christian charity urged by Puritan and Anglican alike was hardly to take a radical—or nostalgic—position against "a new critique of poverty" supposedly introduced by "a 'Protestant ethic,'"[45] or to "critique . . . capitalism" (Cohen, *Drama of a Nation*, 332) itself. For one thing, the "de-sanctification" of the poor actually begins after the High Middle Ages;[46] repressive attitudes toward the idle poor certainly antedate the English Reformation.[47] Historians point out that such attitudes were more likely results of changing economic conditions than of changed religious ideology. There was more famine, more displacement; there were greater numbers of urban poor, more visible vagrants and beggars (see note 8). For another thing, the poor laws, albeit stigmatizing the "idle" poor, and expressing and contributing to negative attitudes toward them, were not simply penal, but concerned with compulsory relief to the very young, very old, and disabled.[48] Furthermore, although it is not entirely clear, for the early seventeenth century, how thoroughly the poor laws were enforced and where,[49] both public poor relief in the form of the poor rate or tax and private charity coexisted.[50] Certainly the Puritan John Downame in 1616 still speaks of daily personal charity to persons personally known to and found worthy by the giver; he does not even altogether exclude giving to beggars at the door, when "the whole stream of men's charity doth not run this way, but [only] some small rivulet," "whilst sufficient order is not taken, and accordingly duly executed by the Magistrate for reformation" of common beggary, and when giving is clearly a matter of necessity (140).[51] Thus we cannot even be sure that in exhibiting Gloucester's act of spontaneous, personal charity, Shakespeare is expressing a regretful nostalgia for a bygone "moral" era of Catholic or Anglican face-to-face charitableness—an era of more humane values as opposed to hard-hearted individualistic and capitalistic ones.[52]

As we have seen, it is particularly improbable to link Gloucester's "distribution" with communism, as reputedly practiced—or preached—by Anabaptists, or any other group, because the most widespread meaning of "distribution" is *charity*—a charity entirely concordant with a ranked society. Even the *loci classici* for Christian communism, Acts 2:44–45 and 4:32–35, where the apostles are said to have had "all things common"—and, in the latter case, to have "distributed unto every man, according as he had need"—are consistently interpreted by most Protestants in a way that denies any communistic implications.[53] Had the apostles given up *all* their private possessions for redistribution, the poor could not have been relieved; therefore distribution must be selective. Calvin fears the doctrine clamored for by "fanatical" Anabaptists who "thought there was no church unless all men's goods were heaped up together and everyone took therefrom as they chose"; he insists that "common sharing . . . must be held in check . . . [so] that the poor should be relieved according as any man have need." The apostles "brought forth their goods and held them in common only with the object of relieving immediate necessity." Commenting on the later passage in Acts, Calvin clears the faithful of communism, too:

[Luke] does not mean that the faithful sold all that they possessed. . . . The rich did not only relieve the poverty of their brethren from the annual revenue of their lands, but in their liberality spared not even the lands themselves. This could be achieved without their wholly impoverishing themselves, and by incurring only a certain reduction of their revenue. . . . The goods were not equally divided, but a reasonable distribution was made, to ensure that no one was burdened with the extremes of poverty. . . . This points us to the meaning of the words that no one counted anything his own, but that they had all things common. For no one held his possessions privately for himself to be selfishly enjoyed to the neglect of others, but they were prepared, as need required, to share them in common.[54]

In complete accordance with this teaching, the marginal commentary of the Geneva Bible on Acts 4:32 ("[N]either any of them said, that anything of that which he possessed, was his own, but they had all things common") is "The goods were not alike divided amongst all, but as every man had want, so was his necessity moderately relieved." [55] Like this commentary on Acts, Leonard Wright's phrasing shows how the idea of "common" charitable sharing according to need, *and* the idea of needs differing according to rank could be voiced at precisely the same time: "The goods of Christians, by right, should be private to no man's lust, but common to every man's need, according to their state and calling." [56] Even John Ponet, whose *Short Treatise of Politic Power* (1556) radically curtails absolute sovereignty, also curtails the "communist" interpretation of Acts; "that all things ought to be in common" is a "foul[] error" of the Anabaptists who "wrest[] scripture to serve their madness" (E8r). "God ordained that man should get his living by the sweat of his brows"; the distinction of mine and thine is likewise ordained by God as the commandments against stealing and coveting one's neighbor's property reveal (E8r–E8v). When "scriptures speaketh of communion of things," it is

not that they ought so to be (for so scripture should be directly against scripture) but that there was such charity among the people, that of their own free will, they gave and sold all they had, to relieve the misery of their poor brethren. . . . Nor of this so given might every man take as much as him lusted, but to every one (according to his necessity) sufficient was distributed. So that it stood in the liberality of the giver, and not in the liberty of the taker. (E8v)

Thus "distribution" and "charity" as used in Reformation discourse specifically exclude egalitarian communal sharing; the explicit injunctions against the Anabaptists in all of the Reformation creeds, including the Forty-two and Thirty-nine Articles of the Anglican Church, deny the idea of common property while urging almsgiving. [57]

Preaching Physic—True Stewardship—to Pomp

If we want to even more fully gauge the degree of "radicalism" implicit in "the superfluous and lust-dieted man" and his "lendings," and in the "distribution" that might "undo excess," we might look at a roughly contemporaneous play with a simpler valorization of plain clothing, a simpler connection of plain clothing to political virtue, and, most importantly, an explicit linkage of pompous clothing to the pillaging of the poor. That play is the anonymous *Thomas of Woodstock*. [58] But even in this politically—if somewhat ambiguously—daring work, no social radicalism, no Anabaptist leveling is advocated.

In the zero-sum game model implicit in *Thomas of Woodstock,* gaudy, gilded court fashions are purchased at direct cost to the commonality, who are taxed to pay for them. The play's central figure is Richard II's uncle, Thomas of Woodstock, duke of Gloucester and lord protector, called, because of his "plain dealing, and his simple clothing," "plain Thomas"; for him "a coat of English frieze" (a coarse woolen cloth) is enough; and he speaks in "plain and honest phrase."⁵⁹ Opposed to him are those who "jet in silk and gold" (1.1.101), who "sit in council to devise strange fashions" (2.3.88) antithetic to "the vulgar fashions of [the] homespun kingdom" (3.1.49):

> French hose, Italian cloaks, and Spanish hats,
> Polonian shoes with peaks a hand full long,
> Tied to their knees with chains of pearl and gold.
> Their plumèd tops fly waving in the air
> A cubit high above their wanton heads.
> (2.3.91–95)

Woodstock castigates such profligate and irresponsible behavior:

> Should this fashion last, I must raise new rents,
> Undo my poor tenants, turn away my servants,
> And guard myself with lace; nay, sell more land
> And lordships too, by th' rood.⁶⁰
> (1.3.104–7)

The upstart favorites Richard keeps in high style close to his throne tax the poor, but, Thomas says, in his own "plain hose [he'll] do the realm more good / Than these that pill the poor, to jet in gold" (2.2.35–36).

Queen Anne is as explicit, or more so:

>   O riotous Richard,
> A heavy blame is thine for this distress,
> That dost allow thy polling flatterers
> To gild themselves with others' miseries.
> (2.3.23–26)

> . . . .
> Fond Richard! thou buildst a hall to feast in,
> And starv'st thy wretched subjects to erect it.
> (2.3.102–3)

Indeed, Queen Anne takes definitive steps toward a charitable distribution that attempts to undo excess and give each man enough, although, even here, no disbanding of a ranked society is implied. She vows "the wealth I have shall be the poor's revenue / As sure as twere confirmed by parliament" (2.3.46–47). A busy administrator, she puts sixty to work to provide for the poor (and thus discourages idleness) The "queen's charity . . . of needful clothing" produced by such labors is directly "distributed amongst the poor" (2.3.59–60). She has "numbered" the "seventeen thousand poor and indigent" in "Essex, Surrey, Kent and Middlesex" and

> to help their wants
> [Her] jewels and plate are turned to coin
> And shared amongst them.
> (2.3.19–22)[61]

The author seems to feel the needs of starving subjects justify the diminishment of the estate of the wealthy—a possibility Downame and other Protestant writers certainly mention.[62]

Thus, as a whole, *Thomas of Woodstock* equates "gorgeous apparel" and the exploitation of the commons. And it is Richard's flagrant violation of good stewardship that motivates the play's sympathetic treatment of political resistance—an unorthodox position by comparison to Shakespeare's more ambiguous treatment of the divinity that hedges a king in *Richard II*. *Thomas of Woodstock* implies, as David Bevington notes, that "under the extremities of royal abuse, armed resistance by the aristocracy may be necessary."[63] There is no condemnation for the risings of Lancaster and York along with the commons against the king or for Lancaster's calling the king "to a strict account" (5.3.20), and forcing "that wanton tyrant to reveal / The death of his dear uncle: harmless Woodstock" (5.3.3–4).

However, even this play, while sanctioning rebellion led by responsible aristocrats against a blatantly irresponsible government, and while insisting on the need for royal charity in a time of destitution, does not espouse any Anabaptist leveling. It is the appearance of upstarts on par with a king that is galling; Lancaster—if perhaps not Woodstock himself—might allow King Richard himself his emperor-like garments:

> We could allow his clothing, brother Woodstock,
> But we have four kings more, are equalled with him:

There's Bagot, Bushy, wanton Green, and Scroop,
In state and fashion without difference.
(3.2.39–42)[64]

To conclude, *Thomas of Woodstock* makes a more radical use of anti-*luxuria* clothing motifs than does *King Lear*. However, both plays maintain an ultimately traditional view of the social order—a view emphasizing the necessity of responsible government and of Christian charity on the part of the socially privileged. The motif of prideful dress that pillages the poor is one that belongs to a shared Christian concern for stewardship, a shared Christian culture.

Christian Charity and the Contract between Governors and Governed: What Limits?

Reformation Protestant social thought, then, encouraged social amelioration within a paternalistic—if often *spiritually* egalitarian—framework; Gloucester (and Lear) hardly demystify Christian charity but exemplify—and in a way exhort—forms of it consistent with current thought and practice. This is not to say that some authorized practices stimulated by the poor's increasing numbers—particularly those addressed toward the presumably "willfull" poor—were not stigmatizing and repressive. Such practices included the requiring of passports and badges, branding, transporting overseas, impressing, summary trial without benefit of jury, and hanging—although some of the more ferocious punishments in the 1572 act (if not the whipping "from tithing to tithing" that Shakespeare's Poor Tom calls our sympathetic attention to [3.4.134]) were removed by later acts.[65] In a society "without a police force, in which the militia proved inadequate to maintain internal order"—albeit one in which martial law could be used against vagrants and rioters—terror was clearly thought an advisable deterrent by many.[66] (Though perhaps not all; Miles Sandys "thought the whole [1572 poor law] 'oversharp and bloody.'")[67] Thus, the 1601 *Ease for Overseers of the Poore*, not untypically, asserts: "The willfull and incorrigible must be constrained to work, in the house of correction, that by applying labour and punishment to their bodies, their froward natures may be bridled, their evil minds may be bettered, and others *terrified* by their example."[68]

It is true that we don't usually get to hear how people of the lowest strata of society felt about such stigmatization. Perhaps, though, we come a little closer than usual in the poetic complaint of Arthur Warren (who had himself been imprisoned for debt), *The Poore Man's Passions* (London, 1605).[69] This complaint is unusual in not stressing that familiar Christian contract between rich and poor, found in so many sources.[70] *The Poore Man's Passions* is also unusual in its scrutiny of the government's stigmatization of the poor, seen as such:

> What i'st to beg, but to be counted base?
> What i'st to borrow, but to be denied?
> When Poor are trespass'd, they learn Ploydon's case,
> And must for recompense content abide,
>   Yet give the Rich but an uncourteous look,
>   It proves a forfeit by their statute book.
>
> . . . .
>
> Degrading us with contumelious spells,
> They touch, attach, and summon us with shames,
> To our discredit ring reproachful bells,
> And catalogue us with inhuman names,
>   Vagabonds, varlets, villains, vassals, slaves,
>   Rogues, caterpillars, runagates, and knaves.[71]

Warren certainly demystifies the relationship of lord and servant, rich and poor:

> Who is the Lord, but he, that hath the luck;
> Who is the man, but he, that hath the muck?
> (D1r)

If someone likely not at the bottom of the social scale — as his versification suggests — may be this overt, surely the illiterate apprentice or chambermaid would be even harsher in his or her judgments?

At this point those who automatically look to radical interpretations may ask: Isn't this Christian charity we've been hearing about, then, only a matter of "false consciousness"? That is, isn't "charity" or "Christian empathy" one of those "illusory beliefs" that are part of "a process of conspiracy on the part of the rulers and misrecognition on the part of the ruled" (Dollimore, *Radical Tragedy*, 9)? I want to suggest that the difficulty with the concept of "ideology" as "false consciousness" is the way it structures debate. Especially in current neo-Marxism, *all* consciousness is inescapably false consciousness.[72] Thus no social ide-

ology—except absolutely egalitarian redistribution produced by a not
yet experienced total class revolution—can really be invulnerable to
the charge of false consciousness. All lesser ideologies and redistributions—whether in our time or Shakespeare's—are by this measure vulnerable.

In the present case, my concern is not with political positions themselves, or with evaluating them as such, but with the linguistic and
cultural systems by means of which political positions would have been
recognized or understood by a contemporaneous audience, and in
terms of which we can reconstruct historically remote understandings.
In describing the limited "redistributions" practiced by the Elizabethan
and Jacobean state or urged by Christian homily, I am neither applaud-
ing them as socially good nor prescribing what individuals or societies
should seek; I am certainly not claiming that such practices and exhortations changed the class structure of English society. I am suggesting
that—whatever political import *King Lear* should have, or should have
had—it is by means of reference to such values and practices that
its political viewpoint was most likely to have been understood in its
time; whatever people should have thought or done around 1606, these
are the kinds of thinking and acts they clearly did do. Perhaps the
"poorer sort" ought to be loyal to people like themselves and not to
lord or prince, locality or country; perhaps the long-term interests of
those who suffer economic injustice are best served by such horizontal
class identifications as opposed to these other vertical ties. Yet people's
identities are often not so simple. The class consciousness of the stigmatized may be accompanied by staunch Protestant nationalism; both
the landlord and the chambermaid may want to avoid disorder. We've
already seen in the case of D'Ewes, that a Puritan antiroyalist could
be a social conservative, and in the case of Hutchinson that a Puritan
and a regicide could also be a traditional landlord. The difficulty with
the postulation of absolutely egalitarian redistribution and total class
revolution as true amelioration, and all else as inescapable "misrecognition," is that it automatically makes irrelevant the discussion of a
range of actual cultural values, practices, events, and linguistic usages,
as well as of the multiple self-identifications of individuals—that is, the
discussion of evidence itself. It also precludes possibly worthwhile distinctions in the discussion of values and practices; for example, one
may want to differentiate between ruthless self-interest, what might be
called enlightened self-interest, and some more extreme altruism.

Political or social egalitarianism was thrown back into the faces of presumed dissidents from early Tudor times. Such frankness seems incompatible with imagining the ruling ideology as a matter of covert conspiracy or self-deluded imprisonment by their own ideological straitjackets — on the part of the rulers — or of misrecognition — on the part of the ruled. Far from being repressed or made unthinkable by that ruling ideology of hierarchy and Christian charity, egalitarian principles seem to be used by the rulers as bogeymen, which they assume are capable of frightening away the masses themselves. Such principles are openly restated, almost with sympathetic understanding, in virtually the same breath as virulent but confident denials that society or the church can be organized any way but hierarchically. In such a manner Bishop Bancroft's *Sermon Preached at Paule's Crosse* (London, 1588), directed against "sectaries and schismatics," including "Anabaptists," and "the Family of Love," argues the fallaciousness of ministerial equality by appeal to the fallaciousness of social equality.

Even as though one should say unto you my brethren of the poorer sort: these gentlemen and wealthier sort of the laity do greatly abuse you: the children of God (you know) are heirs of the world, and these things which the wicked have they enjoy by usurpation. . . . You have an equal portion with the best in the kingdom of God: and will you suffer this unequal distribution of these wordly benefits? Consider how in the Apostles' time the faithful had all things common. They came and laid their goods at the Apostles' feet, and division was therof made according to every man's necessity. You can not but groan under the heavy burden which is laid upon you. Your landlords do wring and grind your faces for the maintenance of their pride in apparel, their excess in diet, their unnecessary pleasures, as gaming, keeping of hawks and dogs, and such like vanities. They enhance your rents, they take great fines, and do keep you in very unchristian slavery and bondage. Why do you not seek for your better release to renew the use which was in the Apostles' times? . . .

Now dearly beloved unto you of all sorts, but especially to you of the richest, I pray you tell me how you like this doctrine. Do you think it is true or meet to be taught? No surely it is not. The whole manner therof is wholly Anabaptistical, and tendeth to the overthrow of all good rule and government.[73]

Though they refute it, the bishops of the Anglican Church seem to have had no problem raising the specter of social egalitarianism. In 1589, Thomas Cooper, in *An Admonition to the People of England*, arguing against "Martin the libeler" and others who would deprive bishops and ministers of their livings and lands, asserts: "At the beginning, (say they), when God had first made the world, all men were alike, there was no principality, there was no bondage or villeinage: that grew afterwards by violence and cruelty. Therefore, why should we live in this miserable slavery under these proud lords and crafty lawyers?" [74] How *are* we to understand these cases where, according to Annabel Patterson, "the system itself records the protests against it" (*Shakespeare and the Popular Voice*, 138)? Patterson argues that in these instances of "reported speech" (she cites the example from Bishop Cooper, ibid., 41–42), the popular voice speaks through "the ventriloquist." Although the authorial voice rehearses these "ethical and pathetic claims" only "in order to refute them," they have a "force" that "linger[s] beyond his powers of persuasion" (ibid., 42).

Now certainly one very likely audience of Bancroft's sermon was the rich, and even the moderately well off, who were encouraged to distribute a little in order not to lose a lot. But, it is probable that a socially varied audience, including the London populace, frequented Paul's Cross; that audience is described by various Reformation contemporaries as "huge," numbering "many thousands of souls." Is it likely that such dire accusations about injustice and oppression would have been made before a popular crowd if the speaker really expected his listeners would reaffirm their sense of being oppressed? Such "reported speech" as Bancroft uses does not seem to have been meant *only* for the ears "of the richest" sort, or even those of the economically comfortable.[75] That is, the "reported speech" of the oppressed—if theirs—seems not simply to have been rhetorically presented—as if it had been overheard by spies—as a warning to the better-off about threats to them from below. The very way in which such texts as these attempt to contain popular "discontentation" (see note 74) suggests confidence that the notion of "all things in common" will be quite unappealing to more than simply the very privileged. Anabaptism seems to have been a successfully stigmatized bogeyman. Bancroft's method of divide and conquer, that is, his allegations that the sectarian laity wants everything for itself and the sectarian ministry wants everything for itself, that they're both using doctrine as a cover for greed, might well have been convincing, especially given the notorious Münster reign of terror; if there was quiet Anabaptist communalism, it got less press.[76]

Statements such as Bancroft's do not necessarily narrowly serve the privileged nor repeat complaints exclusive to refuted or subversive popular complainers. Common discourse could address "need," even if that need was class-based. The relationship between governors and governed, as Theodore B. Leinwand has suggested, might best be understood in terms of negotiation. The rulings of the central government, after all, had to be carried out by local administrators, and they had to adjust their activities according to their sense of "how much pressure [their neighbors and the nation], or they themselves, could bear."[77] The fact that society was "surprisingly stable," even though "patriarchalism" and "the ideology of the rule of law," without a police force, "rested . . . on [nothing] more than persuasion and propaganda" suggests that "the elite's desire for order metamorphoses into the people's desire to avoid disorder."[78] As these examples from Bancroft and Cooper suggest, the pressure of Christian spiritual egalitarianism is strong. But it is not only the very privileged who feel that "superiority" is necessary to avoid chaos, nor only the deprived who understand that good stewardship is the remedy for the "wring[ing]" and "grind[ing]" of the "faces" of the poor.[79] Thus the claims of the exploited are not simply rehearsed to be refuted; even Bancroft says: "These great possessions, lands, and revenues, which the richer sort have in their hands, do (as you see), make them very proud, choke their zeal, hinder them in their virtuous proceedings, and will in deed (if order not be taken) mar and undo them."[80]

It seems plausible, as several social historians suggest, that rich and poor, governors and governed, shared a cultural system of values and ways of explaining hard times such as dearth—a system grounded in the ideals of a paternalistic Christian tradition.[81] "One function of the paternalism explicit in Elizabethan grain policies, for example, was to persuade poor consumers that the government shared their view of the social order and identified the same enemies of the common weal as they did: middlemen above all."[82] Such interpretations provided "both an explanation of the causes of dearth satisfactory to all save the marginal middleman and a guide to the remedial action appropriate to each section of the community. . . . [They] emphasized the dependence of the poor upon powerful social superiors and . . . obliged the powerful to act in the enforcement of regulative measures."[83] Such paternalist measures, historians suggest, were widely, "consistently and conscientiously" enforced, may have saved some from death by starvation, and were crucial to social harmony and the encouragement of deference.[84] The Book of Orders, for example, "was a fairly efficient instrument for redistributing available food supplies; it struck hard at . . . those symptoms of food shortage . . . which often exacerbated serious situations."[85] Attempts to exhort the benevolence of wealthier superiors, via their fasting, for another example, were seriously undertaken with orders widely implemented; city treasurers took great care in distributing monies raised by private benevolence (Archer, *Pursuit of Stability*, 199). Even when price riots occurred in London, they were not "particularly threatening" because of the very fact that they appealed to "values which were shared to some extent by the elite in actions designed to remind the magistrates of their duties" (ibid., 6). It is these shared systems, then, stressing the sufferings of the poor and the obligations of the rich, that permitted those below to put pressure on those above during economic hard times, or when those above defaulted or were perceived to have defaulted on customary obligations. Although "secular-minded twentieth-century historians" are "apt to downplay" the idea that "wealth was held in stewardship," such ideas did influence the behavior of the London oligarchy, according to Ian Archer's study, sufficiently so that "there was no generalised disillusionment with the elite" (57, 56). Similarly, while "the operation of the poor law in the later sixteenth century . . . emphasise[d] the dependence of the poorer members of the community on the wealthy," who could thereby shape their behavior, "the poor could themselves," within limits, "attempt to manipulate the ideal of community and the obligations it imposed on the wealthy" (96, 99).

John Pound credits public poor relief itself with contributing sufficiently to the containment of poverty in normal circumstances that "to say that [it] created a dangerous national situation would be to strain the evidence" (*Poverty and Vagrancy*, 85); Beier says the poor-relief system contributed "to England's long-term social stability compared with other states."[86] Nevertheless, there seems to be some uncertainty in gauging the effectiveness of poor rates in the country as a whole, and, consequently, some uncertainty in gauging their impact on the poor's perception of the stewardship of their superiors. Perhaps rural areas fared better than towns and cities, especially in normal circumstances.[87] Perhaps there was some particular measure of success in those towns whose earlier local initiatives were the model for national legislation.[88] According to Pound, for example, the town of Norwich "provided visible evidence of the success of more humane methods of poor relief"—that is public taxation—at least for a while (*Poverty and Vagrancy*, 57).

Virtually everbody above the status of wage-earner was a contributor. . . .
Most people paid small amounts, almost two-thirds contributing twopence
or less. In contrast, all the city aldermen had to pay one shilling a week
and the Bishop of Norwich was one of the few assessed at the maximum
amount. . . . Throughout most of the 1570s some 950 people were providing support for about 300 regular 'pensioners'. By 1574–5 the annual
receipts for poor relief exceeded £530 and they continued to be above £500
for the rest of the decade. The Norwich chamberlains (financial officials)
received less than this for normal city business, a fair indication of how
seriously the problem of the poor was regarded. (Ibid., 63, 64)[89]

In addition to public poor relief, there was a massive amount of private charity in the form of endowments and trusts, which may have
been a response to exhortations from the pulpit. Subsequent historians
have not been quite as overwhelmed as W. K. Jordan with the extraordinary private beneficence of Reformation Englishmen (because,
unlike him, they have tried to take inflation and the growing numbers
of the poor into account). Yet, though noting the limitations of Jordan's
assessments, Pound concludes:

It is undeniable that the role of private charity in relieving the poor, and
not only in relieving them but in preventing others from sliding into the
same abyss, was paramount in Tudor England. Without the generosity of
the merchant class and, to a lesser extent, other groups in society, Tudor
governments would have found the problem of poor relief far more oner-
ous than in fact it was, and the burden may well have become insupport-
able. (*Poverty and Vagrancy*, 76)

Even Ian Archer, though more critical and statistically sophisticated,
concludes "the scale of the achievement is sufficient to put to flight
Jordan's more pessimistic critics" (*Pursuit of Stability*, 178).[90] It is not possible to even approximately quantify the additional charity dispensed
during the lifetimes of benefactors; in particular parishes for which
there are good documents such as Westminster, such eminences as
Lord Treasurer Burghley are regularly recorded as giving large sums
(ibid., 178–80).

In spite of all of these sources of charity and some positive assessments of their effects and scale, more recent writers, namely Archer
and Slack, specifying about the same percentage of the publicly relieved as their more optimistic historian predecessors (that is, generally

4–5 percent of the population of towns, up to 7 percent in London), do emphasize the *ultimately* marginal nature of both public and private relief.[91] Slack indicates that "the amount raised by poor rates was much smaller" than "the total yield of endowed charities for poor-relief," which itself "amounted to less than 0.25 per cent of the national income."[92] Archer, writing about a large city in a decade of crisis, and warning that it is extremely difficult to gauge actual relief in relation to need, concludes that public poor relief was marginal help, only an "income supplement" to the impotent London poor, while the "under-employed households on the margins of subsistence received only extraordinary relief" (*Pursuit of Stability,* 195, 197). In fact, when there was a great drain on resources by increasing numbers of poor, even large private benevolence had little impact. Much poverty went unrelieved, then, "both because resources were maldistributed, and because the scale of the challenge, particularly in crisis years like the mid 1590s ultimately proved too much for the authorities." Yet, even Archer's conservative evaluation of poor relief and charity suggests it at least worked to promote stability in London—and even in an era of crisis. "The social fabric held in the 1590s in spite of the tensions" (203). And Slack remarks that "in crisis years public measures . . . control of markets, subsidised sales of grain, and increases in outdoor relief" probably had a greater effect than the poor-rate and at least "save[d] some people from starvation, especially in towns."[93]

Especially when the strains were not too great, then, such paternalistic ideology and practice as we have been surveying contributed to social harmony—if most probably of a minimally "satisficing" kind—a harmony which, after all, *most* people might have preferred to disorder.[94] When the strains became too great, or risks were diminished for whatever reasons, this very same cultural system with its strong Christian stress on the godliness of the suffering poor and the obligations of the rich could be among the factors leading to riot—which, in the case of dearth, at least, "were invariably successful in stimulating authoritative action."[95] In short, the kinds of things a Bancroft or Cooper says restate *recognized* grievances of the poor (the more strongly, perhaps, the more strained their situation), but always in a controlling paternalistic framework.

Let us look a little further at that double burden. Robert Wilkinson, preaching after the Midlands Rising of 1607, does indeed "read the lesson of the moral economy" as Patterson says; "the land-lord [should] not . . . rack, but so to rate his tenant that he may live, *not miserably.*"[96] Yet Patterson, in omitting the words that immediately follow, omits the controlling fully hierarchical and paternalistic framework that makes this passage less like one in which the popular voice speaks in its presumed special language and more like many other authoritative ones in which the mutual contract between rich and poor is rehearsed: "but as themselves live plentifully under God, so they sufficiently and contentedly under them." Wilkinson evenly deals with the "Rebellion of the many" and the "Oppression of the mighty," suggesting that to patiently bear oppression at the hands of persecuting "depopulators" is to gain an opportunity for an "honor God . . . offer[s] to us," namely, martyrdom.[97] To take another example: Charles Richardson, in his *Sermon against Oppression and Fraudulent Dealing* (London, 1615), frankly states, "There is oppression in the Church, and in the common-wealth"; he speaks of the sins of cruel landlords and of the hardships of the "oppressed tenant, that riseth early, and goeth late to bed, doth eat the bread of carefulness, and sitteth with many an hungry meal, his poor children . . . crying for food, and all to bring a full diet to his landlord's table." Yet even when he adds "as if these men were slaves and servants"—beginning to sound the note of Christian equality—he does *not* say, 'and not brothers,' but "and not sons."[98]

In the Reformation, apparent radicalism, for example, lament for an age when all things were "in common hold," can coexist with an entirely traditional Christian stress on patient poverty, as it does indeed, even in Arthur Warren's in other ways "demystifying" poem.

> Nature, that first gave life, decreed a law,
> That mortals earth's-fruits should in common hold,
> When time's corruption private profit saw,
> Things gratis given must be bought and sold,
> > And then division strived for a store,
> > To mar what golden age had made before.
> (*The Poore Man's Passions,* C2v)

This does seem a reference to a legendary Ovidian utopia, as opposed to anything more specific or pragmatic, in a poem in which the narrator also seeks refuge among Spenserian savage creatures (including "sylvan satyrs") who are much kinder than men (C2v–C3v). Furthermore, in spite of its partial demystification of the usual Christian view of the relation between "Dives and Lazarus," Warren's poem ends on a pastoral note of pilgrim's contentment:

Come staff, and manage mine unhappy hand,
Scrip, guard my shoulders, burthen light to bear,
Three merry mates we gainst the sun will stand,
Solace to see, that comforts none can hear,
>The lighter purse, the less the cares are found,
>Hark, while I whistle to the winds around.

(E3v)

There is no threat of sedition in this complaint; in fact, Warren seems to blast Catholic "sedition-sowers" or "rabbles of irreligion" who want to be celebrated after their deaths and perhaps have masses sung for them—as in the chantries of old—or want to be delivered posthumously from purgatory.[99] The full title of his 1605 book is *The Poore Man's Passions and Povertie's Patience,* and the latter poem ends most traditionally with "Virtue join[ed] hand in hand with poverty," and the assertion that "we in heaven shall be resident, / To reap the fruits of patience and content" (K1v)—in short, with the poor who are compensated for their suffering by not having to pass through the eye of the needle.

There are other odd bedfellows as well in Reformation beliefs and practices concerning the poor—especially from a modern perspective. Regulation and relief, discrimination against the undeserving and generosity to the deserving coexist. The result of Thomas Cartwright's help with the reformation of poor relief in Warwick in the 1580s was both more rigor in the giving of relief and significantly more help to those deemed worthy.[100] Advocacy of the use of terror and of stigmatization of the poor can coexist with Christian forbearance and spiritual egalitarianism. The *Ease for Overseers* speaks of those terrorizing examples and suggests "the poor of all others are most untractable" ("the poor are by nature much inclined to idleness"), yet this administrative handbook also emphasizes, in the accompanying "Prospect for Rich Men to Induce Them to Give to the Poor" "our being all by birth no better than another" with reference to our "carnal nativity" or original sin, and our being all "brothers in Christ" with reference to our "spiritual nativity."[101] It also urges that overseers not "tyrannize" over the poor: "whom God doth punish with poverty, let no man seek to oppress with cruelty."[102] Finally, it would appear to try to put turning the other cheek into practice in order to keep the peace; although those poor are "most untractable," an officer "must sometime consider what the wise man saith, *It is the glory of a man to pass by an offense:* and let it suffice that God doth punish them with poverty, though man doth not always cross them with severity." [103] Indeed, the Protestant system of values had its own "demystifications" of power, privilege, and self-interest. Thomas Cooper, in *The Art of Giving*, "questioned the appropriateness of providing Christmas entertainment as a way of compensating for neglect of the poor during the rest of the year, a habit that had developed 'among great ones generally, that so they keep jolly rout and riot at that time, they privilege themselves from further hospitality.' " [104] John Downame calls those alms "abominable" which come "out of those goods which are gotten by oppressing the poor": "As is the practice of those cruel, yet vainglorious land-lords, who rack their poor tenants the whole year, and in the twelve days only keep open house, and feast them with some small part of that which is their own" (66–67). Some might perhaps wish to see this as the subversion that guarantees the containment encouraged by the politics of mirth, but one's head spins!

Insofar as fixed-rate poor relief *was* only marginally effective, private benevolence, especially in times of crisis, was that much more crucial; the Protestant minister's exhortations were at least on occasion more compassionate than state policy. Religious writers such as Robert Allen and preachers such as Henry Smith didn't reason the need of even the "idle" poor too much: " '[L]et their bad deeds fall on their own necks, for if they perish for want, we are in danger of God's wrath for them.' " [105] Christopher Hooke in a 1603 sermon sympathetically perceived that there were *laboring* poor who "in this time wanteth work, and therefore wanteth food for [them] and [their] famil[ies] . . . for the sickness thus still continuing, and the winter . . . hard approaching, and none or little work . . . stirring." [106] Perhaps in tune with such empathy, Gloucester knowingly gives to a beggar, one who "has some reason" or "could not beg" (4.1.31)—that is, one who is sane enough to beg, *or* one who has reasons to beg—and therefore whose needs should not be reasoned.

Indeed, no mechanical giving will do. Alms must arise from our love toward God says Downame, and then from our love toward our neighbors. The need for that very heartfelt *empathy* is an entirely traditional Protestant point, almost as passionately urged by ministers as by the language of the play.

The blessed man's bounty in the outward action of the hand, must spring from the inward mercy and compassion of his heart; so that it is not enough to relieve the necessities of the poor, but like a member of the same body, he must do it with a sense and feeling of their misery and penury, as though he suffered together with them. . . . And surely then alone these works of mercy are rightly and throughly performed, when as the outward work proceedeth from the inward habit. . . . Then do we touch these sores of poverty with the softest hand, when as our selves have a feeling of them. (50, 52)

One hardly needs to look as far afield as the Leveller William Walwyn to find sentiments parallel with Lear's compassion for "poor naked wretches."[107]

Whatever the limits of Reformation Protestant social thought, it supplies the moral frame of *King Lear*. Like Arthur Warren, who, finally, seems to be asking for alms at the rich man's gates, for the "crumb[s]," from those who have "choice of cates" ([*Poor Man's Passions*, E2v]), for the "superfluous things" (C2) that could be spared, more than for egalitarian leveling, Shakespeare still views "social inequality from the traditional perspective of Christian charity, with its ideal of an organic, hierarchical state in which all are linked together in brotherly love. The remedy for the sufferings of the poor is that the rich should treat them better, not that they should demand redress of their own initiative."[108] If we still hear, as perhaps some very few members of Shakespeare's audience did, some faint echo of "communalism" in that "distribution" that shall "undo excess," it may well be because Christianity's "distribution" and Marxist redistribution are both concerned to produce a more just society. Some of the paternalistic ideas of the Tudor state having to do with the just price and intervention in the market to avoid middlemen share with Marxism roots in Christian thought.

Robes and Furr'd Gowns Hide All: Mock Trials

and Assaults on Justice

Many critics, recent and not so recent, have commented on the "radicalism" of both the mock-trial scene omitted in the Folio (Q, 3.6.1729–55) and Lear's extended assault on justice, "the great image of authority" (in the Folio, 4.6.2595–615).[1]

Paul Delany, speaking of Lear's powerful meditation in 4.6, argues that "in his second great mad scene Lear progresses to a much more radical critique of the social hierarchy" than he gave in his "poor naked wretches" speech in 3.4.[2] Charles Hobday notes the continuity of egalitarian traditions and of hostility to law, lawyers, and judges from the Peasants' Rebellion in 1381 to the English Revolution and suggests that "Lear's ravings often come near to the thought of the egalitarians." "In his reflections on the theme that big thieves hang little thieves," Lear's sentiments are "precisely similar [to those] expressed in [a] Leveller pamphlet."[3] Christopher Hill, quoting Lear's assault on justice, comments: "[S]ometimes Lear himself gave forcible expression to the lower-class point of view."[4] Walter Cohen connects "handy-dandy, which is the justice, which is the thief" with "similar perceptions . . . commonplace among the Levellers and Diggers." "Winstanley perhaps went furthest in placing the blame on private property, which was obtained 'by murther and theft,' and relatedly, on commodity exchange, which 'makes great murderers and thieves to be imprisoners, and hangers of little ones'" (Drama, 354).[5] Cohen links Lear on "the economics of justice" ("'The usurer hangs the cozener . . . . Plate sin with gold, / And the strong lance of justice hurtless breaks; / Arm it in rags, a pigmy's straw does pierce it'") with Winstanley's question: "'[H]ath not Parliaments . . . made laws . . . to strengthen the rich and the strong, . . . and left oppression upon the backs of the oppressed still?'" (ibid.).[6]

Since the "mock trial" scene of Q 3.6 is omitted in the Folio (where, however, Lear's assault on justice is longer than it is in the Quarto), the "radicalism" of the scenes is also an issue in the discussion of the

reasons for the differences in the texts of *King Lear*. Could political censorship — actual or self-imposed — explain the Folio omission? And how
so, if the assault on justice not only remains but is extended? Gary Taylor concludes that "the Folio's omission of the trial . . . cannot plausibly
be attributed to objections made by the Master of the Revels to the
scene as it stood in Q." [7]

In the mad trial itself, most of what has been omitted in the Folio contains
no political or social comment whatsoever; aside from 'corruption in the
place, / False Justicer why hast thou let her scape[?],'. . . nothing directly
alludes to any fallibility in the legal system. . . . The Duke of Cornwall's
violent abuse of justice, in the very next scene, dramatizes a much more
damning and objectionable instance of political 'legality' at work than anything even hinted in 3.6 — and both texts contain that scene.[8]

Taylor notes the many contemporary plays — including others by
Shakespeare — that satirize justices, and also notes that "those who suggest that 3.6.17–56 suffered from censorship have been able to provide
no examples of political interference in scenes or passages of a similar
nature." In agreement with Roger Warren, he plausibly suggests that
the scene in the Folio is actually much more intense than the "mock
trial"; 4.6 "directly and explicitly formulates the criticism of legal institutions only, at most, implicit" in 3.6. For Taylor, "If the censor had
objected to 3.6, he would have been furious about what apparently replaced it." [9]

   Annabel Patterson, on the other hand, argues that Taylor's arguments are "throughout framed by a premise typical of New Criticism,
that the greater the artist, the less likely he was to have chosen to
deal with the topical and hence to have given the censor any concern."
Against Taylor, Patterson insists it is wrong to conclude that the mock
trial scene was *not* "a major critique of Jacobean justice, [and] that it
did *not* demonstrate dramatically 'that the economically and politically
powerless, deprived of any resort to real justice, must content themselves with fantasies of legal retribution.' " [10]

   Thus, the issue of the "radicalism" of these scenes needs further investigation because that "radicalism" is already deeply embedded in
arguments about censorship, which in turn are deeply embedded in
arguments about the authority of the Quarto and Folio texts of *Lear*.
For these reasons, and because the political criticism mentioned links
these scenes exclusively to radical revolutionary insights, their motifs

and specific language need to be further examined in a wider cultural framework.

The Mock Trial: "Corruption in the Place! / False Justicer, Why Hast Thou Let Her 'Scape?"

In the brief mock trial in *Lear*, his daughters, perhaps clothed in "furr'd gowns," are brought to the bar and tried in the imagination of the mad king. Traditional scenes of the trial of Lady Lucre or Lady Meed and allegories setting Lowliness against Pride resonate behind the mock trial—part of the semiotics of "gorgeous apparel" in the play. The theme of judicial corruption itself—dramatically enacted (in Lear's mind) by the "corrupted" and abruptly abrogated trial in Q 3.6 and meditated on in F 4.6—appears, often in connection with failed trials of one sort or another, in medieval and later dream visions, Tudor morality plays, and Tudor tracts.

There is a long-standing tradition of satirizing veniality, personified as Lady Meed—who is indeed put on trial in Langland's *Piers the Plowman*—and her offspring or sisters. These figures resemble the sumptuously clothed Regan and Goneril put on trial in Q 3.6—a resemblance underscored by the persistent theme of lavish, excessive, or voluminous, sometimes many-folded or "plighted" (pleated) garments, which may hide "cunning" (1.1.282), as opposed to plain, sufficient, and in a sense, guileless clothing. Failures of justice and abruptly abrogated trials also occur in some of the works satirizing Lady Meed or Lady Lucre.

" 'When all treasures are tested,' " Holy Church says in *Piers the Plowman*, "Truth is the best."[11] Lady Meed (or Lady Lucre in some translations), accordingly, is a personification of Treasure, put on trial in passus 2–4. She was about to wed Fraud, but Theology stopped the proceedings, saying that God "intended her for Honest Work" (book 2, 79), since, as reward ("the labourer is worthy of his hire"), meed may be lawful and necessary.[12] The case is taken to Westminster and put before the king, who decides to pardon Lady Meed, provided she will marry his knight Conscience. However, Conscience refuses to marry her, the implication being that she inevitably corrupts. Conscience makes a distinction between the "gift of Heaven which God . . . gives to those who do their work well on earth," and the "lucre without measure, which men in authority grasp at—the bribes they get for supporting evil-doers" (book 3, 89).[13] Langland's Meed is a "fusion of the Whore of Babylon and *Richesse* of the *Roman de la Rose,* Saint John's oriental vision of evil reclothed in courtly medieval splendor."[14] Lady Meed or Lucre's robe "was trimmed with the finest fur in the land. She was crowned with a coronet like a queen's and her fingers were prettily adorned with gold filigree rings. . . . Her dress was gorgeously coloured with rich scarlet dye, set off with bands of bright gold lace studded with gems" (book 2, 76).[15]

Lucre's progeny include the figure "Mede" in a satirical poem of the fifteenth century called "Mede and Muche Thanke" which opposes two men, one clothed in gaudy green, gaily embroidered, the other meanly clothed. Like the disguised Kent, the meanly clad man has done faithful service to his lord, in danger wielding lance and spear, for which he gets only "much thanks"; like the "smiling rogue[]" Oswald (2.2.73), the well-dressed man flatters his lord, for which he grows rich with "Mede."[16] Other relatives are "Sir Nummus" (i.e., money) in Edward Hake's *Newes out of Poule's Churchyarde* (1579), and "Covetousness" in Richard Barnfield's "The Combat, between Conscience and Covetousnesse in the Minde of Man" (1598). Hake's poem is a series of satires (in plodding broken fourteeners) on corruption wrought by meed in various callings (including those of judges, lawyers, clerks, attorneys, merchants, and doctors), and a very traditional lament for the decline of hospitality:

So charity excluded is:
and love is kept aloof.
And right is wronged through reward,
as falleth still in proof;
And usury about the town
is maintained as a trade:
And equity to ease the wrong,
in matters dares not wade.[17]

Barnfield's poem is a dream vision debate or psychomachia. His Conscience, like "Muche thanke" is clothed plainly:

Conscience (me thought) appeared unto me,
Cloth'd with good deeds, with truth and honesty,
Her countenance demure, and sober sad,
Nor any other ornament she had.[18]

Covetousness, in contrast, is "clad in a cassock, like a usurer," and like Avarice in traditional representations, holds a bag of money in his hands from which he cannot take his eyes; his cassock is "made of poor men's skins," and indeed, furred. He boasts that everyone from Prince to simple countryman, including judge and lawyer, is his follower.[19]

Thus, in the brief mock trial in *Lear*, daughters who share traits with the offspring of Lady Meed are brought to the bar and tried as Lady Meed is tried—at least in the imagination of the mad king. And in the meditation of 4.6, justice fails because those luxurious and voluminous "robes and furr'd gowns hide all"—whether these are the robes and furred gowns of the justices themselves, which hide their taking of bribes, or the robes and furred gowns of the economically privileged, which hide their avarice, and which blind justice to their sins.

The themes and antinomies central to these scenes from *Lear*—especially the fallibility of justice, and the opposition of plain and sumptuous garb—are fully developed in a prose work by one F.T. whose long title is revealing: *The Debate betweene Pride and Lowlines, Pleaded to an Issue in Assise: And Howe a Jurie with Great Indifferencie Being Impannelled, and Redy to Have Geven Their Verdict, Were Straungely Intercepted* (1577?). In this work, the theme of the impossibility of earthly justice for the lowly "Cloth Breeches" who dared to strive against his betters and had a misplaced confidence in laws sounds very loudly—virtually unsoftened by any religious hope for heavenly justice. *Pride and Lowlines* shares with Barnfield's "Combat betweene Conscience and Covetousnesse" the defeat of the figure roughly parallel to the simply dressed Conscience.[20] *Pride and Lowlines* also shares with such late moralities as *The Three Ladies of London* (1590) and Thomas Lupton's *All for Money* (1578), the anatomy of earthly justice; it is impossible to find uncorrupted judges or uncorrupted jury members (or to impanel the latter—if they can be found—without hindrance from the "furr'd gowns"); "Lady Lucre" always has friends in high places.

Indeed, it is part of the way of the world in these works that Lady Lucre is immune to the processes of a justice all too willing to be corrupted by her. In *Piers the Plowman*, even after Lady Meed has been tried at Westminster and "branded as a whore by the greater part of the Court," "one of the jurors and a summoner still . . . eagerly" go after her (book 4, 98).[21] In *The Three Ladies of London*, the trial is in fact a type of heavenly judgment (the judge is no man, "Nemo," and the sentences include banishment to the outer darkness where there is gnashing of teeth); however, when the court Clerk asks Lady Lucre whether she pleads guilty or not to adultery with Mercatore (the merchant), robbery of Mercatore, and consenting to the murder of Hospitality, she replies in arrogant tones:

> Not guilty. Where are mine accusers? they may shame to show their
>   faces:
> I warrant you, none comes, nor dare, to discredit my name.[22]

Where everyone is guilty of collusion with Lady Lucre, no one dare accuse her, and she knows it. Goneril rather sounds like her descendant when, confronted by Albany with the evidence of her treachery, she contemptuously responds: "[T]he laws are mine, not thine; / Who can arraign me for't?" (5.3.159–60).[23] Her words echo the insolent tones of the morality play figure who knows how malleable law is because she knows that Lucre ultimately controls it.[24] The corrupted mock trial in *Lear* thus shares the general Christian theme of the imperfection of earthly justice with dream visions and morality plays not all that far removed from it in time.

In *Pride and Lowlines,* the analysis of justice itself depends on clothing metaphors that are developed in a dream vision debate between Cloth Breeches and Velvet Breeches as to who is trespassing on whose territory. They are both instructed:

> Declare and bring your title into light,
> Trespass or disseisin of frank tenement.[25]

Lawful possession of the "tenement" is a metaphor for regaining the position in England which Velvet Breeches, the more litigious of the two, accuses Cloth Breeches of usurping. The examination of a variety of men representing different estates or callings as possible jurors, and the apparent difficulty of impaneling the virtuous permits an analysis of the role that avarice plays in society. Velvet Breeches shows all the marks of conspicuous consumption: these breeches are paned, lined, embroidered with gold lace (A6r). Cloth Breeches, having none of these things—and rather presciently aware of the value of labor—charges Velvet Breeches with taking pride in something that is not his, that is, in the workmanship lavished on his breeches (A8r). Cloth Breeches seems to defend the "virtue is true nobility" tradition against the Italian-born Velvet Breeches. "Pride and vices are most commonly" tied to riches, and rich apparel does not amend or make more virtuous, but in fact only wastes goods, he says, in accordance with that by now very familiar zero-sum view of the good of the commonwealth (A8v). "The more is laid on thee, the more is lost" (ibid.). Velvet Breeches defends himself in a manner somewhat reminiscent of Lady Lucre and her progeny; he claims that he is "the original of laws" (B4v), that he sharpens correction, because money is involved in fines. But Cloth Breeches, like Conscience in *Piers the Plowman*, rejects the idea that all service is done for reward and disdains those who find honor in "arrogance of heart, / In silk and velvet, and in outward show" (B5v). He strongly identifies himself with the contented older generation as opposed to the insatiably avaricious younger generation, thus participating in the common (and maybe timeless) myth that morals, more than economic conditions, have declined—although his analysis of the possible partiality of prospective jurors is based on his understanding of their economic self-interest. In any event, the narrator, who has himself studied fifteen years toward the law, proposes, since "here ye dwellen in a land of peace / And under laws, and under Magistrate," that the case can be justly solved (B1r).

A variety of persons appear and are examined as potential jurors to decide the case between Cloth Breeches and Velvet Breeches. For example, a person comes by who seems to be a squire or knight, but, like Oswald in Kent's eyes, he is tailor-made, in fact, is a tailor. How can he be impartial? asks Cloth Breeches. He gets a lot more work from Velvet Breeches than from Cloth Breeches. On the other hand, when a very Chaucerian knight appears who "had a great deal rather for to see, / Then silk on back, good victuals on his board, / And spend his rent his hospitality" (D2r), Velvet objects:

> This knight was never friend of mine (quoth he),
>> So plain in his apparel and his port:
> The godly he doth more esteem than me,
>> And spend his living on the poorer sort.[26]
> (C8r)

Pride and Lowlines at times broaches issues that look far ahead as well; the husbandman says he's not fit to serve on the jury because he doesn't have a freehold of forty pounds, but Cloth Breeches says that lack of forty pounds is not the same as ignorance or insufficiency (C3v).

What is particularly intriguing is the upshot of the trial. Although, as F.T. says, the cause of Cloth Breeches was so good that "needly must he win: / And that the verdict must needs find his right" (F1r), nevertheless, events take a surprising turn, degenerating into a brawl in which Cloth Breeches is pulled apart with "extreme cruelty" (F1v), until he lies in pieces on the ground. Cloth Breeches's confidence in laws certainly seems to have been misplaced:

> Thou breech of cloth thou weed of lowliness,
> That hast not feared to maintain thy cause:
> Against this garment of such worthiness,
> And all of confidence thou hast in laws.
> (F1v)

He should perhaps have not told, in his defense,

> Such things as were not meet to been iknow
> And better had thou of them kept silence,
> Than tell them to thine utter overthrow.
> (F1v)

Thus he shall be "a memorial, / Of such as with their betters daren strive: / In cause never so just" (F4r). Although *Pride and Lowlines* ends with some words of consolation for Lowliness and suggests that lowliness or humility is necessary—for without it there is no peace (F2v)—and although the narrator asserts truisms about God's favor to the lowly and his making "the proud and haughty come behind" (G4r), the overwhelming impression the work creates is that earthly justice is totally partial. The text bristles with profound resentment of the arrogant rich, who gain their wealth through legacy or fraud. In this work, the hatred may have an anti-Catholic edge, for the narrator insists that God was not fooled by those "proud and haughty" ones, even though "with sacrifice, / And many a ceremony they him sought: / Which (as appeareth well) he did despise" (G4r):

> Shame ye not to make profession,
> Of sacrifice and of religion
> With solemn outward ceremony:
> Hypocrisy and mere derision,
> Where in the heart is not humility.
> (G4r–G4v)

Thus, the trials of Lady Meed or of Cloth Breeches versus Velvet Breeches are part of a widely available and long-standing Christian understanding of the limits of earthly justice and the role that Avarice plays in society. The semiotic system in which the mock trial participates does emphasize the failure of earthly justice; the machinery of justice is quickly abrogated (as it is in *Pride and Lowlines*), because of "corruption [that is, bribery] in the place"; "False justicer[s]" will let the guilty "scape" (3.6.55–56).[27] Ultimate justice appears to be impossible; the law belongs to Lucre, Pride, Velvet Breeches, just as Goneril says it belongs to her in 5.3. Such widely available and long-standing motifs, however — whatever their potential — are not always politically radical ones, held only by lower-class resenters of social superiors and "their" legal system, or tied to revolutionary fervor to catapult that legal system. Not infrequently faults are found at all social ranks in the literature in which these motifs appear (see notes 20 and 82). Hence critical arguments based on the presumed *exclusively* radical — even censorable — nature of such motifs are discredited by their actual wider provenance.

Furthermore, it is by no means clear that the mock trial is exploited in Shakespeare's scene only — or mainly — for legal or social protest, though certainly that is one obvious potential of any mock trial.

Actual Mock Trials and the Dramatic Context

Actual mock trials could be staged as a sort of "charivari" to give voice to tensions in a community. David Harris Sacks gives an example of such a topsy-turvy trial put on in Warwick in 1615. A person convicted of keeping an unlicensed alehouse met with others in such an establishment and set up a parody town court, pretending to summon some of the town's principal burgesses as members of a topsy-turvy jury because they were considered "sufficiently debauched and corrupt" to be impaneled. "Handy-dandy, which is the justice, which is the thief?" (4.6.153–54) indeed.[28] The issue seems to have been a conflict between the town Corporation, which wanted to impose "a strict social discipline," and those who viewed the suppression of the alehouse as the act of "self-serving hypocrites." Apparently this alehouse ridicule made the magistrates seek retribution involving "costly and terrifying proceedings before the Court of Star Chamber to punish their enemies."[29]

The popular ballad, "The Brickmakers' Lamentation from Newgate," appears to be about the fates of those who parody the law, and certainly suggests popular resentment of legal inequities. It rehearses how a brickmaker who steals his mate's bread and cheese is at first given benefit of clergy and merely branded on the hand; subsequently, however, he is tried for treason, hanged, but cut down right away by a mock court of brickmakers. (The plaintiff takes his oath on a brickbat and the jury are similarly sworn in.) The ballad says that some of these mockers were put in Newgate and fined one hundred pounds each (and perhaps this punishment is further parody of the law).[30]

Thus mock trials clearly could serve social protest against magistrate and legal system. However, they also could be nonpolitical bawdy and satiric fun. Mock arraignments were part of law students' Christmas revels at the Inns of Court—"when they set up miniature kingdoms and chose a monarch in direct imitation of the government at Whitehall."[31] In the 1597–98 revels of the ruling Prince d'Amour, for example, a "discontented lover" is "arraigned for bragging that he shifted his mistresses 'as often as he shifts his clothes,' for twisting his words into bawdy puns, and for writing three [ribald] poems."[32] Perhaps the comic possibilities of mock trials are of as much relevance for Q 3.6 as their roles as vehicles of social protest; and perhaps the comic/pathetic effects of Shakespeare's scene merit at least as much attention as its " 'fantasies of legal retribution' " (Patterson, *Censorship,* 62).

Gary Taylor asserts that "Shakespeare marshals his dramatic resources" in this scene "in order to signpost our emotional responses to Lear, rather than to communicate a vision of political reality" that would "challenge the entire social institution of the law." He suggests that the mock-trial scene provokes both laughter and pity, "wrench[ing] pathos from 'unsightly tricks,' snatching tragedy from the edge of risibility."[33] On the one hand, there is a kind of irrelevant and irreverent busyness in the Fool's foolishness. His taking of Goneril for "a join-stool" (3.6.52) allows him to use a "proverbial joke" that "depends upon a pretence of non-recognition" in order to play "a joke on the joke, by using it in a situation where the comic non-recognition is comically justifiable."[34] (In this situation, Goneril "is" a "join-stool.") Indeed, the joint-stool prop feels even less a mockery of justice than the brickbat the plaintiff and jury swear on in "The Brickmaker's Lamentation"; at least the brickbat suggests, in context, that "the rigours of the law are grossly disproportionate to the nature of the offence."[35] Furthermore, the idea of Goneril as a joint-stool comes across as an indictment of her coldness and inhumanity, rather than as a critique of the legal system *qua* system. Thus the Fool's foolish joke hints at his empathy with Lear—perhaps the Fool is humoring Lear by distracting him from his distraction—which further directs attention to the pathos of the king's situation. Moreover, to set up a special mixed "commission" as Lear appears to—a commission such as a king might set up (with justices from various courts) to handle a serious crime against the state—feels pathetically out of proportion to the charge that "[she] kick'd the poor king her father" (47–48).[36] Were it not a question of the royalty of the victim, certainly this would be an offense for a lesser tribunal; Lear's very self-pity and his distracted attempt to salve the personal grief caused by filial ingratitude by means of this grand fantasy of retribution suggest that he is even more aware of the kicked father than of the kicked king. The effect once again is pathos; whatever else we take the mock trial scene as, we cannot help but take it as further evidence of Lear's *personal* anguish. Although the miscarriage of justice is unquestionably a theme that links 3.6 with numerous representations of the corruptions of justice and the general failure of earthly law, it is Lear's individual helplessness, even more than the failings of justice at large, that is foregrounded.

True Local versus False Universal Readings?

As we saw in chapter 5, Leah Marcus, like Annabel Patterson, hears in *Lear* "particularized materials which can easily be interpreted as criticism of King James I" (*Puzzling Shakespeare*, 149). For Marcus, it is particularly "the mock trial in the hovel," "the most flamboyant difference between the quarto and the folio *King Lears*"—a scene "full of pregnant references to issues of royal prerogative" (150)—that seems to make the "1608 quarto version . . . richer in topical details" (149). Marcus's claim will be discussed shortly, but first let us consider more generally the postmodern historicist valorization of contingent meanings.

As Marcus herself suggests in "Localization," the first chapter of *Puzzling Shakespeare*, "as part of our assimilation of poststructuralism and postmodernism, we have developed an appetite for dissonance, for an art which is multicentric, shifting, provisional, implicated in other things" (32). Her own "local reading," as she indicates, has affinities to poststructuralist criticism including British cultural materialism and American new historicism; like them it finds humanist values (30) "more deadening than invigorating" and the notion of "Shakespeare as a symbol for the transcendence and permanance of art . . . confining" (31). Such criticism wants to throw off the Shakespeare for All Time—in the case of British cultural materialism, particularly because he has been enlisted in the cause of conservative politics; it emphasizes the impossibility of "universal" or "transcendent" meanings. In their place, these critics may put "dominant ideologies" and "radical countertendencies" (Dollimore, *Political Shakespeare*, 3), and/or meanings that "may well be multiple or self-cancelling, or both" (*Puzzling Shakespeare*, 37–38). "Topical reading," which Marcus wishes to encourage, "in its very indefiniteness and provisionality . . . cuts across closed, static explanatory systems and closed cultural forms, opening them to the vagaries of historical process" (ibid., 37).[37]

I would like to suggest that the very dichotomy between a proliferation of provisional readings and those "false" fixed "universal" or "transcendent ones"—may sometimes itself be false—and a dichotomy that encourages scanting the *historical* relationship between "local readings" and cultural patterns and values that have a wider than local existence. We have seen how culturally available antinomies such as "excessive adornment" and "appropriate plainness" encode shared values held by a variety of parties within a larger culture, yet may be variously used with different referents and different opposed concepts in mind. For the author of *Pride and Lowlines,* it is the avaricious and ceremonious (and possibly Catholic) rich dressed in velvet who are opposed to the godly and humble poor dressed in cloth. For Robert Greene, on the other hand, who borrows Velvet Breeches and Cloth Breeches for *A Quip for an Upstart Courtier; or, A Quaint Dispute between Velvet Breeches and Cloth-breeches* (1592), the "foreign" usurper concerned with outward show as opposed to inner worth is opposed to the plain true-born Englishman of *almost any rank.* The former "is an upstart come out of Italy, begot of Pride, nursed up by self love, and brought into this country by his companion Newfangledness: . . . a raiser of rents, and an enemy to the commonwealth"; the latter "hath scarce a gown faced [with fur] once in his life," and "hath been *in diebus illis* a companion to kings, an equal with the nobility, a friend to gentlemen and yeomen, and patron of the poor, a true subject, a good housekeeper."[38]

Such broadly shared antinomies and themes—found in the common Christian culture of the sixteenth and seventeenth centuries—are also "historical" as well as "political," that is, capable of being employed by conformist and nonconformist, even Catholic and Protestant for their own purposes in specific situations, as we've seen in earlier chapters. It is by exploring, where possible and plausible, the way in which relatively long-lasting cultural themes—such as the opposition between the gaudily opulent and the appropriately plain, between the Whore of Babylon, or Lady Lucre, and Conscience—get refashioned for and by more or less "local" readers or opposing sides that we can avoid the sometimes meaningless dichotomy of the mystically transcendent and the narrowly particular and shifting (as well as the difficulties entailed in each of *those* possibilities).

All of this is not to say that censorship (or self-censorship) and the evocation of subversive and/or very topically specific political resonances are not possible—in sufficiently volatile particular political situations. Such resonances might even be based on words or passages not normally considered incendiary or seen as targeting existing institutions. As R. Malcolm Smuts says, recent scholars "are certainly correct to insist that early Stuart literature often did have a veiled political significance and not infrequently contained criticism of the royal court," and "Patterson is also correct in arguing that the censorship imposed on writers the need to convey their messages in indirect ways and that readers understood this fact and became adept at finding hidden meanings." However, as Smuts also says, "the problem is that it is generally impossible to determine whether the hidden meanings discovered by a modern critic were intended by the author or recognizable to a seventeenth-century audience."[39] The theoretical understanding of the nature of the "hidden" that forms the basis of some postmodern historical arguments also tends to preclude the relevance of "proof." Nevertheless, at the least (unless the critic in question is claiming only that "anything is possible"), the reader needs to evaluate the evidence adduced and the argument made. Has some particular issue convincingly been shown to receive an unusual weighting? Has some phrase or reference convincingly been shown to be linked elsewhere in the culture with issues pertinent to the proposed reading? Narrowly particular readings are not better than unconvincingly "universal" readings if they themselves are not fully convincing.

To come back to Marcus's argument, then. She makes the specific case that in the mock-trial scene "the wronged king attempts to create a commission of judges very much like a Chancery commission to pronounce on the justice of his daughters' behavior" (*Puzzling Shakespeare*,

150). That aspect of the play's "Stuart referentiality" (151) is important because "by 1606, Chancery had already demonstrated its receptivity to James's ideas about absolutism." Furthermore, she states, by "1608, when the quarto *King Lear* was published, the case of the Post Nati had been tried in the Court of Chancery and the Lord Chancellor himself had issued a lengthy opinion on the Post Nati's right to citizenship on the basis of civil law and equity" (150). Thus, most importantly for our discussion, the arraignment of Lear's daughters is, for Marcus, "a mad-man's eerie echo of James I's actual tactics . . . for attempting to work his will upon recalcitrant subjects" (151).

To begin with, Marcus's positing of King Lear as a stand-in for the oppressor (in contrast to Patterson's view of him as a stand-in for the victims of oppression) does not sit comfortably with the emphasis on Lear's personal anguish and helplessness in the scene—which clearly invites our empathy. Were Lear still powerful and not pathetic, as king he would be able to summon an actual mixed bench—such as may be alluded to in 3.6—appropriate for "examinations . . . of . . . persons thought to be connected with crimes of public importance," when the Privy Council "was reinforced by some of the more outstanding . . . members of the judiciary."[40] Lear seeks redress of injustice by sum-moning an imaginary court; it fails to serve justice, takes bribes, and lets the accused escape ("Stop her there! / . . . Corruption in the place! / False justicer, why hast thou let her scape?" [3.6.54-55]). Would not a topical reading opposed to James's handling of the issue of Scottish naturalization require some dramatic parallel to a *mishandling* of justice *on the part of the king?*

Lear does clearly create a special commission of judges, and as such seems to be summoning a prerogative court. Even if we do put aside our feeling that the plaintiff Lear makes an unlikely oppressor, can we assume that an oblique reference to such a court—whether specifically Chancery or not—*necessarily* implicates a king's "arbitrary" justice in 1606?[41] Were kingly prerogative and rule by law already so saliently and unmistakably opposed in the minds of playgoers? We need not postu-late a harmonious unity among Englishmen on constitutional matters in order to suggest that these issues had perhaps not yet come to the definitive test. Even were such issues generally salient, were they suf-ficiently connected to the case of the Post Nati and to James's stance there to warrant reading a scene in which a king convenes a court in terms of that particular case?

For years English monarchs had resorted to the law to legitimate their doings, thus giving the law a certain preeminence; reciprocally, legislators had legally defined the monarch's prerogative, thus giving regal power a certain preeminence. Law defined when the king could be extralegal.[42] As Johann Sommerville says, "[T]he idea that the royal prerogative was derived from and limited by law was orthodox among Tudor lawyers" and "Tudor monarchs themselves acccepted legal limitations upon their powers in practice, whatever high views of their authority they may have held in theory" (Sommerville, *Politics and Ideology*, 103). In 1615, the jurist William Camden described " 'a certain right of Majesty, called royal prerogative which is not subject to the laws nor yet repugnant to the laws, as the learned in the law have judged.' " [43] Furthermore, "equity," for some jurists, and perhaps for some of the "popular sort" (no lovers of lawyers) as well, may have been thought a useful counterweight to correct the rigor of the common law.[44] Samuel Daniel, in his outspoken, albeit tactful, 1603 verse epistle to Ellesmere, the lord chancellor, certainly regards equity as a hoped-for corrective to the obscurity and harshness of the common law — which is very far from law as it ought to be:

> Whereas it dwells free in the open plain,
> Uncurious, gentle, easy of access;
> Certain unto it self, of equal vane,
> One face, one colour, one assuredness:
> It's falsehood that it is intricate and vain,
> And needs these labyrinths of subtleness:
>
> . . . .
>
> Which thy clear-ey'd experience well descries
> Great *Keeper* of the state of Equity,
> Refuge of mercy, upon whom relies
> The succour of oppressed misery;
> Altar of safeguard, whereto affliction flies
> From th'eager pursuit of severity.[45]

Finally, common lawyers themselves, while possibly resenting the competing jurisdictions of the concilar courts such as Chancery, were not clearly a coherent body opposed to the royal prerogative on principle in the early seventeenth century.[46]

The dates in themselves are not entirely auspicious for the topical reading in question. *King Lear* is commmonly assumed to have been written in 1605–6; it was first performed on December 26, 1606, at Whitehall, entered in the Stationer's Register on November 26, 1607, and printed in the winter of 1607–8.[47] While the naturalization of the Scots was an issue in the Union project from the beginning of James's reign, it was not necessarily a heated issue at the very start;[48] further-more, the major parliamentary debates on the issue were held from February through April 1607, after the performance of the play.[49] Cal-vin's Case itself, the test of the legal position of the Post Nati, although in preparation during the fall of 1607, was not heard until June 1608 (Galloway, 148–49); Ellesmere's speech on the case was not published until February 1609 (ibid., 149).

To regard the verdict itself in Calvin's Case as clear evidence of a per-ceived turn toward arbitrary "prerogative" may also simplify issues on the basis of hindsight. As Bruce Galloway summarizes the case, it did decide "that allegiance in England was owed to the king as a natural person rather than a corporate figurehead," and its "most important facet . . . constitutionally" was "undoubtedly the support it gave to the picture of a king ruling by law of nature, over and above common or municipal laws" (*Union*, 156, 157). Yet he indicates as well that the "im-pact of the case on early seventeenth century thought was indirect" (156).[50] More importantly, Louis A. Knafla argues from Lord Chan-cellor Ellesmere's speech "in the Eschequer Chamber, Touching the *Post-Nati*" (the "lengthy opinion on the Post Nati's right to citizenship on the basis of civil law and equity" to which Marcus refers [*Puzzling Shakespeare*, 150])—that Ellesmere's was very possibly a moderate and actually more accepted view of the royal prerogative than either of the two views usually thought of as dominant in the early seventeenth cen-tury (i.e., the king is sovereign or the law is sovereign).[51] Ellesmere, according to Knafla, believed in "divine right monarchy," but *also* "in the existence of the law of the land as a law unto itself in the name of the King" (*Law and Politics*, 71). Although he argued for allegiance to the "natural body" of the king, his Post Nati position cannot easily be reduced to simple support of a royalist "prerogative" line.

The purpose of monarchy was to guarantee through the royal preroga-tive the expression of the private prerogatives of the people, and to en-sure that the institutions of law and government did not encroach upon them. . . . [The people's] recourse was the King's laws. . . .

The Chancellor also believed, however, that the legal privileges of the

King were binding upon the monarch himself: that the sovereign was charged to observe the laws which he and his predecessors had created. . . . The Chancellor later emphasised this side of the King's absolute prerogatives when he became frustrated with James's policies in governing the State. In addressing the House of Lords in 1614 he turned around nicely the legal privileges of the monarch in declaring that 'the King hath no prerogative but that which is warranted by law and the law hath given him.' (75–76)

Thus Chancellor Ellesmere had an opinion possibly more complex and ambiguous than Marcus allows. It is important to note as well — when the argument about topicality touches on purportedly opposed kinds of law — that Justice Coke, the great champion of the wisdom of the common law, was also on the king's side and found the decision that allegiance was owed to the king concordant with that law.[52] Even if "many believed the verdict had been rigged" — unlike Coke, who stressed the opposite (Galloway, *Union*, 149) — it is also important to remember that attitudes toward the naturalization of the Scots were tied up with the entire problematic Union issue itself, which did not split along clear king/Parliament lines (see above, chapter 5). Thus it is unlikely that objections to naturalization were based simply on a dislike of kingly prerogative or legal procedures. Once again, hindsight may make salient for us what was not yet in focus for Jacobeans — a problem since such arguments as Marcus's about the political allusiveness of the mock trial necessarily presume — among other things — an acute public awareness of such legal issues and a clearer split than seems to have obtained between civil law and royal absolutism, on the one hand, and common law and parliamentary procedure, on the other.

Having dealt with the question of the political valences of the mock trial, let us turn now to consider the same for Lear's plausibly more intense assault on justice.

The Meditation on Corrupt Justice

> [Plate sin] with gold,
> and the strong lance of justice, hurtless breaks:
> Arm it in rags, a pigmy's straw does pierce it.
> (4.6.165–67)[53]

There are several related ideas about the corruption of justice in 4.6.151–73 (F ll. 2595–2615). The poor who cannot bribe get punished for vices, whereas the rich escape because their gold protects them. Those with the power to punish are in fact the bigger thieves and hang men who commit lesser crimes. The very crimes of the judges who punish are disguised by their "robes and furr'd gowns," that is, their insignia of authority, and/or by their actual wealth (of which "fur" is an indubitable marker), which shield them from justice. The crimes of those who should be punished, but are similarly protected by their own robes and furred gowns, go unpunished.

This analysis of justice gone wrong is one available in a variety of kinds of texts from as far back as at least the twelfth century. John Bromyard in the fourteenth-century *Summa Praedicantium*, which was printed several times in the fifteenth and sixteenth centuries, complains: " 'To the man who gives nothing [the law] will be strict,' " but " 'whoever gives freely . . . will find the laws easy.' " The guilty "will be freed and honored, the innocent man with no meed will be condemned." Furthermore, "a rich man able to distribute *munera* can always get his business done at court while a poor man waits." [54] The objection that the punishment for theft does not fit the crime goes back to the Commonwealth men at least; it is voiced by Hytholoday, for example, in More's *Utopia:* " 'This way of punishing thieves is neither just in itself nor good for the public. . . . Simple theft is not so great a crime that it ought to cost a man his life, and no punishment however severe is sufficient to restrain a man from robbery who can find no other livelihood.' " [55] In Thomas Lupton's late morality, *All for Money* (1578), the proverbial "Big thieves hang little thieves" is dramatically enacted. [56] Moneyless steals a few rags, and his rich neighbor threatens him with hanging; once the bribe-taking magistrate All for Money learns he has none, of course he refuses to help him. Moneyless draws the lesson:

> God have mercy on us without a man have money
> He shall be cast away for a trifle we see:
> But the thieves and robbers that with money be stored
> Escape well enough, but the poor thieves be hanged.
> (D2r)

Lupton also wrote *A Dreame of the Divell and Dives. . . Verie Necessarie To Be Read Advisedly . . . Both of Rulers and Inferiours, Rich, and Poore, Younge and Olde, Wise and Simple, That Wish Rather to Dwel in Heaven,*

Then in Hell (1589).[57] In this work one interlocutor tells another how he dreamed of what the devil tells Dives, now in hell. The *Dreame* is an impassioned plea on behalf of the oppressed and a derisive criticism of corrupt lawyers and judges. The devil and Dives see eye to eye on the world's ills, though, of course, it's too late for Dives. The devil disdains "fine fellows that are in their furs, . . . mincing minions, that swim in their silks" (C6v–C7r), who are blind to the poor; Dives derides the sort who "fee [lawyers] largely, to plead against the truth, to hinder the poor man's cause, yea, and to bribe the judges (if they will be bribed) to stand against a true matter, or to delay judgement of the same, when it is plainly proved on the poor man's side" (C6r). Although such remarks are hedged by Christian pieties—that is, it is asserted that there is no redress until Heaven for earthly injustices—they appear to give vent to impassioned class feeling. The devil tells Dives that "the law on the earth is ended by the weight of the purse, not by the truth of the cause"; "the rich may oppress whom they will, and almost do what they will, their gifts and money will tell such a tale against the poor" (E1r, E2v). But, those "rich furred gowns," says Dives, will not make Christ say, "[B]ecause you were rich on earth, I will make you richer in heaven" (C3r).

The very shape of "rich furred gowns" is in itself symbolic of the sins it conceals. Such gowns can "hide all" at least in part because they are many-folded or voluminous—like the ones Regan and Goneril seem to wear. Cordelia, we may remember, is "dismantle[d]" of "so many folds of favor" (1.1.217–18) in the first scene of the play, but her sisters, by her own accusation, are still dressed, as it were, in "plighted cunning" (1.1.280). Avarice, in a tradition that goes at least as far back as the *Psychomachia* of Prudentius, was often portrayed as dressed in a full robe in which she could hide bags of money—rather like Barnfield's usurer, Covetousness.

> They say that Avarice, clothed in ample robe,
> Seized all of worth that Sensuality
> Had left behind. . . .
>
> . . . .
>
> Not satisfied with pockets full, she joys
> To cram with sordid gain her money-bags,
> Which in her robe she hides with her left hand,
> While with the right she gathers up the spoils
> And fills her brazen claws with filthy loot.[58]

The traditional self-defense of the avaricious was that they were being provident and frugal. Thus, in the *Psychomachia:*

> [Avarice] now becomes a Virtue, stern of face
> And dress, and called Frugality, who loves
> To pinch and save, as though she would seize nought
> And had a right to praise for what she feigned.
> (ll. 553–56)

We recall that Goneril argues against the "Epicurism and lust" (1.4.244) that result from Lear's large retinue. In fact, in *The True Chronicle Historie of King Leir* (1605), Goneril quite explicitly exemplifies a hypocritical Avarice who has lavish desires for herself but resents supporting the king.[59]

Dozens of manuals and mirrors for princes, like Thomas Lodge's *The Devill Conjured* (1596), stress that the corrective for justice gone wrong is even-handedness, "equal balance, to rich and poor": the prince must be "aware in [his] kingdom, lest the proud command the humble; the tyrant, the just; the cruel, the pitiful; the dastard, the hardy; the ignorant, the prudent; and the worst thieves, hang the innocent."[60] Andrewes says, "[I]n cases of appeal [the king must] . . . do justice himself; for that it is that must establish his throne . . . and without it . . . 'great kingdoms' are nothing else but 'great robberies'" (*Catechistical Doctrine,* 201). The first tragedy in *The Mirror for Magistrates* (1559), "The Fall of Robert Tresilian Chiefe Justice of Englande," is one

> Where judges and justicers may see, as in a glass,
> What fee is for falsehood, and what our wages was
> Who for our prince's pleasure corrupt with meed and awe
> Wittingly and wretchedly did wrest the sense of law.[61]

Assize sermons likewise reiterate the themes informing Lear's meditation on corrupt justice. For example, Edwin Sandys (1516?–1588), bishop of Worcester, then of London, and finally archbishop of York, issued a warning to judges and princes in one of his sermons:

> He that truly feareth God . . . will not swerve from justice, for fear or favour of any man or thing. . . .
>
> . . . The first thing that judges are especially to take heed of is, that they be not receivers of bribes. Beware of rewards: they are the very bane of upright judgment. . . .
>
> God is no accepter of persons: neither must you in judgment either

favour the rich because of his wealth, or spare the poor for his misery's sake; but weigh their causes in the balance of equity, with an even and steady hand. . . .

You, to whom the sword of justice and judgment is committed, take heed unto it. Let it not spare mighty men; for their sins are mighty sins. If such offend, their fall draweth down others with them. God commanded Moses to hang up the princes of the people upon gibbets, that they might be examples of punishment who had been examples in sinning.[62]

King James's own *Basilikon Doron* (1599) sounds similar notes:

Be diligent therefore to try, and awful to beat down the horns of proud oppressors: embrace the quarrel of the poor and distressed, as your own particular, thinking it your greatest honour to repress the oppressors. . . . Remember when ye sit in judgement, that the throne ye sit on is God's, as Moses saith, and sway neither to the right hand nor to the left; either loving the rich, or pitying the poor. *(Political Works of James I, 21–22)*

Samuel Daniel's *A Panegyrike Congratulatorie to the King*, with which he greeted James—traveling south from Scotland in the spring of 1603— informs the king that "all in-cheering Majesty"

> Shall come to shine at full in all her parts,
> And spread her beams of comfort equally,
> As being all alike to like deserts.[63]

Daniel tells James quite forthrightly that "Plain zeal and truth, free from base flatterings" *will* characterize his court:

> There grace and favour shall not be dispos'd,
> But by proportion, even and upright;
>
> . . . .
>
> All passages that may seem indirect
> Are stopped up now, and there is no access
> By gross corruption, bribes cannot effect
> For th'undeserving any offices;
> Th'ascent is clean, and he that doth ascend
> Must have his means as clean as is his end.
> (1:150, 151)

Perhaps the promise of divine justice should not be seen as simply reinforcing the status quo (the reward of the poor or oppressed will come, but not until heaven) or sending a threatening reminder to mortal kings concerning the limits of their earthly authority. Perhaps the demand for upright, impartial, and responsible judgment, and its converse, the warnings about usurers hanging cozeners, justices being indistinguishable from thieves, robes and furred gowns hiding all should not be imagined simply as *either* platitudinous *or* incendiary. Individual churchmen, even prelates—and occasional poets—certainly believed they were capable of dressing down the mighty, or at least reminding them of their sober responsibilities, and sometimes did; kings themselves—including James—spoke of how God punished kings who transgressed their limits.[64] It is the very applicability to a variety of situations of these biblically supported complaints about the uneven justice suffered by the oppressed at the hands of the privileged that makes various parties have recourse to them; and that continued use by a variety of parties—even opposed parties—is what gives such general motifs their cultural power. Even the most general criticism of injustice might provoke the censor in especially volatile circumstances, or might constitute a "radical" position where severe oppression made silence the norm, but the critic must make a convincing case for a judgment that it did.

Conversely, and also depending on the circumstances, even in so controlled an institutional setting as that of the assize sermon, targeted allegations about rich and poor, oppressor and oppressed, justice and injustice could be made, allegations with some expressed implications for specific institutions. It is not always the case that political and social criticism is extremely covert and can only be teased out by twentieth-century critics. William Kethe's assize sermon, *A Sermon Made at Blandford Forum . . . at the Session Holden There* (1571), attacks "bribing" and seditious Catholics—who even try to bribe God—and the corrupted authorities much too lenient with them, although unlawfully strict with lawful ministers. "Shamefully, and cruelly the poor ministers of this country are misused . . . some are threatened, some imprisoned, I know not by what law, and some put in danger of life, because they will not consent to superstition."[65] The matter at hand concerned "a poor man bringing to light the seditious books of a papist, and delivering them to the Lord Lieutenant," with the result that he was "set by the heels" and driven from his house, and his house "rifled," and he "fain to forsake the town for fear, the offender to be in manner quiet and untouched, saving bound to appear now before you" (10r-10v). The usual warnings about how justice does not "bow to the right hand, nor to the left hand" (Exodus 23:3, [5r]) are here offered in support of rigorous prosecution of papists by magistrates accused of failure to execute justice: "Let honest men upon their oaths, present great crimes, either before the temporal Magistrate, or the spiritual officer, it is oft times seen that the offenders go away less discouraged, than those which present them. What encouragements are these to farther justice, when matters pass so slenderly?" (13r–13v). J. S. Cockburn indicates that judges "had long been subjected, particularly on circuit, to the sombre admonitions of Puritan divines and the equally pious attentions of godly magistrates," yet considers this sermon among those making Elizabethan judges aware of "the extent to which radical doctrines were querying the Establishment and its authority";[66] this minister's "plain speaking" in the cause of more general "discipline" than some of the authorities were willing to support clearly ruffled some conservative's feathers when he gave his sermon.[67] Yet in 1571, when anti-Catholic fever was at a great pitch because of the papal bull excommunicating Elizabeth, the queen and Council were perhaps quite willing to let lenience to Catholics be specifically targeted as injustice—in print.[68]

More strongly "Puritan" attitudes toward injustice than Kethe's are quite tightly tied to class feeling—in a way that anticipates the societal divisions many historians have traditionally associated with a "Puritan Revolution"—in another assize sermon, *A Sermon Preached at Charde,* printed in 1601, and apparently written by George Macey. Like other strong Protestants, Macey reminds magistrates that such as Herod were in "royal apparel" and "sitting on the judgement" seat when they were smitten by the angel of the Lord.[69] "Men of high place and calling have many lets and impediments, many encumbrances that either hinder them from turning into the right way, or clog them that they walk very slowly therein" (4); "by reason of their riches and titles," they "blaspheme the gospel, despise God's ministers, contemn our Church and congregations, set light of holy exercises" (3). However traditional such criticism, this sermon directly criticizes existing political institutions, and it approaches defining "the enemy" as the gentry-controlled state itself. Jurors ill serve the cause of justice, Macey suggests, when a powerful man's own tenants or neighbors are impaneled in his causes. "Men of might" should have such jurors discharged; then "the suspicion of oppression shall be taken away," and "seely men shall be freed from danger, or at least wise from exceeding fear" (24–25). "The next way to purge the land of heinous offences, is to execute the law alike on all" (26), as it was in the time of the Saxons and of William the Conqueror. Oppression by the rich includes the so frequently inveighed against "joining of land to land, and house to house" that drives out the poor husbandmen and tillers without whom "cannot commonweals continue," and such oppression inspires considerable vehemence: "[I]t is no wisdom for the workers of iniquity to eat up God's people as they eat bread" (34)—especially without the "full recompense" (33) (for the "vineyard" he wanted) that even Ahab offered (1 Kings 21:2). Perhaps even more to the point is Macey's possibly politically restive complaint that these poor "be not asked their judgement in the counsel of the people," and are not "high in the congregation," and do not "sit . . . upon the judgement seats" (34). Going beyond this, there is a quite bitter "demystification" of the "common excuses" (Macey's own characterization) of the powerful for enclosure or enlarging domains—reminiscent of Henry Barrow's demystification of the "riot and gluttony" which rich men call "good housekeeping":[70]

If there be no other means, then it must serve to make a park, which will both take away the suspicion of covetousness, and also be a good means to draw in more next adjoining, which after a few years may be employed to uses more profitable for the owner, and also for the commonwealth. Whether it be more reasonable that they that have abundance should be content with their lot, or that such as have but little should depart from all that they possess, judge ye. (33)

Such politically charged specificities may or may not underlie Lear's more general "Thorough tatter'd clothes [small] vices do appear; / Robes and furr'd gowns hide all." Criticism in such terms—like much else in the Christian tradition—*could* become radicalized or revolutionary, and *could* reject paternalist solutions. The Leveller William Walwyn's assertions about the inequities of the old government (in a tract of 1642) are not, of course, unrelated to such long-lived criticism: "[A] murder in one man was not so much punished as a word in another, . . . a poor man was hanged for stealing food for his necessity, and a luxurious courtier of whom the world was never like to have any other fruits but oaths and stabs, could be pardoned after the killing the second or third man."[71] However, it is crucial to note, such terms are not automatically or exclusively revolutionary.

The Dramatic Moment, the Images, the Language

For king and radical alike, then, justice, when corrupted, is partial to the "robes and furr'd gowns" and when uncorrupted, leans neither toward the rich nor poor. Having said this, however, we have not quite finished with Lear's speech itself, nor dealt fully with its emotional effect on us. Of course the social, and, let us not forget, the self-criticism, in F 4.6, is *felt* as sharp, in an enormously moving *dramatic* situation involving a character who enlists our empathy; this analysis of justice gone wrong is enormously affecting because delivered by the suffering Lear, who has shortly before removed his own hand which "smells of mortality" (4.6.133) from Gloucester's lips. Perhaps readers or viewers responding to the emotional intensity of this scene—the sheer derangement and fierce suffering of characters "upon the rack of this tough world" (5.3.315)—look for an ideological analogue to the intensity of Lear's and their own emotion in the most "radical" of political ideas, rather than at the ideas actually expressed—which when pursued, turn up as much or more in the traditional Christian culture as in revolutionary discourse.

Yet, while the mock trial's accusation of "corruption" against the "false justicer" allows for the possibility that some justices are true, Lear here makes a much more incriminating summary statement seemingly implicating an entire system of justice: *all* robes and furred gowns hide corruption. One can certainly understand what prompts Gary Taylor to say that "the censor would have been furious about what apparently replaced" 3.6., *if* he had originally objected to the mock trial.[72] In particular, the "image of authority" itself as "a dog[] obey'd in office"—more than accusations about the preferential treatment of the rich and high-ranked—feels "radical."

The equation of the "image of authority" with the "dog[] obey'd in office" is most immediately related to the metaphor Lear has been developing:

see how yond justice rails upon yond simple thief. . . . Thou hast seen a farmer's dog bark at a beggar?
Glou. Ay, sir.
Lear. And the creature run from the cur? There thou mightst behold the great image of authority: a dog's obey'd in office. (4.6.151–52; 154–59)[73]

The "farmer's dog [that] bark[s] at a beggar" parallels the "justice [who] rails upon yond simple thief"; hence, the "creature [who] run[s] from

the cur" parallels the "simple thief." Lear's metaphor demotes the justice to a barking dog, yet promotes the thief to a beggar not clearly
guilty of the crime of stealing—or, perhaps, it implies that beggars are
automatically, if not necessarily justly, considered thieves. Figured as a
barking dog that scares a beggar, the "image of authority" is here ironically reduced to a brute animal who terrorizes the powerless and not
necessarily criminal beggar (who hasn't even threatened anyone's possessions). The barking dog is instantly obeyed because the insignia of
office—those "robes and furr'd gowns" behind which he hides—spark
immediate blind fear in the powerless upon whom he preys. Like the
"costly ornaments and rich attire" Phillip Stubbes describes, they indeed "strike a terror and fear into the hearts of the people to offend
against the majesty of their callings" (*Anatomy*, 34), but in a particularly
unsettling way. The injunction, "Behold the great image of authority, a
dog's obey'd in office," taken with the assertion that follows a few lines
later, "Robes, and furr'd gowns hide all," presents a horrific discrepancy
between distinguished appearance and subhuman reality: an animal
in a justice's robe. And that image is the most "radical" metaphorical
analysis yet of the corruption of justice. It is an image intensified by
the play's other references to dogs who are sheltered by the fire while
humans are locked outdoors in the howling storm, or to dogs that still
breathe (5.3.307), though Cordelia no longer does. At this point, the
starkest of images do seem to sum up the play: the powerful are dogs
in furred gowns preying upon "poor, bare, fork'd animal[s]" (3.4.107).

The reinvestment of "authority" seems impossible after such extremity. Stage tradition, in interpreting the "fresh garments" (4.7.21) in
which Lear is "arrayed" (4.7.19), after he has been taken into Cordelia's
care, as "a loosely flowing white robe"—which undoubtedly has some
of the aura of the penitent's white garment and new spiritual state,
whatever its other meanings—supports such a feeling.[74] Never again
will Lear wear royal robes, as Leir does in *The True Chronicle Historie*,
even though Cordelia will address him as "my royal lord" and "your
Majesty" (4.7.43), and he will be carried in a chair (in the Folio [4.7.2771]
at least)—as much an indication of his exhausted weakness, perhaps, as
of his former "state."[75]

Yet how radically undermined is social and political authority in
Shakespeare's world by this emotionally wrenching image of corrupt
justice? The big thieves that hang little thieves (so that one can't tell
"which is the justice, which is the thief" [153-54]), the vulnerability of
the patched poor, who cannot bribe, when they stand before their un-

holy judges—all these are present in the literature we have surveyed, often in language quite close to Shakespeare's.[76] However, the discrepancy embodied in the image of dogs in furred robes results from conjoining elements found elsewhere in a combination that seems new and devastating: those profoundly subhuman dogs at the bottom of the scale of creation—least deserving of charity, yet treated better than the poor—and the furred and voluminous gowns that hide the spoils of the avaricious. Can injustice, thus imaged, admit of traditional solutions?

James R. Siemon remarks that Lear, "who accepts the significance of emblem, undergoes a dramatic experience negating the assumptions that had grounded his notions of correspondence. . . . In fact, he manages a rejection of emblem by posing an ultimate antiemblem: 'There thou mightst behold the great image of Authority: / A dog's obeyed in office.'" Before this transformation in Lear's mentality, the "ruling assumption behind such a radical act" as dividing the crown was the "absolute conflation of the symbol with the reality it signifies"; Lear was involved in a "magical valuation of representation over temporal, political process" (Siemon, *Shakespearean Iconoclasm*, 267, 260–61, 261). By this reading, "Authority" is understood as no longer "essential," no longer a thing magically linked to its external signs, but merely a hollow representation, an emblem without an essence—as if Shakespeare's language figures the end of that stage of thinking in which images were intrinsically linked to their referents, outside to inside, word to thing. It is a change that Siemon suggests parallels the movement from an "essentialist" conception of the relation of image and essence to an "arbitrary" one in the post-Reformation understanding of the Eucharist—as if, according to that new understanding, the signs of the Eucharist were only memorial, only signs pointing to something not present (or worse, a theatrical show giving the illusion of something in fact not there), a presumption that oversimplifies the Protestant "real spiritual presence." Yet it is on the basis of this assumed metaphysical radicalism that the debased image of "Authority" is read as politically radical in the play. If "Authority" may be counterfeited by mere robes, mere signs, authority is a counterfeit, a merely conventional sign or image that need have no connection with a truly existent or essential thing.[77]

Finally, however, is it historically plausible and convincing to hear Shakespeare's language in this way? If we want to hear this anatomy of the "image of authority" in a more, if never perfectly, "Renaissance" context, we might look, once again, at Erasmus's use of theatrical imagery in his mirror for princes, *The Education of a Christian Prince*. The appurtenances of authority, the robes and furred gowns, are re- minders of duty:

What does the gold mean, except outstanding wisdom? What significance has the sparkle of the gems, except extraordinary virtues as different as possible from the common run? What does the warm rich purple mean, if not the essence of love for the state? And why the scepter, unless as a mark of a spirit clinging strongly to justice, turned aside by none of life's diver- sions? . . . If a necklace, a scepter, royal purple robes, a train of attendants are all that make a king, what is to prevent the actors who come on the stage decked with all the pomp of state from being called king? . . . The crown, the scepter, the royal robes, the collar, the sword belt are all marks or symbols of good qualities in the good prince; in a bad one, they are accusations of vice. . . .

. . . If you strip [bad princes] of their royal ornaments and inherited goods, and reduce them to themselves alone, you will find nothing left ex- cept the essence of an expert a dice, the victor of many a drinking bout, the fierce conqueror of modesty, the craftiest of deceivers, an insatiable pil- lager; a creature steeped in perjury, sacrilege, perfidy, and every other kind of crime.[78]

It does not seem to me that Erasmus here expects signs to gen- erate realities, that is, that Erasmus magically values "representation over temporal political process," to use Siemon's words once again— although it does seem to me that critics who focus on the change from the "natural sign" to the "arbitrary sign" do often speak rather primitiv- istically about the Renaissance mentality, as if it were naively mystical about such matters. Rather, it seems that Erasmus is simply talking about truth in packaging. It is in the power of the king to use his insig- nia responsibly or not. When he fails, it is not because the symbols fail him—as Siemon implies, when he says that the "emblematic" mode based on correspondences fails Lear. Rather than the symbols failing the king, the king fails the symbols; and when he does, he becomes like an actor with only the appearance of a king, a "vile person gorgeously apparelled [who] represents a king or a prince in a play"—to return to Ridley's image in his discussion of the Eucharist (which was analyzed in chapter 2). For the Protestant—given the central Protestant doctrine of the real spiritual presence—it is a Catholic error to mistake the eucharistic signs themselves for the spiritual reality they represent and with which they are joined. But it is equally false to regard them as equivalent to a theatrical sham or a bare figure, the eucharistic equivalents of "dogs in furred robes" and "bare forked animals." Presence, or essence is still possible. The "image of authority" as a dog obeyed in office is in this context no ultimate "antiemblem" or empty sign, but the image of the debased authority that characterizes the prince who has only the paraphernalia and not the essence of kingship.[79]

Finally, then, we may have to once again mitigate our sense of the "radicalism" of "the image of authority" as a "dog[] obey'd in office." Along with the idea of the oppression of the poor at the hands of the wealthy and privileged, along with the idea of the corruption of earthly courts, even the idea of the utter debasement of "the image of authority" can be used to urge kings and governments to live up to culturally shared ideals of justice, rather than to deny all possibility of justice under present systems. As David Sacks says, "In the ideals of justice . . . we have politically and culturally powerful codes, equally available to the established authorities and to their subjects, that might be used to bring home the wrongs done by those charged with maintaining the right."[80] As such, Lear's terms in 4.6 still leave open the possibility that "false justicers" are implicated more than the entire judicial system, that kings, if they behave according to the counsel urged in the mirror for princes traditions can still be dispensers and abettors of justice.

In roughly contemporaneous morality plays and Protestant dream visions, the patience Lear so clearly lacks is clearly vindicated; injustice is ultimately punished and justice reigns eternal. In *The Trial of Treasure*, "Time" does indeed "reveal what plighted cunning hides"; God's Visitation is weathered only by Just and Trust. A personified Time, who is "the touchstone the just for to try" comes on stage at the denouement to show how Lust and Treasure fade and are punished.

> But whereas Lust and Treasure in time is come to nought,
> Just, possessing Trust, remaineth constantly,
> So that as I Time have revealed their infamy,
> So have I showed the consolation and gain,
> That the just shall receive that justly do reign.[81]

At the very last in *All for Money*, Nemesis intervenes to show the object lessons of Judas and Dives in hell. Godly Admonition, along with

Virtue, Humility, and Charity have the last words urging repentance and the avoidance of the fate of Judas and Dives (E3r–E3v). In *The Dreame of the Divell and Dives,* the attack on earthly injustice and the oppression of the poor by the rich is very powerful, even if the reader is also told that there is no hope of redress until the moment of heavenly judgment. The poor must be patient, awaiting their heavenly reward; they must be comforted by the understanding that the rich will be judged by a true Judge in the life to come. "And as for these lawyers that take such fees, for defending of wrong, and the hindrance of right, they shall get never a lawyer for anything at the last day, that shall plead at their side. . . . And these judges that will be bribed, or defend a false matter, shall be sure at the last day, to have such a true and upright Judge" (C8v).[82]

It has become customary to deny patience's relevance to a secular tragedy that seems to stress metaphysical uncertainty and that offers little hope—heavenly or otherwise—for redress from suffering. Yet, the absence in *Lear* of the morality play's redemptive ending does not necessarily entail the absence of a broadly Christian perspective. Nemesis does operate in *Lear;* evil does undo itself. Cornwall, Goneril, Regan, and Edmund are all in some sense destroyed by the momentum of their own wickedness, even if Lear, Cordelia, and Gloucester are destroyed as well. The Christian promise to the repentant is not fulfilled on earth, nor in a play ending there. Nevertheless—for those whose everyday experience was coded in its terms—that does not necessarily diminish its meaningfulness, and the meaningfulness of the suffering culminating in the mutual humility and charity of Lear and Cordelia.

Conclusion

Political Interpretation versus Dramatic Verisimilitude

and Shared Moral Values

Much recent criticism asks us to choose between a Shakespeare of the left or of the right, a subverter of orthodoxy or a container of subversion; when we are not asked to make such a choice, we are encouraged to think of literary works as "occasions for the jostling of orthodox and subversive impulses" (Greenblatt, *Forms of Power,* 6), or as containing meanings which may be "multiple or self-cancelling" (Marcus, *Puzzling Shakespeare,* 38). Yet each of these Shakespeares often lacks historical convincingness because each seems too much to be constructed from selective evidence. Too often recent political and historical approaches just aren't historical enough about what actually *was* subversive, what orthodox, what marginal, what central. They may make a very ad hoc use of historical data; they may assume rather than fully investigate the ideological characteristics of political and religious opposition; they may argue from the language they assume expressed that opposition, without a sufficient sense of how that language actually was used in a wide variety of texts.[1]

In contrast to many other studies of Shakespeare's politics, this study of the politics expressed through the metaphors and images of the naked and clothed in *King Lear* is grounded in an investigation of the range and nature of those (and related) metaphors in a wide variety of religious, political, and literary texts. That investigation in turn is guided by a theory of communication that recognizes the possibility of cultural sharing, but that in no way precludes individual creativity and freedom with and within cultural parameters. Where semiotic—if not necessarily economic—systems are concerned, human agency consists in choosing, combining, and superimposing available cultural building blocks or codes, in transposing registers, or—we might say—in selecting and recombining elements from various available discourses.[2] Consequently, there is a relationship between particularized meanings—which may be new and creative—and systematic cultural patterns and values with broad applicability. We do not have to chose between radical relativism and positivism, or between "free individuality and cultural totality" (Holstun, "Ranting," 195), "slippery signifier" and "implacable code" (Montrose, "Professing," 21).³ Shared understandings are what enable individual creativity to occur and to communicate, just as Thomas Cartwright communicates when he calls Presbyterian discipline the "chains and bracelets and rings and other jewels [that] adorn [the church] and set her out,"⁴ and Shakespeare's Kent communicates when he punningly combines the register of place names with that of body parts and speaks of getting Oswald "in *Lipsbury* pinfold" (2.2.9, my emphasis), that is, between his teeth (a "pinfold" is a pound for stray animals). Or, for that matter, just as Shakespeare communicates when he combines those lowly dogs—said to be treated better than humans in the homilies exhorting charity—with "robes and furred gowns"—associated with privilege and avarice in dream visions, morality plays, and tracts—in a shocking "image of authority."⁵

Within the universe of expectations about "clothing" and "nakedness" in the Renaissance, certain statements of value are more likely than others. These general parameters, this direction in which the semantic field as a whole leans, is itself part of the meaning of a Renaissance play that uses images and metaphors of nakedness and clothing; the very choice of such images implicates the general shape of the semiotic "system" of "clothing" and "nakedness" as a whole. As we have seen, the frequent statements of value within the cultural universe with which we are concerned recognize the positive function of clothing as a modest or comely covering for a shameful or beggarly nakedness, or, the negative functions of clothing when immodest, inappropriately mean, or wantonly deceitful (in which case the naked truth is preferable). Nakedness itself—strongly associated with loss of dignity—is more often shameful or pitiable than glorious; clothing is faulted only for actually failing to cover nakedness, disguising the true nature of the wearer, or indecently enticing the observer.

At the same time as there is a universe of cultural expectations, there may also be individual or group tendencies toward one or another of the likely statements within that universe. However, opponents may also use the same or similar words (such as "nude and bare," or "comely") and share some of the same broad values encoded in these culturally salient oppositions (such as, "It is better to be covered by 'comely apparel' than to go 'nude and bare'"). Yet, they may have different implicit or explicit referents for those words, and especially for those words creatively used in metaphor — and different ways, in consequence, of interpreting such culturally available oppositions. Thus, they may act on different embodiments of similar values. For conformists, Scripture may be naked and bare without the comely customs of men; for nonconformists, the church may be naked and bare without the godly reformation that adorns it (by stripping it of those very customs). Language is the social compact of people who strive to be understood, even in their disagreement. My emphasis in this book has been on that sharing and those similar values, in part because political criticism has too uncritically focused on apparent differences.

Among the areas in which poststructuralist historicism may not be historical enough is Reformation religious belief; here, selective use of evidence may encourage unhistorical generalizations that tend to put the Reformation on the "early modern" train. Apart from the tendency of the post-Marx, post-Freud critic to regard all Christian values as forms of false consciousness (as the "fataliz[ing]" of "social dislocation," for example, according to Dollimore, *Radical Tragedy*, 194), there seems to be a tendency to misinterpret the metaphysical significance of the Protestant rejection of transubstantiation. Some critics write as if the Protestant rejection of a corporeal real presence were tantamount to the denial of any spiritual presence at all, as if the Protestant suspicion of Catholic "magic" and "theater" were equivalent to an admission that the signs of the Eucharist were merely empty — and as such comparable to "representations" that "mark the absence of a presence that is never fully available in and of itself."[6] It is a short step from this supposedly new "early modern" metaphysics to the claim that royalty, for example, was newly understood as an empty sign magically counterfeited by theater. But such a step is made problematic — at the least — if one understands that the absence of a material presence of the sacred in the Eucharist is not tantamount to the absence of the holy altogether — totally apart from whether or not one subscribes to the notion that royalty, in particular, was a mystical sign to begin with.[7]

A broader — and crucial — point about the lack of historicity of many historicizing critics that emerges from this study concerns the problems that can be created by the parallel-text method and by quick-fix analogical thinking, especially when these replace patient investigation of a wide range of texts and the accumulation of substantial evidence. One verbal parallel between a motif in *Lear* and a similar motif

in a revolutionary writer does not make the motif, or *Lear,* radical—
especially when there are innumerable examples of similar ideas and
language in traditional or orthodox texts. Analogizing is a mode of
thought we all use unreflectively at times, yet analogies should not be
considered automatic determinants of, or constraints on, thought, belief, or feeling. The fact that Milton used the same father-king analogy
that royalists used does not make him a royalist; for different thinkers,
different aspects of fatherhood may underlie the parallel to kingship.

Thus, the new historicist approach to reading religious, political,
and artistic cultural forms as homologous has built-in dangers. In particular, historical and cultural criticism, whether "new historicist" or
"old," is vulnerable to globalizing the Puritan-Anglican opposition between "plainness" and "ceremony" in the church, as if it automatically
extended into all other realms for each side. Analogies linking all the
possible different kinds of "plainness," or all the possible different kinds
of "ceremony" are very much grist for the mill of the critic seeking to
demonstrate, for example, that Puritans who disapprove of ceremony
and hierarchy in the church must disapprove of the same in the state or
the home—assumptions that easily enter into political readings of *Lear.*
But the Puritan or radical Protestant does not inevitably side with the
"plain" or "naked" and their apparent analogues.

In fact, Augustinian Protestant thought as a whole may be said to
weaken the analogy between the spiritual and the civil realms insofar
as it adheres to the idea of the two governments or regiments—spiritual and secular. All "Lords" are not analogous in all respects; Hooker
commented, as we have seen, that linguistic usage requires calling
both Christ and Caesar "Lord," without in any sense rendering them
equivalent. Similarly, all acts of kneeling are not precisely analogous;
Gouge understood that kneeling to a parent did not make the parent
God simply because men also kneel to God. Bradshaw felt that bowing
the knee could be used in both civil "worship" and religious worship
because he did not regard the civil and religious spheres as precisely
analogous; sacred kneeling could be cordoned off from civil kneeling.
More generally speaking, we have seen the sense in which, for Gouge
or Bradshaw, political inequality as a whole did not contradict spiritual
equality. Indeed, there is little evidence that the nonconformist scorn
for "superstitions" forms in religion encouraged a parallel contempt
for civil and domestic forms. Bradshaw did approve the lowliness and
courtesy shown by the bishop's civil servant who wears his livery and

holds up his train; he did *not* approve the spiritual subordination of the minister to the bishop or spiritual lord who commanded him to wear a surplice. Hence Cordelia's scanting of a kind of civil "ceremony" need not connote "Puritanism."

The identification of dramatic characters with clear "sides" polarized along political, religious, and social lines, then — an identification essential to political criticism—often assumes dubious analogical equivalences linking *all* forms of nakedness or plainness and *all* forms of clothing or ceremoniousness. However, even apart from this problem, there are other strong reasons why such identifications are often unconvincing, if not invariably so.[8] To begin with, the political affiliation of particular characters in the play and the political values of the play itself cannot be derived from its metaphors of nakedness and clothing, simply because neither in the play, nor in the culture of which the play is a part, are naked plainness and comely clothing unambiguous clues to good and evil—or to religious position. Tudor and Stuart culture represents value *both* by contrasting appropriate plainness or bareness to deceitful clothing *and* by contrasting appropriate and comely covering to immodest or shameful bareness. It is part of characters' social and human recognizability that, like ourselves, they may cast themselves in culturally available roles in complex or inconsistent ways, and like ourselves as users of language, sometimes valorize one side of a metaphor (e.g., getting down to the "bare bones" of an argument), sometimes another (e.g., "dressing up a point"). Thus, the plain-speaking and true-hearted Cordelia is always described (as Emily Leider points out) in courtly and elegant language, and the Edgar who goes naked as Poor Tom, can also appear "fair and warlike" (5.3.143), in full military regalia, to defend his right in the eloquent language of formal challenge (5.3.127–42). Both plainness and ceremony, simplicity and eloquence are widely held values, while disgraceful bareness and ostentatious flattery are of course disapproved—even if all of these may at times be differently embodied for different groups in the culture.

The identification of characters with political "sides" is also problematic because it suggests that audiences respond to nonallegorical characters suspiciously and intellectually, judging their political credentials.[9] Political readings may underestimate the affective power of theater to sweep audiences into emotional complicity—that is, into sympathetic identification with "good" characters and dislike of "bad." Such broad *moral* evaluations are not directly based on characters' associations with particular societal groups, or even on audience members' own political, religious, or social vested interests, in any narrow sense; rather, they accord with the mechanisms of linguistic communication across "sides," as described in this book.[10] This concluding chapter will end with a brief characterization of the politics of *King Lear*—based on its embodiment of the common cultural values these chapters have shown its language supports. But, first, I want to examine, in relation to dramatic verisimilitude and moral evaluation, the problems of—and alternatives to—lining up the characters of *Lear* with political, religious, or social "sides"—or even with plainness as a value opposed to eloquence.

Two Societies?
Dramatic Verisimilitude versus Ideological Precision

As we saw in chapter 5, historical theories postulating a major transition from one type of society, economy, and social philosophy to another—feudal to bourgeois, subsistence to commercial, Christian to capitalist, Hookerian to Hobbesian, "moral economy" to "possessive individualism"—have been very powerful in generating readings of *Lear*. For example, the contrast between idealized feudal bonds and more legalistic transactions underlies Barish and Waingrow's view of service in *King Lear* ("Service," 353). Rosalie Colie stresses the opposition between "an old ethos of unreckoned generosity, magnificence, and carelessness" exemplified by Lear, Gloucester, and Kent, and "new values" of "greater providence, frugality, and even calculation," a " 'new' world of power and might" in which "Albany, Cornwall, Goneril, Regan, and Edmund are domesticated."[11] Colie's account of a changing aristocratic ethos usefully implies that bourgeois habits of mind were not limited to the bourgeoisie; of course, the land-owning elite reorganized its holdings to make them more commercially profitable, and there were Puritan aristocrats and gentry, as well as Puritan artisans and shopkeepers.[12]

However, even if we agree, with historical hindsight, that the world was changing from the feudal to the bourgeois, there is no reason to expect that pre–Civil War English society polarized into two neat groups (with no ragged edges) in which economic behavior, social position, religious beliefs, and religious practices were perfectly congruent, and hence, that contemporaries would think in such terms. Even today's critics, employing the feudal/bourgeois contrast—so clearly salient for us now—place the same characters on opposite sides. For example, Rosalie Colie's aristocratic ethos includes " 'tolerant indifference to the sins of the flesh,' " placing Gloucester on the feudal side ("Reason and Need," 193).[13] In marked contrast, James H. Kavanagh—viewing the play in an Althusserian Marxist framework—places Gloucester's "weakness and adultery" in the camp of "an individualist ideology that lives the world as a field of calculation, self-gratification and perverse desire," in short, on the bourgeois side ("Shakespeare in Ideology," 145, 156). It is all too easy to find reasons to place characters in either camp. Does the sexual laxity (which Colie links to aristocratic mores) of Goneril and Regan place them on the aristocratic feudal side? Or does their suspicious attitude toward idle and potentially disorderly retainers put them in the Puritan, bourgeois camp?

In fact, the play's contemporaneous resonance could have emerged from its verisimilitude, its portrait of recognizable social attitudes, problems, and practices—which may not map perfectly onto our own (or even *their*) historical dichotomies or generalizations. Such contemporaneous recognizability, furthermore, clearly involves shared attitudes that cut across social and religious groups; this in turn reduces the likelihood that the play spoke particularly—or in different voices—to the nonconformist radicals or the conformist conservatives in a polarized audience. As we have seen, for example, Regan's and Goneril's "gorgeous" robes, linked with the "robes and furr'd gowns" that "hide all," suggest the figure of Avarice, who, like the usurer, is frequently represented with moneybags hidden under furred robes. When Goneril and Regan take on the role of a hypocritical Frugality to Lear's presumed Prodigality, they are enacting an idea much older than the advent of Puritanism and shareable by conformist and nonconformist Christian alike. Now, it is certainly true that Puritans are concerned about idle "riotous servants" who do no work "but to eat, and drink one another under the table," who are the seedbed of disorder, and a hindrance to proper household management (Dod and Cleaver, *Ten Commaundements*, 207)—and this concern seems to echo Goneril's with Lear's "insolent retinue" (1.4.202). Furthermore, strict Puritans may complain in a particularly "Puritan" way that idle retainers "do not eat their own bread . . . and live thievishly . . . out of a calling" (ibid.).[14] Seemingly class-conscious, they may link the idleness of gentlemen with the idleness of their servants.[15] In contrast, Gervase Markham, a gentleman's gentleman who himself served happily as a boy in the "great household" of the Earl of Rutland, effusively praises lordly hospitality to retainers in his *A Health to the Gentlemanly Profession of Serving-Men*.[16] Yet, of course, the concern about the "great train of idle fellows" who are carried about by "noblemen who live idly like drones" also may be found in the first book of More's *Utopia*, and William Harrison — no Puritan — also complained over a half-century later about "great swarms of idle servingmen," "profitable to none," and likely to become beggars in their old age, "because service is none heritage." [17]

Indeed, Goneril's or Regan's "Puritan" reasons for cutting down Lear's wasteful retinue — which include both "charge and danger" (Regan's words, 2.4.239) — recur even in the nostalgic Markham's comment, in his *Health* to the golden age of retainers, that the company of serving men is much "lessened and impaired" in some households lest "the superabundant number of servingmen might grow vicious" (H1v). Although he clearly laments the demise of the cushy life retainers led in a less economically straitened or calculating time, Markham's dislike of excessive spending on vanities is not different from Puritans'. While Puritans emphasize the wastefulness of having retainers, and Markham laments the money *not* spent on hiring appropriate retainers, their complaints about wasteful masters are very similar. "Now these their masters' sports and pastimes, are either turned into covetousness, groping after worldly graith, or else into riotous spending their patrimony in gay clothes, lascivious lewdness, extraordinary gaming, or such like; the godly mean . . . is now banished" (H4v).[18] Markham even allows that "idleness is the root of all mischief" (ibid.).[19] Both Markham and the Puritan writers, then, might agree that masters and servants ought to live less luxuriously. Conformists and nonconformists both, hearing Goneril's remonstrations about Lear's unwieldy retinue, may nod in recognition of a contemporary social problem without actively engaging their possibly politically different analyses of its cause or solution. What makes a piece of dramatic art "work" for a contemporaneous audience is in part simply the overall verisimilitude of the attitudes it implicates, but not necessarily their ideological precision.

Moral Values versus Political Sides

Even if English society were beginning to polarize into groups with ragged edges, it is not likely that sympathy or revulsion for a Lear or an Edmund, a Kent or an Oswald, was simply dependent on polemical identification of such characters with one group or ideology over another. There were still overarching moral values transcending religious and social differences (and exclusively tied neither to the "naked" nor the "clothed") in terms of which characters might have been assessed. Even cultural verisimilitude is probably less crucial for making a piece of dramatic art work, than the audience's sense of whom, in the last estimate, to empathize with and whom to hate, who is good and who is bad. Thus, like ourselves, contemporaneous audiences would judge Goneril not in terms of her attitudes toward household management, but judge her attitudes toward household management in terms of her character, her honesty, and integrity (or the lack thereof). Even were Goneril's attitude toward household management recognizably "Puritan" to both a nonconformist Puritan and a conformist Anglican in the audience, that recognition per se would not determine sympathy or lack of it. The Anglican might well see these frugal "Puritan" attitudes as avaricious hypocrisy because he thinks of Puritans as prone to hypocrisy—as so many of their enemies did. The Puritan would also recognize Goneril's hypocrisy, but he would conclude she therefore could not truly be godly. In other words, Goneril is first understood as a "bad" character; if the "efficiency" she seems to care about is recognizably "Puritan," that Puritanism is recuperated in terms of her badness —either as further indication of it for the anti-Puritan, or as evidence of her lack of true godliness for the Puritan sympathizer. No one regards a "bad" or unsympathetic character as positively representing his or her own political or religious "side"; audiences almost inevitably adjust their perceptions, within broad cultural parameters, to flatter their own self-identifications—and good plays may facilitate such adjustments.

If, for some in the audience, Goneril's attitudes toward household management echo Puritan works, Kent's attitudes toward the tailor-made "base, proud, shallow, beggarly, three-suited, hundred-pound, filthy worsted-stocking" Oswald (2.2.15–17) echo the social attitudes of a contemporary work like Markham's *A Health*. Just as Kent, a self-proclaimed "gentleman of blood and breeding" (3.1.39), contrasts with the Oswald he clearly describes as servile and pretentious (2.3.15–24), so the "gentlemanly servingman, whose life and manners doth equal his birth and bringing up" (F1v) contrasts with the "very officious and diligent" man "of no parts" (G2v), "whose practice and pratling, is not with sincere affection to prefer his master's profit, but thereby to grope for some gain to himself" (G2r), and whose service is "a very servile servitude" (G2v).[20] As gentleman's gentleman, Markham seems to write to reclaim what he describes as a very desirable job from new low-born competitors, "clouted shoes" (H4r), yeomen's sons who "want the gifts of nature and nurture" (G2r), but whose fathers have bribed their ways into the service of impoverished gentlemen with "a couple of fat capons, pig, goose, or lamb" (E4r). Markham is all for "teach[ing] . . . differences." While Kent is more clearly a feudal retainer, a man of the sword, than the gentlemanly servant Markham is concerned with, the overall similarities between the two types of men certainly indicate that *Lear* deals with recognized social tensions.

Yet, once again, our evaluations of these characters are not shaped by their social "side" or our identification with or antipathy toward it. In fact, Shakespeare's exploration of service is complicated by the teasing parallels between the forms of service of the socially opposite servants, Kent and Oswald. There's a certain element of realism about worldly service—whether the service of aristocratic retainer or of low-born parvenu—in the parallels, a realism that keeps us from too neatly categorizing Kent and Oswald in terms of "the two societies" (or of other polarities such as the aristocrat who is "rudely plain and true" as opposed to the social climber who is foppishly "superserviceable" [2.2.18-19]).[21] Nevertheless, in spite of these teasing parallels, our overall evaluations of these characters are not, I think, ambiguated or indeterminate. A crucial reason both for that lack of ambiguity and the limited significance of social or political "sides," is that our ultimate evaluations do not depend on what historical "sides" the characters may suggest, or on their association with plainness or ceremony, or even on what they say they are, but on what we see them do in relation to what they say they are, and to what others say about them.

Kent *is* arrogant and acutely class-conscious, with his "goodman boy" (2.2.45) and other insulting epithets for Oswald. The very neatness of Kent's rejoinder and the very speed of his action when he says "Nor tripped neither" (1.4.86), while actually tripping Oswald— verbally paralleling Oswald's own disclaimer, "I'll not be strucken, my lord" (1.4.85, in response to Lear's striking of him)—convey Kent's possibly too self-pleased sense of his aristocratic privilege.[22] There is also an element of "hitting Oswald when he's down" here (he *has* just been struck) that makes Lear's next lines to Kent, "I thank thee, fellow. Thou serv'st me, and I'll love thee" (1.4.87-88) sound self-serving indeed. There appears to be *some* truth in Oswald's later description of this incident between Kent and himself:

          being down, insulted, railed
And put upon him such a deal of man
That worthied him, got praises of the King
For him attempting who was self-subdued.
(2.2.119–22)[23]

The reservations about Kent as true servant we may have at this point are not too different from the reservations we may have about Lear as true master. When Kent says to the Lear—who has shortly before been irascible and curmudgeonly, "not stay[ing] a jot for dinner" (1.4.8)—"you have that in your countenance which I would fain call master" (1.4.27–28), and to Lear's "What's that?" responds "Authority" (1.4.29–30), we might think that Kent's loyalty to Lear was a "following" "like dogs" (2.2.80), not unlike Oswald's own service as Kent characterizes it.[24] And if Kent is dutiful, and as he says "honest-hearted" (1.4.19), Oswald is perhaps not utterly without his own dutifulness; in spite of Regan's inducements (and the promise of reward from more than one mistress), he will not let her see his mistress Goneril's letter to Edmund (4.4.22)—albeit we feel his reasons have more to do with sticking to the path where he feels his advancement lies.

We might well ask, then, whether anger has the degree of privilege Kent claims (2.2.70) in justifying his beating of Oswald, who does not even draw his sword. When Cornwall says "Know you no reverence?" (2.2.69), doesn't he have a point?[25] Kent's tirade in front of Gloucester's castle (2.2.15–24) makes it evident that Oswald symbolizes the decay of the world for him, but he has not yet fully shared his analysis of why with us.[26] A generous interpretation of Kent's answer, "His countenance likes me not" (2.2.90) to Cornwall's question, "Why dost thou call him knave? What is his fault?" (89) will say that to the world of seeming truths, the "superserviceable" (18–19) world, there is no way to "explain" what's wrong with Oswald; by this point, Kent has spoken of what inspires his instinctive loathing:

          Such smiling rogues as these,
Like rats, oft bit the holy cords a-twain
Which are t'intrinse t'unloose.
(73–75)[27]

In response to Kent's "His countenance likes me not," Cornwall says "No more perchance does mine, nor his, nor hers" (91); his tone of surface "reasonableness" is perhaps fulsomely self-gratulatory enough to corroborate the generous interpretation of Kent's answer.[28] Yet, on the other hand, Kent's "plain," but less than substantive answer, had a certain self-congratulation in it, too, and his ensuing jibe at the faces around him ("Sir, 'tis my occupation to be plain / I have seen better faces in my time / Than stands on any shoulder that I see / Before me at this instant" [92-95]), seems too shallow to clinch his larger point about Oswald. (He has already told Lear he can "deliver a plain message bluntly" [1.4.33-34]; plainness *is* part of his self-conception.) Cornwall's response to this jibe of Kent's, beginning "This is some fellow / Who, having been praised for bluntness, doth affect / A saucy roughness" (2.2.95-97), does not have quite the air of looking around for nods of approval that his previous "No more perchance does mine, nor his, nor hers" had.[29] There *has* been some "saucy roughness" in Kent's jibe. "Pride that she calls plainness"—however incomplete a categorization of Cordelia's behavior in 1.1.—may still ring in some ears. Cornwall seems to have scored a point.

This, then, is one of those moments of so-called indeterminacy, when, *if* one looks at the play not so much as a dramatic text with characters than as an abstract set of oppositional motifs (such as "plain" vs. "eloquent"), it seems that the play is contradicting its own terms or values. Isn't Kent a locus of value and isn't his "plainness" part of that value (as Strier suggests, "Faithful Servants," 117)? If the plainness is questioned with some semblance of justness doesn't that cast doubt on the value?

Kent is, ultimately, a locus of value, but he is also a complex character, not a personification, which makes our evaluation of his "plainness" more complex—although not, I think, indeterminate. When Kent answers Cornwall back in parodically elevated courtly language, he has begun to make the point that really matters in this scene, which is not a point about styles of speech—which finally are seen *as* styles—but a point about moral character, to which either kind of speech is no *sure* guide. "He that beguiled you in a plain accent was a plain knave" (111-12), that is, his knavery, not his plainness is the issue. Just like Henry Barrow, and others in this culture and ours, who know that both the "too nice" garment and the "rough garment" may deceive, Kent knows there can be plain knaves as well as courtly ones.[30] It is a testament to the effectiveness and conviction that Kent's words carry that Cornwall for the first time here turns to question Oswald with the momentary assumption that Kent's story is the correct one: "What was th'offense you gave him?" (114).[31]

Drama does build in corroborations of some of the hypotheses it offers more than of others. It can't do this too quickly and completely, or there's no tension, and no complexity to the characters or themes. We may not be sure that Goneril and Regan were "breeding occasions" with their refusal to entertain their father's retinue.[32] We may feel— because of Lear's peremptoriness and irascibility—the half-rightness of Goneril's complaints about Lear's disordered men. Nevertheless, when Regan, joining in the condemnation of the supposed attempted parricide, Edgar, asks whether he was "companion with the riotous knights / That tended upon my father" (2.1.94-95), and when Cornwall says Kent "is a fellow of the selfsame color / Our sister speaks of" (2.2.138-39)—that is, Goneril speaks of in her forewarning letter to Regan and Cornwall—we begin to see a half-truth become a plot.[33] Even if one is not sure that Kent's extremity of anger has the privilege he suggests, one recognizes that Oswald's immediate response ("This ancient ruffian, sir, whose life I have spared at suit of his gray beard" [2.2.62-63]) to Cornwall's inquiry about what transpired between him and Kent is a self-serving lie; Kent yelled "Draw" three times, but Oswald ran (2.2.35-38). Thus Kent's "That such a slave as this should wear a sword, / Who wears no honesty" (2.3.72-73) is clearly motivated.[34] And certainly Oswald's notion that the King struck at him because he "misconstruct[ed]" his behavior (2.2.117), when Oswald referred to him as "My lady's father" and "bandied" looks with him, also seems to distort the truth.

The description the stocked Kent gives the king of how he came to be stocked contrasts with Oswald's self-serving lies to Cornwall. Kent provides a reason for his own irritation in front of Gloucester's castle ("[Oswald's] welcome I perceived had poisoned mine" [2.4.39]), displays a becoming self-correction ("Having more man than wit about me," as Kent says, he "drew" [42]) and, as well, displays a becoming lack of special pleading. Kent's description also corroborates our suspicion that Oswald's account of the king's "misconstruction" of his behavior is a stark lie, for Kent describes Oswald as "the very fellow which of late / Displayed so saucily against your Highness" (40-41).[35] Later, when Goneril, already having her sights set on Edmund, says of Oswald, "This trusty servant / shall pass between us" (4.2.18-19), she perfectly illustrates Kent's condemnation of Oswald as "one that wouldst be a bawd in way of good service" (2.2.19-20). Like Edmund, though in a different way, Oswald "serve[s] the lust of his mistress' heart" (3.4.86-87).[36] The climactic corroboration of Oswald's moral character, comes, however, when he shouts jubilantly, upon finding Gloucester,

> A proclaim'd prize! Most happy!
> That eyeless head of thine was first framed flesh
> To raise my fortunes.[37]
> (4.6.226-28)

Here Oswald sounds most like Edmund—though he does not even have Edmund's dispossession as a motivation.

That Kent carries with him the prejudices of his class, that he represents a recognizable social "side"—aristocrat versus social newcomer—does not, I think, make it impossible for him to be a locus of value—even for those who belong to the other "side"—because of those overarching moral values that shape audience judgment, and because the opposed "bad" characters are likely to be disassociated from one's own immediate group. The play captures, with verisimilitude, a world in which social values were strongly based on the distinction between gentlemen and nongentlemen, in which many took the opportunity that offered of looking down at those below. Edgar notes that Kent "shunn'd [his own] abhorr'd society" (5.3.211) when he was in his Poor Tom disguise (although it is by no means really clear that he holds this against Kent).[38] Yet Oswald is a better example than Kent of "contempt to inferiors."[39] Coming upon Edgar the "peasant" with his Southwest "rustic" dialect, Oswald (perhaps imitating his own betters), calls him a "peasant," "slave," "dunghill," and "villain" (4.6.231, 236, 243, 246). What makes Kent a locus of value, then, is moral action, and this is more fundamental than whether he speaks plainly or eloquently, represents the subaltern or the aristocrat.

We may now more fully understand the sense in which the values of the play do not necessarily inhere in a simple series of attributes (plainness, silence, the heart, what we feel, nakedness, as opposed to ceremony, speech, the tongue, what we ought to say, gorgeous apparel). We are in a position to understand why the moment when Cornwall "offers a parody of affected plainness" is not really a moment when the "moral moorings of the play threaten to come loose," as Strier claims ("Faithful Servants," 117). The reasons why the "moral moorings of the play" are at no particular risk are that its moral values—rooted in a shared Christian culture—are both more broadly based and more complex than so easy an allegiance to one "side" or another would allow, and that the relation of its characters to those moral values is gradually but clearly revealed through cumulative dramatic clues. Finally, Kent is not good because he is plain, but plain, on occasion, because he is good; and he is still good, though he is accused of affected plainness.

We know from our own experience as audiences that plays can frame a world—values and ethos—quite remote from our own and still enlist our identification with or rejection of characters according to how they play out the apparent values of that world. In such cases we presumably stretch our own values and/or domesticate the values we perceive. Male chauvinist television watchers identify with feminist Roseanne because she's sharp-tongued, quick-witted, and in control; law-abiding citizens find the hit man Vincent (John Travolta) of *Pulp Fiction* appealing because he so well knows "the first law of cool: Don't try to be cool." [40] We are able to applaud shared values, such as bravery or self-awareness, for example, even if they are required in circumstances very different from those to which we might be accustomed. In the case at hand, such values as honesty, integrity, humility, loyal "heart-service" as opposed to "eye-service" only for one's own preferment, and indeed, charity, are certainly supported by the Christian culture as a whole. Plainness is a value when compared to dishonest flattery, and ceremony a value when compared to brutishness or meanness. The culture values both nakedness and proper clothing, both restraint and appropriate pomp; both simple and eloquent styles of speech are capable of appropriate use. Such values may transcend social and religious differences, and are ones with which even a laborer might identify, even when they appear in aristocrat or king. Such transcendence need not automatically be assumed, but neither should it be dismissed out of hand. Part of the appeal of imaginative literature is that it sweeps us into different worlds in which we may see resemblances to our own, sweeps us into emotional complicity with many different kinds of characters. Perhaps indeed "a 'hermeneutics of suspicion,' in and of itself, despite its intellectual sophistication, is as crudely incomplete as a sympathetic imagination divorced from the disciplines of intellectual and historical inquiry." [41]

Shakespearean Politics?

Cumulative dramatic clues, then, gradually establish whether characters are good or bad in terms of an overarching Christian cultural framework. There do exist bridges, of course, between that framework and our own. Even when a Renaissance moral framework is only loosely shared by a present-day viewer or reader, he or she still emotionally understands that Gloucester *is doing a good thing* when he gives his purse to Poor Tom, and that he is expressing values one is supposed to sympathize with when he speaks of the need of the "superfluous . . . man" to "feel," "so that distribution should undo excess" — however he or she choses to interpret "distribution." Nevertheless, the existence of cumulative dramatic cues about the goodness or badness of characters and their actions and the overlap of our present-day moral framework with that of the English Renaissance do not remove the interest or value of the scholarly attempt to recover the historical content of such concepts as "distribution" as precisely as we can. Especially in the current moment, when criticism treats literature as equivalent to political knowledge, we need to understand what that knowledge may have been. As we get more and more removed from the past we tend to understand its artifacts more and more in terms of the present; this tendency makes a self-conscious attempt to recapture former understandings even more important.[42]

It is the conclusion of this book that both "radical" and "traditional" ideas have their basis in the common Renaissance Christian culture that frames the moral judgment of Shakespeare's characters in *Lear*. As we have seen, this culture embodies shared values. It disapproves shameful nakedness where comely clothing is appropriate and approves naked plainness where elaborate clothing would be immodest or deceitful. It disapproves "all anarchy or want of government, and disordered confusion" as well as "all tyrannous . . . and rigorous lordliness and dominion" in kings (and fathers), and would have their "wisdom, love and zeal . . . surmount their authority in commanding," as it also would have the "humility, frank obedience and perfect love" of subjects (and children) "be greater . . . than their civil subjection."[43] In justice, it is alive to the distortion of the law by those "corrupt with meed," as well as to the difficulty of access to overly intricate and obscure law which may require redress by equity. It praises "equal balance to rich and poor," and no sparing of "mighty men" whose "sins are mighty sins."

It appeals publicly to the principle that it is necessary "to execute the law alike on all"; it condemns the corruption that permits "the worst thieves [to] hang the innocent."[44] It urges all "to distribute alms gladly" (for "the alms bestowed upon the poor was bestowed upon [Christ]"), with an urgency made all the more intense by a conception of finite resources ("[I]t is . . . the coat of the naked that thou lockest in thy wardrobe"), and applied as much—or more—to superiors as to the lowly ("Fond Richard! Thou buildst a hall to feast in, / And starv'st thy wretched subjects to erect it.").[45]

Because the values of this culture *are* broadly shared, one can indeed find similar expressions of them in conservatives and revolutionaries. This common Christian culture "form[s] something like a conceptual and practical horizon inside which both [sixteenth- and] seventeenth-century orthodoxy and opposition must fashion themselves."[46] The shared language of mainstream Christian culture can become the language of radicals in a polarized society; it is always available both for the rulers and the ruled, the masters and the servants, for containing discontent, as well as for subverting existing power. Thus those political critics who pronounce *Lear* radical on the basis of parallel ideas in revolutionary writers—such as concern for the downtrodden and contempt for corrupt power—are not convincing, simply because similar ideas are so often expressed with similar passion by conformist or mainstream writers, or the rulers themselves, at the time of the play. Both King James and William Walwyn assert that justice should never be swayed by the bribes of the rich, and that the powerful should not be allowed to oppress the weak.

This shared language and these common values of Renaissance Christian culture, especially considerably before the Civil War, mean that Shakespeare's politics can't be categorized in any easy way as "right" or "left" on a post–Civil War or modern political spectrum; those choices don't map clearly on to the political society of Shakespeare's time and its language as shared by the play. However, neither would it be true to say that Shakespeare's politics are completely indeterminant, either with respect to the political possibilities of the pre–Civil War years broadly considered (and held to include Anabaptism and Levelling, for example, as they certainly are by political critics), or as gauged against the *particular* statements of those "right" or "left" political critics themselves. Let us consider why.

We have seen, in accordance with the semantic theory in this book, that similar language about appropriate nakedness and appropriate clothing can be used by conformist and nonconformist to refer to different things when they metaphorically extend their shared concept of "proper clothing" to discussions of ceremony and government in the church. Similarly, such concepts as "distribution"—metaphorically extended or not—theoretically could have entirely different referents, and Shakespeare's politics—insofar as they rest on the meanings of such concepts—could be inescapably indeterminant as a result. Nevertheless, I do not think they are—however painstaking the effort needed to recover them, and however probabilistic the results. My semantic theory has also shown that certain referents and oppositions are more likely than others in particular cases; this book as a whole has also shown that there is a difference between pervasive cultural evidence for such referents and oppositions and isolated instances—or none. "Distribution," for example—so clearly meaning almsgiving in a multitude of sources—might hypothetically be stretched to refer to "having all things common," insofar as both expressions occur in the text of Acts 4:32-35—looked at in isolation. However, the Geneva Bible gloss on the passage itself rules out this interpretation—not to mention Calvin and a multitude of other exegetes. In Reformation use, "distribution" clearly contrasts with neglect of charity, rather than with concentrations of private property; and the paternalistic context of Gloucester's charitable distribution in the play (as he is served by subordinates, so he is generous to subordinates) supports the core meaning of the concept. In short, there is nothing about the context of the concept's use in *Lear* to suggest that it might there have any newly elastic and unprecedented meaning.

Given the close fit of Shakespeare's play with mainstream, commonly available social and economic thinking that this book has demonstrated, one must also conclude that it is *not* radical by the standards of current radical political criticism. It is not radical in the sense in which Dollimore, for example, regards Elizabethan and Jacobean drama as radical, that is, containing "a knowledge which interrogated prevailing beliefs, submitted them to a kind of intellectual vandalism; radical in the sense of going to their roots and even pulling them up" (*Radical Tragedy*, xxi).

This does not mean, on the other hand, that the play is clearly conservative for its own period, especially in a quietist sense (or should be judged "rightist" by contemporary political critics). Because it is not an

example of radical subversion does not mean that it is an example of
establishment propaganda. The either/or is the problem. *Lear* does not
seem to be socially and economically radical in the sense of proposing
or implying a radical restructuring of society, whether of its present
social hierarchy, or its existing distribution of wealth. For Shakespeare,
as, for example, for Downame, although the need may be reasoned, it
is not the same for beggar and king; the "necessities of one's estate"
are necessities. Nevertheless, *Lear* indeed does powerfully "tak[e] the
traditional order at its word and measur[e] it by its own claims and
standards."[47] The play insists strongly and graphically that Christian
society live up to its ideals to alleviate the suffering of the unfortunate.
In Shakespeare's time, a shared ideology stressing the obligations of
the rich to the poor allowed each to make claims on the other. Elizabethan policies (such as the poor law and the regulation of the supply
of grain in times of dearth) encouraged a paternalist view emphasizing the dependence of the poor on their superiors, but also permitted
the poor to demand some redress in accordance with values the elite
presumably shared. Emerging at some of the play's most intense moments, Shakespeare's concern with "distribution," like Downame's in
his profound and moving *Plea of the Poore,* is a concern that charitable
alms be given in a spirit of unniggling compassion. For Downame, as
for so many contemporaneous Christian urgers of charity in a time of
increased awareness of poverty, the "Persian" or luxurious garments of
the privileged are more likely to encourage sin than not.[48]

Similarly, shared conceptions available to governors and governed
"might be used to bring home the wrongs done by those charged
with maintaining the right" (Sacks, "Searching for 'Culture,' " 485); this
was a society in which stability — in the absence of a police force — depended in part on the willingness of inferiors to obey superiors, and
of superiors to adjust their demands according to what their inferiors would tolerate. Indeed, even if the mainstream Protestant culture
is neither economically nor socially egalitarian — especially in the early
seventeenth century — it does have a built-in potential for resistance to
political tyranny in the ambiguity of its thinking about obedience to
ungodly rulers; the play perhaps gives shape to that potential in the
"better service" (3.7.74) of Cornwall's defiant and then rebellious Servant — even though he pays for his crime.

The thrust of potentially subversive ideas is perhaps not always as
covert as recent political criticism implies — heard only in the words of
conservative repeaters of popular complainers, or in the silences of lan-

guage full of contradictory impulses because of actual or anticipated repression. Bishop Richard Bancroft scuttles Anabaptist egalitarianism in his *Sermon Preached at Paule's Crosse* (while urging the obligations of the rich to the poor); he forthrightly attacks the Scot Buchanan's Protestant antiroyalism in *Dangerous Positions*; such frank ways suggest such ideas were not necessarily restricted only to a heavily camouflaged undercurrent. One can certainly hear the Christian-supported class feeling building in works like *Pride and Lowlines*, Lupton's *Divell and Dives*, Warren's *Poore Man's Passions*, or the writings of Henry Barrow. But it is also interesting and important to note the way in which the strong antigentleman feelings of a writer acutely aware of class privilege like Arthur Warren ("Who is the Lord, but he, that hath the luck; / Who is the man, but he, that hath the muck?"), coexist with, or may even be held in check by anti-Catholic and antisedition Protestant nationalism. And, finally, it is just because of such overlapping self-identifications, that we should be careful not to oversimplify political allegiance in the early seventeenth century.

I hope that the reader of this delimited but comprehensive effort in historical semiotics emerges with a rich and full sense of historical meaning, as well as of the very meaning of meaning. And I certainly hope that that full sense of historical meaning feels more tenable than not *because* of the very fact that it taps into concerns and categorizations at the heart of Reformation Christian culture and dramatically central in *King Lear,* rather than those peripheral or contingent in either. However much disagreement there may be among contemporary literary critics, we probably all do agree that culture at any moment in time crucially influences our values and perception of the world; the question that interests me is precisely *how.* Valorizing the contingent may slight the reality of culture at any one historical moment in the name of the rejection of the falsely "universal." It is to me no discredit to intensely historicist goals to have them result in the unstartling and perhaps unglamorous discovery that a playwright spoke in a language meaningful to superior and inferior, ruler and ruled, master and servant, conformist and nonconformist in a not yet radically polarized culture—if one can demonstrate precisely and comprehensively how that playwright did so. I hope that I have provided that demonstration here, and in doing so convincingly shown that genuine substantive investigation of the past is still possible—if requiring a lot of patience. It is to the restoration of the excitement and the satisfactions and the *meaningfulness* of such investigation that I hope this book will contribute.

Notes

Introduction: History, Language, and Postmodern Criticism
of the Renaissance

1 As Richard Strier notes in *Love Known: Theology and Experience in George Herbert's Poetry* (Chicago: Univ. of Chicago Press, 1983), xv, "while the term 'Puritan' was in actual use in the period, the term 'Anglican' was not." Nevertheless, the concept and term "Anglican," opposed to "Puritan," and including features related to liturgy and church organization has of course been in use in the language of the community of critics of seventeenth-century literature and of historians of the English Reformation for some time. Thus, I do use it as such in this book.

2 Louis Montrose identifies "new historicism or cultural poetics, cultural materialism, feminism, and revisionist forms of Marxism" as "New Historicisms" in his essay of that title (392). See *Redrawing the Boundaries: The Transformation of English and American Literary Studies*, ed. Stephen Greenblatt and Giles Gunn (New York: Modern Language Association of America, 1992), 392–418. When I refer to new historicisms, I include these "intellectual forces" (392), with the exception of feminism. As Montrose says, "Geertzian notions of culture" (including the idea of "generative and restrictive cultural code[s]") and "Foucault's early epistemic history" are influences on new historicism (401). Further references to "New Historicisms" will appear parenthetically in the text.

3 Louis Montrose poses the opposites "implacable code" and "slippery signifier" ("Professing the Renaissance: The Poetics and Politics of Culture" in H. Aram Veeser, ed., *The New Historicism* [New York: Routledge, 1989], 21) in order to suggest the problems of the opposition; nevertheless the terms themselves are problematic as this introduction suggests. See below, chapter 3. Further references to "Professing" will appear parenthetically in the text. For a very interesting study of the *limits* of totalitarian attempts to impose linguistic meaning see Michal Buchowski, David B. Kronenfeld, William Peterman, and Lynn Thomas, "Language, *Nineteen Eighty-Four*, and 1989," *Language in Society* 23, no. 4 (1994): 555–78.

4 "A linguistic unit is like a fixed part of a building, e.g. a column. On the one hand, the column has a certain relation to the architrave that it supports; the arrangement of the two units in space suggests the syntagmatic relation. On the other hand, if the column is Doric, it suggests a mental comparison of this style with others (Ionic, Corinthian, etc.) although none of these elements is present in space: the relation is associative [i.e., paradigmatic]." Ferdinand de Saussure, *Course in General Linguistics,* ed. Charles Bally and Albert Sechehaye, in collaboration with Albert Riedlinger, trans. Wade Baskin (New York: McGraw Hill, 1966), 124–25. Further references will appear parenthetically in the text

5 George Puttenham, *The Arte of English Poesie,* in *Elizabethan Critical Essays,* ed. G. Gregory Smith (London: Oxford Univ. Press, 1964), 2:142.

6 Q has "So distribution should under excesse" (l.1988). For the variants of 4.6.164–65 in F and Q see chapter 8, note 1.

7 For surveys of the diverse theory and practice encompassed by these critical modes, see Montrose, "New Historicisms"; H. Aram Veeser, "The New Historicism," in *The New Historicism Reader,* ed. H. Aram Veeser (New York: Routledge, 1994), 1–32; and H. Aram Veeser, Introduction to *The New Historicism,* ed. H. Aram Veeser (New York: Routledge, 1989), ix–xvi. For a historicizing discussion of American new historicism and British cultural materialism, see Don E. Wayne, "Power, Politics, and the Shakespearean Text: Recent Criticism in England and the United States," in *Shakespeare Reproduced: The Text in History and Ideology,* ed. Jean E. Howard and Marion F. O'Connor (New York: Methuen, 1987), 47–67. Also see Louis Montrose, "Renaissance Literary Studies and the Subject of History," *English Literary Renaissance* 16, no. 1 (winter 1986): 5–12, and "Professing," an expanded version of the previous essay. Marxist and neo-Marxist criticism may both differ from and overlap with these new historicisms. See Catherine Gallagher, "Marxism and the New Historicism," in Veeser, *The New Historicism,* 37–48; also see Walter Cohen, "Political Criticism of Shakespeare," in *Shakespeare Reproduced,* ed. Howard and O'Connor, 18–45.

8 Even Greenblatt suggests there may be something like "containment subverted" in *Lear:* "[T]here are moments in Shakespeare's career—*King Lear* is the greatest example—when the process of containment is stretched to the breaking point" (*Shakespearian Negotiations: The Circulation of Social Energy in Renaissance England* [Berkeley: Univ. of California Press, 1988], 65). Further references to *Shakespearian Negotiations* will appear parenthetically in the text.

9 Richard Strier, *Resistant Structures: Particularity, Radicalism, and Renaissance Texts* (Berkeley: Univ. of California Press, 1995), 5, 6. Strier regards "unthinkability" as a "dangerous" a priori concept (6) which he claims is involved in my essay " 'So Distribution Should Undo Excess, and Each Man Have Enough': Shakespeare's *King Lear*—Anabaptist Egalitarianism, Anglican Charity, Both, Neither?" *ELH* 59 (1992): 755–84, on which chapter 7 of the present book is based. He claims that oppositional conceptions

are ruled out because they are "nonhegemonic or unusual" by critics who attempt to be "historical" and avoid "anachronism," like myself. But it is only in his own a priori assumption that the conceptions at issue are oppositional, or unusual ("radical," in this context, does seem to imply a smaller fringe group, as opposed to the more numerous mainstream); I certainly do not rule them out, since, as I show, they are part of common Christian culture. See below, chapter 7.

10 Frederick Amrine et al., "The Status of Evidence: A Roundtable," *PMLA* III, no. 1 (January 1996): 22.

11 Leah S. Marcus, *Puzzling Shakespeare: Local Reading and Its Discontents* (Berkeley: Univ. of California Press, 1988), 32. Further references will appear parenthetically in the text. See also Brook Thomas: "The most widespread explanation of how the new historicism distinguishes itself from the old is that it has engaged poststructuralist theory" ("The New Historicism and other Old-fashioned Topics," in *The New Historicism*, ed. Veeser, 183). There are also affinities between deconstruction and Marxist demystification in contemporary criticism; see, for example, Jean E. Howard's praise of Dominick La Capra for uniting the two "in the project of fracturing the unified surface of the text to let the multiplicity of its social voices be heard" ("The New Historicism in Renaissance Studies," *English Literary Renaissance* 16, no. 1 [winter 1986]: 30). Further references will appear parenthetically in the text. There are overall similarities in methods used by "critical historicists," i.e., "poststructuralist analysis of the sign, materialist analysis of ideology, and Foucauldian analysis of discursive formations" (Howard Horwitz, " 'I Can't Remember': Skepticism, Synthetic Histories, Critical Action," *South Atlantic Quarterly* 87, no. 4 [fall 1988]: 791). Further references will appear parenthetically in the text.

12 Jaques Derrida, *Of Grammatology*, trans. Gayatri Chakravorty Spivak (Baltimore: Johns Hopkins Univ. Press, 1976), 158. Further references will appear parenthetically in the text.

13 The first quotation is from Jonathan Dollimore, "Introduction: Shakespeare, Cultural Materialism and the New Historicism," in *Political Shakespeare: New Essays in Cultural Materialism*, ed. Jonathan Dollimore and Alan Sinfield (Ithaca: Cornell Univ. Press, 1985), 3. Further references to this essay will appear parenthetically in the text. The remaining quotations are from Stephen Greenblatt, introduction to *The Forms of Power and the Power of Forms in the Renaissance* (Norman, Okla.: Pilgrim, 1982), 6, 5. Further references will appear parenthetically in the text. See Jean Howard on literary texts as "sites where many voices of culture and many systems of intelligibility interact" ("The New Historicism," 30) and quoted above, note 11; also see Carolyn Porter, "History and Literature: 'After the New Historicism,'" *New Literary History* 21 (1990): 253–73, where new historicism is faulted for not emphasizing the possibilities of subversion and demarginalization, i.e., those "multivoiced discourses in which both dominant and oppositional strains are at work" (269).

14 For the valorization of indeterminacy as "the ultimate descent into the politics of silliness," see Gerald Graff, "Co-optation," in *The New Historicism*, ed. Veeser, 174. Also see Howard Horwitz's criticism of Dollimore and Sinfield for "reject[ing] as mystifying and repressive the claim to have a 'right interpretation' of an allegedly given textual fact'" (quoting from their "Foreword: Cultural Materialism," in *Political Shakespeare*, viii), and thus "suggesting that an interpreter's belief in the factuality of a textual feature resembles a criminal indictment, . . . as if accepting the factuality of the world amounts to an endorsement of its present distribution of power" ("'I Can't Remember,'" 794). See Richard Wilson, "Introduction: Historicizing New Historicism," in *New Historicism and Renaissance Drama*, ed. Richard Wilson and Richard Dutton (London: Longman, 1992), 3–4, on the legacy to new historicism from Barthes, Foucault, and French New Philosophy, i.e., that language, classifications, systems, institutions, and reason are all inherently repressive. As Nancy Easterlin and Barbara Liebling say, "Through an endless play of signifiers, the tyrannical world of finite textual meaning was replaced by a free realm of infinite ambiguity" (introduction to *After Poststructuralism: Interdisciplinarity and Literary Theory*, ed. Nancy Easterlin and Barbara Riebling [Evanston, Ill.: Northwestern Univ. Press, 1993], 1).

15 Greenblatt himself recognizes that language is a "collective construction" (*Renaissance Self-Fashioning from More to Shakespeare* [Chicago: Univ. of Chicago Press, 1980], 5), "the supreme instance of a collective creation" (*Shakespearian Negotiations*, 4). Of course, this is a Saussurean principle. Greenblatt, like other new historicists, seems to regard such shared structures as inherently restrictive. Further references to *Renaissance Self-Fashioning* will appear parenthetically in the text and notes.

16 James Holstun suggests that "the new historicism has trouble focusing on categories of collective social being that might mediate between free individuality and cultural totality. . . . The possibility never arises that collective categories such as religion . . . might be something other than the oppressive construct of a dominant system." "Ranting at the New Historicism," *English Literary Renaissance* 19 (1989): 195. Further references will appear parenthetically in the text.

17 Howard and O'Connor, introduction to *Shakespeare Reproduced*, 3.

18 Catherine Belsey, *Critical Practice* (London: Methuen, 1980; reprint, London: Routledge, 1988), 5. Further references will appear parenthetically in the text. Ideology in such descriptions is a prison-house like language, structure, code; it seems to grip the psyche as does the Freudian uncon-scious and to be equally inaccessible to conscious thought.

19 For example, see Jean E. Howard, "The New Historicism," 43: "[C]riti-cism is non-objective, interested and political." Yet she is "not suggesting that it is desirable to look at the past with the willful intention of see-ing one's own prejudices and concerns." Ideology often seems to be that which constrains one's opponent only. As Edward Pechter points out, this thought is not new. See "Against Ideology," in *Shakespeare Left and Right*, ed. Ivo Kamps (New York: Routledge, 1991), particularly 85–87.

20 "On the one hand, [new historicists] claim authority for their recon-structions of literary history by appealing to historical evidence. On the other, they have to admit that their evidence is itself an inevitably partial construction of the past from a present perspective." Thomas, "The New Historicism and other Old-fashioned Topics," 187. For other insightful dis-cussions of these contradictions, see Horwitz, " 'I Can't Remember,' " and David Simpson, "Literary Criticism and the Return to 'History,' " *Critical Inquiry* 14 (summer 1988): 721–47.

21 Stephen Greenblatt, *Learning to Curse: Essays in Early Modern Culture* (New York: Routledge, 1990), 164; I omit the original italics in the first quo-tation. Further references will appear parenthetically in the text. Edward Pechter argues that the early Greenblatt moves from regarding "literature and cultural knowledge . . . as interanimating each other," in the introduc-tion to his *Forms of Power*, to regarding "culture [as] unambiguously deter-mining" in his essay on "*King Lear* and Harsnett's '*Devil Fiction*.' " See "The New Historicism and Its Discontents: Politicizing Renaissance Drama," *PMLA* 102, no. 3 (May 1987): 293. Much of the criticism of new historicism's emphasis on containing structures, codes, power, etc. has been political or moral, that is, concerned that this is a politically quietist model. See, for ex-ample, Holstun, "Ranting," Porter, "History and Literature," and Cohen, "Political Criticism."

22 The contingent conservative Shakespeare is anticipated in Glynne Wickham, "From Tragedy to Tragi-Comedy: 'King Lear' as Prologue," *Shakespeare Survey* 26 (1973): 33–48. For the contingent Shakespeare who is conservative or radical—or both—see Marcus, *Puzzling Shakespeare*, 148–59. A conservative pro-James reading might be tied to the particular cir-cumstances of a particular performance; for example, the liturgical context of St. Stephen's Day—on which *Lear* was performed at court in 1606—might have strengthened the positive aspects of "hospitality" to the out-cast Scots. Also see, among others, Steven Urkowitz, *Shakespeare's Revision of "King Lear"* (Princeton: Princeton Univ. Press, 1980) and Gary Taylor and

Michael Warren, eds., *The Division of the Kingdoms: Shakespeare's Two Versions of "King Lear"* (Oxford: Clarendon, 1983) for their contribution to the "contingent" Shakespeare.

23 See the work of Annabel Patterson: *Censorship and Interpretation: The Conditions of Writing and Reading in Early Modern England* (Madison: Univ. of Wisconsin Press, 1984), esp. 58–73; *Shakespeare and the Popular Voice* (Cambridge, Mass.: Basil Blackwell, 1989); *Reading between the Lines* (Madison: Univ. of Wisconsin Press, 1993). Further references to the first two of these works will appear parenthetically in the text.

24 Christopher Hill, *The Collected Essays*, vol. 2, *Religion and Politics in Seventeenth-Century England* (Brighton: Harvester, 1986), 89–116. See, for cultural materialist criticism of Shakespeare: Jonathan Dollimore, *Radical Tragedy: Religion, Ideology and Power in the Drama of Shakespeare and His Contemporaries*, 2nd ed. (Durham, N.C.: Duke Univ. Press, 1993); Dollimore and Sinfield, *Political Shakespeare*; John Drakakis, ed. *Alternative Shakespeares* (London: Methuen, 1985). References to Dollimore, *Radical Tragedy*, will appear parenthetically in the text.

25 Richard Dutton, "Postscript," in *New Historicism and Renaissance Drama*, ed. Wilson and Dutton, 222. In constructing such radical Shakespeares, new historicists "tacitly draw" on "Whig and Marxist historians," even though "their epistemological premises purport to be very different" (222); they reject the views of revisionist historians who emphasize "the continuities and pragmatic accommodations within the system as it operated" (ibid.) in favor of the Whig emphasis on "corruption, imminent breakdown and revolutionary potential" (221). Leeds Barroll criticizes new historicism's uncritical use of pre-existent narratives. In "A New History for Shakespeare and His Time," *Shakespeare Quarterly* 39, no. 4 (1988): 441–64, he himself provides a fresh investigation of the "locus associating Shakespeare's *Richard II* with the Essex uprising" (442) used by both Greenblatt and Dollimore.

26 Ivo Kamps, "Introduction: Ideology and Its Discontents," in *Shakespeare Left and Right*, 1. Further references will appear parenthetically in the text.

27 "The cry of anachronism, I suggest, almost always serves the interests of a conservative picture of the past" (Strier, *Resistant Structures*, 6).

28 Catherine Belsey, "Literature, History, Politics," in *New Historicism and Renaissance Drama*, ed. Wilson and Dutton, 44.

29 While "critical historicists" as a whole emphasize the ideological nature of all histories, and for this reason refuse to distinguish between "analytic" and "prescriptive" history (Simpson, "Literary Criticism," 727), or "objective" and "moral" models, paradoxically, "new historicists" themselves do

make truth claims—as several recent observers point out—and need to make them insofar as they *are* politically committed. "If one's accounts are not 'right,' how can political recommendations be claimed to be adequate either to history or to the conditions of knowledge? . . . We would not accord a policy political or moral authority were we not persuaded of the basic empirical truth of the account of conditions on which that policy is based. . . . Even when they claim to put into question the status of their interpretations, practitioners of critical historiography do believe in the truth of their accounts of history or literature. . . . One condition of holding beliefs is the conviction that they are true" (Horwitz, " 'I Can't Remember,' " 794, 797).

30 Simpson, "Literary Criticism and the Return to 'History,' " 746.

31 On the issue of the relation of knowledge to ideology, see the insightful essay by Michael Sprinker, "Commentary: 'You've Got a Lot of Nerve,' " in *Shakespeare Left and Right*, ed. Kamps, 115–28.

32 Perhaps Louis Montrose has something similar in mind when he says: "In any situation of signification, the theoretical indeterminacy of the signifying process is delimited by the historical specificity of discursive practices, by the constraints and resources of the reading formation within which that signification takes place" ("New Historicisms," 415).

33 Alan Shapiro, "Horace and the Reformation of Creative Writing," *American Poetry Review* 21, no. 2 (March–April 1992): 12.

34 In fact, the general thrust of this investigation is in accordance with the views of those historians who would reinvent religion as a reason for the Civil War. Even Protestants who disagreed about aspects of ritual and liturgy could be united in their strong nationalistic feelings for Britain as Protestant nation—feelings that were based on their mutual hatred and fear of Catholics. In this view, it was when monarch and episcopate threatened to behave in ways that would reinstate the dreaded papist's religion that Protestant ideas of civil liberty in the cause of religion came into full play. For the importance of the Catholic vs. Protestant antinomy, see, for example, Peter Lake, "Anti-Popery: The Structure of a Prejudice," in *Conflict in Early Stuart England: Studies in Religion and Politics, 1603–1642*, ed. Richard Cust and Ann Hughes (London: Longman, 1989).

35 Rosalie L. Colie, "The Energies of Endurance: Biblical Echo in King Lear," in *Some Facets of "King Lear": Essays in Prismatic Criticism*, ed. Rosalie L. Colie and F. T. Flahiff (London: Heinemann, 1974), 121.

36 Debora K. Shuger, "Subversive Fathers and Suffering Subjects: Shakespeare and Christianity," in *Religion, Literature, and Politics in Post-Reformation England, 1540–1688*, ed. R. Strier and D. Hamilton (Cambridge: Cambridge Univ. Press, 1996), 46.

1 Metaphor and Common Christian Culture

1 Derek Attridge, "Puttenham's Perplexity: Nature, Art, and the Supplement in Renaissance Poetic Theory," in *Literary Theory/Renaissance Texts*, ed. Patricia Parker and David Quint (Baltimore: Johns Hopkins Univ. Press, 1986), 259.

2 Some evidence of the continued vitality of such basic metaphors in our culture might be offered by the sixties vogue for "naked" poetry, or such a discussion as the following, from John Vernon, *Poetry and the Body* (Urbana: Univ. of Illinois Press, 1979), 77. "Donne wasn't a 'naked' poet; he couldn't have conceived of spontaneity taking its own shape. . . . Ceremonies, rituals, and prescribed forms were more than a clothing Donne's culture wore; they were the very body of that culture. That is, the body was assimilated into them, like a body that becomes the clothing it wears."

3 Elaine Pagels, *Adam, Eve, and the Serpent* (New York: Random House, 1988), 12; Frank Bottomley, *Attitudes to the Body in Western Christendom* (London: Lepus, 1979), 25.

4 Bottomley, *Attitudes*, 25–26. For examples of the latter point, see Leviticus 18:7–19. "The nakedness of thy father, or the nakedness of thy mother, shalt thou not uncover: she is thy mother; thou shalt not uncover her nakedness. The nakedness of thy father's wife shalt thou not uncover: it is thy father's nakedness. The nakedness of thy sister," etc. I quote the King James Version because the Geneva Bible uses "shame" for "nakedness."

5 Bottomley, *Attitudes*, 26.

6 I quote from the King James Bible. The Geneva Bible has "filthiness" for "nakedness."

7 Bottomley, *Attitudes*, 26.

8 Peter Brown, *The Body and Society: Men, Women and Sexual Renunciation in Early Christianity* (New York: Columbia Univ. Press, 1988), 315–16.

9 Ibid., 168. This is a description of the thought of Origen on sexuality.

10 Ibid., 49–50.

11 Ibid., 96–97.

12 Henry Chadwick, *Priscillian of Avila: The Occult and the Charismatic in the Early Church* (Oxford: Clarendon, 1976), vii, 139.

13 Norman Cohn, *The Pursuit of the Millennium: Revolutionary Millenarians and Mystical Anarchists of the Middle Ages* (New York: Oxford Univ. Press, 1970), 268. "The new king dressed in magnificent robes and wore rings, chains and spurs made from the finest metal by the most skillful craftsmen in the town. Gentlemen-at-arms and a whole train of officers of the court were appointed. Whenever the king appeared in public he was accompanied by his suite, also splendidly dressed" (272).

14 Ibid., 273–74.

15 Ibid., 169–70. Somewhat similarly, "In the *Arcadia*, Sidney describes a joust involving men 'appareled like shepherds, for the fashion.' The contender has 'furniture . . . dressed over with wool, so enriched with jewels artificially placed, that one would have thought it a marriage between the lowest and the highest.' " J. Z. Kronenfeld, "Social Rank and the Pastoral Ideals of *As You Like It*," *Shakespeare Quarterly* 29, no. 3 (1978): 337, quoting *The Prose Works of Sir Philip Sidney*, ed. A. Feuillerat (Cambridge: Cambridge Univ. Press, 1965), 1:284–85. For the role of such "symbolic marriage[s] between humility and pomp, spareness and plenty, the low and the high" (ibid.) in pastoral literature, see this essay.

16 Horton Davies, *Worship and Theology in England from Cranmer to Hooker, 1534–1603* (Princeton: Princeton Univ. Press, 1970), 75.

17 Richard Hooker, *Of the Laws of Ecclesiastical Polity*, 5.15.1, in *The Works of Mr. Richard Hooker*, compiled by John Keble, 6th ed., 3 vols. (Oxford: Clarendon, 1874), 2:52–53. Further references to book, chapter, and section of *The Laws of Ecclesiastical Polity* (abbreviated *LEP*), as well as to other writings of Hooker in *The Works*, will appear parenthetically in the text.

18 John à Lasco, "The Judgement of Master John à Lasco," from J. B., *The Fortress of Fathers* (1566), in *Elizabethan Puritanism*, ed. Leonard J. Trinterud (New York: Oxford Univ. Press, 1971), 112–13, 116. John Hooper makes the same kind of argument in his debate with Nicholas Ridley, bishop of London, about the vestments; see below, chapter 4.

19 Bartimaeus Andrewes, *Certaine Verie Worthie, Godly and Profitable Sermons, upon the Fifth Chapter of the Songs of Solomon* (1583), 26, quoted in Alan F. Herr, *The Elizabethan Sermon* (New York: Octagon, 1969), 90.

20 *The Sermons of John Donne*, ed. Evelyn M. Simpson and George R. Potter, 10 vols. (Berkeley: Univ. of California Press, 1954), 3:368 (sermon no. 17). Further references will appear parenthetically in the text.

21 See the *OED*. There does seem to be a slant toward "decent, sober, modest, proper," rather than "splendid," in the meanings of the word. For example, in the Geneva Bible, Paul urges "that [women] array themselves in comely apparel, with shamefastness and modesty, not with broided hair, or gold, or pearls, or costly apparel" (1 Timothy 2:9). In the King James Bible the passage has "that women adorn themselves in modest apparel." Among the examples of the use of the word, the *OED* gives a passage from Stubbes's *Anatomy:* "Their hair would . . . overgrow their faces, rather like monsters, than comely sober Christians."

22 *Basilikon Doron*, in *The Political Works of James I*, with an introduction by Charles Howard McIlwain (Cambridge, Mass: Harvard Univ. Press, 1918), 45. Further references will appear parenthetically in the text.

23 Robert Crowley, *A Briefe Discourse against the Outwarde Apparell and Ministring Garmentes of the Popishe Church* ([Emden], 1566), A5v.

24 "Oh Read Over Dr. John Bridges" (known as the "Epistle"), in *The Marprelate Tracts, 1588, 1589*, ed. William Pierce (London: James Clarke, 1911), 18. "A Second Admonition to the Parliament," in *Puritan Manifestoes*, ed. W. H. Frere and C. E. Douglas (London: S.P.C.K., 1954), 84.

25 "Oh Read Over Dr. John Bridges," *Marprelate Tracts*, 135.

26 *The Works of John Whitgift*, ed. John Ayre, 3 vols. (Cambridge: Cambridge Univ. Press, 1851–53), 1:187–88. *The Works of Whitgift* contain *The Defence of the Answer to the Admonition, Against the Reply of Thomas Cartwright*. Cartwright's *Reply* is incorporated, section by section, in Whitgift's *Defence*. Further references will appear parenthetically in the text.

27 Walter Travers, *A Full and Plaine Declaration of Ecclesiastical Discipline* (Zurich, 1574), 128.

28 All Milton quotations in the preceding paragraph are from John Milton, *The Reason of Church Government* (1641), 2.2, in *Complete Prose Works of John Milton*, vol. 1, *1624–1642*, ed. Don M. Wolfe (New Haven: Yale Univ. Press, 1953), 828.

29 *Of Religious Assemblies and the Publick Service of God* (Cambridge, 1642), quoted in Davies, *Worship and Theology*, 206.

30 Richard Strier, *Love Known: Theology and Experience in George Herbert's Poetry* (Chicago: Univ. of Chicago Press, 1983), 129–30. Donne's line is from "A Hymne to God My God, in My Sicknesse"; see *The Complete Poetry and Selected Prose of John Donne*, ed. Charles M. Coffin (New York: Random House, 1952), 272. See John Calvin, *Institutes of the Christian Religion*, 3.11.23, trans. John Allen, 7th ed., 2 vols. (Philadelphia: Presbyterian Board of Christian Education, 1936), 1:821. "Ambrose appears to me to have very beautifully exemplified this righteousness in the benediction of Jacob; . . . he, who had on his own account no claim to the privileges of primogeniture, being concealed in his brother's habit, and invested with his garment, . . . insinuated himself into the favour of his father; . . . so we shelter ourselves under the precious purity of Christ our elder brother, that we might obtain the testimony of righteousness in the sight of God." Further references to book, chapter, and section of Calvin's *Institutes* will appear parenthetically in the text.

31 *A Booke of Christian Prayers* (London, 1578), in *Private Prayers: Put Forth by Authority during the Reign of Qu. Elizabeth*, ed. William Keatinge Clay (Cambridge: Univ. Press, 1851), 442–43.

32 Jonathan Culler, *Structuralist Poetics: Structuralism, Linguistics, and the Study of Literature* (Ithaca: Cornell Univ. Press, 1975; reprint, 1976), 14. Further references will appear parenthetically in the text.

33 Russell A. Fraser, *Shakespeare's Politics in Relation to "King Lear"* (London: Routledge and Kegan Paul, 1962), 110 (my emphasis).

34 Of course, analogy, a rhetorical figure, has long been identified as a notoriously unreliable kind of proof. David Norbrook remarks that Erasmus (in *De Copia*) "points out that some [analogical] material may serve not only diverse but contrary uses." "Rhetoric, Ideology and the Elizabethan World Picture," in *Renaissance Rhetoric*, ed. Peter Mack (New York: St. Martin's, 1994), 142. However, if "bees could be invoked as a model by monarchists, Cromwellians and republicans" (ibid., 143), that is because bee society was seen differently by different political theorists, or, at the least, quite different aspects of bee society were their foci. It is true that analogy permits the same entity to be used in different ways. For this reason, I should state that a framework that goes beyond simple analogy (see below, chapter 3) is involved in my references in this chapter to shared core concepts of "proper clothing" from which metaphoric extension takes place.

35 Quentin Bell, *On Human Finery* (London: Hogarth Press, 1976). Geoffrey Squire alludes to the three Veblen categories and Bell's addition in *Dress, Art and Society, 1560–1970* (London: Studio Vista, 1974), 16. Veblen's book has chapters on "Conspicuous Leisure" and "Conspicuous Consumption," but actually discusses these categories, and "conspicuous waste" in relation to clothing in ch. 7, "Dress as an Expression of the Pecuniary Culture." See *The Theory of the Leisure Class* (1899; reprint, New York: Penguin, 1979).

36 *Quippes for Upstart Newfangled Gentlewomen; or, A Glasse, to View the Pride of Vainglorious Women* (London, 1595), A4v.

37 *Phillip Stubbes's Anatomy of the Abuses in England in Shakspere's Youth, A.D. 1583,* ed. Frederick J. Furnivall (London: N. Trübner, 1877–79), 74. Further references will appear parenthetically in the text.

38 Jane Ashelford, *Dress in the Age of Elizabeth I* (New York: Holmes Meier, 1988), 51, citing *Middlesex County Records*, ed. J. Cordy Jeaffreson (1886), vol. 1 (April 26, 1584).

39 Ibid. Ashelford cites T. S. Willan, *Studies in Elizabethan Foreign Trade* (Manchester: Manchester Univ. Press, 1959), 113.

40 Ashelford, *Dress*, 44, citing John Harrington, *Nugae Antiquae* (1779), vol. 2, for the information about the cost of a winter uniform, and Lawrence Stone, "The Anatomy of the Elizabethan Aristocracy," *Economic History Review* 18, nos. 1 and 2 (1948): 5, for all the other examples of conspicuous consumption in dress.

41 Frances Elizabeth Baldwin, *Sumptuary Legislation and Personal Regulation in England*, Johns Hopkins University Studies in Historical and Political Science, ser. 14, no. 1 (Baltimore: Johns Hopkins Univ. Press, 1926), 194.

42 H. K. Morse, *Elizabethan Pageantry: A Pictorial Survey of Costume and Its Commentators from c. 1560–1620* (London: Studio, 1934), 111.

43 Sir Thomas Elyot, *The Boke Named the Governour*, ed. Henry Herbert Stephen Croft (London: Kegan Paul, Trench, 1883), 2:20–22.

44 George Gascoigne, *The Complete Works of George Gascoigne*, ed. John W. Cunliffe (Cambridge: Cambridge Univ. Press, 1907; reprint, New York: Greenwood, 1969), 2:151, 152.

45 See, for example, Ashelford, *Dress*, 73.

46 On creative uses of cultural norms involving "middle ground"—including the Anglican Church's "middle way" or *via media*—see Joshua Scodel, "The Medium Is the Message: Donne's 'Satire 3,' 'To Sir Henry Wotton' (Sir, More than Kisses), and the Ideologies of the Mean," *Modern Philology* 90, no. 4 (May 1993): 479–511.

47 Lawrence Humfrey's treatise on nobility asserts a similarly modest program: "Be the end of apparel, to shroud the body, to chase cold, having respect of health, strength, honesty, and comeliness." *The Nobles; or, Of Nobilitye* (London, 1563), T4v.

48 George Puttenham, *Arte of English Poesie*, in *Elizabethan Critical Essays*, ed. G. Gregory Smith (London: Oxford Univ. Press, 1964), 2:142, 143. Embroidery was one of the more extraordinary forms of conspicuous expenditure; Lawrence Stone, "Anatomy of the Elizabethan Aristocracy," 5, notes: "In the reign of James a lady at a court ball was reported to be wearing embroidered stuff worth £50 a yard. Even modest country gentlemen like Gervase Holles spent £30 on embroidery for a single suit." Puttenham's treatise was originally published in 1589.

49 St. Thomas Aquinas, *Summa Theologiae*, vol. 41, *Virtues of Justice in the Community*, ed. and trans. T. C. O'Brien (New York: McGraw Hill, 1972), quest. 118, art. 1, p. 243.

50 For associations of Puritanism with egalitarianism, see, for example, Christopher Hill: "The logic of Puritanism called social hierarchy into question" ("Political Discourse in Early Seventeenth-Century England," in *Politics and People in Revolutionary England: Essays in Honour of Ivan Roots*, ed. Colin Jones, Malyn Newitt, and Stephen Roberts [Oxford: Basil Blackwell, 1986], 60). Also see Michael Walzer. "[Puritan writers] replaced the old hierarchy with a collective discipline . . . a new order not natural and inevitable but artificial and purposive. . . . The magic of priesthood was gone and all hierarchies were called into question. . . . Calling and office took the place of birth and status" (*The Revolution of the Saints* [Cambridge, Mass.: Harvard Univ. Press, 1965], 170). Similarly, for William Haller, "This spiritual equalitarianism . . . seized upon the imaginations of men who, no matter what their social rank, had reason to be discontented with the

Stuart regime in church and state, and it thus became the central force of revolutionary Puritanism. Over against the inequalities of an indurated social system and an obsolete form of government, the people learned from preachers inspired by Paul to bear in mind the equality of all men before God and presently to draw the obvious practical inference that God before whom all men are leveled is sure in his own time to uplift the low and humble the great" (*The Rise of Puritanism* [New York: Columbia Univ. Press, 1938; reprint, 1947], 86). "Once the Calvinist preachers admitted that the only true aristocracy was spiritual and beyond any human criterion, they had gone a long way toward asserting that all men in society must be treated alike because only God knows who is superior" (ibid. 178).

51 Richard L. Greaves, *Society and Religion in Elizabethan England* (Minneapolis: Univ. of Minnesota Press, 1981), 505. "Three years before he became bishop of Exeter, John Woolton, a strenuous opponent of the Puritans, charged them with spoiling schools and robbing the patrimony of the church to deck themselves in costly garb. Although he acknowledged the validity of the Puritan position that apparel was a matter of adiaphora, he cited Puritans for abusing indifferent things by their ostentation and prodigal waste. The second Anglican thrust castigated Puritans who dressed in utmost simplicity, wearing flat caps and russet cloaks, 'and well they may: for their religion is a russet religion, good for none but russet coats, and such as favour popular government' " (ibid., 505–6). The quotation appears to be from John Woolton, *The Christian Manuell; or, Of the Life and Maners of True Christians* (London, 1576), 90.

52 Philoponus does add: "[B]ut yet would I wish that what so is superfluous or overmuch, either in the one or in the other, should be distributed to the help of the poor members of Christ Jesus, of whom an infinite number dayly do perish through want of necessary refection and due sustentation to their bodies" (34).

53 *How a Man May Choose a Good Wife from a Bad* (London, 1602), ed. John S. Farmer (Edinburgh: Tudor Facsimile Texts, 1912; reprint, New York: Ams, 1970), G2v–G3r.

54 Quoted from "The Rump Songs" (no citation given), in F. W. Fairholt, *Costume in England: A History of Dress to the End of the Eighteenth Century,* revised by H. A. Dillon (London: George Bell and Sons, 1885; reissue, Detroit: Singing Tree, 1968), 1:308; Fairholt indicates the song's relation to the earlier play (309).

55 C. Willett Cunnington and Phillis Cunnington, *Handbook of English Costume in the Seventeenth Century,* 3rd ed. (London: Faber and Faber, 1972), 11. Their assertion is supported by quotations from Lucy Hutchinson, *The Memoirs of Colonel Hutchinson,* 5th ed. (London: Henry G. Bohn, 1846). Fair-

holt, in *Costume in England*, 1:327, reasserts the close connection of dress and class when he says that the "Dissenter's dress [as shown in a 1646 work concerning differences of opinion between Dissenter and Presbyterian] is in no degree different from the *plain* ordinary one of a gentleman of Charles I's reign." Quentin Bell also suggests that by mid-century, the more sober clothing style of the rank and file of the "industrious sort" was most likely mainly a matter of difference in social class, although there is *some* historic connection to religious motives as well: "It is probably not illegitimate to think of the English middle class of the mid-seventeenth century as reflecting contemporary Dutch models while the Cavalier style, popular though it no doubt was with many gentlemen on the other side, was mainly French. . . . The use of black began in the Burgundian court and is recorded as early as 1468, so that in its origin it can hardly be connected either with the Reformation or counter-Reformation. But such a connection may perhaps be traced in the adoption of this fashion by the Spanish successors of the Burgundians, and certainly the popularity of black among the Dutch Calvinists, who took their style from their Catholic adversaries, may be connected with a religious motive. . . . Both in England and in Holland the more sober style, the style of the 'white-collar worker', remained to some extent as an alternative to the higher sumptuosity of France" (*On Human Finery* [London: Hogarth, 1976], 119–120).

56 Hutchinson, *Memoirs of the Life of Colonel Hutchinson*, 348–49. Further references to Hutchinson will appear parenthetically in the text.

57 Baldwin, *Sumptuary Legislation*, 262.

58 Joan Kent, "Attitudes of Members of the House of Commons to the Regulation of 'Personal Conduct' in Late Elizabethan and Early Stuart England," *Bulletin of the Institute of Historical Research* 46, no. 113 (May 1973): 43, 50. Overt economic rationales having to do with the "imbalance in trade and the depressed state of the cloth industry" (45) were more common reasons for initiating such legislation after 1604 than religious concern about excessive apparel. And opposition was also based on disagreement "about the relative roles of the church and the temporal government in the ordering of men's lives" (46).

59 Ibid., 51, quoting *Journals of the House of Commons*, in *Journals of all the Parliaments of Queen Elizabeth*, ed. Sir Simonds D'Ewes (1682), 1:584, and *The Commons Debates, 1621*, ed. W. Notestein et al., 7 vols. (New Haven, 1935), 4:241.

60 Arthur Dent, *Plaine Man's Pathway to Heaven* (London, 1603), 51.

61 William Bradshaw, "Twelve General Arguments, Proving That the Ceremonies Imposed upon the Ministers of the Gospel in England by

Our Prelates, Are Unlawful," from *Several Treatises of Worship and Cere-monies* (1660), in *Puritanism and Separatism, A Collection of Works by William Bradshaw,* with a new introduction by R. C. Simmons ([Farnborough], England: Gregg International, 1972), [51], 73. "Twelve General Arguments" was originally published in 1605.

62 This point has not, I think, been fully recognized in scholarly discussion of writers' "Puritan" or "Anglican" religious positions. Consider, for example, the assumptions behind such a statement as the following: "[Herbert] was certainly no passive transmitter of orthodox Anglican teaching; he never accepts the forms and festivals of the church merely at their face value. Herbert's testing and internalizing lead him not to reject the set forms but to discover their full significance: They are infused with individual spiritual meaning of a kind that contemporaneous Puritans denied they could possess." Leah S. Marcus, "George Herbert and the Anglican Plain Style," in *"Too Rich to Clothe the Sunne": Essays on George Herbert,* ed. Claude J. Summers and Ted-Larry Pebworth (Pittsburgh: Univ. of Pittsburgh Press), 187–88. The statement implies that "orthodox Anglican teaching" involved accepting forms "at face value," whereas no "insider" would ever speak this way. It is only the enemy Puritan who categorizes the forms as merely having "face value" in contrast with his own—which are of course "infused with . . . spiritual meaning." See below, chapter 4.

63 Bradshaw, "A Treatise of Things Indifferent," from *Several Treatises* (1660), in *Puritanism and Separatism,* 19–20 (my emphasis). This "Treatise of Things Indifferent" was originally published in 1605. Bradshaw's idea of the mean here, although not used to define moral virtue, is, in a broad sense, not unlike Aristotle's idea of the mean "in terms of the thing itself" "which is equi-distant from each of the extremes." "For instance, if ten is many and two is few, six is the intermediate, taken in terms of the object." And Bradshaw's idea of the relativity of this mean seems not completely unlike Aristotle's: "[I]f ten pounds are too much for a particular person to eat and two too little, it does not follow that the trainer will order six pounds; for this also is perhaps too much for the person who is to take it . . . too much for the beginner in athletic exercises." In effect, the "opposite terms" change for the beginner, and so, too, the mean changes. Aristotle, *Ethica Nicomachea,* 2.6, in *The Works of Aristotle,* translated into English under the editorship of W. D. Ross (London: Oxford Univ. Press, 1915; reprint, 1949), vol. 9, *Ethica Nicomachea, Magna Moralia, Ethica Eudemia,* 1106a. Whether Aristotle's ethical mean is one that negates its extremes (e.g., green is neither black nor white), or is composed of them (e.g., grey is both black and white) was apparently debated in the Middle Ages and the Renaissance. (See Scodel, "The Medium Is the Message," 502.) Both such means would clearly be context-dependent, which seems to be Bradshaw's point about "things indifferent."

64 See the quotation from John Ellis on "black vs. white" (*Against Deconstruction* [Princeton: Princeton Univ. Press, 1989], 54) on p. 64.

2 Nakedness and Clothing in Controversy
about the Eucharist

1 John Jewel's phrase in a letter of November 5, 1559, to Peter Martyr, *The Zurich Letters*, ed. Hastings Robinson (Cambridge: Cambridge Univ. Press, 1842), 52.

2 "The Lord God . . . when he brought his own people into the land of *Canaan*: he commanded them, utterly to destroy all those things, that the heathen nations . . . had devised for the furniture of their idol service. . . . Why should not we then fear to give the like occasion to the papists, to think that the true service of Christ can not lack their glittering gear?" Robert Crowley, *A Briefe Discourse against the Outwarde Apparell and Ministring Garmentes of the Popishe Church* ([Emden], 1566), A5v.

3 John Jewel, *An Apologie of the Church of England*, in *English Reformers*, Library of Christian Classics, no. 26, ed. T. H. L. Parker (Philadelphia: Westminster, 1966), 30.

4 Jonas A. Barish, "Exhibitionism and the Antitheatrical Prejudice," *ELH* 36, no. 7 (March 1969): 9.

5 James R. Siemon, *Shakespearean Iconoclasm* (Berkeley: Univ. of California Press, 1985), 58, 260–61, 261, 267. Further references will appear parenthetically in the text.

6 Siemon cites Barish, "Exhibitionism," 5.

7 David Bevington, review of *Shakespearian Iconoclasm*, *Shakespeare Quarterly* 37, no. 1 (1986): 125.

8 Nicholas Ridley, "A Treatise agaynst the Errour of Transubstantiation, and Extracts from His Examinations," in *English Reformers*, ed. T. H. L. Parker, Library of Christian Classics, no. 26 (Philadelphia: Westminster, 1966), 313. The "Extracts" are "from the Disputation at Oxford in April, 1555, between Ridley and a number of opponents" (310).

9 Thomas Cranmer, *An Answer unto a Crafty and Sophistical Cavillation, Devised by Stephen Gardiner*, in *Writings and Disputations of Thomas Cranmer . . . Relative to the Sacrament of the Lord's Supper*, ed. John Edmund Cox (Cambridge: Cambridge Univ. Press, 1844), 36 (my emphasis). The "Answer" was originally published in 1551; the Parker Society *Writings* uses an edition of 1580. Further references will appear parenthetically in the text.

10 Nicholas Ridley, "A Brief Declaration of the Lord's Supper; or, A Treatise against the Error of Transubstantiation Written by Nicholas Ridley . . . During His Imprisonment, A.D. 1555," in *The Works of Nicolas Ridley,* ed. Henry Christmas (Cambridge: Cambridge Univ. Press, 1843), 10.

11 See Huston Diehl, "Graven Images: Protestant Emblem Books in England," *Renaissance Quarterly* 39, no. 1 (spring 1986): 49–66.

12 "The sacrament is one thing, the virtue of the sacrament another." "The sacrament of this thing, namely, of the unity of the body and blood of Christ, is prepared on the Lord's table . . . but the thing itself, of which it is the sacrament, is for every man to life, for no man to destruction, whosever shall have been a partaker therof." *The Works of Aurelius Augustine, Bishop of Hippo,* ed. Marcus Dods, vol. 10, *Lectures or Tractates on the Gospel According to St. John,* bk. 1 (Edinburgh: T. and T. Clark, 1873), 26.11, 15, pp. 374, 378. "The reason these things . . . are called sacraments is that in them one thing is seen, another is to be understood. What can be seen has a bodily appearance, what is to be understood provides spiritual fruit." "Sermon 272," in *The Works of Saint Augustine: A Translation for the Twenty-First Century,* vol. 7, *Sermons 230–272B,* ed. John E. Rotelle, trans. Edmund Hill (New Rochelle, N.Y.: New City, 1993), 300. See *The Encyclopaedia of Religion and Ethics,* ed. James Hastings (New York: Charles Scribner's Sons, 1951), s.v. "Eucharist (to the end of Middle Ages)": While "the sign . . . must be carefully distinguished from that which it signifies," Augustine "shows that the Sacrament is not for him an empty sign. . . . The presence of Christ is, in fact, a spiritual presence. . . . There is no real justification for regarding him as teaching a purely symbolical view" (554).

13 These are the words of Stephen Gardiner, then bishop of Winchester.

14 These are Cranmer's words.

15 Calvin, *Short Treatise on the Holy Supper,* in *Theological Treatises,* Library of Christian Classics, no. 22, trans. J. K. S. Reid (Philadelphia: Westminster, 1954): 162.

16 Calvin, *The Clear Explanation of Sound Doctrine Concerning the True Partaking of the Flesh and Blood of Christ in the Holy Supper,* in *Theological Treatises,* 270 (my emphasis).

17 Calvin, *The Necessity of Reforming the Church,* in *Theological Treatises,* 206.

18 B. A. Gerrish, "The Lord's Supper in the Reformed Confessions," *Theology Today* 23 (1966), 231, 230, 232, 234. Also see Debora K. Shuger, *Habits of Thought in the English Renaissance: Religion, Politics, and the Dominant Culture* (Berkeley: Univ. of California Press, 1990), ch. 1, 37–41. One may certainly feel some tension in such descriptions. Ann Kibbey describes the paradoxes of the Calvinist sacrament as a "double bind": "The ritual negates as well as sanctifies the sacramental *figura,* creating a double bind, because the religious power of the elements is referred to the "spiritual" presence of Christ. . . . The religious virtue of the bread is solely its capacity as a fetish to exhibit or display the spiritual presence. . . . A true fetish, but an "empty token" at the same time, it has a sacredness that always remains derivative, never inhering in the essence of the material element alone. . . . The doctrine of the spiritual presence thus debases the *figura* even as it makes the sacramental object the privileged locus of religious power." *The Interpretation of Material Shapes in Puritanism: A Study of Rhetoric, Prejudice and Violence* (Cambridge: Cambridge Univ. Press, 1986), 49–52.

19 Barish, "Exhibitionism," 9.

20 The metaphor of the tavern's ivy bush being taken for wine itself has considerable longevity as another figure (besides those involving the illusions of theater or theatrical costume) for such an idolatrous mis-taking. It occurs in Tyndale, when he argues that ceremonies were made to serve men, not men ceremonies: "And that trust and confidence, which the ceremonies preached to be given unto God's word and Christ's blood, that same they turned unto the ceremony itself; as though a man were so mad to forget that the bush at the tavern-door did signify wine to be sold within, but would believe that the bush itself would quench his thirst." *An Answer to Sir Thomas More's Dialogue, The Supper of the Lord . . . by William Tyndale,* ed. Henry Walter (Cambridge: Cambridge Univ. Press, 1850), 76. Thomas Jenner, in *The Soule's Solace* (London, 1626), F6v, "depicts the facade of a tavern in an . . . emblem titled 'The foolishness of Transubstantiation.' . . . A human figure climbs a ladder to [the] tavern sign and futilely attempts to eat the image of the grapes. . . . 'In *Christ* alone stands that *spiritual food,*' writes Jenner: 'Which must not of these signs be understood. / For *bread* is *bread,* even after *consecration:* / The work being done for Christ's *commemoration*' " (quoted in Diehl, "Graven Images," 60).

21 Calvin, *Short Treatise on the Holy Supper,* 148 (my emphasis). "For otherwise what would it mean that we eat the bread and drink the wine as a sign that his flesh is our food and his blood our drink, if he gave only bread and wine and left the spiritual reality behind? Would it not be under false colours that he had instituted this mystery?" (ibid.).

22 Calvin, *True Partaking of the Flesh and Blood of Christ,* in *Theological Treatises,* 268.

23 Gordon Leff, *Heresy in the Later Middle Ages* (Manchester: Manchester Univ. Press, 1967), 2:553.

24 Gerrish ("The Lord's Supper," 232) attributes this confession to a team; it is also commonly attributed to Heinrich Bullinger.

25 *The Confescion of the Fayth of the Sweserlandes* (London, 1548), B1v–B2r.

26 Calvin, *Short Treatise on the Holy Supper,* 162.

27 *"Justified by faith* [is he], who, being excluded from the righteousness of works, apprehends by faith the righteousness of Christ, invested in which, he appears, in the sight of God, not as a sinner, but as a righteous man." Calvin, *Institutes of the Christian Religion,* 7th ed., 2 vols., trans. John Allen (Philadelphia: Presbyterian Board of Christian Education, 1936), 3.11.2, 1:793.

28 Henry Bullinger, decade 5, sermon 6, in *Decades* (Cambridge: Parker Society, 1852), 243, quoted in William S. Madsen, *From Shadowy Types to Truth: Studies in Milton's Symbolism* (New Haven: Yale Univ. Press, 1968), 80.

29 See Diehl, "Graven Images."

3 Extensionist Semantics and Its Implications for Criticism

1 Wittgenstein also rejects such a view (see Tullio de Mauro, *Ludwig Wittgenstein: His Place in the Development of Semantics* [Dordrecht, Holland: D. Reidel, 1967], 8–15), but goes even further in the opposite direction than Saussure (see below, note 4).

2 Even in semantic domains such as kinship where one might perhaps naively expect on biological or genealogical grounds that there would be "common, distinctive features of reference that are shared by all the denotata of the term" in question (for example, that everyone called "father" would be one generation above the speaker and that the speaker would be a direct biological descendent, etc.), this "total-category" approach to the meaning of words fails to explain other salient instances of language usage, for example, the "fatherhood" of priests. Floyd Lounsbury, "Language and Culture," in *Language and Philosophy,* ed. Sidney Hook (New York: New York Univ. Press, 1969), 21. See Brent Berlin and Paul Kay, *Basic Color Terms: Their Universality and Evolution* (Berkeley: Univ. of California Press, 1969), 13–14; Eleanor Rosch, "Universals and Cultural Specifics in Human Categorization," in *Cross-Cultural Perspectives on Learning,* ed. Richard W. Brislin, Stephen Bochner, and Walter J. Lonner (New York: John Wiley and Sons, 1975), 179–81; and especially, David B. Kronenfeld, *Plastic Glasses and Church Fathers: Semantic Extension from the Ethnoscience Tradition* (New York: Oxford Univ. Press, 1996), 147–50, 179–84.

3 My examples concerning "cups and glasses" in this chapter, although not specifically the ones given in David B. Kronenfeld, *Plastic Glasses,* are totally indebted to the discussion there, and to my assimilation of this linguistic anthropologist's argument. I have also very much benefited in my understanding of Saussure and semantic theory from discussions with D. B. Kronenfeld. However, he bears no responsibility for my adaptation here of his post-Saussurean semantic theory or for my implementation of it with regard to religious poetry, religious controversy, or literary criticism.

4 "Entities which we commonly subsume under a general term" do not necessarily all have "something in common." Instead, such entities "form a family the members of which have family likenesses. . . . The idea of a general concept being a common property of its particular instances connects up with other primitive, too simple, ideas of the structure of language." Ludwig Wittgenstein, *The Blue and Brown Books* (New York: Harper and Row, 1965), 17. See also Wittgenstein, *Philosophical Investigations* (Oxford: Basil Blackwell, 1968), nos. 65–67. Robert J. Fogelin, *Wittgenstein* (London: Routledge and Kegan Paul, 1976), 118, gives a useful "crude representation":

01	02	03	04	05	06
A	B	C	D	E	F
B	C	D	E	D	A
C	D	E	F	A	B
D	E	F	A	B	C

"01 through 06 is a set of objects; the letters underneath each of them represent properties they possess. Here each object shares three features with two others in the group, but there is no single feature that runs through the lot."

5 On "extensions," see Lounsbury, "Language and Culture," 22; David B. Kronenfeld, *Plastic Glasses*, 5–10, and part 4, "Semantic Extension," 147–94; John Lyons, *Semantics*, 2 vols. (Cambridge: Cambridge Univ. Press, 1977), 1:263–4; Berlin and Kay, *Basic Color Terms*, 13–14. Also see Rosch, "Universals," 181–96, on "degrees of distance."

6 See Lounsbury, "Language and Culture," especially 20, 21; Berlin and Kay, *Basic Color Terms*, especially 2. See particularly, David B. Kronenfeld, *Plastic Glasses*. On the general question of the frequently assumed arbitrariness of linguistic categories, also see Rosch, "Universals," 177–207. Catherine Belsey's citation of color terms as a simple example of language constructivism ("Colour terms, like language itself, form a system of differences, readily experienced as natural, given, but in reality constructed by the language itself." *Critical Practice* [London: Methuen, 1980], 39–40) reveals her lack of awareness of the work of linguistic anthropologists on color universals.

7 "The Windows," from *The Works of George Herbert*, ed. F. E. Hutchinson (Oxford: Clarendon, 1941; reprint, 1959), 67–68. Further quotations from Herbert's poetry and prose are from this edition; page numbers will appear parenthetically in the text.

8 For a detailed treatment of Auden's and Blau's readings, see Judy Z. Kronenfeld, "Probing the Relation between Poetry and Ideology: Herbert's 'The Windows,'" *John Donne Journal: Studies in the Age of Donne* 2 (1983): 55–80.

9 W. H. Auden, introduction to *George Herbert: Selected by W. H. Auden* (London: Penguin, 1973), 11.

10 Sheridan Blau, "George Herbert's Homiletic Theory," *George Herbert Journal* 1, no. 2 (spring 1978): 22, 26. Further references will appear parenthetically in the text.

11 See George Summers, *George Herbert: His Religion and Art* (Cambridge, Mass.: Harvard Univ. Press, 1968), 73: "For the extreme Puritan, the . . . adornments in the church were only sensuous barriers between the naked individual soul and God. . . . The light of the Spirit should reach the individual directly, like sunlight through pure glass; it should not be contaminated by 'externals,' as sunlight was colored by the pictured windows of the Papists." Further references will appear parenthetically in the text.

12 Quotations from Debora K. Shuger, *Sacred Rhetoric: The Christian Grand Style in the English Renaissance* (Princeton: Princeton Univ. Press, 1988), 229, 231, 229. Herbert, as Shuger says, does not "reject[] artistic language, yet . . . so subordinate[s] it to holiness and zeal that the question of the relation between affect and elocutio drops away, although [he], in fact, notes several techniques, including storytelling, apostrophe, and dramatic figures, to make the sermon 'show very Holy'" (95, quoting Herbert, *A Priest to the Temple; or, The Country Parson,* in *The Country Parson, The Temple,* ed. John N. Wall Jr., Classics of Western Spirituality [New York, 1981], 62–64).

13 See Judy Z. Kronenfeld, "Poetry and Ideology," 65–76.

14 Leah S. Marcus, "George Herbert and the Anglican Plain Style," in *"Too Rich to Clothe the Sunne": Essays on George Herbert,* ed. Claude J. Summers and Ted-Larry Pebworth (Pittsburgh: Univ. of Pittsburgh Press, 1980), 191. Further references will appear parenthetically in the text.

15 In attempting to consider some aspects of the semantics of such disagreements I am by no means suggesting that all or most disagreements might be reducible to semantics. We may certainly disagree about the usefulness of our definitions, that is, about whether a label or definition accounts for or captures structures important in the world, as Richard Strier does (*Love Known: Theology and Experience in George Herbert's Poetry* [Chicago: Univ. of Chicago Press, 1983], xv; see above, introduction, note 1). Or, we may disagree about the weighting of relevant features in a definition. For example, I do not agree with Heather Asals that belief in the "real presence" is the most distinguishing important feature of "high Anglicanism" (just as one may or may not feel that being made of glass is the most important feature of the concept "glass"—meaning drinking vessel); the real spiritual presence (which does not involve transubstantiation) is a central Protestant, Calvinist doctrine, and therefore not specifically "Anglican" as opposed to standard "Protestant." (See below, notes 16 and 17, and above, chapter 2.)

Even where definitions or labels are agreed upon and made explicit, critics may of course meaningfully disagree about what constitutes relevant data or whether the facts warrant the label in a particular instance. We may agree that Calvinism may be defined by belief in the doctrines of predestination and salvation by faith alone, yet disagree about whether a particular action or statement constitutes evidence of such a belief.

16 Heather Asals, *Equivocal Predication: George Herbert's Way to God* (Toronto: Univ. of Toronto Press, 1981), 5. Asals says she disagrees "wholeheartedly with Patrick Grant's assertion that Herbert is 'a more assuredly Protestant theologian than Donne' " (5, quoting Grant, *The Transformation of Sin* [Montreal: McGill-Queen's Univ. Press, 1974], 75). She also objects to Barbara Lewalski's and Stanley Fish's "Protestant emphasis in interpreting Herbert," which deemphasizes "outward forms," among other things, "in favour of the inner workings of the heart" (4). Further references to *Equivocal Predication* will appear parenthetically in the text.

17 Among those Asals describes as being on the wrong side of an obvious "polarity," that is, "who believe that we cannot discuss the idea of the Real Presence in Herbert's theology or his poetry" is "Sister Thekla [who] argues . . . that Herbert 'does not assign to the Eucharist the independent reality of Presence' " (5, quoting Sister Thekla, *George Herbert: Idea and Image* [Whitby, England, 1974], 85).

18 Even though there can be some variation in core concepts, or contestation about what features belong to them—especially in the case of more abstract terms—nevertheless, language as a communicative tool in a community of speakers tends to constrain total freedom of usage, to prevent wild divergences. On this issue, see D. B. Kronenfeld, *Plastic Glasses*, 234, and more generally, 203-224.

19 Only by looking for common cores—and not finding them—can we decide that controversialists genuinely differ. Only when we attempt to reconstruct the system of oppositions within which assignments to category on the basis of particular features occur, can we see whether we are really dealing with "family resemblances" or with different but related extensions from shared prototypes. (Of course, even when controversialists implicitly assume such shared meanings, they may not give us enough information for a reconstruction.) The Wittgensteinian position, i.e., that each use of the word "Anglican" has something in common with some other use, is not as extreme as the view that nothing is shared in separate uses but the name. However, Wittgenstein's view, while allowing varying bases for the assignment of verbal labels to things, does not explore the possibility that this variation might be more tightly structured, i.e., more than a chain of independent links.

20 This questioning rests on the Derridean deconstruction of Saussure's so-called phonocentrism; see below, note 28.

21 Hayden White long ago said that "the Absurdist critics [Foucault, Barthes, Derrida]" do not "participate in the attempt of . . . technical linguists to create a science of language. . . . They draw their inspiration from Nietzsche, Mallarmé, and Heidegger. . . . But they dress up their attack on language with a terminology borrowed from Saussure . . . to give it a technical flavor and place conventional critics on the defensive." *Tropics of Discourse: Essays in Cultural Criticism* (Baltimore: Johns Hopkins Univ. Press, 1978), 263. Critics emphasizing indeterminacy (such as Barbara Harman, Jonathan Goldberg, J. Hillis Miller, and Geoffrey Hartman) may practice more or less compelling polysemic interpretation, and may or may not have the particular motive White ascribes to his "Absurdist critics." However, it does seem fair to say that they have been influenced by the Derridean reading of Saussure, deny the referential functions of language, deemphasize or deny the idea that communication depends on the existence of more and less salient contrast sets, codes, or meanings, and accept these ideas without questioning their validity in a more scientific spirit.

22 "The meaning of meaning . . . is infinite implication, the indefinite referral of signifier to signifier. . . . [I]ts force is a certain . . . infinite equivocality which gives signified meaning no respite, no rest, but engages it in its own economy so that it always signifies again and differs." Jaques Derrida, *Writing and Difference*, trans. Alan Bass (Chicago: Univ. of Chicago Press, 1978), 25. In the text, these are rhetorical questions; I have omitted the question marks.

23 For the continuities between deconstruction and new historicisms, see introduction, note 11. A clear explication of *structuralism*'s misunderstanding (much of which passes into poststructuralism) of Saussure, the first I know of, appears in David Kronenfeld and Henry W. Decker, "Structuralism," *Annual Review of Anthropology* 8 (1979): 503–41, particularly, 505–13. This paper grew out of a seminar in which I was a participant. My own 1989 article, "Post-Saussurean Semantics, Reformation Religious Controversy, and Contemporary Critical Disagreement," *Assays: Critical Approaches to Medieval and Renaissance Texts* 5 (1989): 135–65, builds on my understanding of the usefulness of Saussurean principles, and addresses critical misreading of Saussure, as does a later essay, "Yes, Virginia, There

IS a World," *Associated Writing Programs Chronicle* 25, no. 2 (October/No-
vember 1992): 15–18. Similar conclusions have been independently reached
by a number of others. See John M. Ellis, *Against Deconstruction* (Princeton: Princeton Univ. Press, 1989); Raymond Tallis, *Not Saussure: A Critique
of Post-Saussurean Literary Theory* (Basingstoke, England: Macmillan, 1988);
and J. Claude Evans, *Strategies of Deconstruction: Derrida and the Myth of
the Voice* (Minneapolis: Univ. of Minnesota Press, 1991), especially ch. 10.
(I would like to thank Philip F. Williams for making me aware of Tallis's
book.) Ellis remarks that "the usual exchange between proponents and
opponents barely exist[s]" in the case of deconstruction (vii–viii); Tallis
suggests "too much of what has been written about . . . post-structuralism
has been merely scholarly at the expense of actually confronting the underlying ideas" (9). Evans comments that "the deconstructive reading of . . .
Saussure's *Cours* . . . plays a crucial role in *Of Grammatology*, for in Saussure Derrida thinks that he can attack 'the entire uncritical tradition which
[Saussure inherits]' " (Evans, *Strategies*, 152, quoting Derrida, *Of Grammatology*, 46). For a philosophical examination of the antifoundationalism of
poststructuralism, see Horace L. Fairlamb, *Critical Conditions: Postmodernity and the Question of Foundations* (Cambridge: Cambridge Univ. Press,
1994). Nancy Easterlin and Barbara Riebling, eds., *After Poststructuralism:
Interdisciplinarity and Literary Theory* (Evanston, Ill.: Northwestern Univ.
Press, 1993), is a collection of essays radically criticizing some of the tenets
of postmodernism such as infinite intertextuality, and the denial of the
relevance of "all claims to truth, fact, or discernible meaning" (Easterlin
and Riebling, introduction to *After Poststructuralism*, 3).
24 Insofar as Derridean thought encourages the idea that our perception
of the world is mediated by our cultural, linguistic, psychological, and
biological structures of cognition, I applaud it. However, its emphasis on
"representation" or constructivism is of course resolutely antiempirical,
eliminating the possibility that "things in themselves" or "nature" might
have a role to play in *shaping* our perceptions or constructs. See below,
note 38, and see Ellis's lucid example of the concept *warm* as neither simply
"a fact of nature" nor "a fact of language" (*Against Deconstruction*, 56). Easterlin and Riebling, eds., *After Poststructuralism* critiques cultural and linguistic constructivism (see Robert Storey's contribution to the volume, " 'I
Am I Because My Little Dog Knows Me': Prolegomenon to a Theory of
Mimesis") and comments as well on the false choice between positivism
and relativism (see Easterlin and Riebling, introduction, 2). Belsey's *Critical
Practice*—a still influential major work of poststructuralist theory—clearly
incorporates the constructivist view. "The claim that a literary form reflects the world is simply tautological. If by 'the world' we understand the

world we experience, the world differentiated by language, then the claim that realism reflects the world means that realism reflects the world constituted in language. This is a tautology. If discourses articulate concepts through a system of signs which signify by means of their relationship to each other rather than to entities in the world, and if literature is a signifying practice, all it can reflect is the order inscribed in particular discourses, not the nature of the world" (46).

25 The terms are Montrose's; see above, introduction, note 3.

26 Saussure wanted to understand historical change in linguistic forms and meanings; his synchronic linguistics was a means to this end. Systems, as opposed to atomistic entities, move through time.

27 See Mauro, *Ludwig Wittgenstein*, 37. "The linguistic skepticism which was strengthened by the early conclusions of Wittgenstein and Croce . . . is not unrelated to existentialistic skepticism. . . . According to the existentialists, men do not talk, they chatter. . . . Everyday speech consists in putting words together, in hearing words, in repeating them, without any real possibility of communication or comprehension. Incommunicability is the normal condition of the man of the street."

28 One example among many: "In [Saussure's] view, words are not symbols which correspond to referents, but rather are 'signs' which are made up of two parts . . . : a mark, either written or spoken, called a 'signifier', and a concept (what is 'thought' when the mark is made), called a 'signified.'" Raman Selden, *A Reader's Guide to Contemporary Literary Theory* (Lexington: Univ. of Kentucky Press, 1989), 52. Derrida, as J. Claude Evans explains, also misreads a particular Saussurean passage "on the history of the pronunciation of words" (*Strategies*, 159), as if it asserts the intrinsic connection between phonic signifier and concept or signified, "sound and its 'natural bond' [*lien naturel*] with meaning" (*Of Grammatology*, 53) — an idea which of course runs totally counter to Saussure's thought. Derrida can then deconstruct this "phonocentrism," and, along with it, "all the Western methods of analysis, explication, reading or interpretation," by introducing "the radical question of writing" (ibid., 46). See Evans, *Strategies*, 152–65, esp. 158–59.

29 Christopher Norris, for example, while arguing that the split is old news ("post-Saussurian textual theory . . . makes such a startling phenomenon of the split between 'signifier and signified'"), clearly conceives it in these terms ("The rift between sign and referent became a high point of radical theory"). *Deconstruction: Theory and Practice* (London: Methuen, 1982), 130. Of course, Derrida's thought lies at the heart of this misleading practice; signifiers point only to other signifiers and "the signified . . . is merely an illusion that human beings have invented" (Richard Harland, *Super-*

structuralism: The Philosophy of Structuralism and Post-Structuralism [London: Methuen, 1987], 134). I am delighted to see that both Ellis (*Against Deconstruction,* 59) and Tallis (*Not Saussure,* 69) note the same crucial confusion in Derrida and others.

30 See Kronenfeld and Decker, "Structuralism," 506–7, for an excellent analysis, to which I am indebted, of the meanings and misunderstandings of "arbitrariness" in Saussure's theory of language. Some literary critics inconsistently understand arbitrariness. See for example, Robert Scholes, *Structuralism in Literature: An Introduction* (New Haven: Yale Univ. Press, 1974; reprint, 1975), 16 (in spite of his attribution of a nonreferential view of language to Saussure in his later *Semiotics and Interpretation* [New Haven: Yale Univ. Press, 1974; reprint, 1975]): "The arbitrariness of the sign in no way need imply the arbitrariness of the concept or its inadequacy as an image of reality."

31 See Ferdinand de Saussure, *Cours de Linguistique Générale,* ed. Tullio de Mauro, critical edition (Paris: Payot, 1973), 439–41, n. 129. See also D. B. Kronenfeld and H. W. Decker, "Structuralism," 507.

32 On the limitations of the views of the anthropologist Benjamin Lee Whorf for whom language does determine perception, see D. B. Kronenfeld, *Plastic Glasses,* 26, n. 4; 41, n. 11; 151ff., 197; Rosch, 177–78; Lounsbury, 6–13. On the problems of just what Whorfianism postulates, see Max Black, "Some Troubles with Whorfianism," in *Language and Philosophy,* ed. Sidney J. Hook (New York: New York Univ. Press, 1969), 30–35.

33 Saussure says: "If we could embrace the sum of word-images stored in the minds of all individuals, we could identify the social bond that constitutes language. It is a storehouse filled by the members of a given community through their active use of speaking, a grammatical system that has a potential existence in each brain, or, more specifically, in the brains of a group of individuals. For language is not complete in any speaker; it exists perfectly only within a collectivity." *Course in General Linguistics,* ed. Charles Bally and Albert Sechehaye, trans. Wade Baskin (New York: McGraw Hill, 1966), 13–14; also see 73–74, 113.

34 Harland, *Superstructuralism,* 133.

35 Robert Scholes, *Semiotics and Interpretation,* 146. Catherine Belsey speaks of "the signified in its plurality, not the referent in its singular but imaginary presence" ("Literature, History, Politics," 39); for other relevant comments of hers, see above, note 24. Also see Art Berman, *From the New Criticism to Deconstruction: The Reception of Structuralism and Post-Structuralism* (Urbana: Univ. of Illinois Press, 1988): "The neat formula for the sign gives way in poststructuralism to Saussure's further speculation that the linguistic system is composed of terms that have meaning only insofar as they have a collective systematic integrity; and it is concluded that the chain of signifiers cannot yield irreducible signifieds. What language is pointing to is itself: what exists are 'texts.' The idea of a knowable reality independent of language is rejected." Furthermore, "language determines what is (thought to be) known, rather than serving as the medium through which knowledge independent of language is publicly expressed" (173). For a telling deconstruction of such positions, see Tallis, *Not Saussure,* ch. 3, "The Illusion of Reference," and ch. 4, "Reference Restored." These misunderstandings of Saussure are readily applied to texts by critics. See, for example, Francis Barker and Peter Hulme: "in keeping with the Saussurean model of language, no text is intelligible except in its differential relations with other texts" ("Nymphs and Reapers Heavily Vanish: The Discursive Contexts of *The Tempest,*" in *Alternative Shakespeares,* ed. John Drakakis [London: Methuen, 1985], 192).

36 For example, Terence Hawkes, in *Structuralism and Semiotics* (Berkeley: Univ. of California Press, 1977), 17-18, writes: "This new concept, that the *world* is made up of relationships rather than things, constitutes the first principle of that way of thinking which can properly be called 'structuralist'" (my emphasis). Indeed, Hawkes seems to conclude, against his own evidence (for example, from Sapir), that it is a premise of structural linguistics that there is "no such thing as an objective . . . 'real world'" (31). See also Terry Eagleton, *Literary Theory: An Introduction* (Minneapolis: Univ. of Minnesota Press, 1983), 108, "Reality was not reflected by language but *produced* by it."

37 Kronenfeld and Decker, "Structuralism," 507.

38 Lyons, *Semantics,* 1:247. He goes on to say: "For example, the greater salience of variations in luminosity (coupled with the biological importance of the succession of day and night in human life) could account for the universal lexicalization of black and white" (Lyons, 1:248). Ellis (*Against Deconstruction*) addresses the issue of the influence of the facts of nature on linguistic signs; see above, note 24.

39 Whitgift, *The Works of John Whitgift,* ed. John Ayre, 3 vols. (Cambridge: Cambridge Univ. Press, 1851-53), 1: 187-88. See chapter 1, note 26.

40 David Simpson describes a similar model in discussing the problem of the idea—associated with Foucault—"that the individual subject within history is inevitably bound within the limits of the vision imposed by his own local discursive order." He proposes that "we could, for example, explain a large degree of subjective behavior in reference to a particular individual's selection and recombination of various elements from the generally available discourses." "Literary Criticism and the Return to 'History,'" *Critical Enquiry* 14 (summer 1988): 732, 733.

4 Literary Interpretation of the Naked and the Clothed

1 This is a point also developed in Judy Z. Kronenfeld, "Probing the Relation between Poetry and Ideology: Herbert's 'The Windows,' " *John Donne Journal: Studies in the Age of Donne* 2 (1983): 55–80.

2 Heather Asals, *Equivocal Predication: George Herbert's Way to God* (Toronto: Univ. of Toronto Press, 1981), 65, quoting "'Thomas Cestren," *Defence of the Innocencie of the Three Ceremonies of the Church of England* (London, 1618), 91. Peter Milward's *Religious Controversies of the Jacobean Age: A Survey of Printed Sources* (London: Scolar, 1978) indicates this is Thomas Morton, bishop of Chester in 1618, who signed his work "Tho: Cestren" (24).

3 The Statute of Six Articles, 1539, quoted in Clifford William Dugmore, *The Mass and the English Reformers* (London: Macmillan, 1958), 108.

4 See Huston Diehl, "Graven Images: Protestant Emblem Books in England," *Renaissance Quarterly* 39, no. 1 (spring 1986): 55.

5 John Phillips, *The Reformation of Images: Destruction of Art in England, 1535–1660* (Berkeley: Univ. of California Press, 1973), 201 (my emphasis). As Phillips says, "Both Catholics and Protestants had agreed that the second commandment forbids idolatry; yet each disagreed over the issue of when an image becomes idolatrous. . . . In fact, similar arguments could have been invoked by both sides to arrive at opposite conclusions" (201).

6 Laud, *Speech Delivered in the Star Chamber* (London, 1637), 51, quoted in Asals, *Equivocal Predication*, 65.

7 Calvin, *Necessity of Reforming the Church*, in *Theological Treatises*, Library of Christian Classics, no. 22, trans. J. K. S. Reid (Philadelphia: Westminster, 1954).

8 See chapter 1.

9 Phillips, *Reformation of Images*, 160.

10 See, for example, E. C. E. Bourne, *The Anglicanism of William Laud* (London: S.P.C.K., 1947): "The ceremonies of the Church were to him so plainly the natural outward expressions of an inward faith that he simply could not understand how they could possibly be regarded by reasonable folk as the signs of a formalism which checked and thwarted the free outpourings of the spirit" (59). For such statements on Herbert see, for example, Leah S. Marcus, "George Herbert and the Anglican Plain Style," in *"Too Rich to Clothe the Sunne": Essays on George Herbert*, ed. Claude J. Summers and Ted-Larry Pebworth (Pittsburgh: Univ. of Pittsburgh Press, 1980), 187.

11 It is a critical commonplace that Herbert's is a *via media* position. See, for example, Hutchinson's comment on "The British Church" in *Works of Herbert* (Oxford: Clarendon, 1941; reprint, 1959), 515: "The *via media* of the Anglican Church, between Rome and Geneva, both in doctrine and in worship, is often commended by Herbert."

12 Strier, "History, Criticism, and Herbert: A Polemical Note," *Papers on Language and Literature* 17 (1981): 351, 349, 350, my emphasis.

13 "An Admonition to the Parliament," in *Puritan Manifestoes,* ed. W. H. Frere and C. E. Douglas (New York: E. S. Gorham, 1907; reprint, London: S.P.C.K., 1954), 35.

14 Peter Lake argues that Whitgift believed that preaching itself remained the only way to edify "the flock of Christ." The ceremonies edify *per accidens* "because authority had decreed that in order to preach, and hence genuinely to edify, all ministers had to use them." "To 'edify' came to mean little more than to impart the formal content of right doctrine. . . . The need positively to edify was limited to those activities which involved the transfer of information." *Anglicans and Puritans? Presbyterianism and English Conformist Thought from Whitgift to Hooker* (London: Unwin Hyman, 1988), 65, 19, 39.

15 Lake, *Anglicans and Puritans,* 49, 29. Also see 54, 123, 125, 241.

16 Ibid., 29, 30, 48–49.

17 Lake suggests "Hooker saw ceremony and ritual practice as a means of subliminal communication" (*Anglicans and Puritans,* 167).

18 Phillips, *Reformation of Images,* 179, suggests Laud emphasized the former.

19 See Judy Z. Kronenfeld, "Probing the Relation between Poetry and Ideology," 63, 76–77.

20 Fraser, *Shakespeare's Poetics in Relation to "King Lear"* (London: Routledge and Kegan Paul, 1962), 110 (my emphasis).

21 Q has only three repetitions of *never* (l. 2969).

22 Emily W. Leider, "Plainness of Style in *King Lear,*" *Shakespeare Quarterly* 21, no. 1 (1970): 45, 52. Leider does not champion plainness without qualifications; see below, note 68.

23 Sheldon P. Zitner, "*King Lear,* and Its Language," in *Some Facets of "King Lear": Essays in Prismatic Criticism,* ed. Rosalie L. Colie and F. T. Flahiff (London: Heinemann, 1974), 4.

24 Thelma Nelson Greenfield, "The Clothing Motif in *King Lear,*" *Shakespeare Quarterly* 5, no. 3 (1954): 282.

25 Ibid., 285.

26 Ibid., 286, 283.

27 Robert Bechtold Heilman, *This Great Stage: Image and Structure in "King Lear"* (Baton Rouge: Louisiana State Univ. Press, 1948), 76, 82, 86.

28 Richard Strier, "Faithful Servants: Shakespeare's Praise of Disobedience," in *The Historical Renaissance: New Essays on Tudor and Stuart Literature and Culture,* ed. Heather Dubrow and Richard Strier (Chicago: Univ. of

Chicago Press, 1988), 114, 117. Further references to Strier's essay will appear parenthetically in the text.

29 Walter Cohen, *Drama of a Nation: Public Theater in Renaissance England and Spain* (Ithaca: Cornell Univ. Press, 1985), 355. Further references to *Drama of a Nation* will appear parenthetically in the text. Cohen cites Christopher Hill, *The World Turned Upside Down* (Harmondsworth, England: Penguin, 1975), 318, 317 for the first of these assertions, and 369 for the second. The play's possible critiques of plainness, as well as the historical oversimplification involved in the plainness-radical or plainness-Puritan connection will be fully addressed in chapter 5; the issue of the possible unmooring of the play's values at the point Strier identifies will be raised again in the conclusion.

30 Erwin Panofsky, *Studies in Iconology: Humanistic Themes in the Art of the Renaissance* (New York: Harper and Row, 1962), 155. Further references will appear parenthetically in the text. I cannot here fully retrace the argument about Titian's painting that leads Panofsky to conclude that although "the draped woman stands for the loftier principle" in many pictorial traditions, in Titian's painting "the roles are reversed" (ibid., 154–55). Just as I try in this book to understand what the particular evaluations are of malleable concepts in particular situations, Panofsky makes a case for what he thinks is at issue in a particular work; such cases will often include arguments about particular conventions and their historical availability and relevance to the particular content of those works — as will the chapters in the second half of this book.

Although giving the naked figure (Celestial Love) a kind of higher status as "more passionate and ardent," Edgar Wind's neo-Platonic reading of Titian's painting emphasizes that the clothed figure need not be devalued as profane, but should be understood as merely earthly, and not inappropriately so. See *Pagan Mysteries in the Renaissance* (London: Faber and Faber, 1958; reprint, Harmondsworth, England: Penguin, 1967), 142–48 (quotation from 148).

31 Henry Medwall, *Nature, The Seconde Parte*, ll. 15–18, in *The Plays of Henry Medwall*, ed. Alan H. Nelson (Cambridge: D. S. Brewer, 1980), 127. Further references to line numbers will appear parenthetically in the text.

32 See *Nature*, 102, lines 421–27.

33 T. W. Craik, *The Tudor Interlude: Stage, Costume, and Acting* (Leicester: Leicester Univ. Press, 1958), 83.

34 *The Trial of Treasure* (London, 1567), in *Early English Dramatists, Anonymous Plays*, ed. John S. Farmer (London: Early English Drama Society, 1906; reprint, Guildford, England: Charles W. Traylen, 1966), 233, 227.

35 Craik, *Tudor Interlude*, 49.

36 Ibid., 56. He says that Christ so appears in *Wisdom*, and the World so appears in *The Castle of Perseverance* and *Mundus et Infans,* as well as in *Nature.*

37 *The Three Lords and Three Ladies of London,* in *A Select Collection of Old English Plays,* originally published by Robert Dodsley, 1744, 4th ed., revised by W. Carew Hazlitt (1874–76; reissue, New York: Benjamin Blom, 1964), vol. 6:425. Conscience says "Alas! who loads my shoulders with this heavy weed? / Fie! how it stinks: this is perfum'd indeed" (ibid.). Conscience is described as wearing white on 443. In the same play, "Policy," sent from "Dissimulation," "bring'st a gown of glosing, lin'd with lust, / A vardingale of vain boast and fan of flattery, / A ruff of riot and a cap of pride" (434), providing another example of inappropriate clothing.

38 *Three Lords and Three Ladies,* 435. Honest Industry says: "Fair Lucre, lo, what Honest Industry / To thee hath brought, to deck thy dainty self. / Lucre, by Honest Industry achiev'd, / Shall prosper, flourish, and continue long. / Come to thy chamber, to attire thee there." Pure Zeal says: "Pure Zeal hath purchas'd robes to cover Love. / Whiles Love is single, Zeal shall her attire, / With kind affection mortifying lust. / Come Love, with me these garments to put on." Note that "covering" has some of the biblical nuances of covering shame.

39 Ibid., 383.

40 Thomas Lupton, *A Moral and Pitieful Comedie, Intituled, All for Money. Plainely Representing the Manners of Men, and Fashion of the World Noweadayes* (London, 1578; Edinburgh: Tudor Facsimile Texts, 1910; reprint, New York: Ams, 1970). "Learning with money cometh in richly appareled" (B4v); "Money without learning" is "appareled like a rich churl, with bags of money by his sides" (C1r).

41 Ibid., A2v.

42 Godfrey Goodman, *The Fall of Man; or, The Corruption of Nature* (London, 1606), 43.

43 "From the MS. book of Master Hooper, exhibited by him to the king's counsellors, October 3, 1550," taken from "Gloucester Ridley, in his Life of Bishop Ridley, 316, London, 1763," in *The Writings of John Bradford,* ed. Aubrey Townsend (Cambridge: Cambridge Univ. Press, 1853), 373.

44 "Reply of Bishop Ridley to Bishop Hooper on the Vestment Controversy, 1550," in *Writings of Bradford,* 385. *The Oxford Dictionary of the Christian Church,* ed. F. L. Cross and E. A. Livingstone (London: Oxford Univ. Press, 1974), says that the Adamian sect was first mentioned by St. Epiphanius, whose approximate dates are 315–403 (16). At about the same time the ascetic leader Priscillian in Aquitaine followed a practice of praying naked in imitation of Adam and Eve (see above, chapter 1).

45 G. R. Elton, ed. *New Cambridge Modern History,* vol. 2, *The Reformation, 1520–1559* (Cambridge: Cambridge Univ. Press, 1958), 127.

46 Ephraim Pagitt, *Heresiography,* 3rd ed. (London, 1646), 8, 31. Also see

Leah S. Marcus, *Childhood and Cultural Despair: A Theme and Variations in Seventeenth-Century Literature* (Pittsburgh: Univ. of Pittsburgh Press, 1978), 58–59, where she quotes from the 1645 edition. A modern commentator, in a review of several books about misbehavior on the evangelical right, convincingly explains the psychological-theological grounds of a contemporary religious phenomenon that obviously has many antecedents in Reformation (and prior) demonstrations of radical innocence: "What the preacher and those sharing his ecstatic moments feel is the healing of that self-dividedness caused, for people of their theological background, by original sin. The body is uplifted with the spirit, in rapturous accord with it. . . . Sexual potency seems to come at will, and to lose its post-Edenic furtiveness. Spiritual love can be open in its sexuality. That is why so many popular religions swerve at their height into Adamite or antinomian urges, toward naked innocence" (Garry Wills, "The Phallic Pulpit," *New York Review of Books* 36, no. 20 [December 21, 1989], 26).

47 Anthony Anderson, *The Shield of Our Safetie* (London, 1581), T1r–T1v.

48 *A Commentarie of John Calvine, upon the First Booke of Moses Called Genesis,* trans. Thomas Tymme (London, 1578), 79. For the sense in which premodern European propriety involved the individual's feeling of shamefulness about his body even when he was alone, see Philippe Ariès and Georges Duby, *A History of Private Life,* vol. 3, *Passions of the Renaissance* (Cambridge, Mass.: Harvard Univ. Press, Belknap Press, 1989), 185–87. Also note that the Geneva Bible may use "filthiness" or "shame," where the King James uses "nakedness" (see above, chapter 1, notes 4, 6).

49 Henry Holland, *The Historie of Adam* (London, 1606), 5.

50 Gervase Babington, *Certaine Plaine, Briefe, and Comfortable Notes upon Everie Chapter of Genesis* (London, 1592), 8 (my emphasis). Even though such "nakedness of mind" may be here approved, in an age of religion-inspired warfare, the inability of any actually naked Anabaptist to conceal weapons (and pacifism was an Anabaptist tenet) may actually cause suspicion and intolerance, rather than approval. Thomas Drant comments that the Anabaptists, "a people full of frenzy and furor," "would be glad to help themselves in their fancy that no man ought to wear weapon" by means of the example of Adam's innocent "first" and "best state," "without weapon . . . without weed." He clearly thinks that it is necessary to wear weapons for the magistrate. Thomas Drant, *Two Sermons Preached, the One at S. Marie's Spittle . . . 1570 and the Other at the Court at Windsor . . . 1569* (London, [1570?]), 231. The quotations are from the sermon preached at Windsor.

51 "It took the Proto-Renaissance spirit to interpret the nudity of Cupid as a symbol of love's 'spiritual nature,' . . . or to employ an entirely naked figure for the representation of a Virtue." Panofsky, *Studies in Iconology,*

156; also see 157–59. See the appendix, "Renaissance Emblems of Truth and Eloquence" in John Steadman's *The Hill and the Labyrinth: Discourse and Certitude in Milton and His Near-Contemporaries* (Berkeley: Univ. of California Press, 1984), 136–53. Among the many examples of emblems that use nakedness to figure Truth (or a connection with Truth) that Steadman gives is one "representing the differences between grammar, history, rhetoric, and philosophy," in which "History is portrayed as nude in consonance with her simplicity and her association with truth. Rhetoric is clad in a long and ornate gown, in consonance with her resort to "venustis . . . coloribus" (137–38, citing Arthur Henkel and Albrecht Schöne, eds., *Emblemata: Handbuch zür Sinnbildkunst des XVI. und XVIII. Jahrhunderts* [Stuttgart, 1967], cols. 1537–1538). Such an emblem certainly is consonant with Puttenham's way of talking about poetic figures.

52 Stephen Batman, *The Golden Booke of the Leaden Gods* (London, 1577), in *The Renaissance and the Gods*, ed. Stephen Orgel, vol. 13 (New York: Garland, 1976): 7.

53 Steadman, *The Hill and the Labyrinth*, 140. Also see the illustrations from a later edition on 137.

54 See Craik, *Tudor Interlude*, 137, n. 18, where he refers to Man's wearing of "some light clothing" to symbolize his nakedness before being given his garments by World. Craik goes on: "*cf. The Castle of Perseverance*, where Humanum Genus calls himself 'naked' but shortly afterwards says 'bare and poor is my clothing' " (ll. 279, 293). Also see J. Martin Evans, *"Paradise Lost" and the Genesis Tradition* (Oxford: Clarendon, 1968), 194, on the costumes used to signify the "embarrassing but Scriptural fact of Adam and Eve's nakedness" in the twelfth-century French *Mystère d'Adam*.

55 "An Homilie against . . . Idolatrie," in *Certaine Sermons or Homilies Appointed to be Read in Churches in the Time of Queen Elizabeth I (1547–1571)*, facsimile of the 1623 edition, ed. Mary Ellen Rickey and Thomas B. Stroup (Gainesville, Fla.: Scholars' Facsimiles and Reprints, 1968), 71, 69. Further references to homilies in *Certaine Sermons* will be given parenthetically in the text.

56 Margaret Loftus Ranald, *Shakespeare and His Social Context: Essays in Osmotic Knowledge and Literary Interpretation* (New York: Ams, 1987), 192, 202–3.

57 For Foxe's mention of the Pope's "Pontificale," see John Foxe, *The Acts and Monuments*, 4th ed., 8 vols., revised and corrected by Josiah Pratt (London: Religious Tract Society, 1887), 8:76. Further references to *The Acts* will be given parenthetically in the text.

58 The phrase "glittering gear" is Robert Crowley's. See above, chapter 2, note 2.

59 What follows is a brief summary of portions of my argument in "Social

Rank and the Pastoral Ideals of *As You Like It,*" *Shakespeare Quarterly* 29, no. 3 (1978): 333–48.

60 Giovanni Battista Nenna, *Nennio; or, A Treatise of Nobility,* trans. W. Jones (1595; reprint, Jerusalem: Israel Univ. Press, 1967), 74v.

61 Desiderius Erasmus, *The Education of a Christian Prince,* trans. Lester K. Born (New York: W. W. Norton, 1968), 152.

62 See Nancy Lindheim, "*King Lear* as Pastoral Tragedy," in *Facets of "King Lear,"* ed. Colie and Flahiff, 169–84.

63 Humfrey, *The Nobles,* T3v.

64 Woolton, *The Christian Manuell; or, The Life and Maners of True Christians* (London, 1576), H5r.

65 Richard Hooker, "A Learned Sermon of the Nature of Pride," in *The Works of Mr. Richard Hooker,* 6th ed., 3 vols., compiled by John Keble (Oxford: Clarendon, 1874), 3:606.

66 Henry Barrow, *A Brief Discoverie of the False Church* (1590), in *The Writings of Henry Barrow, 1587–1590,* Elizabethan Nonconformist Texts, vol. 3, ed. Leland H. Carlson (London: George Allen and Unwin, 1962): 489.

67 Dean Frye, in contrast, attempts to redress the balance. He finds in Lear's "O reason not the need," for example, "a serious defense of the artificial and, strictly speaking, unnecessary additions that men have made to their natural state," and he points to some of the particularly positive associations of ceremony and decorum in the Renaissance, or at least the felt need for them, even if, as he says, they fail in *Lear.* "The Context of Lear's Unbuttoning," *ELH* 32 (1965): 21.

68 Emily Leider, also, although stressing the contrast of grandiloquent language and "furr'd robes" to simple language and nakedness, is careful to say that she does not "regard plainness as the unchallenged stylistic hero of the play," but as something that "compels our attention . . . partly because it contrasts so sharply with other veins. . . . There is no more striking indication of flexibility than the contrast between Cordelia's near dumbness and the lyric opulence with which she is always described: [she quotes the Gentleman's description]. When such extravagance applies to Cordelia, we reason not the need. The rhetoric we associate with courtly magnificence befits her. She marks the point at which excess and restraint meet." Leider, "Plainness of Style," 52, 53. F omits the entire scene.

69 See for example, Robert Grudin, *Mighty Opposites: Shakespeare and Renaissance Contrariety* (Berkeley: Univ. of California Press, 1979); Norman Rabkin, *Shakespeare and the Common Understanding* (New York: Free Press, 1968); also see Joel B. Altman, *The Tudor Play of Mind: Rhetorical Inquiry and the Development of Elizabethan Drama* (Berkeley: Univ. of California Press, 1978).

5 Sociopolitical Readings and Family Relationships

1 Q has "nor more nor lesse" (l. 81).

2 James H. Kavanagh, "Shakespeare in Ideology," in *Alternative Shakespeares*, ed. John Drakakis (London: Methuen, 1985), 156–57.

3 Yet Cohen sees Cordelia as at least "figuratively connected to the lower classes" (337), and connects her plainness with radical Protestantism. He seems to find her superiority to Lear inhering in *anti*hierarchical attitudes. For him, Lear becomes "at last fully worthy of Cordelia" when "he rejects all hierarchy, insisting instead on his common humanity" (334). One wonders how this can be the same Cordelia who laments that her "poor father" had to "hovel . . . with swine and rogues forlorn / In short and musty straw" (4.7.37–9) and asks "How does my royal lord?" (4.7.43).

4 Franco Moretti, " 'A Huge Eclipse': Tragic Form and the Deconsecration of Sovereignty," in *The Forms of Power and Power of Forms in the Renaissance*, ed. Stephen Greenblatt (Norman, Okla.: Pilgrim Books, 1982), 15.

5 Jonas A. Barish and Marshall Waingrow, " 'Service' in *King Lear*," *Shakespeare Quarterly* 9, no. 3 (1958): 348, 353.

6 Kathleen McLuskie, "The Patriarchal Bard: Feminist Criticism and Shakespeare: *King Lear* and *Measure for Measure*," in *Political Shakespeare: New Essays in Cultural Materialism*, ed. Jonathan Dollimore and Alan Sinfield (Ithaca: Cornell Univ. Press, 1985), 104.

7 Moretti, " 'A Huge Eclipse,' " 30.

8 Walzer, *Revolution of the Saints: A Study of the Origins of Radical Politics* (Cambridge, Mass.: Harvard Univ. Press, 1965), 168, and 214–15, quoting Preston, *The New Covenant* (London, 1629), 331. Also see David Zaret, *The Heavenly Contract: Ideology and Organization in Pre-Revolutionary Puritanism* (Chicago: Univ. of Chicago Press), 1985.

9 John F. Danby, *Shakespeare's Doctrine of Nature: A Study of "King Lear"* (London: Faber and Faber, 1948; reprint, 1965), 129. Further references will be given parenthetically in the text.

10 Conrad Russell, *The Crisis of Parliaments: English History, 1509-1660* (London: Oxford Univ. Press, 1971), 179.

11 Greenblatt, "The Cultivation of Anxiety: King Lear and His Heirs," in *Learning to Curse: Essays in Early Modern Culture* (New York: Routledge, 1990), 97, 96. Further references will appear parenthetically in the text.

12 R[obert] C[leaver], *A Codly [sic] Form of Householde Government: For the Ordering of Private Families* (London, 1598), 347–48 (my emphasis).

13 Bartholmaeus Battus, *The Christian Man's Closet: Wherein Is Contained a Large Discourse of the Godly Training up of Children: As Also Those Duties That Children Owe unto Their Parents*, trans. William Lowth (London, 1581), 72v–73r, 71v. Further references will appear parenthetically in the text.

14 Matthew Griffith, *Bethel; or, A Forme for Families* (London, 1633), 375. Further references will appear parenthetically in the text.

15 John Dod and Robert Cleaver, *A Plaine and Familiar Exposition of the Ten Commaundements* (London, 1606), 191. Further references will appear parenthetically in the text.

16 Barker, *A Learned and Familiar Exposition upon the Ten Commandements* (London, 1633), 255. If the Scythians were emblems of such paradoxical behavior, the grief that underlies Lear's rage may well be underscored by this reference to them. The typical parental comparison: "Even these terrible people have reverence for their parents, and yet you . . . !" Q omits "to my bosom" (l. 108).

17 Geffray Fenton, *A Forme of Christian Pollicie Drawne out of French* (London, 1574), 294. The passage begins by speaking of a *man's* obligation to help his parents as not canceled by his marriage, and ends by talking about "the wife with her husband" helping those made parents by marriage, thus perhaps suggesting to some that the case of a woman is different insofar as she marries into the man's family. Nevertheless, the latter part of the passage does describe relief to those made *their* father and mother by marriage, thus implying that each, wife and husband, will acquire in-laws to whom support is due. If it is claimed that a son ought to continue to aid his own parents, as well as that a son-in-law ought to aid his parents-in-law (as Lear is aided by France), it is certainly implied that a daughter ought to continue to "succour" her own parents, even after marriage, as well as to support her new parents.

18 Walzer, *Revolution*, 214.

19 *The Office of Christian Parents: Shewing How Children Are To Be Governed throughout All Ages and Times of Their Life*, printed by Cantrell Legge, printer to the University of Cambridge (Cambridge, 1616), reports a horrible example of a certain rich mother, negligent in bringing up her son "too gently": "He became a thief, and being brought to the gallows, he saw his mother, with whom when he had requested some secret speech, putting his mouth toward his mother, he pulled off his mother's nose with his teeth; and spitting it on the ground, spake with a loud voice, *O ye citizens, let this be the reward of my mother bringing me up*" (143–44).

20 The *Riverside Shakespeare* gives the reading in F. Q (l. 140) has "To plainnes honours bound when Maiesty stoops to folly."

21 F has "since what I will intend" (ll. 247–48).

22 Q has "since I am sure / My loves more richer then my tongue" (l. 70).

23 *The Office of Christian Parents* (Cambridge, 1616), 236. This work was printed by Cantrell Legge, third in a line of Puritan-associated printers at the University of Cambridge press. "By the early 1580s, Cambridge had become identified as the intellectual centre of presbyterianism." Thomas Thomas, who attempted to print Walter Travers's work, but was stopped by Burghley and Whitgift, was succeeded by John Legate, the "dominant printer of Perkins' prolific output, . . . *ipso facto* a leading puritan printer," whose "authors, like those of his successor Cantrell Legge, showed their hearts on their title-pages, in the styles by which they were presented." Among the authors printed by Legge were Andrew Willet and Thomas Taylor; the latter "made himself notorious by an outspoken attack on Bancroft in the University Church." David McKitterick, *A History of Cambridge University Press,* vol. 1, *Printing and the Book Trade in Cambridge, 1534-1698* (Cambridge: Cambridge Univ. Press, 1992), 93, 95, 128, 129. *Christian Parents* is a work that emphasizes obedience to parents "in all that God commandeth and alloweth, and in other things [urges the child] to prefer his heavenly Father before his earthly parents" (230), and thus a work that qualifies obedience in a manner some critics (such as Danby, as we have seen) associate with "strong" Protestantism. It should be noted, however, that guides to household management are not always written by Puritans, and that the Puritans who wrote them were not always antiroyalist during the civil wars. Matthew Griffith, author of *Bethel; or, A Forme for Families* (1633) was a "royalist divine" (*Dictionary of National Biography,* s.v. "Griffith, Matthew"). William Gouge, author of the best known guide to household management, *Of Domesticall Duties* (London, 1622), was a moderate Puritan on the royalist side during the wars.

24 Lancelot Andrewes, *A Pattern of Catechistical Doctrine,* in *The Works of Lancelot Andrewes* (Oxford: John Henry Parker, 1854; reprint, New York: Ams, 1967), 6:276. The earliest edition of this work, without Andrewes's name, appears to have been printed in 1630 (STC 603). *Halkett and Laing: A Dictionary of Anonymous and Pseudonymous Publications in the English Language, 1475-1640,* 3rd ed., ed. John Horden (Harlow, England: Longman Group, 1980), attributes the work to Andrewes. Further references will appear parenthetically in the text.

25 "A Second Admonition to the Parliament," in *Puritan Manifestoes: A Study of the Origin of the Puritan Revolt,* ed. W. H. Frere and C. E. Douglas (New York: E. S. Gorham, 1907; reprint, London: S.P.C.K., 1954), 109-10.

26 "A Speach, As It Was Delivered . . . in the . . . Parliament . . . on Munday the XIX. Day of March 1603," in *Political Works of James I,* intro. by Howard McIlwain (Cambridge, Mass.: Harvard Univ. Press, 1918), 280.

27 "A Speach to Both the Houses of Parliament . . . Delivered . . . the Last Day of March 1607," in *Political Works of James I,* 290.

28 The *Nouvelle Biographie Générale,* published by Firmin Didot Bros., under the direction of Dr. Hoefer (Paris, 1853-66; reprint, Copenhagen:

Rosendkilde and Bagger, 1963), indicates that Barthelemy Batt (1515–59) was persecuted "pour avoir embrassé le luthéranisme" (746). I have been unable to find any biographical information about Battus's English translator, William Lowth.

29 Battus, *Christian Man's Closet;* 62r follows 63v. Like many strong Protestant or Puritan works, this one stresses the "first table" over the "last" (71v). See J. Sears McGee, *The Godly Man in Stuart England: Anglicans, Puritans, and the Two Tables, 1620–1670* (New Haven: Yale Univ. Press, 1976). Also see R[obert] C[leaver], *A Codly [sic] Form of Householde Government:* "which honor consisteth not in bowing the knee or putting off the cap, or giving to their parents the upperhand only" (346).

30 See Andrewes, *A Pattern of Catechistical Doctrine,* 176–77, where he defines "inward honour" as "that 'good opinion' and reputation that one man hath of another" and "outward honour" as customs that vary with countries and include rising up, uncovering the head, bowing the knee, being silent, using words of submission, etc.

31 Samuel Clarke, *A Collection of the Lives of Ten Eminent Divines* (London, 1662), 446. The relationship between the superior internal "heart" and the inferior external "show" may shift for proponents of "enthusiastic" religion who wear their hearts on their sleeves. Clarke also praises Mrs. Ratcliffe, "silent in her common conversation with the world" for being "eloquent in her intercourse with God." "For such was her holy violence in prayer, as that she seemed not to knock at heaven gate for another to open it, but to make a battery upon it herself, and to break in by the powerful importunity of her supplications." Hers was "no dry devotion, but steeped, and drenched in showers of tears; and though her prudence used as much privacy as might be herein, yet such a gift could not be hid from her servants" (426). Contrast George Herbert: "He as truly repents, who performs the other acts of repentence, when he cannot more, as he that weeps a flood of tears." *A Priest to the Temple,* in *Works of George Herbert,* ed. F. E. Hutchinson (Oxford: Clarendon, 1941; reprint, 1959), 279.

32 William Gouge, *Of Domesticall Duties,* 436. Further references will appear parenthetically in the text.

33 Francis Bunny, *A Guide unto Godlinesse; or, A Plaine and Familiar Explanation of the Ten Commandements* (London, 1617), 121–22. He was prebend at Durham Cathedral (1572), archdeacon of Northumberland (1573), and, finally, rector of Ryton, Durham, from 1578 until his death in 1617. Prior to these positions, Bunny held a chaplaincy to Francis Russell, the strongly Protestant Earl of Bedford. See *Dictionary of National Biography,* s.v. "Bunny, Francis."

34 Q has "pleated" (l. 277).

35 Clement of Alexandria, urging the wearing of simple, white garments for both men and women, comments: "I like the description that the Ceian Sophist gave of . . . good and evil. The one he pictured standing simply, clothed in white, pure: this is virtue, adorned only with her modesty . . . ; the other he describes as just the contrary: wrapped in many robes, decked out in outlandish colors, with a . . . posture best calculated to insure her own enjoyment in company with other shameless women." *Christ the Educator*, trans. Simon P. Wood, Fathers of the Church, no. 23 (Washington, D.C.: Catholic Univ. of America Press, 1954), 184–85.

36 Fritz Saxl, "Veritas Filia Temporis," in *Philosophy and History: Essays Presented to Ernst Cassirer*, ed. Raymond Klibansky and H. J. Paton (Oxford: Clarendon, 1936; reprint, New York: Harper and Row, 1963), 207, quoting John Elder's letter describing the arrival and marriage of King Philip, London, 1555, from John G. Nichols, *The Chronicle of Queen Jane and of Two Years of Queen Mary*, Camden Society Publication no. 48 (1850), 157.

37 Saxl, "Veritas," 207.

38 Ibid., 208–9, quoting John Nichols, *The Progresses . . . of Queen Elizabeth* (London, 1823), 1:50.

39 Saxl, "Veritas," 209.

40 Even a villainness like Regan uses the prime terms of the culture. "In my true heart / I find she names my very deed of love" says Regan, 1.1.69–70, after Goneril speaks, naming both the "true heart" (contrasting implicitly with the false tongue), and the "deed" (contrasting implicitly with mere words or names).

41 Annabel Patterson takes issue with the "commonplace . . . that [*Lear*] represents the transition from a feudal economy or culture to a nascent capitalism." I concur that "the argument that Lear, Kent, and perhaps Cordelia act out the old feudal values or configure . . . a Moral Economy is deeply unpersuasive. Edmund, Goneril and Regan, the figures who supposedly represent the approach of capitalist values, in no way differ from aristocratic predators anywhere in Shakespeare's canon" (*Shakespeare and the Popular Voice* [Cambridge, Mass.: Basil Blackwell, 1989], 108). Graham Holderness also does not approve of the "orthodox reading of our time: that the 'old, patriarchal society has been stripped by the new men, the new, hard materialists'" (Graham Holderness, Nick Potter, and John Turner, *Shakespeare: The Play of History* [Basingstoke, England: Macmillan, 1988], 101, quoting Marvin Rosenberg, *The Masks of King Lear* [Univ. of California Press, 1972], 34).

42 Jack Goody, "Inheritance, Property and Women," in *Family and Inheritance: Rural Society in Western Europe, 1200–1800*, ed. Jack Goody, Joan Thirsk, and E. P. Thompson (Cambridge: Cambridge Univ. Press, 1976), 29.

43 "Settlements of this kind were common in the court rolls of the thirteenth and fourteenth centuries from all parts of England, though they were not always spelt out in great detail." Goody, "Inheritance, Property and Women," 29.

44 George C. Homans, *English Villagers of the Thirteenth Century* (Cambridge: Harvard Univ. Press, 1941; reprint, New York: Harper and Row, 1970), 146, 148.

45 Ibid., 155, quoting *Handlyng Synne*, ed. F. J. Furnivall (Early English Text Society), ll. 1124–6.

46 Homans, *English Villagers*, 154. Homans's note cites *Bracton's Note Book*, ed. F. W. Maitland, no. 1922, as the source of the story of Anseline.

47 Ralph A. Houlbrooke, *The English Family, 1450–1700* (London: Longman, 1984), 10. See Peter Laslett, *Family Life and Illicit Love in Earlier Generations: Essays in Historical Sociology* (Cambridge: Cambridge Univ. Press, 1977) and P. Laslett and R. Wall, eds. *Household and Family in Past Time* (Cambridge: Cambridge Univ. Press, 1972). The question of the "frequency" of nuclear family households is complicated. Depending on the demographics (age at marriage, age of a married couple at the birth of last child, age and marital status of the youngest living child, age at death, frequency of widows or widowers who do not remarry), there could be a strong and faithfully followed extended family model, even while there was an overwhelming preponderance of nuclear family households at any one time.

48 Margaret Spufford, "Peasant Inheritance Customs and Land Distribution," in *Family and Inheritance*, ed. Goody, Thirsk, and Thompson, 175, 174. Also see her *Contrasting Communities: English Villagers in the Sixteenth and Seventeenth Centuries* (Cambridge: Cambridge Univ. Press, 1974). Keith Thomas finds—in spite of Laslett's claim that it is hard to find from the sixteenth century on—that premortem inheritance in exchange for support is not unfamiliar in the Renaissance, even though medieval examples have been more often discussed. See "Age and Authority in Early Modern England," *Proceedings of the British Academy* 62 (1976), 236–37, n. 5. For a discussion of the discrepancies between Spufford's findings and Laslett's see Alan Macfarlane, *Marriage and Love in England: Modes of Reproduction, 1300–1840* (Oxford: Basil Blackwell, 1986), 97ff. Macfarlane suggests that co-residence after marriage might have occurred, but that it was definitely not the norm, and furthermore, that where it did occur it was not because parents and children settled down together after marriage, but because parents who had lived separately for a long time, might come to live with a child, on becoming widows or widowers.

49 Goody, "Inheritance, Property and Women," 32.

50 "Among males of equal degree only the eldest inherited, but females inherited together as coheiresses." Houlbrooke, *English Family*, 229. Also see Kenelm Edward Digby, *An Introduction to the History of the Law of Real Property*, 4th ed. (Oxford: Clarendon, 1892), 419, and A. W. B. Simpson, *An Introduction to the History of the Land Law* (Oxford: Oxford Univ. Press, 1961; reprint, 1964), 55-56.

51 See J. P. Cooper, "Patterns of Inheritance and Settlement by Great Landowners from the Fifteenth to the Eighteenth Centuries," in *Family and Inheritance*, ed. Goody, Thirsk, and Thompson, 209.

52 Q has "sons at perfit age, and fathers declining, his father should be as ward to the sonne, and the sonne mannage the revenew" (ll. 363-65).

53 Geoffrey Bullough, *Narrative and Dramatic Sources of Shakespeare*, vol. 7, *Major Tragedies: Hamlet, Othello, King Lear, Macbeth* (London: Routledge and Kegan Paul, 1973): 270, quoting the letter of [Grace's husband] "Sir John Wildegose and others to Lord Cecil," which is given in full, 309.

54 Also see Battus, *Christian Man's Closet*, 70.

55 Debora K. Shuger makes the same point about love descending in her discussion of parental *storge* or "natural affection" as a "metaphor for divine love" that "replaces eros and *philia*." "Among religious writers, *storge* . . . becomes equivalent to *caritas*, the unmerited and gratuitous love of the higher for the lower, the stronger for the weaker." (*Habits of Thought in the English Renaissance: Religion, Politics, and the Dominant Culture* [Berkeley: Univ. of California Press, 1990], 225-26, 226).

56 Francis Dillingham, *Christian Oeconomy; or, Household Government* (London, 1609), 28, 30.

57 Gervase Babington, *A Very Fruitful Exposition of the Commandements* (London, 1596), 105-6.

58 Dod and Cleaver, *Ten Commaundements*, 202. Dod and Cleaver also stress the foolishness of entailing an estate, thus bypassing daughters, when there is no male heir: "Others . . . offend in the disposing of their lands, that if they have no heir male, but all daughters, the heritage must be put away from them, and given to some other: . . . that the name might continue. . . . How know you that he may not live so, as that he shall be a blot to your name, and to your self, rather than a credit? Why then should one, for a foolish regard of name, break both God's law, and the law of nature too? For God hath appointed, *Numb*, 127. that if there be no son, the land and heritage shall be divided amongst the daughters" (203).

59 John ap Robert, *The Younger Brother His Apologie; or, A Father's Free Power Disputed, for the Disposition of His Lands* (Oxford, 1634), 53, 54. "The first known edition of [this work] was published . . . in 1618." Joan Thirsk, "Younger Sons in the Seventeenth Century," *History* 54 (1969): 364. I keep ap Robert's italics in this quotation since they help the reader hear the echoes of *King Lear*.

60 Only in F.

61 Robert Allen, *A Treasurie of Catechisme; or, Christian Instruction* (London, 1600), 131.

62 See Houlbrooke, *English Family*, 190–91, Thomas, "Age and Authority," 238–42, Macfarlane, *Marriage and Love*, 110–11. Such attitudes appear earlier as well. A story illustrating both the mistreatment of parents by children, and what happens to those children at the hands of *their* children as a result was frequently told. A man's father becomes a burden to him when he has a son of his own; thus he progressively gives the old man less and less, finally asking his son to cover his shivering grandfather with only a sack. At this point the son cuts the sack in half, covers the grandfather with half of it, and shows his father the remaining half to indicate what *his* maintenance is going to be in his old age. Among places where the story occurs are Robert Mannying of Brunne's *Handlying Sinne*, ll. 1121ff., as Homans indicates (*English Villagers*, 155), and Battus, *Christian Man's Closet*, 73.

63 Babington, *Very Fruitful Exposition of the Commandements*, 107.

64 Macfarlane, *Marriage and Love*, 336, 334, 82, 75, 109.

65 McLuskie, "Patriarchal Bard," 104.

66 Both Leah S. Marcus and Annabel Patterson argue for a considerable degree of indeterminacy in accordance with "the importance of localization for defining parameters of meaning" (Marcus, *Puzzling Shakespeare: Local Reading and Its Discontents* (Berkeley: Univ. of California Press, 1988), 158), or with the "hermeneutics of censorship" (Patterson, *Censorship*, 63). For Marcus, "neither text of the play"—that is, neither the First Quarto, which announces it is the play *"As it was played before the Kings Maiestie at Whitehall vpon S. Stephans night in Christmas Hollidayes,"* nor the Folio—"offers a straightforward identification of either King Lear or his enemies with the 'Jacobean line'" (148)—that is, with James's particular forms of self-representation, although the 1608 Quarto "is richer in topical details evoking the royal Project for Union" and "in particularized materials which can easily be interpreted as criticism of King James I" (149). For Patterson, the play is "so deeply ambiguated, so clearly referential in some way to the Union debate, but so utterly resistant to assimilation by either side in the controversy, . . . that it could even, with impunity, be presented before the king" (71). Also see Patterson, *Shakespeare and the Popular Voice*, 107: "There seems little doubt that the Union issue was one major form of the topicality in which *King Lear* is saturated, although, given the reversed mirror in which the issue is visible, it is impossible to decide what solution Shakespeare recommended." Nevertheless, both critics also offer very specific "local" readings implicating James's stance on the Union issue as recognizably authoritarian, recognizably an encroachment on accustomed liberties.

67 For Marcus's connection, see *Puzzling Shakespeare*, 148–49; for Patterson's, see *Censorship*, 59, 64–73. The pioneer new historicist Marie Axton makes the connection in ch. 9 ("The Problem of Union: King James I and 'King Lear'") of *The Queen's Two Bodies: Drama and the Elizabethan Succession* (London: Royal Historical Society, 1997) where she says, "James and his court saw the tragedy against the backcloth of a struggle for Union" (135). The other logical possibility, that James is complimented because his own plan for Union—celebrated in plays and pageants—is the opposite of Lear's—and the mythical Brutus's—division of the realm is put forth in Glynne Wickham's essay, "From Tragedy to Tragi-Comedy: 'King Lear' as Prologue," *Shakespeare Survey* 26 (1973): 33–48.

A logically prior question should proceed the linkage of the presumably negatively seen division by Lear with the presumably negatively seen Union by James. Even if politically unwise for a kingdom, is division per se negative in all relevant contexts? Partible inheritance and/or defiance of male primogeniture were available models, historically and geographically—even in the case of kingdoms, if usually understood as problematic there. See Goody, "Inheritance, Property and Women," in *Family and Inheritance,* 31; John ap Robert, *The Younger Brother His Apologie;* Joan Thirsk, "The European Debate on Customs of Inheritance, 1500–1700," in *Family and Inheritance,* ed. Goody, Thirsk, and Thompson, 177–91.

68 On the Union issue, see R. C. Munden, "James I and 'The Growth of Mutual Distrust': King, Commons, and Reform, 1603–1604," in *Faction and Parliament: Essays on Early Stuart History,* ed. Kevin Sharpe (Oxford: Clarendon, 1978), 62–63. Also see the entire book devoted to a painstaking history of the Union by the Scottish historian Bruce Galloway, *The Union of England and Scotland, 1603–1608* (Edinburgh: John Donald, 1986). Further references to Galloway will appear parenthetically in the text. Munden goes so far as to say "James's actions and intentions have perhaps been more seriously misunderstood and misrepresented by historians in respect of this issue than of any other" (62). Galloway considers the entire treatment of the Project for the Union rife with "Anglocentric" fallacies, such as the belittling of its importance, "considering it . . . irrelevant to the 'real' political issues of the period," in fact as "a personal foible . . . a foolish and ill-considered toy" (161). On James's rational political reasons, including security, for urging Union, see Galloway, *Union* 163–65, 64 (contrast Axton's reading of mystical metaphor, *Queen's Two Bodies,* 133); on James's lack of "browbeating," see Munden, "James I," 63; on his proceeding "cautiously, with leaden foot," see Galloway, *Union,* 166, and also 20–21.

69 "In 1606–7, even loyal servants of the crown are found supporting limitations on naturalisation [of the Scots], and the 'perfect union'. This was why union was defeated. It was not through 'Court vs Country', or even faction, but a general revolt on a specific issue. Union cannot therefore be taken as indicative of normal relations between king and parliament. This cuts both ways. By demolishing the thesis of an organised opposition party, it denies the whig interpretation. On the other hand, it simultaneously demonstrates that, on a political or constitutional issue of particular importance, normal political guidelines ceased to apply. King and Parliament, Lords and Commons might cooperate happily on normal issues, if faction did not intervene; but a 'whiggish' reaction was possible — given the right issue" (Galloway, *Union*, 169).

70 See Richard Cust and Ann Hughes, "Introduction: After Revisionism," in *Conflict in Early Stuart England: Studies in Religion and Politics, 1603–1642*, ed. Richard Cust and Ann Hughes (London: Longman, 1989), 1, on the "linear progression towards liberal democracy," in Whig history; this essay is critical of aspects of revisionism, but attempts a balanced assessment.

71 Barry Coward, "Was There an English Revolution in the Middle of the Seventeenth Century?" in *Politics and People in Revolutionary England: Essays in Honour of Ivan Roots*, ed. Colin Jones, Malyn Newitt, and Stephen Roberts (Oxford: Basil Blackwell, 1986), 16, 17.

72 See Patterson's antirevisionist argument in "The Very Name of the Game: Theories of Order and Disorder," in *Literature and the English Civil War*, ed. Thomas Healy and Jonathan Sawday (Cambridge: Cambridge Univ. Press, 1990), 21–37.

73 Cust and Hughes, "Introduction: After Revisionism," in *Conflict in Early Stuart England*, 17.

74 Johann Sommerville, "Ideology, Property and the Constitution," in *Conflict in Early Stuart England*, ed. Cust and Hughes, 49. Further references will appear parenthetically in the text.

75 Johann Sommerville, *Politics and Ideology in England, 1603–1640* (London: Longman, 1986), 115. Further references will appear parenthetically in the text. Although Sommerville mentions constitutional disagreements in 1610 and 1614 in both this book (e.g., 182) and his later article, "Ideology, Property" (57, 60, 64), many of his statements in the article are about later dates during Charles's reign. For example: "Divisions on constitutional principle, when added to royal incompetence and to religious differences, explain much about politics between 1625 and 1640" (65); "The idea that many clerics advocated arbitrary government and that they were polluting the King's mind with such notions was commonplace by 1628" (59); "The lesson of 1625–40 was that the King's high constitutional views rendered his promises untrustworthy" (66).

76 "Speach to the Lords and Commons . . . 1609," in *Political Works of*

James I, 307. Patterson, referring to the same speech, remarks that by this time "James had become even *more* like Lear, expanding in his own pronouncements on the implications of the patriarchal metaphor, reminding his subjects that the stories of fathers and children are governed by the same rules as the histories of kingdoms" (*Censorship*, 72). Also note: "The king towards his people is rightly compared to a father of children . . . : For as fathers, the good princes, and magistrates of the people of God acknowledged themselves to their subjects. And for all other well ruled commonwealths, the style of *Pater patriae* was ever, and is commonly used to kings." ("The Trew Law of Free Monarchies," *Political Works of James I*, 64).

77 Greenblatt, though making no specific argument about James, says "Cordelia opposes in effect the ethos of the maintenance agreement" "against paternal and monarchal absolutism," an absolutism inherent in the period's conceptions of all power—monarchal, paternal and divine. Lear's "claim to unbounded power" is transformed "into a demand for unbounded love," and only when the direct link between "family and state power has been broken . . . can [he] hope . . . for his daughter's sustaining and boundless love" ("Cultivation of Anxiety," 97, 96, 97, 98).

78 Speaking of the power of the father "of old under the law of nature . . . over their children or family," James says "(I mean such fathers of families as were the lineal heirs of those families whereof kings did originally come:) . . . For kings had their first original from them, who planted and spread themselves in colonies throughout the world." "Speach to the Lords and Commons . . . 1609," in *Political Works of James I*, 308.

79 Peter Laslett, introduction to *Patriarchia and other Political Works*, by Sir Robert Filmer, ed. Peter Laslett (Oxford: Basil Blackwell, 1949), 29.

80 *Bishop Overall's Convocation Book MDC VI Concerning the Government of God's Catholic Church and the Kingdoms of the Whole World* (London, 1690), 3. Sommerville says both that James "suppressed [the Canons] for reasons which are obscure, though he was doubtless aware that the clergy's absolutist ideas would meet with hostility in the House of Commons" (*Politics and Ideology*, 79) and that "James I was unimpressed" by the doctrine that " 'new forms of government' which arose after a rebellion became valid as soon as they were 'thoroughly settled,' " and "this was one reason why he witheld his consent to the canons" (ibid., 26).

81 Filmer, *Patriarchia*, 96.

82 *Political Works of James I*, 63. Similarly, Filmer says, "All kings, even tyrants and conquerors [are] bound to preserve the lands, goods, liberties and lives of all their subjects, not by any municipal law of the land, but by the natural law of a father, which binds them to ratify the acts of their forefathers and predecessors in things necessary for the public good of their subjects" (*Patriarchia*, 103). Johann Sommerville comments: "If God's law of nature gave the king sovereign power, and human laws were valid only inasmuch as they cohered with divine law, it followed that there could be no valid law against absolute monarchy. . . . There were two senses in which the king could be said to be *bound*. He might have a moral obligation not to change the laws, or, on the other hand, he might be bound in the much stronger sense that the laws would remain in force even if he attempted to abrogate them. Plainly the first two Stuarts believed that their duty to abide by the laws was of the first variety" (*Politics and Ideology*, 133).

83 John Hooper, *A Declaration of the Ten Holy Commandments of Almighty God*, in *Early Writings of John Hooper*, ed. Samuel Carr (Cambridge: Cambridge Univ. Press, 1843), 360–61. See note 76 above for a similar passage by James I.

84 Hooper, *Declaration*, 359.

85 Allen, *Treasurie of Catechisme*, 132 (my emphasis). Although divine right theory easily may allow tyranny to slip in, it does not embrace tyranny. James makes this clear in his speech of March 21, 1609 to Parliament, in which he, like Andrewes, refers to Psalm 82: "And therefore a king governing in a settled kingdom, leaves to be a king, and degenerates into a tyrant, as soon as he leaves off to rule according to his laws. . . . And though no Christian man ought to allow any rebellion of people against their prince, yet doth God never leave kings unpunished when they transgress these limits: For in that same psalm where God saith to kings, *Vos Dii estis*, he immediately thereafter concludes, *But ye shall die like men*. The higher we are placed, the greater shall our fall be" (*Political Works of James I*, 309–10).

Sommerville asserts that this speech was intended to "pour oil on troubled waters" after a bishop had asserted that the king had the right to levy taxes without consent; he compares it to more explicit Jamesian statements of his prerogative in 1621. See *Politics and Ideology*, 132–33. The laws James mentions "are properly made by the king only; but at the rogation of the people, the king's grant being obtained thereunto" (*Political Works of James I*, 309), and this does raise the question concerning the sense in which the king is *bound* by his laws (see note 82, above). Insofar as the king is above the law he makes and follows it only of his own free will, out of gracious condescension, for the benefit of his people, he cannot be culpable if he on occasion chooses not to follow it for the same reason. Yet, even Sommerville, who believes there were two different constitutional theories in the early seventeenth century, says: "Of course, is it one thing to believe that you hold supreme power in England and another to govern in a lawless, arbitrary way. Both James and Charles were God-fearing men who thought that they had a duty to rule in an orderly, law-abiding manner. . . . The early Stuart kings believed that they possessed absolute power, but were quite willing to promise that they would rule in the public interest and with the consent of their subjects" (*Politics and Ideology*, 116).

We might note that the Marian martyr Hooper, like James, requires the king to obey the laws *he himself made*: "[Princes] must lead the people and themselves by the law, and not against the law; to be the ministers of the law, and not masters over the law. Cato saith well therein, 'Obey the law that thou madest thyself' " (*Declaration of the Ten Holy Commandments*, in *Early Writings of Hooper*, 362–63). And it is for James a "point wherein a lawful king doth directly differ from a tyrant" that he "prefer[s] the weal of the body and of the whole Commonwealth, in making of good laws and constitutions, to any particular or private ends of [his own], thinking ever the wealth and weal of the Commonwealth to be [his] greatest weal and worldly felicity" ("A Speech, As It Was Delivered . . . in the . . . Parliament . . . on Munday the XIX. Day of March 1603," in *Political Works of James I*, 277).

86 *Political Works of James I*, 65, 55–56. See Shuger, *Habits of Thought*, ch. 6, on "Nursing Fathers," and especially her point that it is an oversimplification to see this image "as an ideological concealment of oppressive power relations" (228).

87 Also see Thomas Floyd, *The Picture of a Perfit Common Wealth* (London, 1600): "Anger in a king is death: grim and terrible is his countenance, when he is puffed with wrath, hurtful to many, odious to all is the sight thereof" (39).

88 John Stockwood, *A Sermon Preached at Paule's Crosse on Barthelmew Day* (London, 1578), 55.

89 Several historians consider that Protestantism actually strengthened the authority of the father within the household. "The household was the inheritor of many of the responsibilities of the parish and the Church; the family head was the inheritor of much of the authority and many of the powers of the priest." Lawrence Stone, *The Family, Sex and Marriage in England, 1500–1800* (New York: Harper and Row, 1977), 141. Laslett comments in his introduction to Filmer's *Patriarchia:* "It is true that extreme Puritanism, especially in the Low Countries and the New World, was ameliorating the position of women and breaking down the bonds which bound the adult son or daughter to the father. Nevertheless the Puritan theology deepened the emotional authoritarianism within the family group" (*Patriarchia*, 24).

90 Shuger, *Habits of Thought*, 241.

91 Fenton, *A Forme of Christian Policy*, 13, quoted in Walzer, *Revolution of the Saints*, 184.

92 R. Malcolm Smuts, *Court Culture and the Origins of a Royalist Tradition in Early Stuart England* (Philadelphia: Univ. of Pennsylvania Press, 1987), 35, 82. At the time of the Spanish match, that is, 1623, "a fissure had appeared . . . that foreboded more serious problems to come if the match was not abandoned" (35). In a country not yet divided "between royalists and parliamentarians," Ben Jonson could be both "the Jacobean court's unofficial laureate" and "the playwright most often accused of writing seditious works" (82).

93 Ibid., 16, 81–82. "In the seventeenth century, royal power and aristocratic privilege had not yet come under the kind of systematic attacks that developed during the Enlightenment and the democratic revolutions of the eighteenth century. The modern habit of blaming moral decadence on reactionary institutions and unjust social systems had not developed, and the belief that human life may be improved by political revolution was not widespread" (ibid., 80).

94 Cust and Hughes, introduction to *Conflict in Early Stuart England,* ed. Cust and Hughes, 17.

6 Hierarchy, Pomp, Service, Authority

1 Q has "handy, dandy, which is the theefe, which is the Iustice" (ll. 2362–63).

2 Q has "The art of our necessities is strange that can, / Make vild things precious" (ll. 1497–98).

3 Margot Heinemann, "'Demystifying the Mystery of State': *King Lear* and the World Upside Down," *Shakespeare Survey* 44 (1992): 80, 79, 82. Further references will appear parenthetically in the text.

4 Strier takes the latter phrase from a chapter heading in John Ponet, *A Short Treatise of Politic Power, 1556* (reprint, Menston, England: Scolar, 1970). Indeed, recent discussion of Renaissance drama as a whole regards it as a prelude to the Civil War. Elizabethan and Jacobean tragedy has been described as based on "a radical social and political realism," as having "subversive preoccupations," including "the demystification of political and power relations" (Jonathan Dollimore, *Radical Tragedy: Religion, Ideology and Power in the Drama of Shakespeare and His Contemporaries,* 2nd ed. [Durham, N.C.: Duke Univ. Press, 1993], 5, 4), as destroying "the fundamental paradigm of the dominant culture," even as "deconsecrat[ing] the king, . . . thus mak[ing] it possible to decapitate him" (Franco Moretti, "'A Huge Eclipse': Tragic Form and the Deconsecration of Sovereignty," in *The Forms of Power and Power of Forms in the Renaissance,* ed. Stephen Greenblatt [Norman, Okla.: Pilgrim Books, 1982], 7, 8.

5 James H. Kavanagh, "Shakespeare in Ideology," in *Alternative Shakespeares*, ed. John Drakakis (London: Methuen, 1985), 158. Further references will appear parenthetically in the text.

6 Old historicist readings of this speech include: an "accusation that his daughter is out of harmony with nature" (Robert Bechtold Heilman, *This Great Stage: Image and Structure in "King Lear"* [Baton Rouge: Louisiana State Univ. Press, 1948], 86) and "a serious defence of the artificial and strictly speaking unnecessary additions that men have made to their natural state" (Dean Frye, "Context of Lear's Unbuttoning," *ELH* 32 [1965]: 21).

7 Kavanagh argues that the "universal" and "variable" "concepts of need," as "incompatible" discourses, "are only made imaginarily compatible in ideology, as a result of ideological work." Thus, "every class subject finds an equally comfortable place" in Lear's address to Regan ("Shakespeare in Ideology," 159). It is not possible to prove that Reformation Christianity does *not* perform such "ideological work"—at least in part because such functions are often assumed to be inaccessible to conscious thought (see this volume, introduction, note 18). However, Christians wrote consciously and passionately about the relationship between "spiritual equality" and "politic inequality"; to regard their work as only significant for what it purportedly conceals drastically oversimplifies it.

8 Q has "Mans life as cheape" (l. 1340).

9 "A Supplycacion to Our Moste Soveraigne Lorde Kinge Henry the Eyght" (1544), in *Four Supplications, 1529–1553 A.D.*, Early English Text Society, e.s., no. 13 (London: Trübner, 1871), 49–50.

10 Tertullian, *Disciplinary, Moral and Ascetical Works*, Fathers of the Church, no. 40 (New York: Fathers of the Church, 1959), 140, 126. Further references to "The Apparel of Women" are from this edition and will appear parenthetically in the text.

11 Clement of Alexandria, *Christ the Educator*, trans. Simon P. Wood, The Fathers of the Church, no. 23 (Washington, D.C.: Catholic Univ. of America Press, 1954), 106. Further references will appear parenthetically in the text.

12 The principle of distinction between necessity and luxury—that is, between "functional" uses of clothing for protection and modesty, for example, and all other uses—is similar to Thomas More's in *Utopia*. Like More, Tertullian and Clement comment favorably on the metaphoric justness of using jewels and gold for privies and workhouse chains. See Tertullian, "Apparel of Women," 125; Clement, *Christ the Educator*, 128–29; More, *Utopia*, trans. and ed. H. V. S. Ogden (New York: Appleton-Century-Crofts, 1949), 43: "Gold and silver have no indispensable qualities. Human folly has made them precious only because of their scarcity. Nature, like a wise and generous parent, has placed the best things everywhere and in the open . . .

but she has hidden vain and useless things." Like More (33), Clement (181) sees no purpose in differentiating between men's and women's clothing. Where any allowance is hinted at at all for the use of precious things, Clement's proviso is that "we use them without attachment or distinction" (193); the incense that is burned and the scent that is sprayed in the dining halls of More's Utopia provide moderate pleasures that can be enjoyed by all.

13 "On the Part Played by Philosophy in the Progress of Man," in *Ad Lucilium Epistolae Morales*, by Seneca, trans. Richard M. Gummere (Cambridge: Harvard Univ. Press, 1953), 2:405. Further page references will appear parenthetically in the text.

14 Clement distinguishes between "rubbing oil on oneself and scenting oneself with it." The former is "a luxury without any useful purpose [which] gives grounds for the charge of being sensual in character, and . . . a drug to excite the passions." The latter is "very beneficial" (*Christ the Educator*, 152).

15 "Even from a medical point of view we should not entirely renounce the pleasures that flowers afford, and the benefit there is in ointments and vapors, for the sake of our health, as well as, at times, by way of moderate relaxation" (ibid., 158).

16 See Lorna Hutson, *Thomas Nashe in Context* (Oxford: Clarendon, 1989), ch. 1, "Consuming Resources: Literature in Economic Context, 1558–1592," 19–26. For example, as Hutson points out (25), the society Stubbes describes in his *Anatomy* "is on its way to being a consumer society, but acknowledgement of this would involve endorsing prodigality and intemperance as the consumer demand on which productivity must henceforward depend. As yet, this was inconceivable. Consumer goods could be praised only from a manufacturing point of view, as the creators of productivity and solvency among individuals."

17 Martin Luther, "Secular Authority: To What Extent It Should Be Obeyed" (1523), in *Martin Luther: Selections from His Writings*, ed. John Dillenberger (New York: Doubleday, 1961), 370, 371.

18 William Perkins, "A Dialogue of the State of a Christian Man," in *The Work of William Perkins*, ed. Ian Breward (Appleford, England: Sutton Courtenay, 1970), 381–82. See Debora K. Shuger's analysis of the effects of this dualism on English Protestant spirituality in *Habits of Thought in the English Renaissance: Religion, Politics, and the Dominant Culture* (Berkeley: Univ. of California Press, 1988), esp. 103–5.

19 Gouge was imprisoned in 1621 for editing a book considered treasonable, and "in 1626 was one of twelve trustees of a scheme for buying up impropriations, in order to foster a puritan ministry. . . . In 1633, as previously in 1618, he refused to read the 'Book of Sports.'" On the other hand, during the Civil War, "he shrank from the king's trial as a breach of the covenant as well as of the constitution." *Dictionary of National Biography*, s.v. "Gouge, William."

20 William Perkins, "Christian Oeconomy; or, A Short Survey of the Right Manner of Erecting and Ordering a Family, According to the Scriptures," in *The Work of William Perkins*, 453.

21 Q has "Stands still in experience" (l. 1919).

22 The passage is a little puzzling. The "whole revenue of their lands" might suggest a gentleman farmer, whose sons might be like those (mentioned later) who spend their whole "patrimony upon pounces and cuts" (105); on the other hand, the "russet coat" that the homilist thinks this person living beyond his station should be compelled to wear suggests a rustic or peasant. It seems unlikely that the homilist would *demote* gentlemen to wearing russet coats, or deny them silks and velvets altogether, however, even if he disapproves of excessive use of silks and velvets.

23 Barrow, *Brief Discoverie*, in *The Writings of Henry Barrow, 1587–1590*, Elizabethan Nonconformist Texts, vol. 3, ed. Leland H. Carlson (London: George Allen and Unwin), 493.

24 See chapter 5, note 3.

25 Heinemann links Shakespeare's Fool with Samuel Rowley's "comic-historical presentation in 1605 of Henry VIII and his famous jester Will Summers [in *When You See Me You Know Me* (London, 1605)], who in this rendering is an iconoclastic, egalitarian, anti-Popish clown and a champion of the poor" ("Demystifying the Mystery of State," 81).

26 Maurice Goldsmith argues that in spite of the "many disagreements about the meanings of their views and proposals" in "recent work on the radicals of the English Revolution," these radicals shared basic egalitarian principles. These principles favored greater political equality or representation (i.e., civil, religious, and political rights) and sometimes favored social or economic equality based on voluntary sharing of property. See "Levelling by Sword, Spade and Word: Radical Egalitarianism in the English Revolution," in *Politics and People in Revolutionary England*, ed. Jones, Newitt, and Roberts, 65–80. Size and coherence of the groups remain issues in the discussion of antinomian religious enthusiasts such as the Ranters and Seekers. J. F. McGregor comments: "There is little objective evidence that either Seekers or Ranters formed coherent movements or that they existed in any considerable numbers. An examination of the source and context of the types of surviving evidence for the two sects suggests that they are largely artificial products of the Puritan heresiographers' methodology; convenient categories in which to dispose of some of the bewildering variety of enthusiastic speculation." "Ranters and Seekers," in *Radical*

Religion in the English Revolution, ed. J. F. McGregor and B. Reay (Oxford: Oxford Univ. Press, 1984), 122.

27 Charles H. George and Katherine George, *The Protestant Mind of the English Reformation, 1570–1640* (Princeton: Princeton Univ. Press, 1961), 350.

28 "The Just Censure and Reproofe of Martin Junior," in *The Marprelate Tracts, 1588, 1589*, ed. William Pierce, 365. On Whitgift's princely habits, see William Pierce, *An Historical Introduction to the Marprelate Tracts* (London: Archibald Constable, 1980), 117–20. "The puritans of Ashby-de-la-Zouche wondered why the bishops could never undertake a journey without 'some great troup of horses', and begged their own diocesan to 'come amongst us sometimes in Christian humility, laying aside all popish lordliness'" (Patrick Collinson, *The Religion of Protestants: The Church in English Society, 1559–1625* [Oxford: Clarendon, 1982], 40, quoting BL Add. MS 27632, fols. 47–48). "The author of a 'plot for reformation' complained that the bishops maintained 'a great rout of people about them like princes, appareling them in chains of gold, silks and other costly apparel, feasting, banqueting and entertaining'" (ibid., 41, quoting "Plot for Reformation," BL Add. MS 48066, fol. 8r).

29 "A Second Admonition to Parliament," in *Puritan Manifestoes: A Study of the Origin of the Puritan Revolt*, ed. W. H. Frere and C. E. Douglas (New York: E. S. Gorham, 1907; reprint, London: S.P.C.K., 1954), 102–3.

30 Ibid., 109–10.

31 *Political Works of James I*, with an introduction by Howard McIlwain, app. C, "James and the Puritans," xc. McIlwain quotes *The Workes of the Most High and Mighty Prince, James* (London, 1616), 175.

32 Henry Brinkelow[?], "A Supplication of the Poore Commons" (1546), in *Four Supplications*, 76–77.

33 Christopher Morris, *Political Thought in England: Tyndale to Hooker* (London: Oxford Univ. Press, 1953), 158. Felicity Heal suggests "there is no reason to believe that the queen had not understood the importance of the connection" between respect for bishops and respect for the sovereign, even though "the articulation of the notion . . . had to wait for [her] impolitic successor" (*Of Prelates and Princes: A Study of the Economic and Social Position of the Tudor Episcopate* [Cambridge: Cambridge Univ. Press, 1980], 210).

34 See Morris, *Political Thought*, 116, and Bancroft, *A Survey of the Pretended Holy Discipline* (London, 1593), 179.

35 Richard Bancroft, *Dangerous Positions and Proceedings, Published and Practised within This Iland of Brytaine, under Pretence of Reformation, and for the Presbiteriall Discipline* (London, 1593), 44.

36 "Again it may justly be feared whether our English nobility . . . would contentedly suffer themselves to be always at the call, and to stand to the sentence of a number of mean persons assisted with the presence of their poor teacher, a man . . . though better able to speak, yet little or no whit apter to judge than the rest: from whom, be their dealings never so absurd, . . . no appeal may be made unto any one of higher power, inasmuch as the order of your discipline admitteth no standing inequality of courts, no spiritual judge to have any ordinary superior on earth, but as many supremacies as there are parishes and several congregations." Hooker, *Of the Laws of Ecclesiastical Polity*, preface, ch. 8, sec. 2, in *The Works of Mr. Richard Hooker*, 6th ed., 3 vols., compiled by John Keble (Oxford: Clarendon, 1874), 1:178.

37 Morris, *Political Thought*, 116–17.

38 Peter Lake, "Anti-Popery: the Structure of a Prejudice," in *Conflict in Early Stuart England: Studies in Religion and Politics, 1603–1642*, ed. Richard Cust and Ann Hughes (London: Longman, 1989), 86.

39 Perez Zagorin, *The Court and the Country: The Beginning of the English Revolution* (New York: Atheneum, 1971), 195. Zagorin cites Laud's remark about "[William] Prynne and his fellows" from W. Knowler, *The Letters and Dispatches of the Earl of Strafforde* (London, 1739), 2:101. Reacting to the writings of the Scottish reformer and Presbyterian John Knox, Archbishop Matthew Parker wrote: " 'If such principles . . . be spread into men's heads . . . and referred to the judgment of the subject, of the tenant, of the servant, to discuss what is tyranny, and to discern whether his prince, his landlord, his master is a tyrant . . . what Lord of the Council shall ride quietly minded in the streets among desperate beasts? What master shall be sure in his bed-chamber?" (Letter 46 [March 1, 1559], "Dr Matthew Parker to Sir Nicholas Bacon," in *Correspondence of Matthew Parker*, ed. John Bruce [Cambridge: Cambridge Univ. Press, 1853], 61).

40 Bancroft, *Dangerous Positions* (London, 1593), 9.

41 See Stuart Barton Babbage, *Puritanism and Richard Bancroft* (London: S.P.C.K., 1962), 39, for the crushing of Puritanism. A 1593 act of Parliament threatened imprisonment for abstainers from authorized services, critics of ecclesiastical authority, and those who associated with unlawful conventicles.

42 Bancroft, *Dangerous Positions*, 29, 13, 29.

43 David Scott Kastan, "Proud Majesty Made a Subject: Shakespeare and the Spectacle of Rule," *Shakespeare Quarterly* 37, no. 4 (1986): 464.

44 Morris, *Political Thought*, 34–35, 156.

45 Lake, "Anti-Popery," 73–74.

46 Ibid., 86.

47 "An Exhortation to the Bishops to Deale Brotherly with Their Brethren," in *Puritan Manifestoes*, ed. Frere and Douglas, 63. Leland H. Carlson makes the case for Job Throkmorton as author of this tract, the "Second Admonition to the Parliament" (1572), the *Marprelate* tracts (1588, 1589), and other works. See *Martin Marprelate, Gentleman: Master Job Throkmorton Laid Open in His Colors* (San Marino, Calif.: Henry E. Huntington Library, 1981).

48 "The Just Censure and Reproofe of Martin Junior" in *The Marprelate Tracts, 1588, 1589*, 373. Carlson indicates this tract "purported to be a rebuke by the older brother of his younger brother for writing 'Martin Junior' ['Theses Martinianae' (1589)]," 17. With study, Martin Junior should be able to "penetrate the prelatical obfuscations" that translate "a petition to redress 'the miseries of the church' " into a petition " 'to seek the overthrow of the State,' " or render " 'a dutiful supplication' " as " 'to rebel against Her Majesty,' " and so forth (18). Martin Senior is of course ironically mimicking Whitgift's characterizations.

49 Zagorin, *The Court and the Country*, 195.

50 Ibid., 196. Zagorin cites Burton, *The Law and the Gospel Reconciled*, 1631, and Lilburne, *Come Out of Here My People*, 1639.

51 Lake, "Anti-Popery," 86–87.

52 John Milton, *Of Reformation in England and the Cawses that Hitherto Have Hindered It*, in *Complete Prose Works of John Milton*, vol. 1, 1624–1642, ed. by Don M. Wolfe (New Haven: Yale Univ. Press, 1953), 598.

53 Although most of the Puritan ministers at Hampton Court presented themselves as moderate reformers, " 'neither as factious men affecting a popular parity in the Church, nor as schismatics aiming at the dissolution of the state ecclesiastical, but as faithful servants of Christ and loyal subjects,' " and although they made no real case against episcopacy, the bishops treated them "at best as men who belonged to the brood of Cartwright's scholars and at worst as Martin Marprelates one and all." Mark H. Curtis, "Hampton Court Conference and Its Aftermath," *History* 46, no. 156 (February 1961): 15. Curtis quotes "Millenary Petition," in Joseph R. Tanner, *Constitutional Documents of the Reign of James I* (Cambridge: Cambridge Univ. Press, 1930), 57. According to Curtis, it was the bishops, in charge of the official accounts of the conference and of putting into effect its recommendations, who disseminated a view of it as inconsequential and put into effect only some "changes in the Book of Common Prayer, the additions to the catechism to explain the sacraments of baptism and the Lord's Supper, and the authorization of a new translation of the Bible" (14). Thus, whether one believes that the aftermath of the conference reflects James's views or the bishops', the result may have been a radicalization of the more moderate reformers.

54 Babbage, *Puritanism and Richard Bancroft*, 372. Bradshaw had been summoned to appear before Archbishop Whitgift and Bishop Bancroft in 1602 because of a report that he held "unsound doctrine"; he had refused to subscribe at around this time, been suspended, and failed to get restored. It is not surprising that his tracts were anonymously printed. See *Dictionary of National Biography*, s.v. "Bradshaw, William."

55 William Bradshaw, "English Puritanism, Containing the Main Opinions of the Rigidest Sort of Those Called Puritans in the Realm of England" (1604), 39, from *Several Treatises* (1660), in *Puritanism and Separatism: A Collection of Works by William Bradshaw*, with a new introduction by R. C. Simmons ([Farnborough], England: Gregg International, 1972). This work is a defense that suggests even "the rigidest sort" do not have harmful opinions.

56 Ibid., 47.

57 Bradshaw, "A Protestation of the Kings Supremacy" (1605), 85, from *Several Treatises* (1660), in *Puritanism and Separatism*.

58 Bradshaw, "A Treatise of Divine Worship, Tending to Prove, That the Ceremonies Imposed upon the Ministers of the Gospel in England, in Present Controversie, Are in Their Use Unlawful" (1604), 5, from *Several Treatises*, in *Puritanism and Separatism*.

59 Ibid., 6. Compare Christopher Hill's opposite approach, in *Society and Puritanism in Pre-Revolutionary England* (New York: Schocken, 1964), 44: "Part of the trouble was that by the seventeenth century some men were coming to question the desirability of exaggerated deference even to their fellow men."

60 Bradshaw, "A Treatise of Divine Worship," 6.

61 Bradshaw, "English Puritanism" (1605), 38.

62 Ibid., 44–45.

63 Aylmer, bishop of London, chief judge in the case of a rector who refused to wear the surplice, said, " 'Are we not the Queen's servants? and is not the surplice the livery which she hath appointed to be worn? And do you think she will be content if we refuse to wear it?' " Pierce, *An Historical Introduction to the Marprelate Tracts* (London: Archibald Constable, 1908), 78. For the surplice as the "Queen's livery," see Hill, *Society and Puritanism*, 44. The quotation about "civil order and comeliness" is taken from "Account of the Examination of Certain Londoners before the Ecclesiastical Commissioners, 20 June 1567," in H. C. Porter, *Puritanism in Tudor England* (London: Macmillan, 1970), 88. This is, as Porter indicates (80), "The true report of our examination and conference . . . had the 20 day of June, Anno 1567, before the Lord Mayor, the Bishop of London, the Dean of Westminster, master Watts, and other Commissioners" which was reprinted in 1593 by Robert Waldegrave (Edinburgh?) in *A Part of a Register: Containing Sundry Memorable Matters, Written by Divers Godly and Learned in*

Our Time, Which Stand for or Desire the Reformation of Our Church. According to Pierce, (*Historical Introduction to the Marprelate Tracts*, 23), the occasion of the mayor's remarks was an examination of "a company of London citizens and their wives" who created their own assembly, "ostensibly to celebrate a wedding, but, in fact, . . . to hear a sermon and to celebrate the Lord's Supper." The examination revealed that their objections were to more than "signing the cross" and that sort of thing; they were against episcopacy itself and wanted pastors appointed through "the choice of the Church itself."

64 Bradshaw, "Twelve General Arguments Proving That the Ceremonies Imposed upon the Ministers of the Gospel in England by our Prelates, Are Unlawful" (1605), 65–66, from *Several Treatises*, in *Puritanism and Separatism*. Bradshaw can wax quite violent about those signs of spiritual homage: "Those that can make a surplice, a cope, a cross . . . to be ornaments of religion and holy ceremonies: can . . . make a shaven crown, a monk's habit, spittle in baptism, holy water, the triple crown, and all the missal rites as holy. . . . Those that have authority to join to the sacrament of baptism the sign of the cross, have authority also . . . to join to the sacrament of the supper, flesh, broth, butter or cheese . . . if they will." "A Treatise of Divine Worship," 10.

65 Bradshaw, "A Treatise of Divine Worship," 13.

66 A. L. Beier, *Masterless Men: The Vagrancy Problem in England, 1560–1640* (London: Methuen, 1985), 3. "Between 1590 and 1620 the aristocracy cut the numbers of their servants from an average of one hundred or so each to three or four dozen—hence the complaints of a 'decline in hospitality' " (Beier, 23). See Walzer, *The Revolution of the Saints: A Study in the Origins of Radical Politics* (Cambridge, Mass.: Harvard Univ. Press, 1965), ch. 6, on social disorganization and Puritanism. Collinson describes it as an age imbued with a "collective paranoia" that led to demonizing the adversary, whether that adversary was "identified with the pope, or the Jesuits, or witches, or 'the great rude unjust rabble' " (Collinson, *Religion of Protestants*, 182)—or in fact with Puritans. (On the "rabble," Collinson cites Paul Slack, "Religious Protest and Urban Authority: The Case of Henry Sherfield, Iconoclast, 1633," in *Schism, Heresy and Religious Protest, Studies in Church History* 9, ed. Derek Baker [Cambridge, 1972], 295–302; see *Religion of Protestants*, 148).

67 Collinson, *Religion of Protestants*, 150. Collinson does not agree with Michael Walzer that Puritanism was " 'the earliest form of political radicalism,' " or that " 'the thrust of Puritan doctrine . . . pointed to the overthrow of the traditional order' " (179, citing Walzer, *Revolution*, 118). He also disagrees with Lawrence Stone's suggestion "that that by erecting an alternative hierarchy of spiritual grace, Calvinism and the puritan conscience sapped respect for rank and title at all levels of the social hierarchy" (187, citing Stone, *The Crisis of the Aristocracy, 1558–1561* [Oxford: Clarendon, 1965] 743, 745). Finally, Collinson disagrees with Christopher Hill's claim that " 'the logic of Protestantism led to an egalitarian individualism' " (188, quoting Hill, *Society and Puritanism*, 477). Hill actually says "radical Protestantism." Collinson notes that Hill quotes Clarendon's complaint that " 'all relations were confounded by the several sects in religion which discountenanced all forms of reverence and respect as relics and marks of superstition.' "

68 Collinson, *Religion of Protestants*, 151.

69 Perkins, "A Treatise of the Vocations or Callings of Men," in *The Works of William Perkins*, 455–56.

70 Collinson, *Religion of Protestants*, 152. Collinson quotes from *A Fruitfull Sermon upon the 3.4.5.6.7. and 8. Verses of the 12 Chapiter of the Epistle of S. Paul to the Romanes* (1584), "anonymously published but widely attributed to Chaderton" (*Religion of Protestants*, 151, n. 36), but gives no page reference.

71 Christopher Hill, *Society and Puritanism*, 462. As Ian W. Archer notes, "The household stood in the front line in the maintenance of order throughout early modern English society," and "the City authorities relied heavily on the commitment of householders to social discipline in stressing the responsibilities of masters for their servants' behaviour" (*The Pursuit of Stability: Social Relations in Elizabethan London* [Cambridge: Cambridge Univ. Press, 1991], 215–16). During the Putney Debates of 1647, "the Leveller Maximilian Petty was willing to admit that 'servants and apprentices . . . are included in their masters' [with regard to the Parliamentary franchise]. Patriarchal attitudes were deeply embedded in social beliefs." Sommerville, *Politics and Ideology*, 29, quoting A. S. P. Woodhouse, *Puritanism and Liberty* (1938), 83.

72 Beier, *Masterless Men*, 23. Masters were able to discipline their servants corporally, if "with moderation" (William Blackstone, *Commentaries on the Laws of England*, facsimile of 1st ed. of 1765–69 [Chicago: Univ. of Chicago Press, 1979], 1:416). However, "if any servant, workman, or labourer, assaults his master or dame, he shall suffer one year's imprisonment, and other open corporal punishment, not extending to life or limb" (ibid.). The servant's time is fully at his master's disposal; the master has a "property . . . in the service of his domestics; acquired by contract of hiring, and purchased by giving them wages" (ibid., 1:417). There was a legal reality to the analogies between sovereign and subject, husband and wife, servant and master and ecclesiastical superior and inferior summed up by the law of "petit treason," which "appeared as a crime . . . in the fourteenth century, and lasted as such until the early nineteenth century." Natalie Zemon Davis, "Women on Top: Symbolic Sexual Inversion and Political Disorder in Early Modern Europe," in *The Reversible World: Symbolic Inversion in Art and Society,* ed. Barbara A. Babcock (Ithaca: Cornell Univ. Press, 1978), 150, n. 6. "Petit treason" occurred when "a servant kill[ed] his master, a wife her husband, or an ecclesiastical person his superior." Blackstone indicates that "the breach of civil or ecclesiastical connections, when coupled with murder, denominates it . . . no less than a species of treason." Thus, "the breach . . . of natural and civil relations" is "ranked in the same class with crimes against the state and the sovereign" (Blackstone, *Commentaries,* 4:203). Puritans writing on the fifth commandment or the art of household maintenance stress the same relationships this law of petit treason embraces, although they replace "bishop/cleric" with "minister/people" and, like most moralists, add "parent/child." See Richard L. Greaves, *Society and Religion in Elizabethan England* (Minneapolis: Univ. of Minnesota Press, 1981), 325, on the similarity of Anglican and Puritan attitudes to master-servant relations.

73 Francis Dillingham, *Christian Oeconomy; or, Household Government* (London, 1609), 44v–45r. See the *Dictionary of National Biography,* s.v. "Dillingham, Francis." He was educated at Christ College, Cambridge, was "richly beneficed at Wilden," and was one of the translators of the authorized Bible in 1611.

74 Henoch Clapham, *Antidoton; Or, A Soveraigne Remedie against Schisme and Heresie* (London, 1600), 25. Patrick Collinson indicates that Clapham was a "reformed separatist" (*Religion of Protestants,* 151, n. 36).

75 See note 63, above.

76 "Account of the Examination of Certain Londoners, 20 June 1567," in Porter, *Puritanism in Tudor England,* 88. See note 63, above. As Debora K. Shuger indicates, "The doctrine of the royal headship effectively incorporated the church into the state. . . . This incorporation could not but affect the holiness of the church" (*Habits of Thought,* 151).

77 Stone, *Family, Sex and Marriage,* 94.

78 I.M., *A Health to the Gentlemanly Profession of Serving-Men, 1598,* Shakespeare Association Facsimiles, no. 3 (London: Oxford Univ. Press, 1931), D3r–D3v. The *Short Title Catalogue* attributes this work to Gervase Markham. Further references will appear parenthetically in the text.

79 Bk. 4, ll. 294–95, of *Paradise Lost,* ed. William G. Madsen (New York: Modern Library, 1969), 101.

80 See Frances Elizabeth Baldwin, *Sumptuary Legislation and Personal Regulation in England,* Johns Hopkins University Studies in Historical and Political Science, ser. 14, no. 1 (Baltimore: Johns Hopkins Univ. Press, 1926).

81 *The Diary of Sir Simonds D'Ewes (1622-1624): Journal d'un étudiant londonien sous le règne de Jacques 1er,* ed. and ann. Elisabeth Bourcier (Paris: Didier, 1974). Further references will appear parenthetically in the text.

82 On August 4, 1622, he notes: "At night a gentleman of our house told me some good news . . . where Justice Hughton spoke how the King disliked a rumour of toleration, and was sorry for his people's fears, and that he himself was far from popery" (89).

83 Ian W. Archer, *The Pursuit of Stability: Social Relations in Elizabethan London* (Cambridge: Cambridge Univ. Press, 1991), 217. Further references will appear parenthetically in the text.

84 See Beier, *Masterless Men,* 24.

85 Ibid. One small example: "Though they know very well that it is their master's pleasure they should speak, yea though they are bidden to speak, yet their stout stomach, and sullen heart will not suffer them to speak: no, though it be never so behoveful for their masters" (Gouge, *Of Domesticall Duties* [London, 1622], 599).

86 The idea that conscience supplants personal loyalty or fear as a result of a change toward a specifically Puritan ethos is Michael Walzer's (see chapter 5 above). But Walzer's description of a "legal or commercial obligation," an "agreement between equals" (*Revolution of the Saints,* 168, 214) does not easily match those of a Puritan such as Gouge, who talks of clear "politic" inequalities, of fear as a motivator of proper service, as well as of the need for those called to service to work to conscientiously fulfill their duties, not for material reward—lest they go unrewarded by God.

87 *Wentworth Papers, 1597-1628,* ed. J. P. Cooper, Camden Fourth Series, vol. 12 (London: Royal Historical Society, 1973), 20, 10, 18, 12. Stone, *Family, Sex and Marriage,* 96, draws attention to the "pessimistic view of human nature," the "basic assumption that no one is to be trusted," commonly found in letters of advice to sons in this period. Wentworth is generally suspicious about relations with superiors, as well as inferiors. "The company of your equals, whose estate is not declining and in whom there is a good conscience and a well-governed tongue, is very fit for you; and for want of such, the company of your inferiors that be of good wealth, humble and discreet in their deeds and words" (12). It might be noted that—for all his worldly-wise advice—Wentworth still urges behavior that sits with a good conscience, including not taking advantage of the poor by usury, mortgages, or bonds (21), even if the behavior he urges is in part urged because of his general suspicion of what may be used against one: "[A] poor man that hateth you may sometime find opportunity to displeasure you greatly" (22).

88 Q has "this forescore—" and leaves out "yeares" (l. 1926).

89 Q has "following it" and "that goes up the hill" (ll. 1141–42, 1142).

90 Being "in service" whether as apprentices, as domestics, or in husbandry, was the major occupation of the young (see Beier, *Masterless Men,* 23); a great many people in almost all ranks had servants (see Peter Laslett's introduction to Sir Robert Filmer, *Patriarchia and other Political Works,* ed. Peter Laslett [Oxford: Basil Blackwell, 1949], 25). Thus, the servant's *might* be a temporary calling—to be followed by the calling of *master*—as opposed to a matter of unalterably fixed social rank: "As [servants and prentices] deal and behave themselves to their masters, mistresses, or dames, and their goods, whilst they are servants, so likewise the Lord in justice will cause their servants to deal and behave themselves to them, when they shall come to be masters or dames themselves, so punishing sin with sin" (R[obert] C[leaver], *A Godlie Forme of Householde Government: For the Ordering of Private Families* [London, 1598], 384).

91 "The Just Censure and Reproofe of Martin Junior," in *Marprelate Tracts,* 354.

92 Giovanni Batista Nenna, *Nennio; or, A Treatise of Nobility,* trans. W. Jones (1595; reprint, Jerusalem: Israel Univ. Press, 1967), 74v.

93 Andrewes, *A Pattern of Catechistical Doctrine* (1630) in *The Work of Lancelot Andrewes,* vol. 6 (Oxford: John Henry Parker, 1854; reprint, New York: Ams, 1967), 182.

94 "That is to say, the king had to be resisted by the whole commonwealth or its representative institutions. . . . No private individual, it was agreed by all, could actively resist his ruler. Applied to English circumstances, this meant that only Parliament could possibly have the authority to resist the first two Stuarts" (Sommerville, *Politics and Ideology,* 75).

95 Cicero seems to judge the deprivation of others in terms of the motivations of the depriver. "For if it is for your own benefit . . . you will have acted inhumanely and against the law of nature. If, however, you are the kind of person who, if you were to remain alive, could bring great benefit to the political community and to human fellowship, and *if for that reason* you deprive someone else of something, that is not a matter for rebuke." *Cicero: On Duties,* ed. M. T. Griffin and E. M. Atkins (Cambridge: Cambridge Univ. Press, 1991), 3.29, 110–11. Further references to book, section, and page will appear parenthetically in the text.

96 "In public affairs wrong is very often done because of the appearance of benefit. . . . The Athenians . . . decreed that the Aeginetans, who had a powerful fleet, should have their thumbs cut off. It seemed to be beneficial, for Aegina was a threat to Piraeus because it was so near. But nothing cruel is in fact beneficial; for cruelty is extremely hostile to the nature of man, which we ought to follow" (3.46, 117).

97 Q omits "well" (l. 1829).

98 Q has "above your Justices" (l. 2076).

99 These lines appear in Q only.

100 These lines appear in Q only.

101 "Though there is little sign that classical learning was exploited to republican ends in the years before 1640, the writings of the ancient Greeks and Romans were used to mount arguments against absolutism. The works of Cicero, Tacitus and Plutarch were staple items in the English gentleman's education. Tacitus' damning analysis of absolute rule appeared in English in the 1590s and was reprinted four times between the accession of James I and the outbreak of Civil War" (Sommerville, *Politics and Ideology*, 58).

102 "Such works as Buchanan's *De jure regni apud Scotos* and the *Vindiciae contra tyrannos* were condemned for putting forward views which were essentially popish, though their authors were Protestant" (Sommerville, *Politics and Ideology*, 44).

103 John Ponet, *A Short Treatise of Politic Power*, 1556 (reprint, Menston, England: Scolar, 1970), G5v. Further references will appear parenthetically in the text.

104 Griffith goes on, "It shall ever be the praise of Saul's servants . . . that they refused to execute Saul's wicked sentence against the Lord's priests" (*Bethel; or, A Forme for Families* [London, 1633], 387). He does talk about the servant being unable to help himself in the case of a personal wrong: "But may not a servant help himself, if he be wronged? God forbid that he should: For . . . *the Magistrate beareth not the sword in vain*" (384). See chapter 5, note 23 for Griffith's royalism. Ponet, *Short Treatise on Politic Power*, D4v, D5r, describes how the "familiar servants" of Saul "(being yet the king's true servants and subjects) denied to obey the king's unlawful commandment," in a long section on passive disobedience or "leaving undone" ungodly commands.

105 *A Declaration of the Ten Commandments*, in *The Early Writings of Hooper*, ed. Samuel Carr (Cambridge: Cambridge Univ. Press, 1843), 359.

106 Certainly the combination of social conservatism and dislike of undue rigor or tyranny was totally plausible for the period. John Hayward, author of *The Life and Raigne of King Henrie IIII* (1599), which was dedicated to Essex and consequently associated with rebellion in the minds of Queen Elizabeth and some of her contemporaries, and which cost Hayward a period of imprisonment until Essex's execution, was, nevertheless, someone who can be understood in such terms. On the one hand, he believed in "traditional values over upstarts, . . . the importance of honour, . . . and government by a talented and hereditary aristocracy, . . . [views] as appealing to [King] James . . . as they had been to the Essex faction" (*The First and Second Parts of John Hayward's "The Life and Raigne of King Henrie IIII,"* ed. John J. Manning [London: Royal Historical Society, 1991], 15). On the other hand, his history of Henry's reign—one looked into by Sir Simonds D'Ewes as well ("because his reign came somewhat near our hard times," *Diary of Sir Simonds D'Ewes,* 138)—while fairly even-handed, does negatively judge "such princes as will be absolute in power, resolute in will, and dissolute in life" (ibid., 167).

7 Distribution: Anabaptist Egalitarianism,
Anglican Charity, Both, Neither?

1 Q has "That stands your ordinance" (l. 1985).
2 Cohen (*Drama of a Nation: Public Theater in Renaissance England and Spain* [Ithaca: Cornell Univ. Press, 1985], 334) quotes from Christopher Hill's suggestion that "there was perhaps a real consistency in the attitude of the [people who] from Spenser's Fox to Winstanley's [Digger] utopia, rejected not only the gentry-controlled state and its law but also the wage-labour system; and opposed to them a backward-looking and idealized communism." Hill, *Change and Continuity in Seventeenth Century England* (London: Weidenfeld and Nicolson, 1974), 204. Hill conflates literary allusion to a legendary English age (with some roots in Ovid's golden one) with usually local popular responses to encroachment on customary rights by enclosure—and these, in turn, with the actions of the small number of Diggers on St. George's Hill.
3 Cohen quotes from Abiezer Coppe, *A Fiery Flying Roll* (London, 1649), B4r.
4 Arnold Kettle, "From *Hamlet* to *Lear,*" in *Shakespeare in a Changing World,* ed. Arnold Kettle (London: Lawrence and Wishart, 1964), 167.
5 Terry Eagleton, *William Shakespeare* (Oxford: Basil Blackwell, 1986), 82 (my emphasis on "redistribution").
6 "The Fool's gibe about monopolies (1:4:158–9), interestingly omitted from the Folio, is not a casual and hence dispensable topicality, but the opening gambit in an analysis of class and economic difference that the Folio, if anything, intensifies" (*Shakespeare and the Popular Voice* [Cambridge, Mass.: Basil Blackwell, 1989], 110). Patterson connects a new role for Parliament "in regulating the economy" (108) and the play's address to economic matters. Insofar as the analysis of economic matters she finds is related to the idea that "the system . . . should combine elements of morality [i.e., something of "the moral economy"] with economic prag-

matism" (108–9), I am in agreement with her. However, much of what she says implies a more radical economic analysis. The nature of that analysis is suggested by her invoking of James Agee, who himself "reinvoked" the critique Shakespeare made "as the inaugural premise of *Let Us Now Praise Famous Men,* his extraordinary study of American rural poverty in the Depression" (108). According to Patterson, Agee places "Lear's ["Poor naked wretches"] speech on the heath opposite another famous radical text, the Communist Manifesto's call to action" (114); Agee "grasped in his own ahistorical manner the radical analysis Shakespeare performed, in disguise, on the economic structure of his own society" (115).

7 Raman Selden in *"King Lear* and True Need," *Shakespeare Studies* 19 (1987), briefly summarizes my essential point when he says: " 'Distribution' . . . in Gloucester's moving lines would have carried no revolutionary implication. Puritans no less than Anglicans interpreted the biblical injunctions on charity as involving no radical adjustment in the social order" (162).

8 Historians on the whole agree on the "role of economic and social changes in triggering official concern about the poor between 1500 and 1650: population growth, rising prices, falling wages, agrarian dislocation, migration and urbanization" all worsened "the lot of the poor" (A. L. Beier, *The Problem of the Poor in Tudor and Early Stuart England* [London: Methuen, 1983], 2). Even revisionist historians largely agree: "If the traditional view of an unparalleled slump in Tudor living-standards needs some revision, as it certainly does, it retains more truth than an alternative which sees no decline at all." "It is plausible to argue from the evidence that conditions were getting worse: there were more vagrants and more paupers with valid claim to public assistance, and both were the result, not just of temporary crises such as dearth and plague, but of long-term economic trends which produced heavy mobility and underemployment" (Paul Slack, "Poverty and Social Regulation in Elizabethan England," in *The Reign of Elizabeth I,* ed. Christopher Haigh [London: Macmillan, 1984], 227, 233). Felicity Heal, studying the abundant literature on "hospitality," notes "the chorus of lamentation" intensifies from the 1580s and then diminishes by the later 1630s ("The Idea of Hospitality in Early Modern England," *Past and Present,* no. 102 [February 1984]: 80). Also see Ian W. Archer, *The Pursuit of Stability: Social Relations in Elizabethan London* (Cambridge: Cambridge Univ. Press, 1991), 9–14, for an assessment of the " 'Crisis' of the 1590s."

9 For example, Matthew 25:35–46, Hebrews 13:16, and Isaiah 58:7.

10 "Ha? here's three on 's are sophisticated" (3.4.105–6).

11 Q has "Our flesh and bloud is growne so vild my Lord" (ll. 1653–54).

12 Q has "mine injurious dogge" (l. 2513).

13 John Downame, *The Plea of the Poore; or, A Treatise of Beneficence and*

Almes-Deeds (London, 1616), 45. Further references will appear parenthetically in the text.

14 Heal, "Idea of Hospitality," 77.

15 Q has "when Ladie oth'e brach" (l. 571).

16 Wilbur K. Jordan, *Philanthropy in England, 1480–1660* (London: George Allen and Unwin, 1964), 158, summarizing an idea in an anonymous work, *The Prayse and Comendacion of Suche as Sought Comenwelthes* (London, 1548?), 2–3.

17 Charles Richardson, *A Sermon against Oppression and Fraudulent Dealing* (London, 1615), 10. These words that Albany speaks in Q do not appear in F at all.

18 Henry Bedel, *A Sermon Exhortyng to Pitie the Poore* (London, 1572), B2r, B3v.

19 E. M. Leonard, *The Early History of English Poor Relief* (Cambridge, 1900; reprint, London: Frank Cass, 1965), 306–7. Examples of this use of the word "distribution" are legion. In Henry Medwall's pre-Reformation morality play, *Nature* (ca. 1530), ll. 1300–1, 1311, Liberality tells Man that he "must give a reckoning / Of all the goods that come to [his] use" which includes "what alms deed or other good distribution" he has made. *Plays of Henry Medwall*, ed. Alan H. Nelson (Cambridge: D. S. Brewer, 1980), 159. Martin Bucer wrote *A Treatise How by the Worde of God Christian Men's Almose Ought To Be Distributed* ([Printed abroad, 1557]).

20 Heal, "Idea of Hospitality," 84; quoting Robert Allen, *Treatise of Christian Beneficence* (London, 1600), 1–3, 36–37.

21 Buchanan Sharp, *In Contempt of All Authority: Rural Artisans and Riot in the West of England, 1586–1660* (Berkeley: Univ. of California Press, 1980), 51. Also see Leonard, *Poor Relief*, app. 5, "Part of a Draft of Orders for Remedying the Scarcity of Corn in 1596," 318–26.

22 Greaves, *Society and Religion*, 565.

23 Q has "your fathers / tenant this forescore—" (ll. 1925–26).

24 Some landlords had something like those "feudal, patriarchal, idyllic" relations with their tenants that Marx and Engels describe the bourgeoisie as putting an end to (*The Communist Manifesto* [New York: Pocket Books, 1964], 61). Keith Wrightson gives documentary evidence for such a one: "Drawing up a list of his tenants, [James Bankes] . . . observed that [one] Margaret Ranford's eight-acre tenement would be better consolidated into his demesne lands, but advised his son to do no harm to her family, for 'the father and the sons have done good service to this house'. The lease should be brought in if possible, but 'place them in some other tenement, in God's name—of the like or better.'" Wrightson quotes from *The Early Records of the Bankes Family at Winstanley*, ed. J. Bankes and Eric Kerridge,

Chetham Society, 3rd ser., vol. 21 (1973), 26–28, in his *English Society, 1580–1680* (New Brunswick: Rutgers Univ. Press, 1982), 59.

25 The mutually beneficial relation of the rich and poor was still symbolically salient: the presence of the poor—clothed at the expense of the deceased—was still desirable at funerals; funeral doles to the poor were often provided, even by Puritans (Archer, *Pursuit of Stability*, 54, 169).

26 Bedel, *Sermon*, B2r, E1r. Again, examples are legion. In Medwall's pre-Reformation morality, *Nature,* Pride is made to say: "Then have I such a short gown, / With wide sleeves that hang adown— / They would make some lad in this town / A doublet and a coat" (ll. 767–70, p. 110). Christopher Sutton, in *Disce Mori: Learne to Die* (London, 1601), dedicated to "one of the ladies of the Queen's Majesty's most honourable privy chamber," asks judgmentally, "is not all scarce sufficient to maintain our excesses[?]. The pride of the world in attire, the needless superfluity in diet hath eaten up hospitality and mercy towards many hungry souls" (176).

27 Leonard, *Early History of English Poor Relief,* 122, quoting John Strype, *The Life of John Whitgift,* bk. 4, app., no. 30 (27 December 1596). The idea of such redistribution—in essence through a kind of morally urged tax on consumption—continues to play a role in schemes for social amelioration. Rice Bush, in *The Poor Man's Friend* (London, 1649), among his other suggestions for supporting the worthy poor by means of maintaining the London Corporation of the Poor, includes, as a last measure, persuading the citizens of London for " 'one year to forbear altering their apparel into other fantastic fashions', the saving to be paid into the stock of the Corporation" (Jordan, *Philanthrophy,* 207, quoting Bush, 20).

28 Henry Arthington, *Provision for the Poore, Now in Penurie* (London, 1597), C1v, D3v. Arthington, a Yorkshire gentleman, was the only repentant survivor of a seditious threesome of religious fanatics involved in the Coppinger plot. See *Dictionary of National Biography,* s.v. "Arthington, Henry." This work was written after the discussions in Parliament that led to the 1598 Poor Law (Jordan, *Philanthropy,* 99).

29 Man in Medwall's *Nature,* ll. 1288–96, is told by Liberality that he does not have to "give away all / And leave [him]self nought!" "I mean not so parde, / For that is waste and sinful prodigality. / Take the mid way, betwixt them two, / And flee th'extremities how so ever thou do. / Thou must thy worldly goods so employ, / In charitable deeds with due compassion, / That thou mayst buy everlasting joy / For the good intent of that distribution" (*Plays of Henry Medwall,* 158).

30 Bedel, *Sermon,* D1r.

31 Thomas Drant, *A Fruitfull and Necessary Sermon, Specially Concernyng Almesgeving* (London, 1572), A8v.

32 Downame urges that "he that hath but a mere competency to supply the necessity of nature and estate, is to give something out of it to relieve those who want necessaries belonging to nature, and those who have only sufficient for nature, are bound to give unto them who are in great and present extremity; unless the like necessity be imminent to themselves" (*Plea of the Poore*, 95).

33 William Vaughan, *The Golden Grove* (London, 1600), bk. 3, Bb4v (my emphasis).

34 "A Treatise of the Vocations or Callings of Men," in *The Work of William Perkins*, ed. Ian Breward (Appleford, England: Sutton Courtenay, 1970), 466. Perkins goes on to say that "sufficiency" must be based on "the example and judgment of the godly and grave men and women of our estate and order." Thus, as a whole he sounds little different from the "Homily against Excesse of Apparrell" (see above, chapter 6). Even when the government intervened in the sale of grain, the amount of corn to spare in each household was to be calculated "upon due consideration of the number of persons which each hath in his house *according to their qualities*" (Leonard, *Poor Relief*, app. 5, 321).

35 As Montaigne has it, "Man is the only forsaken, and out-cast creature, naked on the bare earth . . . having nothing to cover and arm himself withal but the spoil of others. . . . We may be excused for borrowing [from] those which nature had therein favored more than us . . . and under their spoils of wool, of hair, of feathers, and of silk, to shroud us" (Michel de Montaigne, *The Essays*, 1603, trans. John Florio [Menston, England: Scolar, 1969], bk. 2, ch. 12 ["An Apologie of Raymond Sebond"], 262, 280). Or as Pliny described it before: man is "cast[] away on the naked ground, to burst at once into wailing and weeping," without protection of "shells, bark, spines, hides, fur, bristles, hair, down, feathers, scales, fleeces" (Pliny, *Natural History*, trans. H. Rackham [London: Heinemann; Cambridge, Mass.: Harvard Univ. Press, 1947], 2:507).

36 "Prayer for Landlords" (1553), from *The Primer; or, Book of Private Prayer* . . . in *The Two Liturgies . . . and other Documents . . . of King Edward VI* (Parker Society, 1844), 458, reprinted in *Tudor Economic Documents*, ed. R. H. Tawney and Eileen Power, vol. 3 (London: Longmans, Green, 1924; reprint, 1951), 62.

37 See Lorna Hutson, *Thomas Nashe in Context* (Oxford: Clarendon, 1989), ch. 1, and chapter 6 in this volume on sixteenth-century attitudes toward avarice in relation to economic policies favoring English over foreign luxury goods.

38 F.T., *The Debate betweene Pride and Lowlines, Pleaded to an Issue in Assise* (London, [1577?]), D2r. The *Short Title Catalogue* indicates that the attribution to Francis Thynne is erroneous. Even wool—though unquestionably a humbler fabric—if it is especially soft, can be associated with *luxuria*. In Medwall's *Nature*, Pride wears a "bonnet" of "a staring colour of scarlet red," made with "a fine thread / And a soft wool!" (ll. 747–50, 110).

39 George More, *A Demonstration of God in His Workes* (London, 1597), 9. Slack, "Poverty and Regulation," 237, provides the information on More.

40 Foxe, *Acts and Monuments*, 8:88. See above, chapter 4.

41 Humfrey, *The Nobles; or, Of Nobilitye* (London, 1563), T5v–T6r. Perhaps "renoumeth" is an error for "renowneth," with the older meaning of "to celebrate."

42 Drant, *Two Sermons Preached, the One at S. Maries Spittle . . . 1570 and the Other at the Court at Windsor, . . . 1569* (London, 1570?), I2v, I4r. "Garboil" and "ruffle" are words meaning "tumult" or "disturbance"; "hoisting" seems to refer to lifting someone on the back of another in order for that someone to receive a punishment—such as flogging. Further references to Drant's *Two Sermons* will appear parenthetically in the text.

43 Drant was the chaplain of Edmund Grindal (see Richard L. Greaves, *Society and Religion in Elizabethan England* [Minneapolis: Univ. of Minnesota Press, 1981], 519), bishop of London, who, later, while archbishop of Canterbury, sufficiently remonstrated against Elizabeth for her efforts to prevent the "prophesyings" to be suspended from his functions. Drant generally seems to be aware that he is taking on a rather dangerous subject. Using his chosen text, he daringly admonishes courtiers for their assumption that they are removed from preacherly admonition: "And generally in kings' houses, of the preachers this is true which Martial the poet said of his friends. *My friends, ye will me to speak the truth. . . . The truth is this, that you cannot abide to hear the truth*" (K6v).

44 Like Eagleton and Danby, like Patterson, and like Dollimore and Cohen (by implication), Dieter Mehl, in "*King Lear* and the 'Poor Naked Wretches,'" (*Deutsche Shakespeare-Gesellschaft West Jahrbuch* [Heidelberg: Quelle and Meyer, 1975]) interprets Gloucester's as a "plea for a just distribution of wealth" (155), "a utopian longing for an even distribution of the world's riches" (156). Like Danby and Cohen, Mehl places "Lear's prayer for the poor within the context of a long popular tradition of radical social comment, usually associated with extreme situations and with social outsiders" (158). However, Mehl says, "[T]he modern reader is easily tempted to overestimate their seriousness and their subversive purpose" (158); "[i]t seems . . . mistaken to claim on the strength of these passages that Shakespeare's ideas . . . were particularly progressive or even very definite" (159). I do agree with him when he says the play presents Lear's prayer as a matter of "taking the traditional order at its word and measuring it by its own claims and standards" (161).

45 Beier, *Masterless Men: The Vagrancy Problem in England, 1560–1640* (London: Methuen, 1983), 5. Beier argues the main cause of the growing criticism of poverty was the growth of poverty and vagabondage.

46 Ibid., 4.

47 The 1531 Act Concerning Punishment of Beggars and Vagabonds, for example, stipulates punishments for any vagrant person "being whole and mighty in body and able to labour" that include "to be tied to the end of a cart naked and be beaten with whips throughout the same market town or other place till his body be bloody by reason of such whipping: and after such punishment and whipping had, the person so punished . . . shall be enjoined upon his oath to return forthwith without delay in the next and straight way to the place where he was born, or where he last dwelled before the same punishment by the space of three years, and there put himself to labour like as a true man oweth to do" (*English Historical Documents, 1485–1448*, ed. C. H. Williams, vol. 5 of *English Historical Documents*, ed. David C. Douglas [New York: Oxford Univ. Press, 1967], 1026).

48 "Contemporary understanding of the causes of poverty was, with a few exceptions, not sufficiently sophisticated to allow for the possibility that men could be unemployed through no fault of their own. Therefore as unemployment increased and more people took to the road in search of work, the existence of a subculture of the idle and work-shy, however illusory it may have been in reality, was more widely perceived" (Archer, *Pursuit of Stability*, 164).

49 See introduction to *Order and Disorder in Early Modern England*, ed. Anthony Fletcher and John Stevenson (Cambridge: Cambridge Univ. Press, 1985), 14, for a late-seventeenth-century date for full institutionalization; also see Slack, "Poverty and Social Regulation," 222–23. Note that Archer criticizes Jordan's "remarks about the relative balance of private charity" as "based on the astonishing fallacy that those few poor accounts which have survived represent all the rates levied in the counties under review" (*Pursuit of Stability*, 164). "Jordan's argument that the poor rate contributed only 7 per cent of the money spent on poor relief was one of his sillier contributions to the discussion about the role of philanthropy in the relief of the poor" (ibid., 181).

50 Private charity included endowments and bequests as well as gifts made to the living—including to beggars, licensed or not. See Heal, "Idea of Hospitality," 84; Beier, *Problem of the Poor*, 15; Archer, *Pursuit of Stability*, ch. 5, "Social Policy"; Slack, "Poverty and Regulation," 235. As Beier points out in *Masterless Men*, "local mendicancy was officially condoned in the poor laws" even if "it was commonly assumed that many who carried papers were actually vagrant frauds, and there was some truth to these assertions" (110–11).

51 The "order" that Downame refers to is presumably the institutionalization of poor rates with the concomitant licensing of worthy beggars, and
restraint, punishment, or "setting to work" of the unworthy.

52 For the similarity of Anglican and Puritan attitudes toward charity, see
Greaves, *Society and Religion*, ch. 13, "Wealth and Poverty"; Heal, "Hospitality"; and Beier, *Problem of the Poor*. Archer indicates that Reformation
Protestants stressed acts of charity as much as their predecessors, at least
in part to prove the superiority of Protestantism to the old religion (*Pursuit of Stability*, 168). "The polarity between harsh repression and generous
toleration [*re* the poor] assumed in the Tawney model [of Puritanism] is
as misconceived as the contrast which has been assumed to exist between
'Puritan' and 'Anglican' social thought more generally" (Slack, "Poverty
and Social Regulation," 237).

53 Similarly, perhaps, many Protestant ministers avoided the literal meaning of Luke 3:11 ("He that hath two coats, let him part with him that hath
none"). On the allowance of more than mere necessity in clothing, see
Greaves, *Society and Religion*, 510.

54 John Calvin, *The Acts of the Apostles, 1-13*, vol. 1, trans. John W. Fraser
and W. J. G. McDonald (Grand Rapids: Eerdmans, 1965-66), in *Calvin's
Commentaries*, ed. David W. Torrance and Thomas E. Torrance, 6:87, 88,
129-30. Calvin says we "must beware of two extremes." "For many on
a pretext of civil order conceal what they possess and defraud the poor,
thinking that they are doubly righteous so long as they do not seize another
man's goods. Others are carried away to the opposite error, desiring to
have everything mingle together" (129).

55 Like Calvin, Radulpe Gualthere [Rudolph Walther], in his enormous
tome, *An Hundred, Threescore and Fiftene Homelyes or Sermons, uppon the
Actes of the Apostles* (London, 1572), objects to the Anabaptists and "divers
such newfangled and factious fellows" who would "bring in *Plato* his communion of all things" (143), and finds no support for such in the passages at
issue: "There was here no disordinate communion of goods, no confusion
of things, no violent usurping of other men's goods, such as the phrenetic
and seditious imagine" (225). Like Calvin, Walther says that Luke is not
saying that men should not be householders able to care for their own
with their own possessions ("[Paul] saith that they which provide not for
their family and house, are worse than infidels" [143]). Like Calvin, he
refers to the proverb "All things are common among friends" to substanti-
ate that this was a voluntary, need-prompted sharing, but not a giving up
of ownership (224): "Wherefore by this word (common) is understanded
nothing, but a voluntary contribution, whereby every man gave, as seemed
him good, after his ability, to the relief and maintenance of the poor lest

through impatiency and poverty they should take any naughty ways, or turn to their Jewish religion and superstition again" (144).

56 Leonard Wright, *A Summons for Sleepers* ([London], 1589), 4.

57 "The riches and goods of Christians are not common, as touching the right, title, and possession of the same; as certain Anabaptists do falsely boast. Notwithstanding, every man ought, of such things as he possesseth, liberally to give alms to the poor, according to his ability" (*Creeds of the Churches,* 3rd ed., ed. John H. Leith [Atlanta: John Knox Press, 1982], 280).

58 The likely date of the play is between 1591 and 1594–95 (*Woodstock, A Moral History,* ed. A. P. Rossiter [London: Chatto and Windus, 1946], 16; *Thomas of Woodstock,* ed. George Parfitt and Simon Shepherd [Nottingham: Nottingham Univ. Press, 1977], iii; David Bevington, *Tudor Drama and Politics: A Critical Approach to Topical Meaning* [Cambridge: Harvard Univ. Press, 1968], 250).

59 1.1.100, 1.1.99, 1.1.102; 1.3.18, in *Thomas of Woodstock,* ed. Rossiter. Further references to act, scene, and line nos. of this play are to Rossiter's edition and will appear parenthetically in the text. For the play's rearrangements of history see Rossiter's preface, 18ff.

60 See also Woodstock's complaint that "[t]o make my horse more tire, / Ten acres of good land are stitched up here" (1.3.97–98) which parallels Burton's comment: "So ridiculous, moreover, we are in our attires, and for cost so excessive, that, as Hierome said of old . . . 'tis an ordinary thing to put a thousand oaks and an hundred oxen into a suit of apparel, to wear a whole manor on his back." Robert Burton, *The Anatomy of Melancholy* (London: J. M. Dent, 1932; reprint, New York: Vintage, 1977), pt. 3, sec. 2, mem. 2, subsec. 3, p. 98.

61 Such numbering suggests the censuses and listings of the poor that were made—at least in part to determine the deserving—at the end of the sixteenth century. See Slack, "Poverty and Social Regulation," 230.

62 See note 32 for Downame on such cases.

63 Bevington, *Tudor Drama and Politics,* 251. But such radical positions do not come without struggle: the martyr-hero also speaks orthodox doctrine, consistent with the "Homilie against Disobedience and Wilfull Rebellion": "His youth is led by flatterers much astray. / But he's our king: and God's great deputy; / And if ye hunt to have me second ye / In any rash attempt against his state, / Afore my God, I'll ne'er consent unto it. / I ever yet was just and true to him, / And so will still remain: what's now amiss / Our sins have caused . . . and we must bide heaven's will" (4.2.143–50, 143).

64 Bevington says: "To the extent that the play's heroes are noblemen who believe in rank, *Woodstock* is hierarchically orthodox. Far from indulging in . . . anti-aristocratic jibes, . . . *Woodstock* upholds an ideal of old-fashioned nobility as England's best hope for justice. No Cade or Tyler spouts leveling doctrines. In its use of metaphor *Woodstock* views the universe itself as one of order and degree" (*Tudor Drama and Politics*, 250–51). "In its view of taxation and of criticizing the government for manifest abuses," however, "*Woodstock* is an outspoken defense of the rights of free men," but "within the existing social order" (ibid., 252). In Robert Greene's *A Quip for an Upstart Courtier; or, A Quaint Dispute between Velvet Breeches and Clothbreeches. Wherein is Plainely Set Downe the Disorders in All Estates and Trades* (London, 1592), (in *The Life and Complete Works in Prose and Verse of Robert Greene*, ed. Alexander B. Grosart [New York: Russell and Russell, 1964], vol. 11, *Prose*), as in *Woodstock*, rich clothing is allowed for the truly noble, but disallowed for upstarts. However, Greene is careful not to offend his gentlemen readers who wear velvet breeches: he "twits not the weed but the vice, not the apparel when tis worthily worn, but the unworthy person that wears it, who sprang of a peasant will use any sinister means to climb to preferment, being then so proud as the fop forgets like the ass that a mule was his father" ("To the Gentlemen Readers' Health," 211). Cloth Breeches is no "precise" Puritan; it's the "new" social upstarts or pretenders who "don't belong" that he resents: "I am not so precise directly to inveigh against the use of velvet, . . . nor will I have men go like John Baptist, in coats of camel's hair. Let princes have their diadems, and Caesar what is due to Caesar, let noblemen go as their birth requires, and gentlemen as they are born or bear office: I speak . . . for the ancient gentility and yeomanry of England, and inveigh against none, but such malapert upstart as raised up from the plough, or advanced for their Italian devises, or for their witless wealth, covet in bravery to match, nay to exceed the greatest noblemen in this land" (231–32). In connection with such attitudes, see Frank Whigham, *Ambition and Privilege: The Social Tropes of Elizabethan Courtesy Theory* (Berkeley: Univ. of California Press, 1984). *A Quip* also strikes the familiar notes of lament for the idealized past of simplicity and hospitality to the poor: then "K. Stephen wore a pair of cloth breeches of a noble a pair, and thought them passing costly: then did he count Westminster hall too little to be his dining chamber, and his alms was not bare bones, instead of broken meat, but lusty chines of beef fell into the poor man's basket" (234).

65 Beier, *Masterless Men*, 158–64; John Pound, *Poverty and Vagrancy in Tudor England* (London: Longman, 1971), 50. See above, note 47. Further references to Pound will appear parenthetically in the text.

66 Sharp, *In Contempt*, 46; on martial law, see Beier, *Masterless Men*, 152–53.

67 Slack, "Poverty and Social Regulation," 234, quoting from T. E. Hartley, ed., *Proceedings in the Parliaments of Elizabeth I*, vol 1, *1558–1581*, 219.

68 *An Ease for Overseers of the Poore* (Cambridge, 1601), 19 (my emphasis).

69 For Warren's imprisonment, see Jordan, *Philanthropy*, 193.

70 "God hath given riches to many to see how they will use them, and he hath made many poor as his instruments to prove them" (*Ease for Overseers*, 35).

71 Arthur Warren, *The Poore Man's Passions and Povertie's Patience* (London, 1605), C4v. Further references will appear parenthetically in the text. Presumably "Ploydon's case" in the first passage refers to the proverb "[T]he case is altered, quoth Plowden," attributed to the jurist Edmund Plowden (1518–85). See *Dictionary of National Biography*, s.v. "Plowden, Edmund."

72 Jonathan Dollimore regards "a process of conspiracy on the part of the rulers and misrecognition on the part of the ruled" as a "direct sense" of ideology, or "a system of illusory beliefs held in the state of so-called false consciousness." However, as he says, the "inadequacy" of this view has been stressed recently: "Ideology becomes not a set of false beliefs capable of correction by perceiving properly, but the very terms in which we perceive the world . . . the condition and grounds of consciousness itself" (*Radical Tragedy: Religion, Ideology, and Power in the Drama of Shakespeare and His Contemporaries*, 2nd ed. [Durham, N.C.: Duke University Press, 1993], 9).

73 Bishop Richard Bancroft, *A Sermon Preached at Paule's Crosse* (London, 1588), 3, 25–6.

74 Thomas Cooper, *An Admonition to the People of England* (London, 1589), title page, 157. The passage is also quoted in Patterson, *Shakespeare and the Popular Voice*, 42. This frank throwing back of egalitarianism into the faces of religious or other dissidents goes back into early Tudor times. Edmund Dudley, a casualty of the transition from the realm of Henry VII to Henry VIII, attempted to buy his pardon by writing *The Tree of Commonwealth*, an argument for absolute monarchy, while he was in the Tower in 1509–10. Like Bancroft's sermon, this treatise tells the people that they are deceived by such egalitarian arguments; Dudley has his own version of "politic inequality and spiritual equality": "The name of the second messenger [after Discontentation] is Arrogancy. . . . He will show you that you be made of the same mold and metal that the gentles be made of. Why then should they sport and play and you labour and till? . . . Why should they have so much of the prosperity and treasure of this world, and ye so little? . . . Why should they have this great honour, royal castles and manors with so much lands and possessions, and you but poor tenements and cottages? He will show you also why that Christ bought as dearly you as them, and with one manner of price, which was his precious blood. Why then should you be of so poor estate, and they of so high degree? Or why should you do them so much honour and reverence with crouching and kneeling, and they take it so high and stately on them? . . . Why then should they have of you so great authority and power to commit to prison, to punish and to judge you? . . . Therefore mind you not this purpose or intent, that is the equality of the molds between the nobles and you, nor the cognisance of the pedigree from Adam, nor the indifferency of their souls in their creations. . . . But let us all consider that god hath set a due order by grace between himself and angels, and between angel and angel, and by reason between angel and man, and between man and man, and man and beast, and by nature only between beast and beast; which order, from the highest point to the lowest god willeth us fervently to keep." "Dudley's Warning to the People Against Rebellion, 1509-10," excerpt from *The Tree of Commonwealth*, in *Tudor Economic Documents*, 3:14-16. Even one of the widely disseminated homilies, "An Exhortation Concerning Good Order, and Obedience to Rulers and Magistrates," does not scruple to remark: "Take away kings, princes, rulers, magistrates, judges and such estates of God's order, no man shall ride or go by the high way unrobbed, no man shall sleep in his own house or bed unkilled, no man shall keep his wife, children and possession in quietness, all things shall be common." *Certaine Sermones or Homilies Appointed to be Read in Churches in the Time of Queen Elizabeth I (1547-1571)*, facsimile reproduction of the 1623 edition, ed. Mary Ellen Rickey and Thomas B. Stroup (Gainesville, Fla.: Scholars' Facsimilies and Reprints, 1968), 69.

75 Millar MacLure, *The Paul's Cross Sermons, 1534-1642* (Toronto: Univ. of Toronto Press, 1958), 8. Among the economically comfortable were the city aldermen and their wives for whose "comfort and convenience" seating provision was made at Paul's Cross (8).

76 For John of Leyden's reign at Münster, see Norman Cohn, *The Pursuit of the Millennium: Revolutionary Millenarians and Mystical Anarchists of the Middle Ages* (New York: Oxford Univ. Press, 1970), 261-80.

77 Theodore B. Leinwand, "Negotiation and New Historicism," *PMLA* 105, no. 3 (May 1990), 483.

78 Fletcher and Stevenson, introduction to *Order and Disorder*, ed. Fletcher and Stevenson, 38; Leinwand, "Negotiation," 482.

79 Interestingly, even the Münster Anabaptists resorted to "an absolutely authoritarian code" in an attempt to maintain order: "death was . . . the punishment for every kind of insubordination—of the young against their parents, of a wife against her husband, of anyone against God and God's representatives, the government of Münster" (Cohn, *Pursuit of the Millennium*, 269).

80 Bancroft, *Sermon Preached at Paule's Crosse*, 26.

81 See E. P. Thompson, "The Moral Economy of the English Crowd in the Eighteenth Century," *Past and Present*, no. 50 (1971): 76–136; and John Stevenson, "The 'Moral Economy' of the English Crowd: Myth and Reality," in *Order and Disorder*, ed. Fletcher and Stevenson, 218–35.

82 Slack, "Poverty and Social Regulation," 240.

83 John Walter and Keith Wrightson, "Dearth and the Social Order in Early Modern England," in *Rebellion, Popular Protest and the Social Order in Early Modern England*, ed. Paul Slack (Cambridge: Cambridge Univ. Press, 1984), 120.

84 Sharp, *In Contempt*, 55; Slack, "Poverty and Social Regulation," 224, 239; Archer, *Pursuit of Stability*, 201.

85 Sharp, *In Contempt*, 57.

86 Beier, *Problem of the Poor*, 29.

87 Pound asserts that "the really destitute in a rural parish were usually supported without any difficulty, a fact which becomes abundantly clear as more and more churchwardens' and overseers' accounts are unearthed from the parish chests" (*Poverty and Vagrancy*, 80). Slack indicates that "it was only in the generation after the 1598 statute that [poor rates] spread to a majority of rural parishes," although they "became more common after the Act of 1572" ("Poverty and Social Regulation," 235).

88 As well as in London, "compulsory taxes for the poor had been instituted in . . . Norwich, Ipswich and York in the later 1540s and 1550s. Temporary expedients to begin with, they were well established there and in other towns such as Exeter, Cambridge and Chester before the Act of 1572" (Slack, "Poverty and Social Regulation," 223).

89 Pound speaks of other successes as well, in Norfolk, Essex, and Bedfordshire, where relief only became inadequate during the crises of the 1590s. "Sometimes extraordinary forms of taxation were devised. Thus in 1599 at Bunwell in Norfolk 106 people were assessed at the rate of one penny for each acre of land owned, with the intention of providing stocks of materials for the local poor, and fifty of them paid a further penny for each six acres owned to provide support for the impotent" (*Poverty and Vagrancy*, 81).

90 Archer compares two time periods, 1570–73 and 1594–97 in London. "Taking endowments and cash bequests together, private charity grew by 111 per cent and 54 per cent in real terms. In order to appreciate the significance of these changes to potential recipients it is necessary to take into account the increase in the City's population in the intervening period. The overall increase in per capita real terms was 13 per cent, and the net gain to recipients was probably further eroded by the fact that the proportion of the poor in the City population was increasing. Thus the gain to individuals was very limited" (178). For other discussions of Jordan's findings in *Philanthropy*, see Beier, *Problem of the Poor*, 21–22; Pound, *Poverty and Vagrancy*, 70–72. Paul Slack says that Jordan's "conclusion that in aggregate charitable giving was much more voluminous [than income from the poor rates] remains persuasive for Elizabeth's reign" ("Poverty and Social Regulation," 287 n. 28).

91 "About 7 per cent of [London] householders were dependent on regular parish support and a further 18 per cent in need of occasional help and threatened with destitution in crisis years. As a proportion of the population the poor were about 14 per cent. These figures are consonant with Paul Slack's conclusions in relation to provincial towns, 'that 4 or 5% of the population of a town commonly received relief in the sixteenth century, and that another 10 or 15% was recognized to be "poor" and liable at some time to claim it.' " Archer, *Pursuit of Stability*, 153–54, quoting Slack, "Poverty and Social Regulation," 232. Pound agrees: "Ultimately, after considerable experiment, it was accepted that responsibility must be taken for both the impotent and the unemployed poor, but the numbers regularly supported rarely exceeded 4 or 5 per cent of the population. Many that might have joined them were bolstered by the charitable bequests of all classes of society" (*Poverty and Vagrancy*, 84).

92 Slack, "Poverty and Social Regulation," 239.

93 Ibid.

94 I borrow the term "satisficing" from economic theory to refer to a minimal or good enough solution just above the unacceptable, as opposed to a best or optimal solution. See, for the original use of the term (opposed to "maximizing"), Herbert A. Simon, *Models of Man: Mathematical Essays on Rational Human Behavior in a Social Setting* (New York: John Wiley and Sons, 1957), 204–5, 271.

95 Walter and Wrightson, "Dearth and the Social Order," 127. Riot was not necessarily the first step, either. "Since government and governed alike subscribed to a common consensus on the proper ordering of the economy in the face of dearth and on the role of the authorities dictated by it, the initial reaction of the poor was not one of riot but of appeal to the local authorities to act. Petitions preceded riots" (ibid.). This is not to say that government action was successful in more than minimal ways.

96 Patterson, *Shakespeare and the Popular Voice*, 139, quoting Robert Wilkinson, *A Sermon Preached at North-Hampton the 21 of June Last Past . . . upon the Occasion of the Late Rebellion and Riots in Those Parts Committed* (1607), D2r (her emphasis).

97 Wilkinson, *Sermon Preached at North-Hampton* (London, 1607), D2r; A3v; F1r.

98 Richardson, *A Sermon against Oppression*, 9, 12 (my emphasis).

99 Although "Truth should them scandal's sepulcher give," "These Purgatorians, though forgot in grave, / Ora pro nobis must remembered have" (E2v).

100 Slack, "Poverty and Social Regulation," 237.

101 *An Ease for Overseers of the Poore* (Cambridge, 1601), 28, 25, 32. Here, as opposed to in the passage from Charles Richardson quoted above, brotherhood is stressed. However, the control on taking this too far toward social egalitarianism appears in the emphasis on "carnal nativity" and "spiritual nativity," as opposed to, e.g., social nativity.

102 *Ease for Overseers*, 28, 20.

103 Ibid., 28.

104 Heal, "Idea of Hospitality," 83, quoting Thomas Cooper, *The Art of Giving* (1571), 61. The *Short Title Catalogue* reveals that this is not Bishop Thomas Cooper who wrote the *Admonition to the People of England*.

105 Archer, *Pursuit of Stability*, 179, quoting H. Smith, *The Poore Men's Teares Opened in a Sermon* (1592), 13. Slack quotes a similar sentiment from Robert Allen (*A Treatise of Christian Beneficence* [London, 1600], 41, 126–27): "[I]n the end it was better 'that alms should be cast away, then any creature should perish for want of relief' " ("Poverty and Social Regulation," 234).

106 Archer, *Pursuit of Stability*, 183, quoting Christopher Hooke, *Sermon Preached in Paule's Church* (1603), C3v.

107 Cohen, *Drama*, 353, does just this, citing Walwyn "[If] one suffer, all ought to suffer with that one, even by having a sympathy and fellow feeling of his misery, and helping to bear his burden" ("England's Lamentable Slaverie," in *The Levellers in the English Revolution*, ed. G. E. Aylmer [Ithaca, N.Y.: Cornell Univ. Press, 1975], 64).

108 Paul Delaney, "*King Lear* and the Decline of Feudalism," *PMLA* 92, no. 3 (May 1977): 435.

8 Mock Trials and Assaults on Justice

1 Q has the shorter assault on justice, ll. 2361–73. I continue to quote from *The Riverside Shakespeare*'s composite text, which includes (with some emendations) the mock trial from the Quarto, as well as (with some emendations) the longer version of the assault on justice that appears in the Folio. As usual, I will give variant readings in the notes. F has "the great image of Authoritie" (l. 2602) and "Thorough tatter'd cloathes great Vices do appeare: Robes, and Furr'd gownes hide all" (ll. 2606–8); Q has "through tottered raggs, smal vices do appeare, robes and furd-gownes hides all" (ll. 2370–1).

2 Paul Delany, "*King Lear* and the Decline of Feudalism," *PMLA* 92, no. 3 (May 1977), 435. Delany cites pre-Glasnost Soviet approval "of Lear's social analysis," but himself qualifies the degree of radicalism involved by saying that Lear is "at this point intermittently mad" and that he speaks as "a Christian radical," with no "rational scheme of social reconstruction" (436).

3 Charles Hobday, "Clouted Shoon and Leather Aprons: Shakespeare and the Egalitarian Tradition," *Renaissance and Modern Studies* 23 (1979): 75. Hobday goes on to quote from "More Light Shining in Buckinghamshire," in *The Works of Gerrard Winstanley*, ed. G. H. Sabine (1941), 633. Hobday concludes more broadly: "Shakespeare . . . was familiar with the egalitarian tradition, and could use its language now ironically, now sympathetically. Much the same can be said of his use of more orthodox political ideas" (76).

4 Hill, "The Pre-Revolutionary Decades," in *Collected Essays of Christopher Hill*, vol. 1, *Writing and Revolution in Seventeenth-Century England* (Brighton: Harvester, 1986), 16.

5 Cohen quotes *The Works of Gerrard Winstanley*, ed. George H. Sabine (Ithaca, N.Y.: Cornell University Press, 1941), 274.

6 Cohen quotes from Winstanley, *Works*, 557.

7 Gary Taylor, "Monopolies, Show Trials, Disaster, and Invasion: *King Lear* and Censorship," in *The Division of the Kingdoms: Shakespeare's Two Versions of "King Lear,"* ed. Gary Taylor and Michael Warren (Oxford: Clarendon, 1983), 101.

8 Ibid., 88–89.

9 Ibid., 89. See Roger Warren, "The Folio Omission of the Mock Trial," in *Division of the Kingdoms*, 52–53. Warren argues for the omission of the mock trial from the Folio on artistic grounds, as does Taylor—although Taylor says the anticipation of censorship might have contributed to a "structural uncertainty" in the scene ("Monopolies, Show Trials," 92–93). Even if F 4.6 is more intense than Q 3.6, one should not forget that a good deal of the Folio diatribe on injustice is in fact present in Q 4.6, thus even further complicating arguments about censorship and the texts of *Lear*.

10 Patterson, *Censorship and Interpretation: The Conditions of Writing and Reading in Early Modern England* (Madison: Univ. of Wisconsin Press, 1984), 61 (my emphasis), 62 (quoting Taylor, "Monopolies, Show Trials," 90).

11 "Whan alle tresors ben tried, treuþe is þe beste." *Piers Plowman: The B Version. Will's Visions of Piers Plowman, Do-Well, Do-Better and Do-Best*, edition of Trinity College Cambridge MS B.15.17, corrected and restored, with variant readings, by George Kane and E. Talbot Donaldson, vol. 2 of *Piers Plowman: The Three Versions* (London: Athlone, 1975), passus 1, l. 207, 254. The original Middle English passages, which will be given in the notes, are from this edition. The translation is from William Langland, *Piers the*

Ploughman, trans. J. F. Goodridge (Harmondsworth, England: Penguin, 1959; reprint, 1964), bk. 1, 72. Passages in modern English are from this edition; references will be given parenthetically in the text.

12 "God graunte[d] to gyve Mede to truþe" (passus 2, l. 120, 262).

13 "That oon god of his grace [gyveþ] in his blisse / To [hem] þat [werchen wel] while þei ben here" (passus 3, ll. 232-33, 284); "Ther is [a] Mede mesurelees þat maistres desireþ; / To mayntene mysdoers Mede þei take" (passus 3, ll. 246-47, 285). See John A. Alford, "The Design of the Poem," in *A Companion to "Piers Plowman,"* ed. John Alford (Berkeley: Univ. of California Press, 1988), 36-39.

14 John A. Yunck, *The Lineage of Lady Meed: The Development of Mediaeval Venality Satire* (Notre Dame, Ind.: University of Notre Dame Press, 1963), 289.

15 "Purfiled wiþ Pelure, þe [pureste on] erþe, / Ycorouned [in] a courone, þe kyng haþ noon bettre. / Fetisliche hire fyngres were fretted with gold wyr. . . . Hire Robe was ful riche, of reed scarlet engreyned, / Wiþ Ribanes of reed gold and of riche stones" (passus 2, ll. 9-11, 15-16, 255, 256).

16 See Yunck, *Lineage,* 272-73, and "Mede and Muche Thank," in *Twenty-Six Political and Other Poems,* ed. J. Kail, Early English Text Society, o.s., no. 124 (London: K. Paul, Trench, Trübner, 1904), 6-9.

17 Edward Hake, *News out of Powle's Churchyarde* (London, 1579), G8r. Hake indicates he has praised judges in a former work; all degrees have both good and bad. "So then, some chief and so besides / so smally ponder meed, / That where they sit in common sway, / there, Justice doth proceed" (B6r).

18 Richard Barnfield, "The Combat, between Conscience and Covetousnesse in the Minde of Man," in *The Poems of Richard Barnfield* (London: Fortune, 1936), 120. See Job 29:14, Isaiah 61:10.

19 Barnfield, "The Combat," 120, 121. This was, as Barnfield says, "no common fur"; it's not clear what he means when he says, "Or if it were, himself he was the fur" (120). Perhaps, since the cloak is made of the skins of poor men, it is furred with their hair. Barnfield also wrote "The Encomion of Lady Pecunia; or, The Praise of Money" (London, 1598). To the list of the progeny of Lady Meed one must, of course, add Spenser's Lady Munera in book 5 of *The Faerie Queene,* "Containing, The Legend of Artegall, or of Justice." She "meant him to corrupt with goodly meed . . . great sacks with endless riches." Ibid., 5.2.23, in *The Poetical Works of Edmund Spenser,* ed. J. C. Smith and E. de Selincourt (London: Oxford Univ. Press, 1963), 283.

20 However, in accordance with the estates literature theme so often linked with the trial of Lady Lucre, all groups are at fault: both "young and old, the rich and poor" "shut their door" against Conscience and he returns to heaven whence he came ("The Combat," 124).

21 "For þe mooste commune of þat court called hire an hore. / Ac a Sisour and a Somonour sued hire faste" (passus 4, ll. 166–167, 303). In Lang-land's poem as well as in *Lear*, justice seems to fail, even in the highest court. "It is the king acting as an individual and listening only to his inter-nal Conscience and Reason, who decides to punish Wrong [that is Fraud] and Meed and to attack the lawyers who have sided with them against Truth. . . . One can see this as an absolutist solution . . . but it is perhaps truer to see it as an apolitical solution." Anna P. Baldwin, "The Historical Context," in *Companion to Piers Plowman*, 83.

22 *The Three Ladies of London* (London, 1584), in *A Select Collection of Old English Plays* (originally published by Robert Dodsley, 1744; 4th ed., rev. W. Carew Hazlitt, 1874–76; reissue, New York: Benjamin Blom, 1964), 6:365.

23 Q has "who shal arraine me for't" (l. 2817).

24 In Lupton's *All for Money*, the character of that name becomes the "ruler or magistrate" who promises to save the thieves, adulterers and murderers willing to bribe him; as judge, "All for Money" indeed has the "power to seal the accuser's lips" (*Lear*, 4.6): "They that should give evidence shall be all tongue tied, / And the twelve men shall find her guiltless, let her not be afraid" (D1v).

25 F. T., *The Debate betweene Pride and Lowlines, Pleaded to an Issue in Assise* (London, [1577?]), B2r. The *Short Title Catalogue* indicates that the attri-bution to Francis Thynne is erroneous. Further references will be given parenthetically in the text.

26 In the version printed in *Early Prose and Poetical Tracts Illustrative of the Drama and Literature of the Reign of Queen Elizabeth*, vol. 2 (London: Shake-speare Society, 1853), 39, the line "And spend his rent his hospitality" reads "And spend his rent in hospitality."

27 Of course, these lines appear only in Q, since the mock-trial scene does not appear in the Folio. Robert Greene's *A Quip for an Upstart Courtier; or, A Quaint Dispute between Velvet Breeches and Cloth-breeches* (London, 1592), in *The Life and Complete Works in Prose and Verse of Robert Greene*, vol. 11, *Prose* (New York: Russell and Russell, 1964), lacks the passionate indictment of the rich and of the abuse and injustice suffered by the poor found in *Pride and Lowlines*. In Greene's more lighthearted dream vision, Cloth-breeches wins the case; justice has a rather fanciful success.

28 David Harris Sacks, "Searching for 'Culture' in the English Renais-sance," *Shakespeare Quarterly* 39, no. 4 (winter 1988): 484. Q has "which is the theefe, which is the Justice" (ll. 2362–63).

29 Sacks, "Searching for 'Culture,' " 484, 485.

30 James Sharpe, "The People and the Law," in *Popular Culture in Seven-teenth Century England*, ed. Barry Reay (London: Croom Helm, 1985), 261–

62. Sharpe suggests that the authorities found this sort of parody unacceptable.

31 Marie Axton, *The Queen's Two Bodies: Drama and the Elizabethan Succession* (London: Royal Historical Society, 1977), 6. "Details of two such English trials survive" (ibid.). "To my knowledge the Queen punished no Inns of Court dramatist or actor for displeasing her or her government with a play" (3).

32 Philip J. Finkelpearl, *John Marston of the Middle Temple* (Cambridge, Mass.: Harvard Univ. Press, 1969), 60, quoting from Benjamin Rudyerd, *Le Prince d'Amour* (London, 1660), 69. These consistently bawdy and witty revels "simultaneously mock legal language and satirize [Petrarchan] fashions in lovemaking" (Finkelpearl, *John Marston,* 57); the young wits also satirize "the wealthy idlers, rakes, clotheshorses, and fools among whom they lived" and are "not above overt didacticism to improve their time-wasting colleagues" (61). All this goes along with expressions of devotion and compliment to the queen here and in the other surviving Inns of Court revels, the *Gesta Grayorum* (see Finkelpearl, *John Marston,* 59, 44). In the latter revels of 1594–95, "a mock-arraignment was conducted to determine the cause of the mix-ups on the night when *The Comedy of Errors* was offered" (ibid., 42). Among the charges: "[H]e [a sorcerer or conjuror] had foisted a company of base and common fellows, to make up our disorders with a play of errors and confusions; and that the night had gained to us discredit, and it self a nickname of errors. All which were against the crown and dignity of our sovereign lord, the Prince of Purpoole." *Gesta Grayorum; or, The History of the High and Mighty Prince Henry Prince of Purpoole,* ed. Desmond Bland (Liverpool: Liverpool Univ. Press, 1968), 33.

33 Taylor, "Monopolies, Show Trials," 92, 90, 96 (citing G. Wilson Knight, "*King Lear* and the Comedy of the Grotesque," in *The Wheel of Fire* [1930, rev. ed. 1949], 160–76). Knight's remarks about tragedy and risibility apply to the play as a whole.

34 Taylor, "Monopolies, Show Trials," 94.

35 Ibid., 95. I borrow the words Taylor uses to characterize folk plays (which influenced the mock-trial scene) where there is an "absurd application of legal procedure to kitchen utensils."

36 Q omits "she" (l. 1748). See below, note 41.

37 See, for example: Patterson, *Censorship,* 61, where she objects to Gary Taylor's presumed concern with " 'a potentially timeless work of art' " over the " 'political restraints of a particular time and place' " (Patterson quotes Taylor, "Monopolies, Show Trials," 75); Jonathan Dollimore, *Radical Tragedy: Religion, Ideology, and Power in the Drama of Shakespeare and His Contemporaries,* 2nd ed. (Durham, N.C.: Duke Univ. Press, 1993), 8, where he objects to the elimination of the "socio-political context and (content)" from literature, in favor of "supposedly timeless values which become the *universal* counterpart of man's *essential* nature, the underlying human essence"; Stephen Greenblatt, introduction to *The Forms of Power and the Power of Forms in the Renaissance* (Norman, Okla.: Pilgrim Books, 1982), 6, where he talks of literary works "as fields of force, places of dissension and shifting interests, occasions for the jostling of orthodox and subversive impulses."

38 *A Quip for an Upstart Courtier,* 294, 269. This prose dream vision/debate shares with many late moralities of the sixteenth century a jingoistic attitude toward foreigners, especially Catholic foreigners, on whom many of the troubles of the country are blamed. See Bevington, *Tudor Drama and Politics,* especially 134–40.

39 R. Malcolm Smuts, *Court Culture and the Origins of a Royalist Tradition in Early Stuart England* (Philadelphia: Univ. of Pennsylvania Press, 1987), 111, n. 35.

40 George Williams Keeton, *Shakespeare's Legal and Political Background* (New York: Barnes and Noble, 1958), 6. The case of the Post Nati to which Marcus refers is "Calvin's Case," which involved one "Robert Colville" (Galloway, *Union,* 148), a Post Natus, that is, a Scotsman born after James's accession to the throne. At issue was whether Colville was an alien or a naturalized citizen with rights to ownership of English land. James's project for the Union of England and Scotland—which involved many issues including that of the naturalization of the Scots—was of course debated in Parliament before this particular case was tried in the prerogative courts.

41 Marcus seems to assume that this commission is "very much like a Chancery commission" because " 'yokefellows of equity' were judges in the court of Chancery" (*Puzzling Shakespeare: Local Reading and Its Discontents* (Berkeley: Univ. of California Press, 1988), 150). However, it has not been clear to all readers that *all* the judges are from Chancery. See O. Hood Phillips, *Shakespeare and the Lawyers* (London: Methuen, 1972), 90, and Keeton, *Shakespeare's Legal and Political Background,* 16. Moreover, whatever the number of "yokefellows of equity," is it indisputably clear that the word "equity" refers only to Chancery judges? The term "equity" came gradually to be "confined to the justice, independent of the common law, administered by the Privy Council, Chancery, the Star Chamber and the Court of Requests" (Edward Hake, preface to *Epieikeia: A Dialogue on Equity in Three Parts,* ed. D. E. C. Yale [New Haven: Yale University Press, 1953], vii). However, the term was not unambiguous; William J. Jones notes that a contemporaneous jurist asserted that "the word 'equity' was used in respect of all courts (*The Elizabethan Court of Chancery* [Oxford: Clarendon Press, 1967], 419, n. 2). Edward Hake's treatise *Epieikeia* (ca. 1600) is divided into sections on "Equity in General," "Equity of the Common Lawes of England," and "Equity of the High Courte of Chauncery." Of course, insofar as a prerogative court is alluded to in the scene, all this may be moot. In the case of the Post Nati, according to Galloway, simultaneous suits in the King's Bench (a common law court) and Chancery were "adjourned . . . into the Exchequer-Chamber" (a court of appeal) where the judges comprised "all the King's Bench and Common Pleas justices, the Exchequer-Barons and the Lord Chancellor" (Bruce Galloway, *The Union of England and Scotland, 1603–1608* (Edinburgh: John Donald, 1986), 148–49). Marcus indicates something similar (*Puzzling Shakespeare,* 124), but emphasizes Chancery in her discussion of the mock trial.

42 "To solve immediate political crises, and to enhance the effectiveness of government, Privy Councilors and parliamentarians passed act after act that increased the King's prerogatives. At the same time, moreover, these very statutes afforced, by implication, the principles of political, or public, law. . . . By the 1590s [kings and queens] had accorded the rule of law statutory, judicial, and regal recognition. For the Tudor time-being, this principle served to balance regal power and political law and to give to this antinomy a congruity." William Huse Dunham Jr., "Regal Power and the Rule of Law: A Tudor Paradox," *Journal of British Studies* 3 (1964): 24–25.

43 William Camden, *Annales Rerum Anglicarum et Hibernicarum Regnante Elizabeta* (London, 1615), 266 [Latin ed.]; (London, 1625), 369 [English ed.], quoted in Dunham, "Regal Power and the Rule of Law," 51.

44 See Dunham, "Regal Power and the Rule of Law," 55. Also see Eric W. Ives, "The Reputation of the Common Lawyers in English Society, 1450–1550," *University of Birmingham Historical Journal* 7 (1959–60): 130–61.

45 "To Sir Thomas Egerton Knight, Lord Keeper of the Great Seale of England," ll. 53–58, 61–66, from *Certain Epistles,* in *The Complete Works in Verse and Prose of Samuel Daniel,* ed. Alexander B. Grosart, 4 vols. (1885; reprint, Ann Arbor, Mich.: University Microfilms, 1981), 1:193.

46 See Sir Charles Ogilvie, *The King's Government and the Common Law, 1471–1641* (Oxford: Basil Blackwell, 1958), 129, 130, 142.

47 See *The Parallel King Lear,* prepared by Michael Warren (Berkeley: Univ. of California Press, 1989), xi–xii.

48 Galloway points out that "there was universal agreement in 1604 about the legal status of the *Post-Nati*" (106). The issue was the status of the Ante Nati (see Galloway, *Union,* 71), those born before James's accession in 1603.

49 See ibid., 103–19.

50 He only mentions it having "briefly returned to public attention in a polemical tract" much later on, during the Civil War; this tract attempted to justify resistance to Charles I in terms of allegiance to the body politic (ibid., 160, n. 104).

51 See Louis A. Knafla, *Law and Politics in Jacobean England: The Tracts of Lord Chancellor Ellesmere* (Cambridge: Cambridge Univ. Press, 1977). The speech is given on pp. 202–53. Further references to Knafla's book will appear parenthetically in the text. The two views Knafla defines are: the view of those common lawyers who "placed sovereignty in the common law, and the law over the King"; on the other, of those "civilians and politicians [who] conceived of a monarch who was totally absolute, dispensing a natural or divine law to his subjects," and who therefore "exalted the undivided power and sovereignty of the King" (70, 71). As such, these are similar to the "two markedly different constitutional theories . . . voiced throughout [early Stuart England]" according to Johann Sommerville ("Ideology, Property, and the Constitution," in *Conflict in Early Stuart England: Studies on Religion and Politics, 1603–1642*, ed. Richard Cust and Ann Hughes (London: Longman, 1989), 49).

52 See Galloway, *Union*, 148–57, which includes a discussion of allegiance to the king vs. to the body politic as a constitutional issue in Calvin's Case. Also see Samuel Gardiner, *History of England from the Accession of James 1 to the Disgrace of Chief-Justice Coke, 1603–1616* (London: Hurst and Blackett, 1863), 317.

53 F has "Place sinnes with Gold, and the strong Lance of Justice, hurtlesse breakes: Arme it in ragges, a Pigmies straw do's pierce it" (ll. 2608–10).

54 Yunck, *Lady Meed*, 239, for the information on the printing; 247, quoting Bromyard, *Summa Praedicantium* (Venice, 1586), "Aquisitio," 23, and summarizing generally from Bromyard on "Aequitas," 4.

55 Thomas More, *Utopia*, trans. and ed. H. V. S. Ogden (New York: Appleton-Century Crofts, 1949), 7.

56 Among the seventeenth-century citations that Morris Palmer Tilley gives for the proverb "The great thieves hang the little ones" in *A Dictionary of the Proverbs in England in the Sixteenth and Seventeenth Centuries* (Ann Arbor: Univ. of Michigan Press, 1950), 656, are Randle Cotgrave, *A Dictionarie of the French and English Tongues* (1611) ("Les gros larrons pendent les petits"), and Giovanni Torriano, *Piazza Universale di Proverbi Italiani; or, A Common Place of Italian Proverbes* (1666) ("Great thieves cause small ones to be hanged").

57 Thomas Lupton, *A Dreame of the Divell and Dives . . . Verie Necessarie to Be Read Advisedly, and Heard Attentivelie, Both of Rulers and Inferiours, Rich, and Poore, Younge and Olde, Wise and Simple, That Wish Rather to Dwel in Heaven, Then in Hell* (London, 1589). Further references will appear parenthetically in the text.

58 "The Spiritual Combat (*Psychomachia*)," ll. 454–56, 459–63; in *The Poems*

of *Prudentius,* vol. 2, *Apologetic and Didactic Poems,* trans. Sister M. Clement Eagan (Washington, D.C.: Catholic Univ. of America Press, Inc., 1965), Fathers of the Church, no. 52, 95, 98. For the tradition of Avarice disguised as Frugality, also see Thomas H. Bestul, *Satire and Allegory in "Wynnere and Wastoure"* (Lincoln: Univ. of Nebraska Press, 1974), 20–21.

59 She resents supporting the king "of almn / Who is not able for to keep himself" and also "that my sister Ragan should go free, / To whom he gave as much, as unto me." As if the king were "our better," she says, he checks her desires for "a new fashioned gown . . . set forth with more than common cost" or to "make a banquet extraordinary / To grace [her] self, and spread [her] name abroad." The king's "old doting doltish withered wit / is sure to give a senseless check" for the gown, and the "old fool" says that "the cost" of the banquet "would well suffice for twice." She immediately takes the advice that the favor-currying counselor Skalliger gives to reduce the "allowance" the king has from her: "Therefore abridge it half, and you shall see, / That having less, he will more thankful be: / For why, abundance maketh us forget / The fountains whence the benefits do spring." *The True Chronicle History of King Leir,* sc. 9, ll. 778–79, 792–93, 779, 782–83, 786–87, 784–85, 788–789, 801–4, in *Sources of Shakespeare,* ed. Geoffrey Bullough (London: Routledge and Kegan Paul, 1973), 7:356–57. Avarice also appears disguised as Frugality in such works closer to Shakespeare's time as the morality play, *New Custom* (1573). See *Early English Dramatists, Anonymous Plays,* 3rd ser., ed. John S. Farmer (London: Early English Drama Society, 1906; reprint, Guildford, England: Charles W. Traylen, 1966), 190.

60 Thomas Lodge, *The Divell Conjured* (London, 1596), in *The Complete Works of Thomas Lodge,* 4 vols. (New York: Johnson Reprint, 1966), 3:88.

61 "The Fall of Robert Tresilian, Chiefe Justice of Englande," ll. 11–14, in *The Mirror for Magistrates,* ed. Lily B. Campbell (Cambridge: Cambridge Univ. Press, 1938; reprint, New York: Barnes and Noble, 1960), 73.

62 "The Twelfth Sermon: A Sermon Preached at an Assizes," in *The Sermons of Edwin Sandys,* ed. John Ayre (Cambridge: Cambridge Univ. Press, 1841; New York: Johnson Reprint, 1968), 225–27. Sandys, like some Genevan exiles, was "an obstinate and conscientious puritan at a time when those in authority wished that men with Romish leanings should be treated indulgently." Yet, he "was one of those who signed the order on 12 Dec. 1573 for the arrest of Cartwright," and "as bishop of London . . . he had a very difficult part to play. He had belonged to the early puritan party, and yet had to join with Archbishop Parker in trying to secure uniformity." *Dictionary of National Biography,* s.v. "Sandys, Edwin," 773, 774.

63 Samuel Daniel, "A Panegyrike Congratulatorie to the King" (1603), in *Complete Works in Verse and Prose,* 1:155.

64 See the quotation from the speech of James to Parliament, March 21, 1609, above, chapter 5, note 85.

65 William Kethe, *A Sermon Made at Blandford Forum, in the Countie of Dorset . . . at the Session Holden There, before the Honorable and the Worshyppefull of That Shyre* (London, 1571), 7v. Further references will be given parenthetically in the text. After the first sigs. with letters, the book has page nos.

66 J. S. Cockburn, *A History of English Assizes, 1558–1714* (Cambridge: Cambridge Univ. Press, 1972), 222. Of course, the assize sermon was generally a nonincendiary genre: "Most local preachers, called upon by the sheriff to deliver a maximum of two assize sermons, probably welcomed the chance to augment their stipends, masking their feelings with well-worn platitudes and inoffensive generalizations on tolerance, suffering, and the peace of God" (66). Control tightened in the Stuart period in that the Privy Council itself took notice of appointments; "under the early and restored Stuarts the sermon, in common with almost all public utterances at assizes, was utilized as a vehicle for propaganda" (ibid.).

67 Kethe makes clear in the dedication to Lord Ambrose, earl of Warwick, that "sundry, not only of the multitude, but some of higher calling so much misliked my said sermon, that they thought I spake somewhat more then became me. . . . When occasion was offered to speak plainly before your honor and the rest, and yet not forgetting I trust, before whom I spake, yea and when I saw that great necessity so required, and that duty drave me thereto, I practiced (your honour well knoweth) a certain kind of discipline, even upon those, that by birth and parentage were far above me" (*Sermon*, A2v–A3v).

68 Not dissimilarly, the serious criticism made in *The Mirror for Magistrates* of Richard II (a historical king, long-dead, whose defeat was part of a Tudor myth of victory) right after the reign of Bloody Mary—herself a tyrant from the Protestant point of view—and at the beginning of the reign of a Protestant queen, was unlikely to be threatening to that Protestant queen. This might not have been the case in Elizabeth's last years, however. The degree to which Elizabeth identified herself with Richard, or was so identified, is obviously an important question for political criticism. Her famous comment that she herself was Richard ("I am Richard II. Know ye not that?"), made after the failed Essex rebellion in 1601, and connected with presumed street performances of Shakespeare's *Richard II* is, of course, often mentioned as prime evidence for the salience of topical political meanings of drama. However, see Leeds Barroll, "A New History for Shakespeare and His Time," *Shakespeare Quarterly* 39 (1988): 441–64, for a careful assessment of the more complex historical circumstances surrounding the performance of *Richard II*.

69 George Macey, *A Sermon Preached at Charde in the Countie of Somerset, the Second of March 1597, Being the First Day of the Assizes There Holden* (London, 1601), 37. Further references will be given parenthetically in the text. I identify the author according to Cockburn; see, *History of English Assizes,* 222, and 222, n. 2.

70 Barrow, *Brief Discoverie,* in *The Writings of Henry Barrow, 1587–1590,* Elizabethan Nonconformist Texts, vol. 3, ed. Leland H. Carlson (London: George Allen and Unwin), 493.

71 "Some Considerations Tending to the Undeceiving Those, Whose Judgments Are Misinformed," in *The Writings of William Walwyn,* ed. Jack R. McMichael and Barbara Taft (Athens: Univ. of Georgia Press, 1989), 70.

72 Gary Taylor, "Monopolies, Show Trials," 89 (my emphasis). Roger Warren, "The Folio Omission of the Mock Trial," 53, makes similar points.

73 Q has "behold the great image of authoritie, a dogge, so bade in office" (l. 2366). F has:

> See how
> yond Justice railes upon yond simple theefe. . . .
> Thou hast seene a Farmers dogge barke at a Beggar?
> *Glou.* I Sir.
> *Lear.* And the Creature run from the Cur: there thou migh'st behold the great image of Authoritie, a Dogg's obey'd in Office. (ll. 2595–96, 2598–2603)

74 The robe is "something like the *candidatus,* or gown of humility, in which both Coriolanus and Titus Andronicus solicit the votes of the people." Maurice Charney, " 'We Put Fresh Garments on Him': Nakedness and Clothes in *King Lear,*" in *Some Facets of "King Lear": Essays in Prismatic Criticism,* ed. Rosalie L. Colie and F. T. Flahiff (London: Heinemann, 1974), 80.

75 Leir is clearly restored to the kingship in both Monmouth and *The True Chronicle Historie of King Leir.* As far as I know, only W. Gordon Zeeveld believes that Shakespeare's Lear, however, is "reinvested in his royal robes, symbols of his restitution." According to Zeeveld, "the turn to tragedy is held off until Lear has been reinstated in the kingship. It is crucial that when he appears on stage with the dead Cordelia in his arms he be invested." W. Gordon Zeeveld, *The Temper of Shakespeare's Thought* (New Haven: Yale Univ. Press, 1974), 70.

76 F has "which is the Justice, which is the theefe" (ll. 2597–98).

77 Here I paraphrase David Kastan's "[The theater's] counterfeit of royalty raises the possibility that royalty is a counterfeit" ("Proud Majesty Made a Subject: Shakespeare and the Spectacle of Rule," *Shakespeare Quarterly* 37, no. 4 [1986]: 464). In quoting Siemon, I have let stand his quotation from Shakespeare, in which, as in F, "Authority" is capitalized.

78 Erasmus, *Education of a Christian Prince*, trans. Lester K. Born (New York: W. W. Norton, 1968), 152.

79 Although even radical Protestants (like Ponet) warn that Christian liberty should not be misinterpreted as freedom from obedience to the secular power, in a sense, Reformation Protestantism may contribute to a devaluation of temporal authority. The "kingdom of God" is superior to the "kingdom of the world." "And if all the world were composed of real Christians, that is, true believers, no prince, king, lord, sword, or law would be needed." Luther, "Secular Authority: To What Extent It Should Be Obeyed," in *Martin Luther: Selections from His Writings*, ed. John Dillenberger (New York: Doubleday, 1961), 368, 369. However, too few led a genuine Christian life; Luther, of course, also vehemently opposed resistance and insisted that God had commanded obedience to rulers.

80 Sacks, "Searching for 'Culture,' " 485.

81 *The Trial of Treasure* (London, 1567), in *Early English Dramatists, Anonymous Plays*, 245.

82 In this work, it is only at the very last, after many passionate indictments of Dives, that, rather suddenly, fault is found with those who live "impatiently, enviously, idly, and sinfully, as do the most part of the poor especially the most beggarly sort" (G4v). These can be as surely shut out of heaven as Dives. "The poor should consider the advantages of their estate and practise patience; if hungry and naked, they should call on God for food and clothes, and if homeless, look to their home in heaven" (ibid.).

Political Interpretation versus Dramatic Verisimilitude and Shared Moral Values

1 See Nancy Easterlin and Barbara Riebling, eds., *After Poststructuralism: Interdisciplinarity and Literary Theory* (Evanston, Ill.: Northwestern Univ. Press, 1993) on the general poststructuralist tendency to choose theories "not on the basis of [their] cogency . . . but according to . . . [their] utility for . . . political or critical projects" (introduction, 4). Frederick Crews comments in the foreword that "the empirical spirit . . . has been neglected and disdained in the heyday of poststructuralism" (x).

2 See above, chapter 3, note 40.

3 James Holstun comments on Greenblatt's well-known reflection about human subjects as "remarkably unfree" (*Renaissance Self-Fashioning from More to Shakespeare* [Chicago: Univ. of Chicago Press, 1980], 256): "the only choice seems to be between seeing humans as free and sovereign subjects, and seeing them as cultural artifacts produced by the social system" ("Ranting at the New Historicism," *English Literary Renaissance* 19 (1989): 194–95).

4 In *The Works of John Whitgift*, 1:187. See above, chapter 1, note 26.

5 Perhaps Greenblatt's discussion of the "circulation of social energy," the "extended borrowings" and "collective exchanges" made "by moving certain things—principally ordinary language but also metaphors, ceremonies, dances, emblems, items of clothing, well-worn stories, and so forth—from one culturally demarcated zone to another," in ch. 1 of *Shakespearean Negotiations: The Circulation of Social Energy in Renaissance England* (Berkeley: Univ. of California Press, 1988), 7, has something in common with the ideas about the relation of individual creation to cultural codes I advance here. Yet Greenblatt's arguments about transpositions from one register to another deliberately stress the contingent and peripheral rather than the culturally and dramatically central; these "half-hidden cultural transactions" do not to my mind convincingly come across as those "through which great works of art are empowered" (4). There are possible overlaps, as well, between Greenblatt's counterposed "totalizing society" and "total artist" (2) and the idea of cultural code and individual creation. Yet my language-based view of the relation of individual creation to enabling codes may be less problematic than the relation between Greenblatt's more reified entities, especially insofar as he begins with "certain abjurations" that my model makes unnecessary, e.g., "There can be no appeals to genius as the sole origin of the energies of great art" or "There can be no autonomous artifacts," or even "There can be no transcendent or timeless or unchanging representation" (12).

6 David Scott Kastan, " 'The King Hath Many Marching in His Coats'; or, What Did You Do During the War, Daddy?," in *Shakespeare Left and Right*, ed. Ivo Kamps (New York: Routledge, 1991), 252. Kastan is using Derrida in his discussion of the representations of royal power and authority in *1 Henry IV.*

7 See above, chapter 2.

8 Of course where a play is an *allegory* of political figures in a specific contemporary political situation like Thomas Middleton's *A Game at Chess* of 1624 (which pits England and the Protestant cause against Spain, Catholicism, and the Jesuits), viewers certainly appear to have been interested in decoding it. And in a politically sensitive situation, undoubtedly audiences could regard history plays, for example, allegorically, i.e., could make the link between past and current disliked royal favorites. In these cases, such themes seem more central and more salient than those in some of the "local" readings of *Lear* with which I've been concerned in this book. See A. R. Braunmuller, " 'To the Globe I Rowed': John Holles Sees *A Game at Chess*," *English Literary Renaissance* 20, no. 2 (spring 1990): 340–56.

9 See above, note 8.

10 See William E. Cain, "The Crisis of the Literary Left: Notes toward a Renewal of Humanism," in *After Poststructuralism*, ed. Easterlin and Riebling, for some related pedagogical suggestions about "teaching that highlights differences but that also details a moral inquiry at work in literary texts that does not depend on race, gender, or ethnicity to make itself meaningful" (138–39).

11 Rosalie Colie, "Reason and Need: *King Lear* and the 'Crisis' of the Aristocracy," in *Some Facets of "King Lear,"* ed. Colie and Flahiff, 212, 196. Further references to "Reason and Need" will appear parenthetically in the text.

12 Among many good descriptions of this reorganization, see Roger B. Manning, "Agrarian Change and Common Rights," ch. 1 of *Village Revolts: Social Protest and Popular Disturbances in England, 1509–1640* (Oxford: Clarendon, 1988), 9–30. Annabel Patterson remarks on the difficulty of such divisions as Barish and Waingrow's and Colie's when applied to the play. "It has become something of a commonplace in discussions of *King Lear* that it represents the transition from a feudal economy or culture to a nascent capitalism; or . . . the decline of a moral in the face of a market economy. But the argument that Lear, Kent, and perhaps Cordelia act out the old feudal values or configure (semi-allegorically) a Moral Economy is deeply unpersuasive. Edmund, Goneril and Regan, the figures who supposedly represent the approach of capitalist values, in no way differ from aristocratic predators anywhere in Shakespeare's canon; while it is Lear himself, by promoting a land transfer tax to be paid in professions of love, who introduces marketability into a simple because arbitrary principle of aristocratic inheritance" (*Shakespeare and the Popular Voice* [Cambridge, Mass.: Basil Blackwell, 1989], 108). Of course, insofar as aristocrats could have "bourgeois" habits of mind (as her own remarks about Lear—and Colie's—imply), newly emergent "capitalist values" could be represented by "aristocratic predators" found anywhere in Shakespeare.

13 Here Colie makes use of one of the features of the aristocratic ethos as it is described by Lawrence Stone (in his *Crisis of the Aristocracy, 1558–1641* [Oxford: Clarendon, 1965], 9) in order to characterize "the noble ethos in the process of erosion during the Renaissance" ("Reason and Need," 196).

14 Thus it is particularly necessary for the master of a house to make sure that everyone has real work to do, to give everyone his appointed task, "else the house may be full of servants, and yet full of confusion, and nothing be well done or in any good order" (John Dod and Robert Cleaver, *A Plaine and Familiar Exposition of the Ten Commaundements* [London, 1606], 213).

15 "Who are the seedsmen of all mischief in our country, but these children of gentlemen, who have not been taught and trained up in learning, or some occupation, while they were young?" R[obert] C[leaver], *A Codly [sic] Form of Householde Government* (London, 1598), 275.

16 F. N. L. Poynter, *A Bibliography of Gervase Markham, 1568?–1637* (Oxford: Oxford Bibliographical Society, 1962), 9. "Men of gentle birth," before the Civil War, were "found among the upper servants of the nobility"; "[C]onvention still decreed that young men of good social standing should receive part of their training by attending on nobles of recognized power and reputation." Dorothy Marshall, *The English Domestic Servant in History* (London: George Philip and Son, 1949), 4.

17 *Utopia*, 8. William Harrison, *The Description of England*, ed. Georges Edelen (Ithaca: Cornell Univ. Press, 1968), 119. Harrison is described in the introduction as in "total sympathy with Elizabeth's highly pragmatic attempts to achieve religious stability" (xxviii), and as "stifl[ing] latent sympathy with the Puritan attacks upon the episcopacy" because he is a supporter of conformity (xxix).

18 "Graith" means *gear* or *dress*.

19 This idea is mobilized in support of the properly industrious servant's busyness. F. N. L. Poynter in fact says Markham's "firm religious belief developed as he grew older into a simple and austere but not harsh Puritanism, which led him to condemn all kinds of extravagance and excess" (*Bibliography of Markham*, 30–31).

20 The line "I am a Gentleman of blood and breeding" appears only in Q (l. 1415). Richard Strier comments that Jonathan Dollimore (in *Radical Tragedy: Religion, Ideology, and Power in the Drama of Shakespeare and His Contemporaries*, 2nd ed. [Durham, N.C.: Duke Univ. Press, 1993], 201) is wrong in considering Kent's attitude toward Oswald as snobbery based on differences in wealth; Strier's grounds are that the position of steward in a noble household was one of respect that could "open the way to 'gentle' status and to yet further advancement" and that Oswald "is certainly not to be imagined as poor" ("Faithful Servants," 130, n. 48). Whatever Oswald's degree of material wealth, Kent's attitude seems to be *class* snobbery, which has certainly rested on attributes other than wealth per se in England.

21 The word appears only in F (l. 1091).

22 Q has "Ile not be struck my Lord" (l. 548).

23 Q has ". . . that, / That worthied him" (l. 1006–7).

24 Q has "like dayes" (l. 968).

25 Q has "you beastly Knave you have no reverence" (l. 957).

26 Of course, whether Cornwall's point about Kent's lack of "reverence" has any validity will depend on directorial decisions: how insolently Oswald exits (1.4.45) with his murmured "So please you—"; how peremptory the tone Lear takes when summoning Oswald back (1.4.46–47); how insolent the looks are that Oswald bandies with Lear after Oswald has referred to him as "My lady's father" (1.4.79); whether Oswald is clearly perceived as pretending not to recognize Kent in a cowardly way at the beginning of 2.2.; and even—after Cornwall has attacked Kent's lack of reverence—what exact look Oswald wears while Kent lambasts Oswald's servility, his "following" like dogs ("A plague upon your epileptic visage! / Smile you my speeches, as I were a fool?" [2.2.81–82]). One does suspect that look is a facetious grin; Oswald knows who's in the saddle, and he's not too worried about the direction things are likely to take.

27 Q has "What's his offence" (l. 976). The *Riverside Shakespeare* follows F for 2.2.73–75; Q has "those cordes in twaine, / Which are to intrench, to inloose" (ll. 963–64).

28 Q has "or his, or hers" (l. 978).

29 The *Riverside Shakespeare* follows F; Q has "This is a fellow" (l. 983).

30 Barrow, *Brief Discoverie*, in *The Writings of Henry Barrow, 1587–1590*, Elizabethan Nonconformist Texts, vol. 3, ed. Leland H. Carlson (London: George Allen and Unwin), 493.

31 The *Riverside Shakespeare* follows F; Q has "What's the offence you gave him?" (l. 1001). Compare the irate tone of most of Cornwall's previous words to Kent, such as: "Why dost thou call him knave? What is his fault?" (89).

32 "I would breed from hence occasions" appears only in Q, ll. 474–75.

33 For 2.1.94–95, Q has "the ryotous knightes, that tends upon my father?" (ll. 865–66).

34 Q has "That weares no honesty" (l. 961).

35 Q has "Being the very fellow that of late" (l. 1121).

36 When Edmund accepts the favor Goneril gives him, becoming her servant, he illustrates Poor Tom's almost Theophrastian description of the proud and wicked servingman who obeys commands he should refuse, who "wore gloves in his cap" and "served the lust of his mistress' heart" (3.4.86–87).

37 Q leaves out "first" (l. 2423).

38 This line appears only in Q (l. 2870).

39 Patrick Collinson (in *Religion of Protestants*, 152) cites this phrase from Lawrence Chaderton, *A Fruitfull Sermon upon the 3.4.5.6.7. and 8. Verses of the 12 Chapter of the Epistle of S. Paul to the Romans* (1584). See above, chapter 6, note 70.

40 Anthony Lane, "Degrees of Cool," *New Yorker* (October 10, 1994): 97.

41 Alan Shapiro, "Horace and the Reformation of Creative Writing," *American Poetry Review* 21, no. 2 (March–April 1992), 12.

42 R. A. Foakes distinguishes between emotional "understanding" on the part of the ordinary contemporary viewer, and scholarly or historical "interpretation" in *Hamlet versus Lear: Cultural Politics and Shakespeare's Art* (Cambridge: Cambridge Univ. Press, 1993), especially 137–45. He also makes a distinction somewhat less relevant here between the *aesthetic experience of the literary work (dependent in part on formal values)*, and the treatment of literature as a source of political or other knowledge.

43 The first quotations ("anarchy," "dominion") are from Robert Allen, *A Treasure of Catechisme; or, Christian Instruction* (London, 1600), 132. The second quotations ("wisdom," "subjection") are from Geffray Fenton, *A Forme of Christian Policy*, 13, quoted in Walzer, *The Revolution of the Saints: A Study in the Origins of Radical Politics* (Cambridge, Mass.: Harvard Univ. Press, 1965), 184.

44 The first quotation is from "The Fall of Robert Tresilian, Chiefe Justice of Englande," l. 13, in *The Mirror for Magistrates*, ed. Lily B. Campbell (Cambridge: Cambridge Univ. Press, 1938; reprint, New York: Barnes and Noble, 1960), 73. The second ("equal balance") and last ("worst theeves") are from Thomas Lodge, *The Divell Conjured* (London, 1596), in *The Complete Works of Thomas Lodge*, 4 vols. (New York: Johnson Reprint), 3:88. The third quotation ("mighty men") is from Sandys, "The Twelfth Sermon: A Sermon Preached at an Assizes," in *The Sermons of Edwin Sandys*, ed. John Ayre (Cambridge: Cambridge Univ. Press, 1841; New York: Johnson Reprint, 1968), 227. The fourth ("the law alike") is from George Macey, *A Sermon Preached at Charde in the Countie of Somerset, the Second of March 1597, Being the First Day of the Assizes There Holden* (London, 1601), 26.

45 The first quotation is from "An Homilie of Almes Deedes," in *Certaine Sermons or Homilies Appointed to Be Read in Churches in the Time of Queen Elizabeth I 1547–1571*, facsimile reproduction of the 1623 edition, ed. Mary Ellen Rickey and Thomas B. Stroup (Gainesville, Fla.: Scholars' Facsimiles and Reprints, 1968), 155–56. The second is from Henry Bedel, *A Sermon Exhortyng to Pitie the Poore* (London, 1572), B2r. The third is from *Woodstock, A Moral History*, ed. A. P. Rossiter (London: Chatto and Windus, 1946), 2.3.102–3.

46 Here I borrow James Holstun's words about the Scriptures ("Ranting," 216).

47 Dieter Mehl, "King Lear and the 'Poor Naked Wretches,'" in *Deutsche Shakespeare-Gesellschaft West Jahrbuch* (Heidelberg: Quelle und Meyer, 1975), 161.

48 The lines implicated are Lear's to Edgar: "You, sir, I entertain for one of my hundred; only I do not like the fashion of your garments. You will say they are Persian, but let them be chang'd" (3.6.78–81). Q has "youle say, / They are Persian attire" (ll. 1773–74).

Works Cited

Primary Sources

"An Admonition to the Parliament." In *Puritan Manifestoes*, edited by Frere and Douglas.
—————. *A Treasurie of Catechisme; or, Christian Instruction.* London, 1600.
Anderson, Anthony. *The Shield of Our Safetie.* London, 1581.
Andrewes, Lancelot. *A Pattern of Catechistical Doctrine.* In *The Works of Lancelot Andrewes*, vol. 6. Oxford: John Henry Parker, 1854. Reprint, New York: Ams, 1967.
Ap Robert, J. *The Younger Brother His Apologie; or, A Father's Free Power Disputed, for the Disposition of His Lands.* Oxford, 1634.
Aquinas, Thomas. *Summa Theologiae.* Vol. 41, *Virtues of Justice in the Community*, edited and translated by T. C. O'Brien. New York: McGraw Hill, 1972.
Aristotle. *Ethica Nicomachea.* In *The Works of Aristotle.* Translated into English under the editorship of W. D. Ross. Vol. 9, *Ethica Nicomachea, Magna Moralia, Ethica Eudemia.* Oxford: Oxford Univ. Press, 1915. Reprint, 1949.
Arthington, Henry. *Provision for the Poore, Now in Penurie.* London, 1597.
Augustine. *The Works of Aurelius Augustine, Bishop of Hippo.* Edited by Marcus Dods. Vol. 10, *Lectures or Tractates on the Gospel According to St. John*, bk. 1. Edinburgh: T. and T. Clark, 1873.
—————. *The Works of Saint Augustine: A Translation for the Twenty-First Century.* Vol. 7, *Sermons 230–272B*, edited by John E. Rotelle, translated by Edmund Hill. New Rochelle, N.Y.: New City, 1993.
Babington, Gervase. *Certaine Plaine, Briefe, and Comfortable Notes upon Everie Chapter of Genesis.* London, 1592.
—————. *A Very Fruitful Exposition of the Commandements.* London, 1596.
Bancroft, Richard. *Dangerous Positions and Proceedings, Published and Practised within This Iland of Brytaine, under Pretence of Reformation, and for the Presbiteriall Discipline.* London, 1593.
—————. *A Sermon Preached at Paule's Crosse.* London, 1588.
—————. *A Survay of the Pretended Holy Discipline.* London, 1593.
Barker, Peter. *A Learned and Familiar Exposition upon the Ten Commandements.* London, 1633.
Barnfield, Richard. *The Poems of Richard Barnfield.* London: Fortune, 1936.

Barrow, Henry. *The Writings of Henry Barrow, 1587–1590*. Elizabethan Non-conformist Texts, vol. 3. Edited by Leland H. Carlson. London: George Allen and Unwin, 1962.

Batman, Stephen. *The Golden Booke of the Leaden Gods*. London, 1577. In *The Renaissance and the Gods*, edited by Stephen Orgel, vol. 13. New York: Garland, 1976.

Battus, Bartholomaeus. *The Christian Man's Closet: Wherein Is Conteined a Large Discourse of the Godly Training Up of Children: As Also Those Duties That Children Owe unto Their Parents*. Translated by William Lowth. London, 1581.

Bedel, Henry. *A Sermon Exhortyng to Pitie the Poore*. London, 1572.

Bishop Overall's Convocation Book MDC VI Concerning the Government of God's Catholic Church and the Kingdoms of the Whole World. London, 1690.

Blackstone, William. *Commentaries on the Laws of England*. Facsimile of 1st ed. of 1765–69. 4 vols. Chicago: Univ. of Chicago Press, 1979.

A Booke of Christian Prayers. London, 1578. In *Private Prayers: Put Forth by Authority during the Reign of Qu. Elizabeth*. Edited by William Keatinge Clay. Cambridge: Cambridge Univ. Press, 1851.

The Book of Common Prayer, 1559. Edited by John E. Booty. Charlottesville: Univ. Press of Virginia, 1976.

Bradford, John. *The Writings of John Bradford*. Edited by Aubrey Townsend. Cambridge: Cambridge Univ. Press, 1853.

Bradshaw, William. *Puritanism and Separatism, A Collection of Works by William Bradshaw*. With a new introduction by R. C. Simmon. [Farnborough], England: Gregg International, 1972.

Bullough, Geoffrey, ed. *Narrative and Dramatic Sources of Shakespeare*. Vol. 7, *Major Tragedies: Hamlet, Othello, King Lear, Macbeth*. London: Routledge and Kegan Paul, 1973.

Bunny, Francis. *A Guide unto Godlinesse; or, A Plaine and Familiar Explanation of the Ten Commandements*. [London], 1617.

Burton, Robert. *The Anatomy of Melancholy*. London: J. M. Dent, 1932. Reprint, New York: Vintage, 1977.

Calvin, John. *The Acts of the Apostles, 1–13*, vol. 1, translated by John W. Fraser and W. J. G. McDonald. In *Calvin's Commentaries*, edited by David W. Torrance and Thomas E. Torrance, vol. 6. Grand Rapids: Eerdmans, 1965.

———. "The Clear Explanation of Sound Doctrine Concerning the True Partaking of the Flesh and Blood of Christ in the Holy Supper." In Calvin, *Theological Treatises*.

———. *A Commentarie of John Calvine, upon the First Booke of Moses Called Genesis*. Translated by Thomas Tymme. London, 1578.

————. *Institutes of the Christian Religion.* 7th ed. 2 vols. Translated by John Allen. Philadelphia: Presbyterian Board of Christian Education, 1936.

————. "The Necessity of Reforming the Church." In Calvin, *Theological Treatises.*

————. "Short Treatise on the Holy Supper." In Calvin, *Theological Treatises.*

————. *Theological Treatises.* Library of Christian Classics, no. 22. Translated by J. K. S. Reid. Philadelphia: Westminster, 1954.

Certaine Sermons or Homilies Appointed to Be Read in Churches in the Time of Queen Elizabeth I (1547–1571). Facsimile reproduction of the 1623 edition. Edited by Mary Ellen Rickey and Thomas B. Stroup. Gainesville, Fla.: Scholars' Facsimiles and Reprints, 1968.

Cicero: On Duties. Edited by M. T. Griffin and E. M. Atkins. Cambridge: Cambridge Univ. Press, 1991.

Clapham, Henoch. *Antidoton; Or, A Soveraigne Remedie against Schisme and Heresie.* London, 1600.

Clarke, Samuel. *A Collection of the Lives of Ten Eminent Divines.* London, 1662.

R[obert] C[leaver]. *A Codly [sic] Form of Householde Government: For the Ordering of Private Families.* London, 1598.

————. *A Godlie Forme of Householde Government: For the Ordering of Private Families.* Compiled by R.C. London, 1598.

Clement of Alexandria. *Christ the Educator.* Translated by Simon P. Wood. The Fathers of the Church, no. 23. Washington, D.C.: Catholic Univ. of America Press, 1954.

The Confescion of the Fayth of the Sweserlandes. London, 1548.

Cooper, Thomas. *An Admonition to the People of England.* London, 1589.

Cranmer, Thomas. *An Answer unto a Crafty and Sophistical Cavillation Devised by Stephen Gardiner.* In *Writings and Disputations of Thomas Cranmer . . . Relative to the Sacrament of the Lord's Supper.* Edited by John Edmund Cox. Cambridge: Cambridge Univ. Press, 1844.

Crowley, Robert. *A Briefe Discourse against the Outwarde Apparell and Ministring Garmentes of the Popishe Church.* [Emden], 1566.

Daniel, Samuel. *The Complete Works in Verse and Prose of Samuel Daniel.* Edited by Alexander B. Grosart. 4 vols. 1885. Reprint, Ann Arbor, Mich.: University Microfilms, 1981.

Dent, Arthur. *The Plaine Man's Pathway to Heaven.* London, 1603.

Derrida, Jaques. *Of Grammatology.* Translated by Gayatri Chakravorty Spivak. Baltimore: Johns Hopkins Univ. Press, 1976.

————. *Writing and Difference.* Translated by Alan Bass. Chicago: Univ. of Chicago Press, 1978.

D'Ewes, Sir Simonds. *The Diary of Sir Simonds D'Ewes (1622-1624): Journal d'un étudiant londonien sous le règne de Jacques 1er.* Edited and annotated by Elisabeth Bourcier. Paris: Didier, 1974.

Dillingham, Francis. *Christian Oeconomy; or, Houshold Government.* London, 1609.

Dod, John, and Robert Cleaver. *A Plaine and Familiar Exposition of the Ten Commaundements.* London, 1606.

Donne, John. *The Complete Poetry and Selected Prose of John Donne.* Edited by Charles M. Coffin. New York: Random House, 1952.

———. *The Sermons of John Donne.* 10 vols. Edited by Evelyn M. Simpson and George R. Potter. Berkeley: Univ. of California Press, 1953-1962.

Downame, John. *The Plea of the Poore; or, A Treatise of Beneficence and Almes-Deeds.* London, 1616.

Drant, Thomas. *A Fruitfull and Necessary Sermon, Specially Concernyng Almesgeving.* London, 1572.

———. *Two Sermons Preached, the One at S. Marie's Spittle . . . 1570 and the Other at the Court at Windsor, . . . 1569.* London, [1570?].

Dudley, Edmund. "Dudley's Warning to the People against Rebellion, 1509-10." Excerpt from *The Tree of Commonwealth.* In *Tudor Economic Documents,* edited by Tawney and Power, vol. 3.

Early English Dramatists, Anonymous Plays. 3rd ser. Edited by John S. Farmer. London: Early English Drama Society, 1906. Reprint, Guildford, England: Charles W. Trayler, 1966.

An Ease for Overseers of the Poore. Cambridge, 1601.

Elyot, Thomas. *The Boke Named the Governour.* 2 vols. Edited by Henry Herbert Stephen Croft. London: Kegan Paul, Trench, 1883.

English Historical Documents, 1485-1548. Edited by C. H. Williams. Vol. 5 of *English Historical Documents,* edited by David C. Douglas. New York: Oxford Univ. Press, 1967.

Erasmus, Desiderius. *De Civilitate Morun* [sic] *Puerilium . . . A Lytell Booke of Good Maners for Chyldren, with Interpretation in to the Englysshe Tonge,* by R. Whtyngton. London, 1532.

———. *The Education of a Christian Prince.* Translated by Lester K. Born. New York: W. W. Norton, 1968.

"An Exhortation to the Bishops to Deale Brotherly with Their Brethren." In *Puritan Manifestoes,* edited by Frere and Douglas.

Fenton, Geffray. *A Forme of Christian Pollicie Drawne out of French.* London, 1574.

Filmer, Robert. *Patriarchia and Other Political Works.* Edited by Peter Laslett. Oxford: Basil Blackwell, 1949.

Floyd, Thomas. *The Picture of a Perfit Common Wealth.* London, 1600.

Four Supplications, 1529–1553 A.D. Early English Text Society, e.s., no. 13. London: Trübner, 1871.

Frere, W. H., and C. E. Douglas, eds. *Puritan Manifestoes: A Study of the Origin of the Puritan Revolt. With a Reprint of the Admonition to Parliament and Kindred Documents, 1572.* New York: E. S. Gorham, 1907. Reprint, London: S.P.C.K., 1954.

Foxe, John. *The Acts and Monuments.* 4th ed. 8 vols. Revised and corrected by Josiah Pratt. London: Religious Tract Society, 1887.

Gascoigne, George. *The Complete Works of George Gascoigne.* Edited by John W. Cunliffe. Vol. 2. Cambridge: Cambridge Univ. Press, 1907. Reprint, New York: Greenwood, 1969.

The Geneva Bible: A Facsimile of the 1560 Edition. Madison: Univ. of Wisconsin Press, 1969.

Gesta Grayorum; or, The History of the High and Mighty Prince Henry Prince of Purpoole. Edited by Desmond Bland. Liverpool: Liverpool Univ. Press, 1968.

Gibbon, Charles. *A Work Worth the Reading.* London, 1591.

Goodman, Godfrey. *The Fall of Man; or, The Corruption of Nature.* London, 1606.

Gouge, William. *Of Domesticall Duties.* London, 1622.

Greene, Robert. *A Quip for an Upstart Courtier; or, A Quaint Dispute between Velvet Breeches and Cloth-breeches.* (London, 1592). In *The Life and Complete Works in Prose and Verse of Robert Greene,* vol. 11, *Prose.* New York: Russell and Russell, 1964.

Griffith, Matthew. *Bethel; or, A Forme for Families.* London, 1633.

Gualthere, Radulpe [Rudolph Walther]. *An Hundred, Threescore and Fiftene Homelyes or Sermons, uppon the Actes of the Apostles.* London, 1572.

Edward Hake, *Epieikeia: A Dialogue on Equity in Three Parts.* [c. 1600]. Edited by D. E. C. Yale. New Haven: Yale Univ. Press, 1953.

———. *News out of Powle's Churchyarde.* London, 1579.

Harrison, William. *The Description of England.* Edited by Georges Edelen. Ithaca: Cornell Univ. Press, 1968.

Hayward, John. *The First and Second Parts of John Hayward's "The Life and Raigne of King Henrie IIII."* Edited by John J. Manning. London: Royal Historical Society, 1991.

Herbert, George. *A Priest to the Temple.* In *The Works of George Herbert,* edited by Hutchinson.

———. *The Works of George Herbert.* Edited by F. E. Hutchinson. Oxford: Clarendon, 1941. Reprint, 1959.

Holland, Henry. *The Historie of Adam.* London, 1606.

The Holy Bible . . . Translated out of the Original Tongues . . . by His Majesty's Special Command. Cambridge: Cambridge Univ. Press, [1611].

Hooker, Richard. *The Works of Mr. Richard Hooker.* 6th ed. 3 vols. Compiled by John Keble. Oxford: Clarendon, 1874.

Hooper, John. *Early Writings of John Hooper.* Edited by Samuel Carr. Cambridge: Cambridge Univ. Press, 1843.

How a Man May Choose a Good Wife from a Bad. London, 1602. Edited by John S. Farmer. Edinburgh: Tudor Facsimile Texts, 1912. Reprint, New York: Ams, 1970.

Humfrey, Lawrence. *The Nobles; or, Of Nobilitye.* London, 1563.

Hutchinson, Lucy. *Memoirs of the Life of Colonel Hutchinson.* 5th ed. London: Henry G. Bohn, 1846.

James I. *Basilikon Doron.* In *The Political Works of James I.*

―――. "The Trew Law of Free Monarchies." In *The Political Works of James I.*

―――. *The Political Works of James I.* With an introduction by Howard McIlwain. Cambridge, Mass.: Harvard Univ. Press, 1918.

Jewel, John. *An Apologie of the Church of England.* In *English Reformers,* edited by Parker.

Kethe, William. *A Sermon Made at Blandford Forum, in the Countie of Dorset.* . . . London, 1571.

Langland, William. *Piers the Ploughman.* Translated by J. F. Goodridge. Harmondsworth, England: Penguin, 1959. Reprint, 1964.

―――. *Piers Plowman: The B Version. Will's Visions of Piers Plowman, Do-Well, Do-Better and Do-Best.* Edition of Trinity College, Cambridge, MS B.15.17, corrected and restored, with variant readings, by George Kane and E. Talbot Donaldson. Vol. 2 of *Piers Plowman: The Three Versions,* edited by George Kane. London: Athlone, 1975.

Lasco, John à. "The Judgement of Master John à Lasco," from J. B., *The Fortress of Fathers,* 1566. In *Elizabethan Puritanism,* edited by Trinterud. New York: Oxford Univ. Press, 1971.

Leith, John H., ed. *Creeds of the Churches.* 3rd ed. Atlanta: John Knox, 1982.

Lodge, Thomas. *The Divell Conjured.* London, 1596. In *The Complete Works of Thomas Lodge,* 4 vols., Glasgow, 1883. Reprint, New York: Johnson Reprint, 1966.

Lupton, Thomas. *A Dreame of the Divell and Dives.* . . . London, 1589.

―――. *A Moral and Pitieful Comedie, Intituled, All for Money. Plainely Representing the Manners of Men, and Fashion of the World Noweadayes.* London, 1578. Edinburgh: Tudor Facsimile Texts, 1910. Reprint, New York: Ams, 1970.

Luther, Martin. *Martin Luther: Selections from His Writings.* Edited by John Dillenberger. New York: Doubleday, 1961.

M., I. [Gervase Markham] *A Health to the Gentlemanly Profession of Serving-*

Men, 1598. Shakespeare Association Facsimiles, no. 3. London: Oxford Univ. Press, 1931.

Macey, George. *A Sermon Preached at Charde in the Countie of Somerset, the Second of March 1597. . . .* London, 1601.

The Marprelate Tracts, 1588, 1589. Edited by William Pierce. London: James Clarke, 1911.

Marx, Karl, and F. Engels. *The Communist Manifesto*. New York: Pocket Books, 1964.

Medwall, Henry. *The Plays of Henry Medwall*. Edited by Alan H. Nelson. Cambridge: D. S. Brewer, 1980.

Milton, John. *The Complete Prose Works of John Milton*. Vol. 1, *1624–1642*. Edited by Don M. Wolfe. New Haven: Yale Univ. Press, 1953.

———. *Paradise Lost*. Edited by William G. Madsen. New York: Modern Library, 1969.

The Mirror for Magistrates. Edited by Lily B. Campbell. Cambridge: Cambridge Univ. Press, 1938. Reprint, New York: Barnes and Noble, 1960.

Montaigne, Michel de. *The Essays, 1603*. Translated by John Florio. Menston, England: Scolar, 1969.

More, George. *A Demonstration of God in His Workes*. London, 1597.

More, Thomas. *Utopia*. Translated and edited by H. V. S. Ogden. New York: Appleton-Century-Crofts, 1949.

Nenna, Giovanni Battista. *Nennio; or, A Treatise of Nobility*. Translated by W. Jones. 1595. Reprint, Jerusalem: Israel Univ. Press, 1967.

New Custom. In *Early English Dramatists, Anonymous Plays*, 3rd series, edited by John S. Farmer. London: Early English Drama Society, 1906. Reprint, Guildford, England: Charles W. Traylen, 1966.

The Office of Christian Parents: Shewing How Children Are to Be Governed throughout All Ages and Times of Their Life. Cambridge, 1616.

Pagitt, Ephraim. *Heresiography*. 3rd ed. London, 1646.

Parker, Matthew. *Correspondence of Matthew Parker*. Edited by John Bruce. Cambridge: Cambridge Univ. Press, 1853.

Parker, T. H. L., ed. *English Reformers*. Library of Christian Classics, no. 26. Philadelphia: Westminster, 1966.

Perkins, William. *The Work of William Perkins*. Edited by Ian Breward. Appleford, England: Sutton Courtenay, 1970.

Pliny. *Natural History*. Translated by H. Rackham. London: Heinemann; Cambridge, Mass.: Harvard Univ. Press, 1947.

Ponet, John. *A Short Treatise of Politic Power, 1556*. Reprint, Menston, England: Scolar, 1970.

Porter, H. C. *Puritanism in Tudor England*. London: Macmillan, 1970.

Prudentius. *The Poems of Prudentius*. Vol. 2, *Apologetic and Didactic Poems*.

Translated by Sister M. Clement Eagan. The Fathers of the Church, no. 52. Washington, D.C.: Catholic Univ. of America Press, 1965.

Puttenham, George. *The Arte of English Poesie.* 1589. In *Elizabethan Critical Essays,* vol. 2, edited by G. Gregory Smith. London: Oxford Univ. Press, 1964.

Quippes for Upstart Newfangled Gentlewomen; or, A Glasse, to View the Pride of Vainglorious Women. London, 1595.

Richardson, Charles. *A Sermon against Oppression and Fraudulent Dealing.* London, 1615.

Ridley, Nicholas. "A Brief Declaration of the Lord's Supper; or, A Treatise against the Error of Transubstantiation Written by Nicholas Ridley . . . During His Imprisonment, A.D. 1555." In *The Works of Nicholas Ridley,* edited by Henry Christmas. Cambridge: Cambridge Univ. Press, 1843.

———. "A Treatise agaynst the Errour of Transubstantiation, and Extracts from his Examinations." In *English Reformers,* edited by Parker.

Sandys, Edwin. *The Sermons of Edwin Sandys.* Edited by John Ayre. Cambridge: Cambridge Univ. Press, 1841. Reprint, New York: Johnson Reprint, 1968.

Saussure, Ferdinand de. *Course in General Linguistics.* Edited by Charles Bally and Albert Sechehaye, in collaboration with Albert Riedlinger; translated by Wade Baskin. New York: McGraw Hill, 1966.

———. *Cours de Linguistique Générale,* critical edition. Edited by Tullio de Mauro. Paris: Payot, 1973.

"A Second Admonition to the Parliament." In *Puritan Manifestoes,* edited by Frere and Douglas.

Seneca. *Ad Lucilium Epistulae Morales.* 3 vols. Translated by Richard M. Gummere. Cambridge: Harvard Univ. Press, 1953.

Shakespeare, William. *The Parallel King Lear, 1608–1623.* Prepared by Michael Warren. Berkeley: Univ. of California Press, 1989.

———. *The Riverside Shakespeare.* Boston: Houghton Mifflin, 1974.

Spenser, Edmund. *The Poetical Works of Edmund Spenser.* Ed. J. C. Smith and E. de Selincourt. London: Oxford Univ. Press, 1963.

Stockwood, John. *A Sermon Preached at Paule's Cross on Barthelmew Day.* London, 1578.

Stubbes, Phillip. *Phillip Stubbes's Anatomy of the Abuses in England in Shakspere's Youth, A.D. 1583.* Edited by Frederick J. Furnivall. London: N. Trübner, 1877–79.

Sutton, Christopher. *Disce Mori: Learne to Die.* London, 1601.

T., F. *The Debate betweene Pride and Lowlines, Pleaded to an Issue in Assise.* London, [1577?].

Tawney, R. H., and Eileen Power, eds. *Tudor Economic Documents: Being*

Select Documents Illustrating the Economic and Social History of Tudor England. Vol. 3. London: Longmans, Green, 1924. Reprint, 1951.

Tertullian. *Disciplinary, Moral, and Ascetical Works*. The Fathers of the Church, no. 40. New York: Fathers of the Church, 1959.

Thomas of Woodstock. Edited by George Parfitt and Simon Shepherd. Nottingham: Nottingham Univ. Press, 1977.

The Three Ladies of London (London, 1584). In *A Select Collection of Old English Plays*, vol. 6. Originally published by Robert Dodsley, 1744; 4th ed. revised by W. Carew Hazlitt, 1874-76. Reissue, New York: Benjamin Blom, 1964.

The Three Lords and Three Ladies of London (London, 1590). In *A Select Collection of Old English Plays*, vol. 6. Originally published by Robert Dodsley, 1744; revised by W. Carew Hazlitt, 1874-76. Reissue, New York: Benjamin Blom, 1964.

Tilley, Morris Palmer. *A Dictionary of the Proverbs in England in the Sixteenth and Seventeenth Centuries*. Ann Arbor: Univ. of Michigan Press, 1950.

Travers, Walter. *A Full and Plaine Declaration of Ecclesiastical Discipline*. Zurich, 1574.

The Trial of Treasure (London, 1567). In *Early English Dramatists, Anonymous Plays*. Edited by John S. Farmer. London: Early English Drama Society, 1906. Reprint, Guildford, England: Charles W. Traylen, 1966.

Trinterud, Leonard, ed. *Elizabethan Puritanism*. New York: Oxford Univ. Press, 1971.

Twenty-Six Political and Other Poems. Edited by J. Kail. Early English Text Society, o.s., no. 124. London: K. Paul, Trench, Trübner, 1904.

Tyndale, William. *An Answer to Sir Thomas More's Dialogue, The Supper of the Lord . . . by William Tyndale*. Edited by Henry Walter. Cambridge: Cambridge Univ. Press, 1850.

Vaughan, William. *The Golden Grove*. London, 1600.

Walwyn, William. *The Writings of William Walwyn*. Edited by Jack R. McMichael and Barbara Taft. Athens: Univ. of Georgia Press, 1989.

Warren, Arthur. *The Poore Man's Passions and Povertie's Patience*. London, 1605.

Wentworth Papers, 1597-1628. Edited by J. P. Cooper. Camden Fourth Series, vol. 12. London: Royal Historical Society, 1973.

Whitgift, John. *The Works of John Whitgift*. 3 vols. Edited by John Ayre. Cambridge: Cambridge Univ. Press, 1851-53.

Wilkinson, Robert. *A Sermon Preached at North-Hampton the 21 of June Last Past . . . upon the Occasion of the Late Rebellion and Riots in Those Parts Committed*. London, 1607.

Winstanley, Gerrard. *The Law of Freedom and other Writings*. Edited by Christopher Hill. Harmondsworth, England: Penguin, 1973.

Wittgenstein, Ludwig. *The Blue and Brown Books.* New York: Harper and Row, 1965.

———. *Philosophical Investigations.* Oxford: Basil Blackwell, 1968.

Woodstock, A Moral History. Edited by A. P. Rossiter. London: Chatto and Windus, 1946.

Woolton, John. *The Christian Manuell; or, Of the Life and Maners of True Christians.* London, 1576.

Wright, Leonard. *A Summons for Sleepers.* [London], 1589.

The Zurich Letters. Edited by Hastings Robinson. Cambridge: Cambridge Univ. Press, 1842.

Secondary Sources

Alford, John A., ed. *A Companion to "Piers Plowman."* Berkeley: Univ. of California Press, 1988.

Altman, Joel B. *The Tudor Play of Mind: Rhetorical Inquiry and the Development of Elizabethan Drama.* Berkeley: Univ. of California Press, 1978.

Amrine, Frederick, et al. "The Status of Evidence: A Roundtable." *PMLA* 111, no. 1 (January 1996): 21–31.

Archer, Ian W. *The Pursuit of Stability: Social Relations in Elizabethan London.* Cambridge: Cambridge Univ. Press, 1991.

Ariès, Philippe, and Georges Duby, eds. *A History of Private Life.* Vol. 3, *Passions of the Renaissance.* Cambridge, Mass.: Harvard Univ. Press, Belknap Press, 1989.

Asals, Heather. *Equivocal Predication: George Herbert's Way to God.* Toronto: Univ. of Toronto Press, 1981.

Ashelford, Jane. *Dress in the Age of Elizabeth I.* New York: Holmes and Meier, 1988.

Attridge, Derek. "Puttenham's Perplexity: Nature, Art, and the Supplement in Renaissance Poetic Theory." In *Literary Theory/Renaissance Texts,* edited by Patricia Parker and David Quint. Baltimore: Johns Hopkins Univ. Press, 1986.

Auden, W. H. Introduction to *George Herbert: Selected by W. H. Auden.* London: Penguin, 1973.

Axton, Marie. *The Queen's Two Bodies: Drama and the Elizabethan Succession.* London: Royal Historical Society, 1977.

Babbage, Stuart Barton. *Puritanism and Richard Bancroft.* London: S.P.C.K., 1962.

Baldwin, Anna P. "The Historical Context." In *Companion to "Piers Plowman,"* edited by Alford.

Baldwin, Frances Elizabeth. *Sumptuary Legislation and Personal Regulation in England.* Johns Hopkins University Studies in Historical and Political Science, ser. 14, no. 1. Baltimore: Johns Hopkins Univ. Press, 1926.

Barish, Jonas A. "Exhibitionism and the Antitheatrical Prejudice." *ELH*, 36, no. 7 (March 1969): 1–29.

Barish, Jonas A., and Marshall Waingrow. "'Service' in *King Lear.*" *Shakespeare Quarterly* 9, no. 3 (1958): 347–55.

Barker, Francis, and Peter Hulme. "Nymphs and Reapers Heavily Vanish: the Discursive Con-Texts of *The Tempest.*" In *Alternative Shakespeares,* edited by Drakakis.

Barroll, Leeds. "A New History for Shakespeare and His Time." *Shakespeare Quarterly* 39, no. 4 (1988): 441–64.

Beier, A. L. *Masterless Men: The Vagrancy Problem in England, 1560–1640.* London: Methuen, 1985.

———. *The Problem of the Poor in Tudor and Early Stuart England.* London: Methuen, 1983.

Bell, Quentin. *On Human Finery.* London: Hogarth, 1976.

Belsey, Catherine. *Critical Practice.* London: Methuen, 1980. Reprint, London: Routledge, 1988.

———. "Literature, History, Politics." In *New Historicism and Renaissance Drama,* edited by Wilson and Dutton.

Berlin, Brent, and Paul Kay. *Basic Color Terms: Their Universality and Evolution.* Berkeley: Univ. of California Press, 1969.

Berman, Art. *From the New Criticism to Deconstruction: The Reception of Structuralism and Post-Structuralism.* Urbana: Univ. of Illinois Press, 1988.

Bestul, Thomas H. *Satire and Allegory in "Wynnere and Wastoure."* Lincoln: Univ. of Nebraska Press, 1974.

Bevington, David. Review of *Shakespearean Iconoclasm* by James R. Siemon. *Shakespeare Quarterly* 37, no. 1 (1986): 125–26.

———. *Tudor Drama and Politics: A Critical Approach to Topical Meaning.* Cambridge, Mass.: Harvard Univ. Press, 1968.

Black, Max. "Some Troubles with Whorfianism." In *Language and Philosophy,* edited by Hook.

Blau, Sheridan. "George Herbert's Homiletic Theory." *George Herbert Journal* 1, no. 2 (spring 1978): 17–29.

Bottomley, Frank. *Attitudes to the Body in Western Christendom.* London: Lepus, 1979.

Bourne, E. C. E. *The Anglicanism of William Laud.* London: S.P.C.K., 1947.

Braunmuller, A. R. "'To the Globe I Rowed': John Holles Sees *A Game at Chess.*" *English Literary Renaissance* 20, no. 2 (spring 1990): 340–56.

Brown, Peter. *The Body and Society: Men, Women and Sexual Renunciation in Early Christianity.* New York: Columbia Univ. Press, 1988.

Buchowski, Michal, David B. Kronenfeld, William Peterman, and Lynn Thomas. "Language, *Nineteen Eighty-Four,* and 1989." *Language in Society* 23, no. 4 (1994): 555–78.

Cain, William E. "The Crisis of the Literary Left: Notes toward a Renewal of Humanism." In *After Poststructuralism,* edited by Easterlin and Riebling.

Carlson, Leland H. *Martin Marprelate, Gentleman: Master Job Throkmorton Laid Open in His Colors.* San Marino, Calif.: Huntington Library, 1981.

Chadwick, Henry. *Priscillian of Avila: The Occult and the Charismatic in the Early Church.* Oxford: Clarendon, 1976.

Charney, Maurice. " 'We Put Fresh Garments on Him': Nakedness and Clothes in *King Lear.*" In *Some Facets of "King Lear,"* edited by Colie and Flahiff.

Cockburn, James S. *A History of English Assizes, 1558–1714.* Cambridge: Cambridge Univ. Press, 1972.

Cohen, Walter. *Drama of a Nation: Public Theater in Renaissance England and Spain.* Ithaca: Cornell Univ. Press, 1985.

———. "Political Criticism of Shakespeare." In *Shakespeare Reproduced,* edited by Howard and O'Connor.

Cohn, Norman. *The Pursuit of the Millennium: Revolutionary Millenarians and Mystical Anarchists of the Middle Ages.* New York: Oxford Univ. Press, 1970.

Colie, Rosalie L. "The Energies of Endurance: Biblical Echo in *King Lear.*" In *Some Facets of "King Lear,"* edited by Colie and Flahiff.

———. "Reason and Need: *King Lear* and the 'Crisis' of the Aristocracy." In *Some Facets of "King Lear,"* edited by Colie and Flahiff.

Colie, Rosalie L., and F. T. Flahiff, eds. *Some Facets of "King Lear": Essays in Prismatic Criticism.* London: Heinemann, 1974.

Collinson, Patrick. *The Religion of Protestants: The Church in English Society, 1559–1625.* Oxford: Clarendon, 1982.

Cooper, J. P. "Patterns of Inheritance and Settlement by Great Landowners from the Fifteenth to the Eighteenth Centuries." In *Family and Inheritance,* edited by Goody, Thirsk and Thompson.

Coward, Barry. "Was There an English Revolution in the Middle of the Seventeenth Century?" In *Politics and People in Revolutionary England,* edited by Jones, Newitt, and Roberts.

Craik, T. W. *The Tudor Interlude: Stage, Costume, and Acting.* Leicester: Leicester Univ. Press, 1958.

Cross, F. L., and E. A. Livingstone. *The Oxford Dictionary of the Christian Church.* London: Oxford Univ. Press, 1974.

Culler, Jonathan. *Structuralist Poetics: Structuralism, Linguistics, and the Study of Literature.* Ithaca: Cornell Univ. Press, 1975. Reprint, 1976.

Cunnington, C. Willet, and Phillis Cunnington. *Handbook of English Costume in the Seventeenth Century.* 3rd ed. London: Faber and Faber, 1972.

Curtis, Mark H. "Hampton Court Conference and Its Aftermath." *History* 46, no. 156 (February 1961): 1–16.

Cust, Richard, and Ann Hughes, eds. *Conflict in Early Stuart England: Studies in Religion and Politics, 1603–1642.* London: Longman, 1989.

Danby, John F. *Shakespeare's Doctrine of Nature: A Study of "King Lear."* London: Faber and Faber, 1948. Reprint, 1965.

Davies, Horton. *Worship and Theology in England from Cranmer to Hooker, 1534–1603.* Princeton: Princeton Univ. Press, 1970.

Davis, Natalie Zemon. "Women on Top: Symbolic Sexual Inversion and Political Disorder in Early Modern Europe." In *The Reversible World: Symbolic Inversion in Art and Society,* edited by Barbara A. Babcock, Ithaca: Cornell Univ. Press, 1978.

Delany, Paul. "*King Lear* and the Decline of Feudalism." *PMLA* 92, no. 3 (May 1977): 429–40.

Diehl, Huston. "Graven Images: Protestant Emblem Books in England." *Renaissance Quarterly* 39, no. 1 (spring 1986): 49–66.

Digby, Kenelm Edward. *An Introduction to the History of the Law of Real Property.* 4th ed. Oxford: Clarendon, 1892.

Dollimore, Jonathan. *Radical Tragedy: Religion, Ideology, and Power in the Drama of Shakespeare and His Contemporaries.* 2nd ed. Durham, N.C.: Duke Univ. Press, 1993.

Dollimore, Jonathan, and Alan Sinfield, eds. *Political Shakespeare: New Essays in Cultural Materialism.* Ithaca: Cornell Univ. Press, 1985.

Drakakis, John, ed. *Alternative Shakespeares.* London: Methuen, 1985.

Dugmore, Clifford William. *The Mass and the English Reformers.* London: Macmillan, 1958.

Dunham, William Huse, Jr. "Regal Power and the Rule of Law: A Tudor Paradox." *Journal of British Studies* 3 (1964): 24–56.

Dutton, Richard. "Postscript." In *New Historicism and Renaissance Drama,* edited by Wilson and Dutton.

Eagleton, Terry. *Literary Theory: An Introduction.* Minneapolis: Univ. of Minnesota Press, 1983.

———. *William Shakespeare.* Oxford: Basil Blackwell, 1986.

Easterlin, Nancy, and Barbara Riebling, eds. *After Poststructuralism: Interdisciplinarity and Literary Theory.* Evanston, Ill.: Northwestern Univ. Press, 1993.

Ellis, John M. *Against Deconstruction.* Princeton: Princeton Univ. Press, 1989.

Elton, G. R., ed. *The New Cambridge Modern History.* Vol. 2, *The Reformation, 1520–1559.* Cambridge: Cambridge Univ. Press, 1958.

Evans, J. Claude. *Strategies of Deconstruction: Derrida and the Myth of the Voice.* Minneapolis: Univ. of Minnesota Press, 1991.

Evans, J. Martin. *"Paradise Lost" and the Genesis Tradition.* Oxford: Clarendon, 1968.

Fairholt, F. W. *Costume in England: A History of Dress to the End of the Eighteenth Century.* Revised by H. A. Dillon. London: George Bell and Sons, 1885. Reissue, Detroit: Singing Tree, 1968.

Fairlamb, Horace L. *Critical Conditions: Postmodernity and the Question of Foundations.* Cambridge: Cambridge Univ. Press, 1994.

Finkelpearl, Philip J. *John Marston of the Middle Temple.* Cambridge, Mass.: Harvard Univ. Press, 1969.

Fletcher, Anthony, and John Stevenson, eds. *Order and Disorder in Early Modern England.* Cambridge: Cambridge Univ. Press, 1985.

Foakes, R. A. *"Hamlet" versus "Lear": Cultural Politics and Shakespeare's Art.* Cambridge: Cambridge Univ. Press, 1993.

Fogelin, Robert J. *Wittgenstein.* London: Routledge and Kegan Paul, 1976.

Fraser, Russell A. *Shakespeare's Poetics in Relation to "King Lear."* London: Routledge and Kegan Paul, 1962.

Frye, Dean. "The Context of Lear's Unbuttoning." *ELH* 32 (1965): 17–31.

Gallagher, Catherine. "Marxism and the New Historicism." In *The New Historicism,* edited by Veeser.

Galloway, Bruce. *The Union of England and Scotland, 1603–1608.* Edinburgh: John Donald, 1986.

Gardiner, Samuel. *History of England from the Accession of James 1 to the Disgrace of Chief-Justice Coke, 1603–1616.* London: Hurst and Blackett, 1863.

George, Charles H., and Katherine George. *The Protestant Mind of the English Reformation, 1570–1640.* Princeton: Princeton Univ. Press, 1961.

Gerrish, B. A. "The Lord's Supper in the Reformed Confessions." *Theology Today* 23 (1966): 224–43.

Goldsmith, Maurice. "Levelling by Sword, Spade and Word: Radical Egalitarianism in the English Revolution." In *Politics and People in Revolutionary England,* edited by Jones, Newitt, and Roberts.

Goody, Jack, Joan Thirsk, and E. P. Thompson, eds. *Family and Inheritance: Rural Society in Western Europe, 1200–1800.* Cambridge: Cambridge Univ. Press, 1976.

Goody, Jack. "Inheritance, Property and Women." In *Family and Inheritance,* edited by Goody, Thirsk, and Thompson.

Graff, Gerald. "Co-optation." In *The New Historicism,* edited by Veeser.

Grant, Patrick. *The Transformation of Sin.* Montreal: McGill-Queens Univ. Press, 1974.

Greaves, Richard L. *Society and Religion in Elizabethan England.* Minneapolis: Univ. of Minnesota Press, 1981.

Greenblatt, Stephen. *The Forms of Power and the Power of Forms in the Renaissance.* Norman, Okla.: Pilgrim Books, 1982.

—. *Learning to Curse: Essays in Early Modern Culture.* New York: Routledge, 1990.

—. *Renaissance Self-Fashioning from More to Shakespeare.* Chicago: Univ. of Chicago Press, 1980.

—. *Shakespearean Negotiations: The Circulation of Social Energy in Renaissance England.* Berkeley: Univ. of California Press, 1988.

Greenblatt, Stephen, and Giles Gunn, eds. *Redrawing the Boundaries: The Transformation of English and American Literary Studies.* New York: Modern Language Association of America, 1992.

Greenfield, Thelma Nelson. "The Clothing Motif in *King Lear.*" *Shakespeare Quarterly* 5, no. 3 (1954): 281–86.

Grudin, Robert. *Mighty Opposites: Shakespeare and Renaissance Contrariety.* Berkeley: Univ. of California Press, 1979.

Haigh, Christopher, ed. *The Reign of Elizabeth I.* London: Macmillan, 1984.

Haller, William. *The Rise of Puritanism.* New York: Columbia Univ. Press, 1938. Reprint, 1947.

Harland, Richard. *Superstructuralism: The Philosophy of Structuralism and Post-Structuralism.* London: Methuen, 1987.

Hastings, James, ed. *The Encyclopaedia of Religion and Ethics.* New York: Charles Scribner's Sons, 1951.

Hawkes, Terence. *Structuralism and Semiotics.* Berkeley: Univ. of California Press, 1977.

Heal, Felicity. "The Idea of Hospitality in Early Modern England." *Past and Present*, no. 102 (February 1984): 66–93.

—. *Of Prelates and Princes: A Study of the Economic and Social Position of the Tudor Episcopate.* Cambridge: Cambridge Univ. Press, 1980.

Heilman, Robert Bechtold. *This Great Stage: Image and Structure in "King Lear."* Baton Rouge: Louisiana State Univ. Press, 1948.

Heinemann, Margot. " 'Demystifying the Mystery of State': *King Lear* and the World Upside Down." *Shakespeare Survey* 44 (1992): 75–83.

Herr, Alan F. *The Elizabethan Sermon.* New York: Octagon, 1969.

Hill, Christopher. *Change and Continuity in Seventeenth-Century England.* London: Weidenfeld and Nicolson, 1974.

—. *The Collected Essays of Christopher Hill.* Vol. 1, *Writing and Revolution in Seventeenth-Century England.* Brighton: Harvester, 1985.

—. *The Collected Essays of Christopher Hill.* Vol. 2, *Religion and Politics in Seventeenth-Century England.* Brighton: Harvester, 1986.

—. "Political Discourse in Early Seventeenth-Century England." In *Politics and People in Revolutionary England,* edited by Jones, Newitt, and Roberts.

————. *Society and Puritanism in Pre-Revolutionary England.* New York: Schocken, 1964.

————. *The World Turned Upside Down: Radical Ideas During the English Revolution.* London: Temple Smith, 1972.

Hobday, Charles. "Clouted Shoon and Leather Aprons: Shakespeare and the Egalitarian Tradition." *Renaissance and Modern Studies* 23 (1979): 63–78.

Holderness, Graham, Nick Potter, and John Turner. *Shakespeare: The Play of History.* Basingstoke, England: Macmillan, 1988.

Holstun, James. "Ranting at the New Historicism." *English Literary Renaissance* 19 (1989): 189–225.

Homans, George C. *English Villagers of the Thirteenth Century.* Cambridge: Harvard Univ. Press, 1941. Reprint, New York: Harper and Row, 1970.

Hook, Sidney, ed. *Language and Philosophy.* New York: New York Univ. Press, 1969.

Horden, John, ed. *Halkett and Laing: A Dictionary of Anonymous and Pseudonymous Publications in the English Language, 1475-1640.* 3rd ed. Harlow, England: Longman Group, 1980.

Horwitz, Howard. "'I Can't Remember': Skepticism, Synthetic Histories, Critical Action." *South Atlantic Quarterly* 87, no. 4 (fall 1988): 787–820.

Houlbrooke, Ralph A. *The English Family, 1450-1700.* London: Longman, 1984.

Howard, Jean E. "The New Historicism in Renaissance Studies." *English Literary Renaissance* 1986, no. 1 (winter 1986): 13–43.

Howard, Jean E., and Marion F. O'Connor, eds. *Shakespeare Reproduced: The Text in History and Ideology.* New York: Methuen, 1987.

Hutson, Lorna. *Thomas Nashe in Context.* Oxford: Clarendon, 1989.

Ives, Eric W. "The Reputation of the Common Lawyers in English Society, 1450-1550." *University of Birmingham Historical Journal* 7 (1959–60): 130–61.

Jones, Colin, Malyn Newitt, and Stephen Roberts, eds. *Politics and People in Revolutionary England: Essays in Honour of Ivan Roots.* Oxford: Basil Blackwell, 1986.

Jones, William J. *The Elizabethan Court of Chancery.* Oxford: Clarendon, 1967.

Jordan, Wilbur K. *Philanthropy in England, 1480-1660.* London: George Allen and Unwin, 1964.

Kamps, Ivo, ed. *Shakespeare Left and Right.* New York: Routledge, 1991.

Kastan, David Scott. "'The King Hath Many Marching in His Coats'; or, What Did You Do During the War, Daddy?" In *Shakespeare Left and Right*, edited by Kamps. New York: Routledge, 1991.

————. "Proud Majesty Made a Subject: Shakespeare and the Spectacle of Rule." *Shakespeare Quarterly* 37, no. 4 (1986): 459–75.

Kavanagh, James H. "Shakespeare in Ideology." In *Alternative Shakespeares*, edited by Drakakis.

Keeton, George Williams. *Shakespeare's Legal and Political Background*. New York: Barnes and Noble, 1958.

Kent, Joan. "Attitudes of Members of the House of Commons to the Regulation of 'Personal Conduct' in Late Elizabethan and Early Stuart England." *Bulletin of the Institute of Historical Research* 46, no. 113 (May 1973): 41–71.

Kettle, Arnold. "From *Hamlet* to *Lear*." In *Shakespeare in a Changing World*, edited by Arnold Kettle. London: Lawrence and Wishart, 1964.

Kibbey, Ann. *The Interpretation of Material Shapes in Puritanism: A Study of Rhetoric, Prejudice and Violence*. Cambridge: Cambridge Univ. Press, 1986.

Knafla, Louis A. *Law and Politics in Jacobean England: The Tracts of Lord Chancellor Ellesmere*. Cambridge: Cambridge Univ. Press, 1977.

Kronenfeld, David B. *Plastic Glasses and Church Fathers: Semantic Extension from the Ethnoscience Tradition*. New York: Oxford Univ. Press, 1996.

Kronenfeld, David B., and Henry W. Decker. "Structuralism." *Annual Review of Anthropology* 8 (1979): 503–41.

Kronenfeld, Judy Z. "Post-Saussurean Semantics, Reformation Religious Controversy, and Contemporary Critical Disagreement." *Assays: Critical Approaches to Medieval and Renaissance Texts* 5 (1989): 135–65.

——. "Probing the Relation between Poetry and Ideology: Herbert's 'The Windows.'" *John Donne Journal: Studies in the Age of Donne* 2 (1983): 55–80.

——. "Social Rank and the Pastoral Ideals of *As You Like It*." *Shakespeare Quarterly* 29, no. 3 (1978): 333–48.

——. *So Distribution Should Undo Excess, and Each Man Have Enough*: Anabaptist Egalitarianism, Anglican Charity, Both, Neither? *ELH* 59 (1992): 755–84.

——. "Yes, Virginia, There IS a World." *Associated Writing Programs Chronicle* 25, no. 2 (October/November 1992): 15–18.

Lake, Peter. "Anti-Popery: The Structure of a Prejudice." In *Conflict in Early Stuart England*, edited by Cust and Hughes.

——. *Anglicans and Puritans? Presbyterianism and English Conformist Thought from Whitgift to Hooker*. London: Unwin Hyman, 1988.

Lane, Anthony. "Degrees of Cool." *New Yorker* (October 10, 1994): 95–97.

Laslett, Peter. *The English Family, 1450–1700*. London: Longman, 1984.

——. Introduction to *Patriarchia and Other Political Works* by Robert Filmer, edited by Peter Laslett. Oxford: Basil Blackwell, 1949.

Laslett, Peter, and R. Wall, eds. *Household and Family in Past Time*. Cambridge: Cambridge Univ. Press, 1972.

Leff, Gordon. *Heresy in the Later Middle Ages.* 2 vols. Manchester: Manchester Univ. Press, 1967.

Leider, Emily W. "Plainness of Style in *King Lear.*" *Shakespeare Quarterly* 21, no. 1 (1970): 45–53.

Leinwand, Theodore B. "Negotiation and New Historicism." *PMLA* 105, no. 3 (May 1990): 477–90.

Leonard, E. M. *The Early History of English Poor Relief.* Cambridge, 1900. Reprint, London: Frank Cass, 1965.

Lindheim, Nancy. "*King Lear* as Pastoral Tragedy." In *Facets of "King Lear,"* edited by Colie and Flahiff.

Lounsbury, Floyd G. "Language and Culture." In *Language and Philosophy,* edited by Hook.

Lyons, John. *Semantics.* 2 vols. Cambridge: Cambridge Univ. Press, 1977.

Macfarlane, Alan. *Marriage and Love in England: Modes of Reproduction, 1300–1840.* Oxford: Basil Blackwell, 1986.

McGee, J. Sears. *The Godly Man in Stuart England: Anglicans, Puritans, and the Two Tables, 1620–1670.* New Haven: Yale Univ. Press, 1976.

McGregor, J. F., and B. Reay, eds. *Radical Religion in the English Revolution.* Oxford: Oxford Univ. Press, 1984.

McKitterick, David. *A History of Cambridge University Press.* Vol. 1, *Printing and the Book Trade in cambridge, 1534–1698.* Cambridge: Cambridge Univ. Press, 1992.

MacLure, Millar. *The Paul's Cross Sermons, 1534–1642.* Toronto: Univ. of Toronto Press, 1958.

McLuskie, Kathleen. "The Patriarchal Bard: Feminist Criticism and Shakespeare: *King Lear* and *Measure for Measure.*" In *Political Shakespeare,* edited by Dollimore and Sinfield.

Madsen, William G. *From Shadowy Types to Truth: Studies in Milton's Symbolism.* New Haven: Yale Univ. Press, 1968.

Manning, Roger B. *Village Revolts: Social Protest and Popular Disturbances in England, 1509–1640.* Oxford: Clarendon, 1988.

Marcus, Leah S. *Childhood and Cultural Despair: A Theme and Variations in Seventeenth-Century Literature.* Pittsburgh: Univ. of Pittsburgh Press, 1978.

————. "George Herbert and the Anglican Plain Style." In *"Too Rich to Clothe the Sunne": Essays on George Herbert,* edited by Claude J. Summers and Ted-Larry Pebworth. Pittsburgh: Univ. of Pittsburgh Press, 1980.

————. *Puzzling Shakespeare: Local Reading and Its Discontents.* Berkeley: Univ. of California Press, 1988.

Marshall, Dorothy. *The English Domestic Servant in History.* London: George Philip and Son, 1949.

Mauro, Tullio de. *Ludwig Wittgenstein: His Place in the Development of Semantics.* Dordrecht, Holland: D. Reidel, 1967.

Mehl, Dieter. "*King Lear* and the 'Poor Naked Wretches.'" In *Deutsche Shakespeare-Gesellschaft West Jahrbuch*. Heidelberg: Quelle and Meyer, 1975.

Milward, Peter. *Religious Controversies of the Jacobean Age: A Survey of Printed Sources*. London: Scolar, 1978.

Montrose, Louis. "New Historicisms." In *Redrawing the Boundaries*, edited by Greenblatt and Gunn.

———. "Professing the Renaissance: The Poetics and Politics of Culture." In *The New Historicism*, edited by Veeser.

———. "Renaissance Literary Studies and the Subject of History." *ELR* 16, no. 1 (winter 1986): 5–12.

Moretti, Franco. "'A Huge Eclipse': Tragic Form and the Deconsecration of Sovereignty." In *Forms of Power*, edited by Greenblatt.

Morris, Christopher. *Political Thought in England: Tyndale to Hooker*. London, Oxford Univ. Press, 1953.

Morse, Harriet K. *Elizabethan Pageantry: A Pictorial Survey of Costume and Its Commentators from c. 1560–1620*. London: Studio, 1934.

Munden, R. C. "James I and 'The Growth of Mutual Distrust': King, Commons, and Reform, 1603–1604." In *Faction and Parliament*, edited by Sharpe.

Norbrook, David. "Rhetoric, Ideology and the Elizabethan World Picture." In *Renaissance Rhetoric*, edited by Peter Mack. New York: St. Martin's, 1994.

Norris, Christopher. *Deconstruction: Theory and Practice*. London: Methuen, 1982.

Nouvelle Biographie Générale. Published by Firmin Didot Bros., under the direction of Dr. Hoefer. Paris, 1853–66. Reprint, Copenhagen: Rosenkilde et Bagger, 1963.

Ogilvie, Sir Charles. *The King's Government and the Common Law, 1471–1641*. Oxford: Basil Blackwell, 1958.

Pagels, Elaine. *Adam, Eve, and the Serpent*. New York: Random House, 1988.

Panofsky, Erwin. *Studies in Iconology: Humanistic Themes in the Art of the Renaissance*. New York: Harper and Row, 1962.

Patterson, Annabel. *Censorship and Interpretation: The Conditions of Writing and Reading in Early Modern England*. Madison: Univ. of Wisconsin Press, 1984.

———. *Reading between the Lines*. Madison: University of Wisconsin Press, 1993.

———. *Shakespeare and the Popular Voice*. Cambridge, Mass.: Basil Blackwell, 1989.

———. "The Very Name of the Game: Theories of Order and Disorder."

In *Literature and the English Civil War,* edited by Thomas Healy and Jonathan Sawday. Cambridge: Cambridge Univ. Press, 1990.

Pechter, Edward. "Against Ideology." In *Shakespeare Left and Right,* edited by Kamps.

―――. "The New Historicism and Its Discontents: Politicizing Renaissance Drama." *PMLA* 102, no. 3 (May 1987): 202–303.

Phillips, John. *The Reformation of Images: Destruction of Art in England, 1535–1660.* Berkeley: Univ. of California Press, 1973.

Phillips, O. Hood. *Shakespeare and the Lawyers.* London: Methuen, 1972.

Pierce, William. *An Historical Introduction to the Marprelate Tracts.* London: Archibald Constable, 1908.

Porter, Carolyn. "History and Literature: 'After the New Historicism.'" *New Literary History* 21 (1990): 253–73.

Pound, John. *Poverty and Vagrancy in Tudor England.* London: Longman, 1971.

Poynter, F. N. L. *A Bibliography of Gervase Markham, 1568?–1637.* Oxford: Oxford Bibliographical Society, 1962.

Rabkin, Norman. *Shakespeare and the Common Understanding.* New York: Free Press, 1968.

Ranald, Margaret Loftus. *Shakespeare and His Social Context: Essays in Osmotic Knowledge and Literary Interpretation.* New York: Ams, 1987.

Rosch, Eleanor. "Universals and Cultural Specifics in Human Categorization." In *Cross-Cultural Perspectives on Learning,* edited by Richard W. Brislin, Stephen Bochner, and Walter J. Lonner. New York: John Wiley and Sons, 1975.

Russell, Conrad. *The Crisis of Parliaments: English History, 1509–1660.* London: Oxford Univ. Press, 1971.

Sacks, David Harris. "Searching for 'Culture' in the English Renaissance." *Shakespeare Quarterly* 39, no. 4 (1988): 465–88.

Saxl, Fritz. "Veritas Filia Temporis." In *Philosophy and History: Essays Presented to Ernst Cassirer,* edited by Raymond Klibansky and H. J. Paton. Oxford: Clarendon, 1936. Reprint, New York: Harper and Row, 1963.

Scholes, Robert. *Semiotics and Interpretation.* New Haven: Yale Univ. Press, 1982.

―――. *Structuralism in Literature.* New Haven: Yale Univ. Press, 1974. Reprint, 1975.

Scodel, Joshua. "The Medium Is the Message: Donne's 'Satire 3,' 'To Sir Henry Wotton' (Sir, More Than Kisses), and the Ideologies of the Mean." *Modern Philology* 90, no. 4 (May 1993): 479–511.

Selden, Raman. "*King Lear* and True Need." *Shakespeare Studies* 19 (1987): 143–69.

―――. *A Reader's Guide to Contemporary Literary Theory.* Lexington: Univ. of Kentucky Press, 1989.

Shapiro, Alan. "Horace and the Reformation of Creative Writing." *American Poetry Review* 21, no. 2 (March–April 1992): 7–13.

Sharp, Buchanan. *In Contempt of All Authority: Rural Artisans and Riot in the West of England, 1586–1660.* Berkeley: Univ. of California Press, 1980.

Sharpe, James. "The People and the Law." In *Popular Culture in Seventeenth Century England,* edited by Barry Reay. London: Croom Helm, 1985.

Sharpe, Kevin, ed. *Faction and Parliament: Essays on Early Stuart History.* Oxford: Clarendon, 1978.

Shuger, Debora K. *Habits of Thought in the English Renaissance: Religion, Politics, and the Dominant Culture.* Berkeley: Univ. of California Press, 1990.

―――. *Sacred Rhetoric: The Christian Grand Style in the English Renaissance.* Princeton: Princeton Univ. Press, 1988.

―――. "Subversive Fathers and Suffering Subjects: Shakespeare and Christianity." In *Religion, Literature, and Politics in Post-Reformation England, 1540–1688,* edited by R. Strier and D. Hamilton. Cambridge: Cambridge Univ. Press, 1996.

Siemon, James R. *Shakespearean Iconoclasm.* Berkeley: Univ. of California Press, 1985.

Simon, Herbert A. *Models of Man: Mathematical Essays on Rational Human Behavior in a Social Setting.* New York: John Wiley and Sons, 1957.

Simpson, A. W. B. *An Introduction to the History of the Land Law,* Oxford: Oxford Univ. Press, 1961. Reprint, 1964.

Simpson, David. "Literary Criticism and the Return to 'History.'" *Critical Inquiry* 14 (summer 1988): 721–47.

Slack, Paul. "Poverty and Social Regulation in Elizabethan England." In *The Reign of Elizabeth I,* edited by Haigh.

―――, ed. *Rebellion, Popular Protest and the Social Order in Early Modern England.* Cambridge: Cambridge Univ. Press, 1984.

Smuts, R. Malcolm. *Court Culture and the Origins of a Royalist Tradition in Early Stuart England.* Philadelphia: Univ. of Pennsylvania Press, 1987.

Sommerville, Johann. "Ideology, Property and the Constitution." In *Conflict in Early Stuart England,* edited by Cust and Hughes.

―――. *Politics and Ideology in England, 1603–1640.* London: Longman, 1986.

Sprinker, Michael. "Commentary: 'You've Got a Lot of Nerve.'" In *Shakespeare Left and Right,* edited by Kamps.

Spufford, Margaret. *Contrasting Communities: English Villages in the Sixteenth and Seventeenth Centuries.* Cambridge: Cambridge Univ. Press, 1974.

―――. "Peasant Inheritance Customs and Land Distribution." In *Family and Inheritance,* edited by Goody, Thirsk, and Thompson.

Squire, Geoffrey. *Dress, Art and Society, 1560–1970.* London: Studio Vista, 1974.

Steadman, John. *The Hill and the Labyrinth: Discourse and Certitude in Milton and His Near-Contemporaries.* Berkeley: Univ. of California Press, 1984.

Stevenson, John. "The 'Moral Economy' of the English Crowd: Myth and Reality." In *Order and Disorder,* edited by Fletcher and Stevenson.

Stone, Lawrence. "Anatomy of the Elizabethan Aristocracy." *Economic History Review,* 18, nos. 1 and 2 (1948): 1–53.

———. *Crisis of the Aristocracy, 1558–1641.* Oxford: Clarendon, 1965.

———. *The Family, Sex and Marriage in England, 1500–1800.* New York: Harper and Row, 1977.

Strier, Richard. "Faithful Servants: Shakespeare's Praise of Disobedience." In *The Historical Renaissance: New Essays on Tudor and Stuart Literature and Culture,* edited by Heather Dubrow and Richard Strier. Chicago: Univ. of Chicago Press, 1988.

———. "History, Criticism, and Herbert: A Polemical Note." *Papers on Language and Literature* 17 (1981): 347–52.

———. *Love Known: Theology and Experience in George Herbert's Poetry.* Chicago: Univ. of Chicago Press, 1983.

———. *Resistant Structures: Particularity, Radicalism, and Renaissance Texts.* Berkeley: Univ. of California Press, 1995.

Summers, George. *George Herbert: His Religion and Art.* Cambridge, Mass.: Harvard Univ. Press, 1968.

Tallis, Raymond. *Not Saussure: A Critique of Post-Saussurean Literary Theory.* Basingstoke, England: Macmillan, 1988.

Taylor, Gary. "Monopolies, Show Trials, Disaster, and Invasion: *King Lear* and Censorship." In *Division of the Kingdoms,* edited by Taylor and Warren.

Taylor, Gary, and Michael Warren, eds. *The Division of the Kingdoms: Shakespeare's Two Versions of "King Lear."* Oxford: Clarendon, 1983.

Thirsk, Joan. "The European Debate on Customs of Inheritance, 1500–1700." In *Family and Inheritance,* edited by Goody, Thirsk, and Thompson.

Thomas, Brook. "The New Historicism and Other Old-Fashioned Topics." In *The New Historicism,* edited by Veeser.

Thomas, Keith. "Age and Authority in Early Modern England." *Proceedings of the British Academy* 62 (1976): 205–48.

Thompson, E. P. "The Moral Economy of the English Crowd in the Eighteenth Century." *Past and Present,* no. 50 (1971): 76–136.

Urkowitz, Steven. *Shakespeare's Revision of "King Lear."* Princeton: Princeton Univ. Press, 1980.

Veblen, Thorstein. *The Theory of the Leisure Class.* 1899. Reprint, New York: Penguin, 1979.

Veeser, H. Aram, ed. *The New Historicism.* New York: Routledge, 1989.

———, ed. *The New Historicism Reader.* New York: Routledge, 1994.

Vernon, John. *Poetry and the Body.* Urbana: Univ. of Illinois Press, 1979.

Walter, John, and Keith Wrightson. "Dearth and the Social Order in Early Modern England." In *Rebellion, Popular Protest and the Social Order in Early Modern England,* edited by Paul Slack. Cambridge: Cambridge Univ. Press, 1984.

Walzer, Michael. *The Revolution of the Saints: A Study in the Origins of Radical Politics.* Cambridge, Mass.: Harvard Univ. Press, 1965.

Warren, Roger. "The Folio Omission of the Mock Trial." In *Division of the Kingdoms,* edited by Taylor and Warren.

Wayne, Don E. "Power, Politics and the Shakespearean Text: Recent Criticism in England and the United States." In *Shakespeare Reproduced,* edited by Howard and O'Connor.

Whigham, Frank. *Ambition and Privilege: The Social Tropes of Elizabethan Courtesy Theory.* Berkeley: Univ. of California Press, 1984.

White, Hayden. *Tropics of Discourse: Essays in Cultural Criticism.* Baltimore: Johns Hopkins Univ. Press, 1978.

Wickham, Glynne. "From Tragedy to Tragi-Comedy: 'King Lear' as Prologue." *Shakespeare Survey* 26 (1973): 33–48.

Wills, Garry. "The Phallic Pulpit." *New York Review of Books* 36, no. 20 (Dec. 21, 1989): 26.

Wilson, Richard. "Introduction: Historicizing New Historicism." In *New Historicism and Renaissance Drama,* edited by Wilson and Dutton.

Wilson, Richard, and Richard Dutton, eds. *New Historicism and Renaissance Drama.* London: Longman, 1992.

Wind, Edgar. *Pagan Mysteries in the Renaissance.* London: Faber and Faber, 1958. Reprint, Harmondsworth, England: Penguin, 1967.

Wormuth, Francis D. *The Royal Prerogative, 1603–1649.* Ithaca: Cornell Univ. Press, 1939.

Wrightson, Keith. *English Society, 1580–1680.* New Brunswick, N.J.: Rutgers Univ. Press, 1982.

Yunck, John A. *The Lineage of Lady Meed: The Development of Mediaeval Veniality Satire.* Notre Dame, Ind.: University of Notre Dame Press, 1963.

Index

207, 211, 221–22, 249, 331 n.38, 338 n.8; ritual of, 41, 45, 47, 85
Catholics versus Protestants, 3, 41, 43, 46, 50, 85
Censorship, 212, 221; and the texts of *Lear*, 201, 224, 327 n.9
Ceremonies, 140, 144, 160; as "apparel of religion at the heart," 26; "attire" of, in sacrament, 22; Bradshaw and, 147–50, 306 n.64; and children's behavior toward parents, 103–4; in the church, 21, 26, 38–39; and edification, 72–74; as "externals," "middle ways," or "extremes," 68; justified by Pauline injunctions, 70; as more than "clothing," 258 n.2; "polluted clothing of," 28
Certaine Sermons or Homilies: "Against Disobedience and Wilfull Rebellion," 161; "Against Excess of Apparrell," 127, 130–31, 135–37, 177, 316 n.34; "Against Perill of Idolatry," 51, 85; and economic policy, 131; "Of Almes Deedes," 173
Chaderton, Laurence, 152
Chancery, Court of, 212–14, 331–32 n.41
Charity, Christian, 172–79, 182–90, 194–95, 198–99, 319 n.52; rank-based, 178–79, 182, 315 n.29, 316 n.34. *See also* Distribution; Poor: and fasts of rich; Poor: and poor laws; Poor: and private charity
Charles I, 146
Christian culture: and language of *Lear*, 12; and moral frame of *Lear*, 199, 238, 245; and oppositional conceptions, 252–53 n.9; radical and conservative possibilities of, 7; and "secular" drama, 13, 229; as system of

shared signs, 7–8; and traditional versus revolutionary ideas in *Lear*, 224
Christian culture, shared values of: against avarice, 236; and Catholics and Protestants, 68–69, 87, 107, 181; charity, 173, 182, 236, 244, 319 n.52; against confusion of degree, 133; and Cordelia, 97–100; deeds over words, 103; against idle retainers, 236–37; against idolatry, 68–69; inner truth versus externals, 104–5; inward and outward honor, 106; justice, 228; against levelling, 178–79; nakedness and proper clothing, 244; not simple attributes, 243; obeying God versus man, 166–67; and Pauline injunctions (1 Corinthians 14: 26, 40), 70, 72; plainness, 103; plainness and ceremony, 234, 244; plainness versus excessive adornment, 211; and present-day reader, 245; against rebellion, 166; resistance to tyranny, 248; stewardship, 187; summary of, 245–46. *See also* Equality, spiritual: and political inequality; Paternalism; "Truth the daughter of time"
Cicero: *De Officiis*, 162–65, 310 nn.95–96
Civil War, 10, 246, 261 n.34, 301–2 n.26; and question of polarization in early seventeenth century, 122, 295 n.77, 298 n.92; and Renaissance drama, 298 n.4; Whig versus revisionist history and, 115–16, 293–94 n.69
Clarke, Samuel: "The Life and Death of Mrs. Jane Ratcliffe," 104
Cleaver, Robert, 98

Craik, T. W., 80
Cranmer, Thomas (archbishop
of Canterbury), 43–44, 48–49,
87–88, 181
Creativity, linguistic, 9, 65–66,
230–31, 338 n.5; and metaphor,
30–31, 50–53, 62
Culler, Jonathan, 29, 64
Cultural materialism, 4–10,
210–11, 251 n.2, 252 n.7; and
deconstruction, 61
Cultural semiotics. *See* Nakedness
versus clothing, as semiotic
system
Culture, coded in language: as
shared, 2, 6–7, 65, 231, 235,
254 n.15 (*see also* Agency;
Creativity); as a system of
signs, 7

Dalechamp, Caleb, 174
Danby, John F., 97–98, 170–71,
178, 317 n.44
Daniel, Samuel: *Panegyricke Con-
gratulatorie to the King,* 220; "To
Sir Thomas Egerton," 214
Debate betweene Pride and Lowlines
(F.T.), 204–8, 211, 249, 316–17
n.38, 329 n.27
Deconstruction, 1–2, 5, 61–62, 66,
253 n.11
Deferral of meaning. *See* Indeter-
minacy
Definition of terms: and "cup[s]
and glass[es]," 53–55, 59; by
distinctive features, problems
of, 53–54, 59, 269 n.2, 271–72
n.15
Delany, Paul, 200
Dent, Arthur: *Plaine Man's
Pathway to Heaven,* 38
Demystification, 11, 138, 170, 172,
187–88, 196, 198, 223, 253 n.11,
298 n.4

Derrida, Jacques, 5, 17, 338 n.6;
misunderstanding of Saussure,
61–65
D'Ewes, Sir Simonds, 155–56, 189
Diehl, Huston, 51
Diggers, 124, 138–39, 171, 200, 301
n.26
Dillingham, Francis, 152, 308 n.73
Disobedience. *See* Resistance
Distribution, 170–78, 182–86,
189, 193, 199, 245–48, 313 n.7,
314 n.19, 315 n.27, 319–20 n.55;
versus communism, 248.
See also Charity, Christian;
Communism, Christian
Divestment: and degradation,
86–88; and pastoral, 89–90
Dod, John, 99
Dollimore, Jonathan, 7, 170, 172,
232, 247, 317 n.44, 322 n.72, 340
n.20
Donne, John, 22, 28, 30–31
Downame, John: *Plea of the Poore,*
174–79, 186, 198, 248, 316 n.32,
319 n.51
Dramatic characters, general
verisimilitude versus precise
political identification of,
235–39
Dramatic characters, moral
evaluation of: based on cumulative dramatic clues, 241–45;
not indeterminate, 239, 241;
versus polemical identification,
238, 241–44; when from remote
worlds, 244–45
Drant, Thomas, 317 n.43; *Fruitfull
and Necessary Sermon,* 178; *Two
Sermons,* 181, 282 n.50, 317 n.43
Dudley, Edmund: *Tree of Commonwealth,* 322–23 n.74

Eagleton, Terry, 172, 277 n.36, 317
n.44

Judy Kronenfeld teaches in

the Department of Creative Writing at

the University of California,

Riverside.

The following articles are incorporated in revised form in this volume; they originally appeared in these publications and are used by permission:

"Post-Saussurean Semantics, Reformation Religious Controversy, and Contemporary Critical Disagreement," in *Assays: Critical Approaches to Medieval and Renaissance Texts*, vol. 5, pp. 135–65, Peggy A. Knapp, ed., © 1989 by University of Pittsburgh Press. Reprinted by permission of the University of Pittsburgh Press.

"Probing the Relation between Poetry and Ideology: Herbert's 'The Windows'" *John Donne Journal: Studies in the Age of Donne* 2, no. 1 (1983): 55–80.

"'So Distribution Should Undo Excess and Each Man Have Enough': Shakespeare's *King Lear*—Anabaptist Egalitarianism, Anglican Charity, Both, Neither?" *ELH* (1992): 755–84.

"Yes, Virginia, There IS a World," *The Associated Writing Programs Chronicle* 25, no. 2 (1992): 15–18.

Library of Congress Cataloging-in-Publication Data

Kronenfeld, Judy.
King Lear and the naked truth: rethinking the language of religion and resistance / Judy Kronenfeld.
p.   cm.
Includes bibliographical references and index.
ISBN 0-8223-2027-4 (cloth : alk. paper). — ISBN 0-8223-2038-x (pbk. : alk. paper)
   1. Shakespeare, William, 1564-1616. King Lear.   2. English language—
Early modern, 1500-1700—Semantics.   3. Lear, King (Legendary character),
in literature.   4. Christianity and literature—England—History.   5. Literature and history—England—History.   6. Language and culture—England—
History.   7. Dissenters, Religious, in literature.   8. Social ethics in literature.
9. Costume in literature.   10. Nudity in literature.   I. Title.
PR2819.K76   1998
822.3'3—dc21   97-29429